'This refreshingly engaging book with multidimensional perspectives is a must-read for all. It is an outstanding contribution to global discourse on women's equality and empowerment in the crucial area of peace and security. The substantive, powerful and well-articulated writings add to a comprehensive understanding of the women, peace and security agenda which enters its third decade.'
Ambassador Anwarul K. Chowdhury, *Former Under-Secretary-General of the United Nations and President of the UN Security Council in March 2000*

'If you have been waiting for a pragmatic book on gender and security, this is it. Every fact-filled chapter is organized around the obstacles, drivers, and strategies for improving gender-based security, focusing on the "gender balance of power" as "the ultimate balance of power in human affairs."'
Jack Snyder, *Robert and Renée Belfer Professor of International Relations, Columbia University, USA*

'Global security in all its dimensions can never be achieved until the security community takes gender and women's equality seriously. The authors of this fine book tell us why. A must-read for those in the security community – scholars, activists and policymakers alike who aspire to creating a more peaceful world.'
J. Ann Tickner, *Distinguished Scholar in Residence, American University, USA*

'This edited volume features an all-star line-up of some of the most articulate voices within the Women, Peace, and Security community today. One could not ask for a more approachable, one-stop shop of all things WPS. An extremely useful contribution that will surely have a long shelf life!'
Valerie M. Hudson, *Professor and George H.W. Bush Chair, Texas A & M University, USA*

THE GENDER AND SECURITY AGENDA

This book examines the gender dimensions of a wide array of national and international security challenges.

The volume examines gender dynamics in ten issue areas in both the traditional and human security sub-fields: armed conflict, post-conflict, terrorism, military organizations, movement of people, development, environment, humanitarian emergencies, human rights, governance. The contributions show how gender affects security and how security problems affect gender issues.

Each chapter also examines a common set of key factors across the issue areas: obstacles to progress, drivers of progress and long-term strategies for progress in the 21st century. The volume develops key scholarship on the gender dimensions of security challenges and thereby provides a foundation for improved strategies and policy directions going forward. The lesson to be drawn from this study is clear: if scholars, policymakers and citizens care about these issues, then they need to think about both security and gender.

This will be of much interest to students of gender studies, security studies, human security and International Relations in general.

Chantal de Jonge Oudraat is President of Women In International Security (WIIS). She has held senior positions at the US Institute of Peace, the Carnegie Endowment for International Peace and the United Nations Institute for Disarmament Research in Geneva.

Michael E. Brown is Professor at George Washington University's Elliott School of International Affairs, USA.

Routledge Studies in Gender and Security
Series Editors:
Laura Sjoberg, *University of Florida,* and Caron E. Gentry,
University of St. Andrews

This series looks to publish books at the intersection of gender studies, international relations, and Security Studies. It will publish a broad sampling of work in gender and security – from private military companies to world wars, from food insecurity to battlefield tactics, from large-N to deconstructive, and across different areas of the world. In addition to seeking a diverse sampling of substantive work in gender and security, the series seeks a diverse author pool – looking for cutting-edge junior scholars alongside more established authors, and authors from a wide variety of locations and across a spectrum of backgrounds.

NATO, Gender and the Military
Women Organising from Within
Katharine A. M. Wright, Matthew Hurley and Jesus Gil Ruiz

Gender and Drone Warfare
A Hauntological Perspective
Lindsay C. Clark

Gender and Civilian Victimization in War
Jessica L. Peet and Laura Sjoberg

The Gender and Security Agenda
Strategies for the 21st Century
Edited by Chantal de Jonge Oudraat and Michael E. Brown

For more information about this series, please visit: www.routledge.com/Routledge-Studies-in-Gender-and-Security/book-series/RSGS

THE GENDER AND SECURITY AGENDA

Strategies for the 21st Century

Edited by Chantal de Jonge Oudraat and Michael E. Brown

Routledge
Taylor & Francis Group

LONDON AND NEW YORK

First published 2020
by Routledge
2 Park Square, Milton Park, Abingdon, Oxon OX14 4RN

and by Routledge
52 Vanderbilt Avenue, New York, NY 10017

Routledge is an imprint of the Taylor & Francis Group, an informa business

British Library Cataloguing-in-Publication Data
A catalogue record for this book is available from the British Library

Library of Congress Cataloging-in-Publication Data
Names: Jonge Oudraat, Chantal de, editor. | Brown, Michael E. (Michael
    Edward), 1954– editor.
Title: The gender and security agenda : strategies for the 21st century /
    edited by Chantal de Jonge Oudraat and Michael E. Brown.
Description: Abingdon, Oxon ; New York : Routledge, [2020] | Series:
    Routledge studies in gender and security | Includes bibliographical
    references and index.
Identifiers: LCCN 2020004590 (print) | LCCN 2020004591 (ebook) |
    ISBN 9780367466510 (hardback) | ISBN 9780367466503 (paperback) |
    ISBN 9781003030232 (ebook)
Subjects: LCSH: Women and the security sector. | Security sector. |
    Human security.
Classification: LCC UB416 .G46 2020 (print) | LCC UB416 (ebook) |
    DDC 355/.0335082—dc23
LC record available at https://lccn.loc.gov/2020004590
LC ebook record available at https://lccn.loc.gov/2020004591

ISBN: 978-0-367-46651-0 (hbk)
ISBN: 978-0-367-46650-3 (pbk)
ISBN: 978-1-003-03023-2 (ebk)

Typeset in Bembo
by Apex CoVantage, LLC

MIX
Paper from
responsible sources
FSC
www.fsc.org   FSC™ C013985

Printed in the United Kingdom
by Henry Ling Limited

CONTENTS

List of tables   ix
List of figures   x
Acknowledgments   xi
List of contributors   xiii
List of abbreviations   xv

1 Gender and security: framing the agenda   1
   Chantal de Jonge Oudraat and Michael E. Brown

2 Gender and armed conflict   28
   Kathleen Kuehnast

3 Gender and peacebuilding   47
   Anne Marie Goetz and Rob Jenkins

4 Gender and terrorism   72
   Jeannette Gaudry Haynie

5 Gender and military organizations   90
   Ellen Haring

6 Gender and population movements   113
   Jane Freedman

 7 Gender, development and security   135
    Jeni Klugman

 8 Gender and environmental security   155
    Edward R. Carr

 9 Gender, humanitarian emergencies and security   176
    Tamara Nair

10 Gender, human rights and security   196
    Corey Levine and Sari Kouvo

11 Gender, governance and security   214
    Jacqui True and Sara E. Davies

12 Promoting gender and security: obstacles, drivers
    and strategies   235
    Chantal de Jonge Oudraat and Michael E. Brown

    Index   *266*

TABLES

1.1   The Women, Peace and Security Agenda   13
5.1   Women as a Percentage of the Total Force   94
12.1 Gender Policy Tactics of Patriarchs and Progressives   245

FIGURES

7.1   Gender Equality and Human Development   137
7.2   The Best and Worst Performers on the WPS Index   140
7.3   Gender Equality and GDP   141
7.4   Gender Discrimination by Region   143

ACKNOWLEDGMENTS

This book is a product of an ongoing initiative by Women In International Security (WIIS) to bridge the divide between the traditional security studies community and security policy establishments, on the one hand, and gender studies and the Women, Peace and Security communities, on the other.

This book is the result of an exceptionally collaborative effort from a spectacular group of supporters, scholars and colleagues. First, we would like to thank the Carnegie Corporation of New York and the John D. and Catherine T. MacArthur Foundation for funding the WIIS *Women Peace and Security + Gender Peace and Security Initiative* that included this book project.

Second, we would like to thank the outstanding scholars who wrote the issue-focused chapters that comprise the heart of this book. Each of these ten topics deserves a book-length study of its own. Drawing on decades of experience and expertise, our authors produced concise, chapter-length summaries and sharp analytical assessments of complex problems.

Third, we would like to thank several sets of colleagues who provided valuable feedback at various stages of this project. The participants of the WIIS Next Generation WPS+GPS Symposium contributed many good ideas at the project's launch workshop in November 2017. An exemplary group of external readers – Virginia Haufler, Christopher A. Kojm, Mona Lena Krook and Paul D. Williams – reviewed first drafts and provided constructive guidance at the project's second workshop in April 2018. We are also grateful to renowned scholar J. Ann Tickner for her invaluable insights at this workshop. In addition, we would like to thank the scholars who reviewed the book manuscript for Routledge. All of these suggestions have helped to improve the book.

Fourth, we would like to thank our outstanding colleagues at WIIS who have helped at critical stages in the development of this book project. In particular, we would like to convey our great appreciation to Beatriz Carboni, Nadia Crevecoeur,

Kayla McGill, Madeline Purkerson, Hannah Proctor and Brooke Stedman for their commitment and many contributions to this effort. We would also like to thank Jennifer Ginsburg, who provided valuable research assistance in the early stages of this project.

Last, we would like to thank Nigel Mullins for permission to use an image of his painting *Continuum II* for the cover of the book and Gregory R. Staley for his photograph of the painting. We also would like to thank the Routledge team, Andrew Humphrys and Bethany Lund-Yates, for their help in advancing our book quickly and smoothly through the publication process.

We would like to convey our deep gratitude and appreciation to everyone who contributed to the production of this book.

CONTRIBUTORS

Michael E. Brown is Professor of International Affairs and Political Science at George Washington University's Elliott School of International Affairs.

Edward R. Carr is Professor and Director of the International Development, Community and Environment Department at Clark University.

Sara E. Davies is Associate Professor at the Centre for Governance and Public Policy, School of Government and International Relations, Griffith University. She is a co-editor of *The Oxford Handbook on Women, Peace and Security*.

Chantal de Jonge Oudraat is President of Women In International Security (WIIS).

Jane Freedman is Professor of Politics at the University of Paris 8.

Jeannette Gaudry Haynie is Senior Fellow and Director of the Athena Project at WIIS. She is a Lieutenant Colonel in the US Marine Corps Reserves.

Anne Marie Goetz is Clinical Professor at the Center for Global Affairs, New York University.

Ellen Haring is Senior Fellow and Director of the Combat Integration Initiative at WIIS.

Rob Jenkins is Professor of Political Science, Hunter College and The Graduate Center, City University of New York.

Jeni Klugman is Managing Director at the Georgetown Institute for Women, Peace and Security. She is the lead author of the *WPS Index*.

Sari Kouvo is Associate Professor at the Department of Law at Gothenburg University.

Kathleen Kuehnast is Director of Gender Policy and Strategy at the US Institute of Peace.

Corey Levine is a human rights and humanitarian law policy expert, researcher and writer, with a specialization in gender.

Tamara Nair is Research Fellow at the Centre for Non-Traditional Security Studies at the S. Rajaratnam School of International Studies, Nanyang Technological University.

Jacqui True is Professor of Politics and International Relations and Director of the Centre for Gender, Peace and Security at Monash University. She is a co-editor of *The Oxford Handbook on Women, Peace and Security*.

ABBREVIATIONS

A4P	Action for Peacekeeping
AADMER	ASEAN Agreement on Disaster Management and Emergency Response
AICHR	ASEAN Intergovernmental Commission on Human Rights
AIIB	Asian Infrastructure Investment Bank
AoR	Area of Responsibility
APEC	Asia-Pacific Economic Cooperation
ASEAN	Association of Southeast Asian Nations
AU	African Union
BRI	Belt and Road Initiative
C-Fam	Center for Family and Human Rights
CEDAW	Convention on the Elimination of All Forms of Discrimination against Women
CERD	Convention on the Elimination of All Forms of Racial Discrimination
CERF	Central Emergency Relief Fund
CPEC	China-Pakistan Economic Corridor
CSO	Civil Society Organization
CST	Cultural Support Teams
CSW	Commission on the Status of Women
CT	Counter Terrorism
CVE	Countering Violent Extremism
DAC	Development Assistance Committee
DfiD	Department for International Development (UK)
DOD	Department of Defense (US)
ECOSOC	Economic and Social Council (UN)
EU	European Union

EVAW	Elimination of Violence Against Women
FARC	Revolutionary Armed Forces of Colombia
GAD	Gender and Development
GBV	Gender-Based Violence
GDP	Gross Domestic Product
GIZ	Gesellschaft für Internationale Zusammenarbeit (Germany)
HRC	Human Rights Council (UN)
ICC	International Criminal Court
ICCPR	International Covenant for Civil and Political Rights
ICESCR	International Covenant for Economic, Social and Cultural Rights
ICTR	International Criminal Tribunal for Rwanda
ICTY	International Criminal Tribunal for Yugoslavia
IDF	Israeli Defense Force
IDP	Internally Displaced Person
IEG	Informal Experts Group (UN Security Council)
ILO	International Labour Organization
IMAGES	International Masculinity and Gender Equality Survey
IMF	International Monetary Fund
IOM	International Organization for Migration
IPCC	Intergovernmental Panel on Climate Change (UN)
ISAF	International Security Assistance Force
ISIS	Islamic State in Iraq and Syria
JICA	Japan International Cooperation Agency
M&E	Monitoring and Evaluation
MDG	Millennium Development Goal
MILF	Moro Islamic Liberation Front
MP	Member of Parliament
NAP	National Action Plan
NATO	North Atlantic Treaty Organization
NGO	Non-Governmental Organization
NPA	New People's Army (Philippines)
OECD	Organization for Economic Co-operation and Development
OPAPP	Office of the Presidential Advisor on the Peace Process (Philippines)
OSCE	Organization for Security and Co-operation in Europe
OSD	Office of the Secretary of Defense (US)
PBF	Peacebuilding Fund (UN)
PFA	Platform for Action
PFLP	Popular Front for the Liberation of Palestine
PIRA	Provisional Irish Republican Army
PSVI	Prevention of Sexual Violence Initiative
PVE	Preventing Violent Extremism
R2P	Responsibility to Protect
RAP	Regional Action Plan
SAARC	South Asian Association of Regional Cooperation

SDG	Sustainable Development Goal
SEA	Sexual Exploitation and Abuse
SGBV	Sexual and Gender-Based Violence
SIGI	Social Institutions and Gender Index
SOAWR	Solidarity for African Women's Rights
SVAC	Sexual Violence in Armed Conflict
UDHR	Universal Declaration of Human Rights
UK	United Kingdom
UN	United Nations
UNDP	United Nations Development Program
UNESCO	United Nations Educational, Scientific and Cultural Organization
UNFPA	United Nations Population Fund
UNHCR	United Nations High Commissioner for Refugees
UNISDR	United Nations International Strategy for Disaster Reduction
UNOCHA	United Nations Office for the Coordination of Humanitarian Affairs
UNODC	United Nations Office on Drugs and Crime
UNSCR	United Nations Security Council Resolution
US	United States
USAID	United States Agency for International Development
USG/ERC	Under-Secretary General and Emergency Relief Coordinator
WHO	World Health Organization
WID	Women in Development
WIIS	Women In International Security
WPS	Women, Peace and Security

1

GENDER AND SECURITY

Framing the agenda

Chantal de Jonge Oudraat and Michael E. Brown

Over the last few decades of the 20th century and the first two decades of the 21st century, political leaders around the world have made a series of grand public declarations and formal commitments to gender equality in general and the advancement of the role of women in security issues in particular. Unfortunately, there is still an enormous gap between these pronouncements and aspirations, on the one hand, and real-world progress, on the other.

The public proclamations about these issues have been impressive. In 1975, the United Nations (UN) convened the first world conference on the status of women (held in Mexico City), focusing on gender discrimination, gender equality and the roles of women in development and security. In 1979, the UN General Assembly adopted the Convention on the Elimination of All Forms of Discrimination against Women (CEDAW), an international bill of rights for women. Since then, 188 of the UN's 193 member states have ratified and become parties to the CEDAW.[1] In 1995, the fourth World Conference on Women (in Beijing) adopted a Declaration and Platform for Action that specified a series of strategic goals and policy actions for the advancement of women across twelve issue areas, including development, the environment, human rights, armed conflict and participation in decisionmaking.

Spurred by the advocacy of women's groups, the UN Security Council adopted Resolution 1325 on Women, Peace and Security (WPS) in 2000. This landmark resolution formally called on member states and the Secretary-General to increase the participation of women in conflict prevention and conflict resolution processes; it called for the integration of gender perspectives in the negotiation and implementation of peace agreements; and it called for special measures to protect women and girls from gender-based violence in conflict settings. Nine subsequent UN Security Council resolutions in the 2000s and 2010s have reinforced and refined the WPS agenda. This included a recognition that rape and other forms of sexual violence, which have been employed as tactics of war, constitute war crimes and crimes against humanity.

Regional organizations as diverse as the African Union (AU), the European Union (EU), the North Atlantic Treaty Organization (NATO) and the Organization for Security and Co-operation in Europe (OSCE) have developed organization-wide policies and Regional Action Plans (RAPs) to incorporate the guidance from United Nations Security Council Resolution (UNSCR) 1325 into their deliberations and actions. At the national level, approximately 43 percent of UN member states have developed National Action Plans (NAPs) to implement and advance the WPS agenda.[2] In 2014, Sweden adopted an explicitly feminist foreign policy. It was the first country in the world to do so.[3] In 2015, the 193 member states of the United Nations unanimously adopted a set of Sustainable Development Goals (SDGs) for 2030, including a stand-alone goal that contained an array of commitments to gender equality, the empowerment and participation of women in political and economic affairs, as well as an end to all forms of discrimination and violence against "all women and girls everywhere."[4]

Enunciating these goals has been an important step forward. Reaffirming these goals through additional international and national proclamations has been very valuable. All of this has been necessary for progress, but it has not been sufficient. Progress has been limited and uneven. Even where progress has been made, many of the gains are vulnerable and potentially reversible. Problems persist in traditional national and international security areas, such as security policymaking and conflict settings, as well as in areas where non-military and security issues are intertwined.

The underrepresentation of women in national and international security deliberations remains glaring. Between 1992 and 2018, women constituted only three percent of mediators, 13 percent of negotiators and four percent of witnesses and signatories in major peace processes.[5] Gender perspectives are insufficiently integrated into analyses of national and international security challenges: gender perspectives are usually afterthoughts, if they are thought about at all.

Violence against women and girls has continued at horrifying levels, especially in conflict settings. Since the start of the civil war in South Sudan in 2013, thousands of South Sudanese have been subjected to sexual violence, including rape, gang rape, sexual slavery, sexual mutilation and sexual torture. In one survey, 72 percent of women at UN protection sites reported they had been raped since the onset of the conflict. According to survivors, sexual violence was used as a weapon of war; individuals were often targeted based on their ethnicity or perceived political allegiance.[6] In 2017, rape was used as a weapon by the Myanmar military in its forced expulsion campaign and genocide against the country's Rohingya minority.[7] In Syria, detained political opponents were gang raped by government forces.[8] Although conflict cases like these stand out, scholars have emphasized that sexual violence is not limited to conflict settings and that gender-based violence takes many forms. The World Health Organization (WHO) estimated that more than one in three women (35 percent) worldwide have experienced physical and/or sexual violence – often perpetrated by male intimate partners. Because of limitations in available data, it is difficult to determine whether wartime sexual violence and other forms of gender-based violence are increasing, but there is no doubt that these problems are widespread and severe.[9]

Gender inequalities also persist in political, economic and legal matters. In the political arena, women are underrepresented in the executive, legislative and judicial branches of government at all levels, from national to local, in most countries around the world. As of January 2019, only 24 percent of all national parliamentarians were women; as of June 2019, only 12 women were serving as Head of Government.[10]

Inequalities are multidimensional and intense in the economic realm. A World Bank study has determined that, in 115 out of 131 countries surveyed, women face legal and financial restrictions that men do not face when running a business: 45 percent of countries have laws constraining the types of jobs a woman can occupy; 40 percent of countries limit women's property rights; and nearly 30 percent of countries restrict women's freedom of movement. The World Bank has calculated that, on average, women have only three-quarters of the legal rights of men. Countries in the Middle East and North Africa provide women with only half of the legal rights enjoyed by men. Only six countries provide women and men with equal legal standing – Belgium, Denmark, France, Latvia, Luxembourg and Sweden.[11] Women also face persistent gender pay gaps. The International Labor Organization (ILO) has determined that women earn about 20 percent less than men.[12] The McKinsey Global Institute has calculated that advancing women's equality could add $28 trillion (26 percent) to the global economy in 2025.[13] The World Economic Forum has estimated that, at the current rate of progress, it will take 257 years to close the economic gender gap.[14]

The reasons for the sub-optimal policy record on gender equality and the WPS agenda will be explored issue by issue in the chapters that follow. A few fundamental propositions can be established at the outset.

Gender inequalities exist in the first place because of the ideas people had, and still have, about the roles men and women should play in human affairs – at home and at work, in business and economic affairs, in community and social life and in politics and governance. Gender roles and norms are learned and enforced through institutions – families, schools, religious institutions, local communities, ethnic groups, government agencies, the media – that shape and govern the way people live. Deeply entrenched patriarchal beliefs, cultures and institutions have perpetuated regressive gender stereotypes that, in turn, have perpetuated power asymmetries and gender inequalities in a multitude of issue areas. If the goal is promoting gender equality globally or the specific policy goals of the WPS agenda, multiple arrays of human institutions and cultures will have to be transformed. This is a massive, multi-generational task.

Second, national and international security policy establishments are comprised of and run mainly by men. These policy establishments focus on traditional security threats that are analyzed through traditional lenses and familiar policy frameworks. National security policy establishments are especially attached to traditional threat assessments and traditional policy responses. Intellectual frameworks, organizational cultures, bureaucratic interests and policymaking processes in general tend to be highly resistant to change. Pushing national security establishments to focus on gender-related issues is an especially formidable proposition. Although some states have made declarations in support of gender equality and the WPS agenda, many national security policy establishments continue to treat gender issues as secondary or tertiary issues, and they have been slow to bring women into staff and policy-making positions, especially if this would displace men. Most national security poli-cymaking establishments are lacking in gender expertise and well-informed gender perspectives, and they have a long way to go in mainstreaming gender issues. This is bad for the WPS agenda and the gender equality agenda more generally, but it is also bad for national and international security – which policymakers profess to care about.

A third problem is that the gender equality and WPS agendas have been held back because they have been explicitly framed in terms of "women." This has made it easy for security policy establishments to echo the prevailing nomenclature, pigeonhole these issues as "women's" issues and put them on a back burner. The gender equality and WPS agendas have consequently been marginalized in most national security discussions. In addition, UN Security Council resolutions and national political leaders have repeatedly conflated women's rights and WPS agen-das with "women and children," "women and girls" or "women and youth." This infantilizes women, reinforces the idea that women have no agency and bolsters the prevailing pattern that excludes women from participating in national and interna-tional security policymaking.

This book examines the gender dimensions of a wide array of national and international security challenges. We seek to advance understanding of the con-nections between gender issues, on the one hand, and national and international security problems, on the other. These connections are complex, and they run both ways: gender affects security, and security problems affect gender issues. The causal diagram is not a simple one-way proposition. In looking at national and interna-tional security concerns, we believe it is essential for scholars and policymakers to understand the gender dimensions of these issues. Similarly, in looking at gender problems around the world, we believe it is important to understand the security dimensions of these problems. Our goal is to contribute to scholarship that will, in turn, provide lessons and guidance for the development of strategies that will advance international peace and security as well as gender equality.

From a security perspective, the gender-security agenda is critical because gen-der expands the scope of the agenda and injects additional complexities into the policy equation. For example, the gender-security agenda includes the role of gen-der in the causes and resolution of armed conflict; the impact of gender on the causes, paths and dangers of migration; the role of women in military organizations and the other issues examined in this book. Many of these issues would not be included on a traditionally framed security policy list. Gender also adds tremen-dously to the complexities and difficulties of security problems. To the extent that traditionalists consider these issues, they usually start by thinking about the special dangers faced by women and girls in armed conflicts. These are vital issues, to be sure, but the key to gender analysis is to also think about the agency and power women have – or should have – in all of these security settings. A gender perspective also has to examine the impact of patriarchies on policy problems. As a result, the gender-security agenda is both especially important and especially complicated.

In this book, we build on the important work that has been done to develop and advance the gender equality and WPS agendas. First, this book broadens the lens from "women" to "women and gender." We argue that an emphasis on women is necessary but not sufficient. Indeed, the WPS framework makes it easier for security policy establishments to treat this agenda as a "women's" issue. This, in turn, makes it easier for security establishments to marginalize and neglect these issues. Focusing on gender also facilitates the inclusion of men and masculinities in the analytic equation. This is essential to understanding the problems as well as developing policy solutions. Thinking about gender in an inclusive way is valuable both analytically and politically.

Second, this book broadens the lens by examining the role of gender in an array of traditional security areas as well as non-traditional, human security issues. Too often the discussion about gender and security is confined to a discussion about the WPS agenda or armed conflict. In addition, many studies focus on one single issue or problem. Very few studies bridge the divide between traditional security issues (the dynamics of armed conflict and the behavior of military organizations, for example) and human security issues (such as development, environmental security, humanitarian emergencies, human rights and governance). These are all important issues, they all merit close attention, and they have more in common than is usually understood. Examining gender dynamics in traditional and non-traditional human security areas gives us a broader analytical foundation for developing general conclusions about gender and security issues. It also reinforces the point that gender really matters in national and international security affairs.

Third, to give the book a sharp analytic focus, each of the ten issue-oriented chapters focuses on three key factors: the *obstacles to progress* in these areas, the *drivers of progress* and *strategies for progress* in the future. These substantive chapters make important contributions to our understanding of these issues. Collectively, these chapters provide the basis for developing broad, comparative judgments about the state of and priorities for the gender-security agenda.

Finally, this book seeks to bridge the existing divide between security policy establishments and traditional security studies communities, on the one hand, and the WPS and gender studies communities, on the other. Our goal is to produce a book that advances thinking and scholarship on the gender dimensions of important peace and security challenges, but one that will also be accessible to generalists and policymakers. We hope that this, in turn, helps to enhance and mainstream gender considerations in security policy deliberations.

In this chapter, we frame the book's discussion of gender and security. We begin by defining gender and security. We then review the main gender and security policy initiatives that have been undertaken to date, especially since the end of the Cold War.

Defining gender

The debate over the definition of *gender* is often framed as a question of nature versus nurture – a clash between essentialist and constructivist views.[15] Essentialists define gender in terms of biological differences between men and women. They believe these differences are inherent and immutable. Constructivists see gender as a set of social constructs that have developed over the course of human history and have been passed down from generation to generation through an array of social institutions. They see gender as a human construct and, therefore, potentially fluid.

The biological/essentialist view of gender was challenged by social scientists starting in the 1950s. Most social scientists believe that the most important gender differences are socially constructed rather than biologically determined.[16] Although men and women have obvious biological differences, socially constructed norms, roles and expectations are far more important than biology when it comes to understanding gender dynamics in social, economic and political affairs. Anne Fausto-Sterling and other scientists have argued, moreover, that the traditional biological binary is actually a multidimensional matrix. Indeed, even biological sex is difficult to define by "the presence or absence of a particular gene." It is better seen as a "balance of power among gene networks acting together or in a particular sequence."[17]

Candace West and Don Zimmerman have argued that gender as a social construct is not "a simple property of individuals but an integral dynamic of social orders."[18] Gender also intersects with other identity markers such as race, ethnicity, class, sexual orientation and age. Understanding how gender and these other identity markers are operationalized within societies "can reveal the mechanisms by which power is exercised and inequality is reproduced."[19] Indeed, gender is all about power. Gender structures power in every arena (education, economics, politics, security), at every level (local, national, regional, global) and through multiple mechanisms (family, society, culture, organizations). When scholars and policymakers talk about gender in any issue area, it is important to focus on power and how power dynamics unfold in that setting.

As social and cultural constructs, gender roles and gender relations can change over time. Even so, established gender-based norms and roles have been persistent and durable. Gender stereotypes have helped to keep gender hierarchies in place. Gender stereotypes related to war and peace – seeing the feminine as soft, caring and linked to peace; seeing the masculine as strong, violent and linked to war – have also persisted.

Gender norms and roles are ideas propagated and perpetuated by a powerful array of human institutions – families, community and ethnic groups, religious institutions, schools, government agencies and the media. These ideas evolve into ideologies that become institutionally and inter-generationally entrenched. Although change is possible, it has to be brought about through changes in these ideological, institutional and foundational structures. This requires individual, societal and systemic transformation. Change is possible, but it is difficult because of ideological and institutional inertia as well as social and political resistance. Changing gender roles entails change in the gender balance of power and, as we have seen in international and national politics, established powers generally do not give up their privileged positions willingly. The gender balance of power is the ultimate balance of power in human affairs.

In the 1990s, the idea of gender as a social construct became widely adopted by international organizations. In 1995, the idea of mainstreaming gender perspectives in policies and programs to promote gender equality was formally endorsed in the Beijing Declaration and Platform for Action. In 1997, the UN's Economic and Social Council (ECOSOC) defined gender mainstreaming as:

> the process of assessing the implications for women and men of any planned action. . . . It is a strategy for making women's as well as men's concerns and experiences an integral dimension of the design, implementation, monitoring and evaluation of policies and programmes . . . so that women and men benefit equally and inequality is not perpetuated. The ultimate goal is to achieve gender equality.[20]

Most international organizations – including the AU, the EU, NATO and the OSCE – have adopted gender equality and gender mainstreaming as policy priorities. On paper, these organizations are in remarkable agreement: gender is seen as a cross-cutting, socially constructed concept. Many organizational definitions emphasize that gender and "gender systems are established in different socio-cultural contexts which determine what is expected, allowed and valued in a women/man and girl/boy in these specific contexts."[21] They also emphasize that gender roles and norms are learned, which means they can change over time and across socio-cultural contexts.[22]

In practice, however, essentialist views of gender are still widely held in international organizations and even more so in national and international security establishments. In international policy discussions, the term *gender* is often used interchangeably with *women*. The WPS resolutions themselves are unclear on this issue. Although they mostly focus on women (rather than gender), the texts often oscillate between an understanding of the role of women and gender as a social construct and the role of women and gender as biologically determined. Similarly, many national and international programs focused on gender issues have been based on essentialist assumptions – with women seen as victims, weak and peaceful, and men seen as perpetrators, strong and aggressive.

Despite lofty political commitments to gender equality and the WPS agenda, most national and international policymakers have not embraced or even employed the frameworks that might help them understand the gender dynamics of security challenges. Champions of the WPS agenda have stated repeatedly (and correctly) that it is essential to include gender perspectives in security policy analyses, security policy deliberations and security policy actions. Unfortunately, security policy establishments only occasionally – and almost always reluctantly – agree with this. And then, instead of considering a broad-based, sophisticated analysis of the gender issues at hand, the security establishment's default approach is to reduce "including gender perspectives" to "focusing on women's issues momentarily" or, even worse, "getting a woman's point of view."

A proper gender analysis should focus on people and power and analyze patterns of inclusion and exclusion based on gender and other markers of identity (including race, class, age and sexual orientation). A gender perspective helps to identify structural factors within societies – including stereotypical notions of femininity and masculinity as well as institutional practices – that lead to gender imbalances as well as unequal access to resources and opportunities. In addition, gender perspectives should be mainstreamed: gender should be a regular, normal, constant, legitimate, central consideration – for scholars and analysts, and especially for policymakers.

Defining security

Security has been a central human concern for eons. For most of human history, security has predominantly been a personal, local issue. Hunter-gatherer tribes, for example, focused on what we now refer to as food and water security, and they worried about local threats from other human groups. The agricultural revolution changed the dynamics of food and group protection, but security problems were still primarily local in nature. Groups and individuals were preoccupied with what is now known as community security and personal security. As Emma Rothschild observed, the Latin noun securitas referred to the inner condition of individuals – "tranquility of spirit, freedom from care" – and the feeling of being secure.[23]

The security concerns of larger political entities – dynasties and empires – and the dangers posed by long-distance military threats became increasingly important over time. However, as Rothschild argued, these state-level military concerns became dominant preoccupations only after the Revolutionary and Napoleonic Wars in Europe. Starting in the 1800s, European leaders focused on external military threats to their states and dynastic regimes.[24] The emergence of professional military organizations and academies in the 1800s reinforced the increasingly dominant fixation on military threats to state-level security.[25]

For most of the 20th century and especially during the Cold War, the theory and practice of security in most of the major powers was grounded in this state-centric, military-centric view. In NATO countries during the Cold War, security problems were defined overwhelmingly in military terms, with an intense focus on military balances – the nuclear balance, the conventional balance on the Central Front, the naval balance and the prospects for technological developments that could affect any of these balances. Scholars, strategists and policymakers in NATO and many allied countries shared this common outlook.[26] Barry Buzan and Richard Ullman, writing separately in 1983, were among the few at the time who suggested that a broader array of non-military factors – including economic, political, societal and environmental securities – should be incorporated into the security equation.[27]

The end of the Cold War, followed by the breakup of the Soviet Union in 1991, led to profound changes in international politics and a split in thinking about the nature of security in the contemporary world. Two main schools of thought have emerged about the scope and focus of the security agenda: (1) a traditionalist school that continues to emphasize the primacy of inter-state politics, the centrality of national (state-level) security and the use of national military forces; and (2) a human security school that argues for a broader conception of security problems, including non-military problems faced by non-state actors, such as community groups and individuals.[28]

In the traditionalist camp, realists argue that the main features of the international system have not changed, even though the Cold War has ended and globalization has become a growing force in international relations. Kenneth Waltz argued that the world "has not been transformed" by the end of the Cold War. Rather, "the structure of the system has simply been remade by the disappearance of the Soviet Union." A true transformation in international relations, he wrote, "awaits the day when the international system is no longer populated by states that have to help themselves." In the meantime, he maintained, "the essential continuity of international politics" is intact.[29] Similarly, John Mearsheimer argues that "international anarchy – the driving force behind great-power behavior – did not change with the end of the Cold War, and there are few signs that such change is likely any time soon. States remain the principal actors in world politics."[30] The future, it is said, will therefore look much like the past: "The state system is alive and well, and although regrettable, military competition between sovereign states will remain the distinguishing feature of international politics for the foreseeable future."[31]

For realists, the most important security problems are issues involving states, and they involve the threat, use or potential use of military force. For realists, the most important issues on the security agenda today are the same issues that have been on the agenda for centuries: the search by states for security; competitions among states for security; and the inter-state competitions, confrontations, arms races and wars that result from these quests.[32] Sophisticated realists understand that there are other conflict problems in the world – at the intra-state level, for example – but they believe that the security landscape is dominated by inter-state problems that have prominent military dimensions.

Many national security policymaking establishments have been grounded in this framework for decades, even centuries, and they remain grounded in this worldview today. This is understandable to some extent, because national leaders have a responsibility to look out for national security; this is their fiduciary obligation, and external military threats are still part of the threat matrix for most major powers. It is also true that established belief systems and organizational ideologies are highly resistant to change – even in the face of systemic transformations.[33]

Other scholars have developed a more expansive conception of the security agenda. Many have contended that intra-state, transnational and an array of non-military problems should be added to the agenda. Writing in the early 1980s, Richard Ullman was one of the first to argue that "defining national security merely (or even primarily) in military terms conveys a profoundly false image of reality." This is dangerous, he wrote, because "it causes states to concentrate on military threats and to ignore other and perhaps more harmful dangers."[34] In 1992, Edward Kolodziej argued that it had become misguided to confine the security agenda to "state-centric analysis."[35]

The publication of the United Nations Development Program (UNDP) *Human Development Report* in 1994 was a milestone in the development of post-Cold War thinking about security issues. It argued for a fundamental reformulation:

> The concept of security has for too long been interpreted narrowly: as security of territory from external aggression, or as protection of national interest in foreign policy or as global security from the threat of a nuclear holocaust. It has been related more to nation-states than to people. . . . Forgotten were the legitimate concerns of ordinary people who sought security in their daily lives. For many of them, security symbolized protection from the threat of disease, hunger, unemployment, crime, social conflict, political repression and environmental hazards. With the dark clouds of the cold war receding, one can now see that many conflicts are within nations rather than between nations.[36]

UNDP proposed a new human security framework with seven components: (1) economic security; (2) food security; (3) health security; (4) environmental security; (5) personal security; (6) community security; and (7) political security. As Emma Rothschild observed, this new formulation was actually a return to the security priorities of earlier eras. However, given the state-centric, military-centric paradigm then in place, UNDP's human security approach represented a radical transformation in the geometry of the security agenda. As Rothschild noted, the human security framework extended the agenda horizontally to include an array of non-military factors. It also extended the agenda downward to include individual, community and group security at different levels. And it extended the agenda upward to include problems that pose threats to humanity and global security more generally: mounting environmental problems, population growth, international migration, transnational trafficking and terrorism.[37]

Although the human security framework substantially expanded the scope of the international security agenda and the security studies field, it did not, in its first formulation, explicitly and specifically highlight gender security as a priority. This is a major failure, but also a telling omission: one of the most progressive policy formulations of its time ignored women and gender.

The human security conception of security has been adopted more enthusiastically at the international level than the national level. The human security approach provided the conceptual foundation for the 2004 report of the UN Secretary-General's High-Level Panel on *Threats, Challenges, and Change*, which outlined a framework for thinking about security in the 21st century. This report carefully balanced attention to traditional security problems (nuclear, chemical and biological weapons, for example) with an emphasis on growing intra-state conflict problems and the dangers posed by poverty, infectious disease and environmental degradation.[38] Many of these poverty, development, economic, health, education and environmental issues are pillars of the *2030 Agenda for Sustainable Development*, adopted by the UN General Assembly in 2015.

At the regional level, the EU embraced a broad conception of security in its *Global Strategy for Foreign and Security Policy*, adopted in 2016. Along with traditional security threats posed by Russia and armed conflict, the EU also emphasized the long-term challenges posed by population trends, economic problems and climate change, as well as weak states and bad governance in neighboring countries and regions. As the EU's strategy noted: "When violent conflicts erupt, our shared vital interests are threatened. The EU will engage in a practical and principled way in peacebuilding and foster human security through an integrated approach."[39] Significantly, although the EU has emphasized the promotion of gender equality among member states within the Union, the EU's *Global Strategy* for external relations mentioned women and gender equality only in passing.[40] This is striking: the EU expanded its conception of security to include human security considerations, but even in the 2010s, this relatively progressive regional organization did not emphasize gender issues in its external strategy.

Security and gender have been two of the most central human preoccupations since the dawn of time. Yet, remarkably, the connections between these two fundamentally important human concerns received little attention – from scholars or policymakers – until the latter years of the 20th century. In the 1980s and 1990s, J. Ann Tickner was one of the first scholars to push for more conceptual and analytical work on the security-gender nexus.[41] Over subsequent decades, the impetus for security-gender analysis has come overwhelmingly from feminist and gender scholars. The top academic and policy journals in the security studies field have published only a handful of articles on security-gender issues in the 21st century.[42] The security studies field has taken steps to broaden its agenda since the end of the Cold War, especially with respect to human security concerns. Unfortunately, gender has not yet been mainstreamed in the security studies field, and it has not been mainstreamed in most national security policymaking establishments.

Gender and security policy initiatives: the WPS agenda

Gender equality has been recognized as a core principle of human rights in many foundational legal texts. In 1945, the UN Charter 1945 affirmed its faith in "fundamental human rights," including "the equal rights of men and women."[43] The Universal Declaration of Human Rights (adopted by the UN General Assembly in 1948) set human rights standards that explicitly apply to every human being "without distinction of any kind, such as race, colour, sex, language, religion, political or other opinion, national or social origin, property, birth or other status."[44] In

1979, CEDAW went much farther in defining gender-based discrimination and specifying the measures state parties are obligated to undertake, including in areas of law, political life, economic affairs, education, health, marriage and family life.

The internal conflicts in the 1990s – in particular, the widespread use of rape as a weapon of war in the Balkan and Rwandan genocides – helped draw international attention to the gendered effects of war. From the Balkans to Africa and around the world, women mobilized for peace and demanded to have a significant role in peace negotiations and post-conflict actions.[45]

Galvanized by the advocacy of women's groups in conflicted countries and elsewhere, the fourth World Conference on Women (held in Beijing in 1995) adopted a Declaration and Platform for Action that called for the participation of women in conflict resolution deliberations and decisions, the protection of women in conflict and gender mainstreaming.[46] For the first time, an international conference recognized the important role of women as actors in advancing international peace and security, and not just as victims in need of protection.

In 1996, ECOSOC instructed the UN Commission for the Status of Women (CSW) to take the lead in monitoring and reviewing progress on the implementation of the Beijing Platform for Action. In 1997, ECOSOC adopted directives for gender mainstreaming within the United Nations.[47] Although some progress was made in advancing gender equality and gender mainstreaming in some parts of the United Nations in the mid-1990s, the UN bodies responsible for international peace and security (the Security Council, the General Assembly's First Committee and the Secretariat) largely ignored the messages of the Beijing Platform for Action, including its Chapter on Women and Armed Conflict. This led a number of women's advocacy groups to focus their efforts more specifically on the Security Council – the main organ of the United Nations responsible for the maintenance of international peace and security.[48]

The annual meeting of the CSW in March 2000 coincided with its review of the 1995 Beijing Platform for Action and helped to consolidate women's advocacy efforts on an approach to the UN Security Council. They achieved a significant victory on March 8, 2000, when the President of the UN Security Council (Bangladesh's Ambassador Anwarul Chowdury) issued a statement on behalf of the Council recognizing that "peace is inextricably linked with equality between women and men."[49] Encouraged by this progress, women's advocacy groups intensified their lobbying of UN Security Council members. This led the Security Council to take up the issue in October 2000, with an open session on women, peace and security and the introduction of what would become Resolution 1325.

With the adoption of UNSCR 1325 on October 31, 2000, the UN Security Council for the first time formally recognized the importance of gender equality in achieving peace and security. This resolution and nine follow-up resolutions passed in the 2000s and 2010s frame what is now known as the WPS agenda. (See Table 1.1.)

With UNSCR 1325, Security Council members recognized that war and armed conflicts have different effects on men and women. The Council urged national

TABLE 1.1 The Women, Peace and Security Agenda

The UN Security Council adopted ten resolutions on Women, Peace and Security (WPS) in the 2000s and 2010s.	
UNSCR 1325 October 31, 2000	*Recognizes* the disproportionate and unique impact of armed conflict on women. *Urges* member states and the United Nations to increase the representation and participation of women at all decisionmaking levels in the prevention and resolution of conflicts, including in field-based operations. *Affirms* the importance of integrating gender perspectives in all negotiations and operations. *Calls* for measures to protect women and girls from gender-based violence.
UNSCR 1820 June 19, 2008	*Recognizes* sexual violence as a tactic of war. *Declares* that "rape and other forms of sexual violence can constitute war crimes, crimes against humanity, or a constitutive act with respect to genocide."
UNSCR 1888 September 30, 2009	*Establishes* a mandate for the Special Representative on Sexual Violence in Conflict. *Calls* for the appointment of Women Protection Advisors in all peacekeeping missions.
UNSCR 1889 October 5, 2009	*Calls* for the development of indicators to measure the implementation of UNSCR 1325.
UNSCR 1960 December 16, 2010	*Calls* for a monitoring, analysis and reporting arrangement on conflict-related sexual violence. *Establishes* a "naming and shaming" mechanism for perpetrators of sexual violence. *Recommends* referral to UN Sanctions Committees.
UNSCR 2106 June 24, 2013	*Focuses* on the national responsibility of all states to protect civilians and prevent sexual violence in conflict. *Recognizes* men and boys as victims of sexual violence.
UNSCR 2122 October 18, 2013	*Commits* to focus attention on women's leadership and participation in conflict resolution and peacebuilding. *Asks* the UN Secretary-General to undertake a global study on the implementation of UNSCR 1325. *Calls* for humanitarian aid to include the full range of medical, legal, psychosocial and livelihood services to women affected by armed conflict.
UNSCR 2242 October 13, 2015	*Recognizes* terrorism as part of the WPS agenda and gender as a crosscutting issue within the counter-terrorism and counter-violent extremism agendas. *Recognizes* the importance of integrating WPS across all country situations. *Establishes* an Informal Experts Group (IEG) on WPS.
UNSCR 2467 April 23, 2019	*Calls* for a survivor-centered approach in the prevention and response to conflict-related sexual violence. *Recognizes* the importance of civil society organizations in addressing conflict-related sexual violence and the need to pay special attention to children born of sexual violence in armed conflict.
UNSCR 2493 October 29, 2019	*Requests* the UN Secretary-General to provide further information on progress and remaining challenges in the WPS agenda.

and international actors to incorporate gender perspectives into their policy deliberations and programs so that these efforts would not perpetuate or create gender inequalities. In addition, the Council emphasized the need to protect women from violence, particularly sexual violence, and it acknowledged the need to expand the role of women in field-based operations, including military operations. Most importantly, the Council recognized that women need to participate in greater, equal levels in peace negotiations and every aspect of national and international peace and security policymaking.

Unfortunately, the momentum developed around UNSCR 1325 was dampened by the September 11, 2001 terrorist attacks in the United States. For the next several years, the US government, many US allies and other countries, and the UN Security Council became preoccupied with terrorism and counter-terrorism efforts and the US-led wars in Afghanistan and Iraq. Although the UN Security Council continued to hold annual discussions on UNSCR 1325 every October, these were often routine and somewhat perfunctory exercises. WPS issues were rarely mentioned in other UN Security Council statements and resolutions. Within the UN Secretariat, UNSCR 1325 was a low priority.

In 2004, the United Kingdom's (UK) Permanent Representative to the United Nations (also serving as President of the Council) encouraged member states to adopt National Action Plans (NAPs) for implementing UNSCR 1325.[50] Few states responded at that time.[51] Attention to the WPS agenda picked up in 2007, when US government officials and the public were mobilized by reports of widespread rape in the Democratic Republic of the Congo (DRC) and Sudan. Some reports estimated that more than 433,000 people (mostly women) had been sexually assaulted over a one-year period in the DRC alone.[52]

The United States subsequently introduced UNSCR 1820 (2008), which recognized that sexual violence has been used as a tactic of war and that this constitutes a threat to international peace and security. This resolution was followed by UNSCR 1888 (2009), which called on the UN Secretary-General to appoint a Special Representative to monitor implementation of UNSCR 1820. In UNSCR 1889 (2009), the Security Council asked the UN Secretariat to develop a framework to measure progress on the implementation of UNSCR 1325 and the WPS agenda.[53]

Drawing on these WPS resolutions, the UN Secretariat identified four main pillars of the WPS agenda:[54]

1   The *prevention* of all forms of violence against women, including sexual and gender-based violence;
2   The *participation* of women at all levels of decisionmaking related to peace and security, including in security institutions (military and police);
3   The *protection* of women's physical security and their political, social and economic rights, including access to justice;
4   Access to *relief and recovery* support for women who need assistance.[55]

Since 2010, this four-pillar framework has been widely used by states and Non-Governmental Organizations (NGOs) to describe and define the WPS agenda. It is important to note that, in 2000, UNSCR 1325 placed a great deal of emphasis on increasing the representation and participation of women in peace negotiations, peace processes and field-based operations. This was featured early and often in the text of the resolution. By 2010, the participation pillar was just one of four pillars in the emerging WPS agenda.

The tenth anniversary of UNSCR 1325 in 2010 did not generate any new WPS resolution from the Security Council, but the General Assembly established a new UN Women office that consolidated and elevated various agencies and bodies within the United Nations that worked on women's issues.[56] Although UN Women did not have an explicit mandate with respect to UNSCR 1325, it would quickly establish itself as a key player on the WPS agenda.[57]

Between 2010 and 2015, the Security Council focused mainly on the issue of conflict-related sexual violence, despite efforts by civil society organizations and UN Women to emphasize the issue of participation and representation.[58] In the run-up to the 15th anniversary of UNSCR 1325, the Security Council asked the Secretary-General to commission a comprehensive, global study of the implementation of UNSCR 1325.[59] This review coincided with two other, related reviews: one on UN peace operations and the other on the UN's peacebuilding architecture.[60] All three reviews recognized the changing security environment. They acknowledged that contemporary security challenges were interconnected and would require whole-of-society approaches that would emphasize the security of people.

When introducing the 417-page review of the implementation of UNSCR 1325 – generally known as the *Global Study* – UN Women's Executive Director Phumzile Mlambo-Ngcuka noted the existence of a "crippling gap between the ambition of our commitments and actual political and financial support."[61] The study itself confirmed that the many declarations that had been made over the years in support of gender equality and the WPS agenda had not been matched by effective implementation actions.

Following the review, the Security Council adopted UNSCR 2242 (2015). The resolution recognized that women remained underrepresented in "many formal processes and bodies related to the maintenance of international peace and security." The Council endorsed many of the recommendations of the *Global Study*, including better integration of the WPS agenda in its work and the creation of an Informal Experts Group on WPS, also known as the IEG or 2242 Group.[62] It also took note of the gender recommendations made by the High-Level Independent Panel on Peace Operations, including the need to improve gender-responsiveness of peace operations, the integration of gender expertise within mission staffing structures and promoting better gender balance in UN military and police contingents.

UNSCR 2242 also widened the WPS agenda to include international efforts to counter terrorism and violent extremism. Since 2001, the campaign against terrorism had become a major policy priority for the United States and its allies. With the rise of the Islamic State in Iraq and Syria (ISIS) and its declaration of an ISIS caliphate in 2014, the United States recognized that it needed a comprehensive approach to terrorism that would address radicalization and violent extremism. This led the United States and others to develop a greater appreciation of the role that gender was playing in ISIS recruitment efforts – aimed at both men and women. This, in turn, led some governments to reach out to women's organizations and reconsider the WPS agenda.[63]

Around this time, world leaders were also assessing the accomplishments of the Millennium Development Goals (MDGs) – adopted in 2000 – which aspired to promote global development and eradicate extreme poverty. The MDGs focused on gender inequalities in several important areas, including health, education and economic and political opportunities. The follow-on set of Sustainable Development Goals, adopted in 2015, placed an even stronger emphasis on gender issues by including a stand-alone goal on gender equality and the empowerment of women. The SDGs also recognized the importance of tackling structural barriers to gender equality and considering gender equality as a priority across all issue areas.

Unfortunately, this surge of momentum did not last. The establishment of the IEG helped to deepen awareness of Council members to gender-related issues, especially in the Council's country-specific work. It also allowed civil society actors greater access to members of the Council, particularly when Council members went on fact-finding visits. At the same time, the adoption of UNSCR 2242 revealed important political divisions within the Security Council. China and Russia had always been lukewarm about the WPS agenda; over time, they became increasingly wary about expansion of this agenda and its possible infringement on state sovereignty.

The WPS agenda lost an important ally in 2017, with the change in US administrations. This had an impact at the annual UN discussions on conflict-related sexual violence and WPS in 2019, when the United States threatened to veto any resolution that mentioned women's sexual and reproductive health. China and Russia, for their part, were fiercely opposed to any mention of human rights defenders. They were also opposed to any expansion of the Council's involvement in the WPS area, including the establishment of a working group on sexual violence in conflict or formal recognition of the IEG. As a result, negotiations leading up to the April and October 2019 resolutions (UNSCR 2467 and 2493) were difficult. This ultimately led to watered-down resolutions – not strong statements of support. The frustrating debates in the Security Council, particularly the US stance against sexual and reproductive health rights, left some civil society actors questioning the wisdom of pursuing a new resolution.[64] These meetings also showed that progress on the WPS agenda is not a given and can easily be reversed.

Assessing the track record

The overall track record of international actors to mainstream gender and integrate gender perspectives in national and international security policies – including efforts to implement the WPS agenda – is mixed. Some actors have been serious and supportive of the WPS agenda; others have not. Some implementation efforts have been correspondingly serious and sustained; others have not. Some actors have been apathetic toward some or all aspects of the WPS initiative; some have been openly hostile. Assessing this track record involves commitments and actions primarily at the international and national levels.[65]

International level

Since the adoption of UNSCR 1325, UN member states have focused largely on the protection of women in conflict, particularly prevention and protection from sexual violence. In 2008, the UN Security Council recognized sexual violence as a tactic of war and a crime against humanity. The Council also asked the UN Secretary-General to appoint a Special Representative on Sexual Violence in Conflict.[66] In 2013, the G-8 launched an initiative to prevent sexual violence in conflict. This was followed in 2014 by the UK Prevention of Sexual Violence Initiative (PSVI). All of these initiatives have focused on legal accountability measures and other efforts that can help survivors deal with the aftermath of sexual violence.

The frameworks put into place by these initiatives and other UN Security Council resolutions are important. However, these initiatives have fallen short in five important ways.

First, the international community has paid little attention to the structural factors, including gender inequality, that promote and condone sexual and gender-based violence in situations outside of war. The lack of attention to gender and the narrow focus on conflict-related sexual violence as a tactic of war have limited the impact of the policy initiatives adopted in the wake of UNSCR 1325. In addition, many of these initiatives inadvertently reinforced gender stereotypes by portraying women solely as victims or survivors and men solely as perpetrators of violence. The "weapon of war" frame also leaves out other vulnerable populations, such as boys and the LGBTQ community.[67]

Second, although the UN Security Council and other international actors have focused their efforts on conflict-related sexual violence, UN peacekeepers have not been held sufficiently accountable for the crimes they have committed – including sexual violence, exploitation and abuse – while carrying out UN peace operations.[68] Although this problem was first raised in 1993 in conjunction with the UN's peacekeeping mission in Cambodia, shocking reports of sexual abuse involving peacekeepers and children in the Central African Republic appeared in 2017.[69] A 2019 study reported on the Sexual Exploitation and Abuse (SEA) by UN personnel in Haiti.[70] The United Nations has not taken sufficient action and is itself still part of the problem.

Third, data on conflict-related sexual violence is notoriously incomplete.[71] The data that exists suggests that sexual violence remains a problem throughout the world. The United Nations has identified 50 parties (non-state actors, terrorist groups and states) that have committed conflict-related sexual violence.[72]

However, the lack of precise data impedes accountability. Indeed, prosecutions and convictions for conflict-related sexual violence are rare, due in part to the lack of accurate data.

Fourth, the relief and recovery pillar of the WPS agenda has been insufficiently developed. Many UN entities have adopted policy guidance documents for humanitarian emergencies that recognize the importance of gender perspectives. For example, the UN's World Humanitarian Summit in 2016 contained many calls for gender equality in humanitarian actions, but the gap between policy documents and actual implementation remains wide. Even the most basic steps to prevent sexual and gender-based violence in humanitarian emergencies – lighting, locks and latrines: the "three L's" – are unevenly implemented.[73]

Lastly, the focus on protection and on a narrow definition of prevention – as prevention of sexual violence, not armed conflict – has meant that an important component of the WPS agenda (the participation of women in peace and security) has not been sufficiently advanced. Indeed, women remain underrepresented in the halls of power, in peace negotiations and in security institutions, as discussed earlier. Most of the peace agreements that have been signed since 1990 have no female signatories.[74] Women were underrepresented in the 2016 Myanmar Union Peace Conference, constituting only seven of 75 delegates. The 2017 Central African Republic peace talks had no women participants. In the 2017 UN Security Council debate on WPS, the executive director of UN Women reported an overall decline in female participation in UN-led peace processes.[75] In 2018, women were included in 14 out of 19 delegations participating in UN-led negotiations, but the overall percentage of women remained low. In addition, the vast majority of peace agreements do not address gender equality or the rights of women.[76] In UN peace operations, women have comprised only four percent of military personnel and ten percent of police personnel UN peacekeepers.[77] The UN's aspirational goals in this area are modest: the United Nations aims to have 15 percent of its military forces and 20 percent of its police forces be comprised of women.

In sum, while the UN Security Council and UN member states have made multiple rhetorical commitments to women's representation and participation in peace and security affairs, almost all of their attention to date has focused on the three passive pillars of the WPS agenda: prevention of sexual violence, protection from sexual violence and relief and recovery. These three pillars can be described as "passive pillars" because they all frame women and girls as victims in need of protection; they conform to existing gender stereotypes in male-dominated security and policymaking establishments. They do not disrupt prevailing views and power dynamics, and they have consequently been supported (imperfectly) by the UN and national policy establishments.

The participation pillar has not made great progress because it has been neglected and opposed by policy establishments. This pillar has received a very different reception because it challenges prevailing gender stereotypes in male-dominated security and policymaking circles. Advancing the participation pillar would increase female participation in peace and security policymaking and would challenge the

prevailing balance of gender power. Increasing the participation and representation of women in peace and security deliberations and operations would threaten
male-dominance and male-employment opportunities in these organizations. The
participation pillar has therefore been suppressed for ideational, ideological and
social reasons as well as political and economic reasons. Advancing the participation
pillar is essential to advancing the broader gender and security agenda, but it has
faced and will continue to face a perfect storm of opposition. Unfortunately, the
WPS agenda will continue to fall short unless and until there is equal representation
in peace and security decisionmaking and policymaking, in peace negotiations and
operations, in security institutions and on missions in the field. Peace and security
will consequently suffer.

National level

Starting in 2004, the UN Security Council has encouraged implementation of the
WPS agenda at the national level through the adoption of National Action Plans.[78]
National governments have been slow to develop, adopt and implement these plans.
By 2005, only one country – Denmark – had developed and adopted a NAP. By
2008, only 12 states had developed NAPs.[79] The run-up to UNSCR 1325's tenth
anniversary in 2010 saw a spike of activity, with an additional 32 states adopting
NAPs, including the United States. The run-up (and aftermath) to UNSCR 1325's
fifteenth anniversary in 2015 also saw an increase in NAP adoption, though not as
extensive as in 2010. As of January 2020, 83 states had adopted NAPs.[80]

Since 2010, the UN's four-pillar framework has been widely used by states and
civil society organizations to define and organize the WPS agenda. Many NAPs
have been based on this framework.[81] Although one might expect that this would
lead to a fair amount of uniformity and standardization around the world, the reality
is that the WPS agenda has been interpreted very differently in different countries.

National goals and expectations have varied widely. This became clear during the
2015 global review of the WPS agenda. Several issues have stood out. First, NAPs
have varied widely in terms of their focus and scope. For many states in the Global
North, NAPs have been developed to guide national interventions abroad. Many
of these plans are outward-looking. For conflict states, NAPs have been conceived
as national governance plans, and they are consequently inward-looking. Many
conflict countries have received support and encouragement from donor countries
to develop NAPs. This has led to a paradox: strong gender equality frameworks have
been developed in some countries and cultures that might not have been receptive
to gender equality initiatives. At the same time, many high-income, low-conflict
countries have not developed NAPs, even though these countries would seem to
be more supportive of gender equality. More generally, most NAPs have not been
integrated into broader national security policies. For many states, the WPS agenda
remains an add-on initiative, not an integrated policy priority.

Second, NAPs have varied widely in terms of civil society's roles in development,
monitoring and implementation. The range goes from formal co-responsibilities

for NAP development and implementation to informal consultations with civil society. Third, NAPs have varied in terms of accountability measures. Some NAPs have clear benchmarks and monitoring and evaluation measures, but most have none. Fourth, NAPs have varied widely in terms of resources allocated to implementation. Some NAPs have dedicated resources, but most do not have significant resources for sustained implementation: only 22 percent of all NAPs have had a budget for implementation.[82]

Finally, there have been tensions between governments and civil society organizations over the prevention pillar. For most governments, the prevention pillar is defined in passive terms and focused on the prevention of sexual violence. For many civil society activists and organizations, the prevention pillar is seen in broad and proactive conflict prevention terms, as well as involving broader questions regarding the militarization of societies.[83] Many feminist scholars and activists have been critical of the evolution of the WPS agenda. In 2000, many activists hoped that UNSCR 1325 and the WPS agenda would constitute first steps toward the demilitarization of societies and the development of anti-militarist policies.[84] Cora Weiss, one of the drafters of UNSCR 1325, lamented the bureaucratization of the WPS agenda, including initiatives to end sexual violence in conflict. She argued that "we cannot pluck rape out of war and let the war go on. We must not make war safe for women. It is time to abolish war."[85] Similarly, some feminist activists have criticized the WPS emphasis on increasing the number of women in military organizations and law enforcement. Sanam Anderlini has argued that the WPS agenda should push for peace and not "to enable our daughters to be drafted into armies on equal footings as our sons. Rather [we should] ensure that neither our daughters nor our sons have to bear witness or engage in the horrors of war."[86]

Focus and organization of the book

The chapters in this book focus on a common set of problems and factors that are important in understanding gender-security dynamics. This provides a framework for assessing progress in each issue area, and it provides a foundation for developing general conclusions and lessons in the book's final chapter. The scholarly and analytical literatures have not focused specifically on *obstacles to progress*, *drivers of progress* and *strategies for progress*. Focusing on these factors will be a valuable contribution to our collective understanding of these issues.

Each chapter provides an overview of the importance of gender and an outline of the main issues that comprise this particular field of study. The chapters "frame the field" and show how gender and security are interconnected in each area. This is followed by a review and assessment of the policy track record in each area since the early 1990s. Although many issues have deep historical roots, it is useful to focus primarily on international and national policy actions since the end of the Cold War. How have gender-security issues been addressed (or not addressed) in each area? What are the most important policy failures? What have been the main obstacles to progress? What progress has been made? What have been the main drivers of progress? The final section of each chapter develops the policy lessons that should be derived and applied in each issue area. But, instead of proposing near-term policy recommendations that will quickly be overtaken by events, the authors take a longer-term view and outline strategies for progress in that area.

This book begins with chapters that examine gender-security issues that are at the traditional end of the security spectrum: the dynamics of armed conflict, the dangers of terrorism and the behavior of military organizations. The chapters that follow examine issues that are usually categorized as human security problems: population movements, development, environmental security, humanitarian emergencies, human rights and governance challenges.

Kathleen Kuehnast examines the relationship between gender and armed conflict. She analyzes the role of gender and gender inequalities in the onset of armed conflicts. She notes that a growing body of scholarship has demonstrated a strong connection between a society's treatment of women and the prospects for war and peace. She also considers how gender is used and manipulated during conflict, paying particular attention to the issue of conflict-related sexual violence. She concludes with an assessment of international policy responses since the early 1990s and the advancement of the WPS agenda.

Anne Marie Goetz and Rob Jenkins review the obstacles to gender-responsive peacebuilding. They argue that successful implementation of gender-responsive peacebuilding and the future of the WPS agenda will be shaped by three trends in the international system: the backlash against liberal norms in affluent democracies; the growing tendency of influential regional powers in the developing world to adopt "authoritarian modes of conflict management" when addressing insurgencies, terrorism and other security problems within their borders; and the growing role of China as a provider of foreign assistance and purveyor of development models.

Jeannette Gaudry Haynie examines the lack of gender perspectives in counter-terrorism policies, which has been highly problematic. She develops a comprehensive framework for thinking about gender and terrorism. Through a case study of Mohamed Atta and a discussion of Incel terrorism, she shows how gender and notions of masculinity are key. All of this should inform research and policy. She notes that one of the keys for policy communities will be the recruitment of a more diverse cohort of leaders, who will have a better appreciation of the roles of men and women in enabling and countering terrorism.

Ellen Haring analyzes gender and military organizations. Military organizations are based on bifurcated notions of men as warrior-protectors and women as the protected. These ideas are deeply imbedded in organizational cultures and policies. There is no room in this construct for women who want to join national militaries. The result is that women have faced systemic discrimination and mistreatment in recruitment, training, job opportunities, promotion and retention. She shows how the main driver of progress has been organizational necessity: military organizations have been more open to accepting women when this has been an operational imperative due to wartime and security needs.

Jane Freedman explores the gender dimensions of population movements, including migration, refugee flows and human trafficking. Population movements are both the result of and a cause of instability and conflict; they reached record highs in the late 2010s, and they might become even larger in the future due to climate change. Gender is a central factor in the dynamics of population movements. Gender influences who migrates, how people migrate, the dangers they face during migration and the dangers they face at borders and in host countries. She highlights the lack of sophisticated gender perspectives in most refugee and migration policies.

Jeni Klugman examines a range of development challenges – including economic opportunities, education, health and leadership – with a gender and security lens. She analyzes the gender dimensions of these issues, the underlying problems and what scholars and policymakers have learned in order to close gaps and advance gender equality, development and security. Although the problems are multidimensional and formidable, the good news is that concerted efforts can change norms, laws, policies and the facts on the ground. Top priorities include the expansion of educational and leadership opportunities for girls and women.

Edward Carr examines the connections between gender and environmental security, analyzing two key issues in detail: water security, and climate change and security. He notes that the study of environmental security issues has evolved from a traditional security approach (focusing on states, stability and armed conflict problems) to a broader human security approach (focused more on resource problems). Even so, too little attention has been paid to the role of gender, and some framings rely on stereotypical ideas about gender. This has been detrimental to the development of effective policies.

Tamara Nair investigates the role of gender in humanitarian emergencies caused by natural disasters. She begins by noting that natural events become humanitarian emergencies only when they effect human communities. Humanitarian emergencies are social constructs with many gendered dimensions. Unfortunately, the gender dimensions of disasters have not received much attention at the national level, in particular. A key question for international actors is whether they should shift the humanitarian assistance paradigm from resilience and restoration (including restoration of gender inequalities) to transformation.

Corey Levine and Sari Kouvo review the evolution of international human rights law and women's rights since World War II. They argue that progress on women's rights has been driven by determined advocacy by women's rights activists. These efforts have also been galvanized by international developments, such as the conflict-related atrocities of the 1990s. The authors argue that human rights laws are critically important, but formal declarations are not sufficient. They show how the "war on terror" has been a major setback for international human rights progress, including women's rights.

Jacqui True and Sara Davies examine the interconnections between gender, governance and security. The authors argue that gender balances can be facilitated through quotas and other mechanisms. However, numerical balances are not sufficient to bring about optimal policy outcomes. Women must have meaningful participation in government, gender perspectives have to be mainstreamed in policy processes, and gender equality agendas must be genuine policy priorities. As in other issue areas, women's civil society organizations and coalitions have been major drivers of progress.

In the concluding chapter, the editors of the book consolidate key insights and lessons in these issue areas. We develop several sets of analytic and policy lessons, focusing on obstacles to progress, drivers of progress and strategies for progress.

Notes

1 As of December 2019, the United States and Palau have signed but not ratified CEDAW. Iran, Somalia and Sudan have not signed CEDAW.
2 As of January 2020, 83 states have adopted NAPs.
3 See Ministry of Foreign Affairs, *Handbook: Sweden's Feminist Foreign Policy* (Stockholm: Government of Sweden, 2019). Canada adopted a feminist international assistance policy in 2017. France and Mexico also adopted feminist foreign policies.
4 SDGs, Goal 5.
5 See Council on Foreign Relations (CFR), *Women's Participation in Peace Processes* (New York: CFR, January 2019, interactive database @ cfr.org).
6 Amnesty International, *Do Not Remain Silent* (London: Amnesty International, July 2017).
7 *Report of the UN Secretary-General on Conflict-Related Sexual Violence*, S/2019/280 (New York: United Nations, March 29, 2019).
8 Ibid.
9 Ibid. See also chapter 2 in this book.
10 See UN Women, *Facts and Figures: Leadership and Political Participation* (New York: UN Women, June 2019).
11 World Bank, *Women, Business and the Law 2019: A Decade of Reform* (Washington, DC: World Bank, 2019), p. 8.
12 See *Report of the Secretary-General on SDG Progress 2019* (New York: United Nations, 2019).
13 McKinsey Global Institute, *The Power of Parity: How Advancing Women's Equality Can Add $12 Trillion to Global Growth* (New York: McKinsey, September 2015).
14 World Economic Forum (WEF), *Global Gender Gap Report 2020* (Geneva: WEF, December 2019). See also Gita Sen, "Gender Equality and Women's Empowerment: Feminist Mobilization for the SDG's," *Global Policy*, Vol. 10, No. S1 (January 2019), pp. 28–38.
15 See Francis Fukuyama, "Women and the Evolution of World Politics," *Foreign Affairs*, Vol. 77, No. 5 (September–October 1998). For a critique, see Barbara Ehrenreich et al., "Fukuyama's Follies: So, What If Women Ruled the World," *Foreign Affairs*, Vol. 78, No. 1 (January–February 1999); J. Ann Tickner, "Why Women Can't Run the World: International Politics According to Francis Fukuyama," *International Studies Review*, Vol. 1, No. 3 (Autumn 1999), pp. 3–11.
16 See Naomi Ellemers, "Gender Stereotypes," *Annual Review of Psychology*, Vol. 69 (2018), pp. 277–278; Janet Shibley Hyde, "The Gender Similarities Hypothesis," *American Psychologist*, Vol. 60, No. 6 (September 2005); Jenifer R. Lightdale and Deborah A. Prentice, "Rethinking Sex Differences in Aggression: Aggressive Behavior in the Absence of Social Roles," *Personality and Social Psychology Bulletin*, Vol. 20, No. 1 (February 1994), pp. 34–44.
17 Anne Fausto-Sterling, "Why Sex Is Not Binary," *New York Times* (October 25, 2018). See also Anne Fausto-Sterling, "Gender/Sex, Sexual Orientation, and Identity Are in the Body: How Did They Get There?" *Journal of Sex Research*, Vol. 56, Nos. 4–5 (2019), pp. 529–555.

18 Candace West and Don H. Zimmerman, "Doing Gender," in Michael Kimmel and Amy Aronson, eds., *The Gendered Society Reader*, 5th ed. (Oxford: Oxford University Press, 2014), p. 133.

19 See Candace West and Sarah Fenstermaker, "Doing Difference," in Michael Kimmel and Amy Aronson, eds., *The Gendered Society Reader*, 5th ed. (Oxford: Oxford University Press, 2014), p. 135. See also Cecilia Ridgeway, *Framed by Gender: How Gender Inequality Persists in the Modern World* (Oxford: Oxford University Press, 2011).

20 ECOSOC, *Agreed Conclusions 1997/2*, A/52/3 (July 18, 1997).

21 Office of the Special Adviser on Gender Issues and the Advancement of Women, *Important Concepts Underlying Gender Mainstreaming* (New York: United Nations, August 2001).

22 Ibid.

23 Emma Rothschild, "What Is Security?" *Daedalus*, Vol. 124, No. 3 (Summer 1995), p. 61.

24 Ibid., pp. 60–65.

25 See Samuel P. Huntington, *The Soldier and the State: The Theory and Politics of Civil-Military Relations* (Cambridge, MA: Harvard University Press, 1957).

26 See Joseph S. Nye, Jr. and Sean M. Lynn-Jones, "International Security Studies: A Report of a Conference on the State of the Field," *International Security*, Vol. 12, No. 4 (Spring 1988), pp. 5–27.

27 See Barry Buzan, *People, States and Fear: The National Security Problem in International Relations* (Brighton: Wheatsheaf, 1983); Richard H. Ullman, "Redefining Security," *International Security*, Vol. 8, No. 1 (Summer 1983), pp. 129–153.

28 See Richard H. Schultz, Jr., Roy Godson and George H. Quester, eds., *Security Studies for the 21st Century* (Washington, DC: Brassey's, 1997); Steven E. Miller, "*International Security* at Twenty-Five: From One World to Another," *International Security*, Vol. 26, No. 1 (Summer 2001), pp. 5–39; Michael E. Brown, "Security Problems and Security Policy in a Grave New World," in Michael E. Brown, ed., *Grave New World: Security Challenges in the 21st Century* (Washington, DC: Georgetown University Press, 2003), pp. 305–327; Michael E. Brown et al., eds., *New Global Dangers: Changing Dimensions of International Security* (Cambridge, MA: MIT Press, 2004).

29 Kenneth N. Waltz, "Structural Realism After the Cold War," *International Security*, Vol. 25, No. 1 (Summer 2000), p. 39.

30 John J. Mearsheimer, *The Tragedy of Great Power Politics* (New York: Norton, 2001), p. 361.

31 John J. Mearsheimer, "Disorder Restored," in Graham Allison and Gregory F. Treverton, eds., *Rethinking America's Security: Beyond Cold War to New World Order* (New York: Norton, 1992), p. 214.

32 See Stephen P. Walt, "The Renaissance of Security Studies," *International Studies Quarterly*, Vol. 35, No. 2 (June 1991), pp. 211–239.

33 See Robert Jervis, *Perception and Misperception in World Politics* (Princeton, NJ: Princeton University Press, 1976); Irving L. Janis, *Victims of Groupthink: A Psychological Study of Foreign Policy Decisions and Fiascoes* (Boston: Houghton Mifflin, 1972).

34 See Ullman, "Redefining Security," p. 129.

35 See Edward A. Kolodziej, "Renaissance in Security Studies? Caveat Lector!" *International Studies Quarterly*, Vol. 36, No. 4 (December 1992), p. 422.

36 UNDP, "New Dimensions of Human Security," in *Human Development Report, 1994* (New York: United Nations, 1994), p. 22. See also Gunhild Hoogensen Gjørv, "Human Security," in Paul D. Williams and Matt McDonald, eds., *Security Studies: An Introduction*, 3rd ed. (London: Routledge, 2018), pp. 221–234. For a critique, see Roland Paris, "Human Security: Paradigm Shift or Hot Air?" *International Security*, Vol. 26, No. 2 (Fall 2001), pp. 87–102.

37 See UNDP, "New Dimensions of Human Security," pp. 34–40; Rothschild, "What Is Security?" p. 55.

38 See UN Secretary-General's High-Level Panel on Threats, Challenges and Change, *A More Secure World: Our Shared Responsibility* (New York: United Nations, December 2004).

39 EU, *Shared Vision, Common Action: A Stronger Europe. A Global Strategy for the European Union's Foreign and Security Policy* (Brussels: EU, June 2016), p. 9.

40 In December 2018, the EU committed to integrate gender perspectives in all its policies, including the *EU Global Strategy*. See EU, *Women, Peace and Security: Council Conclusions*, 15086/18 (Brussels: EU, December 10, 2018).

41 See J. Ann Tickner, *A Feminist Voyage Through International Relations* (Oxford: Oxford University Press, 2014); J. Ann Tickner, *Gender in International Relations: Feminist Perspectives on Achieving Global Security* (New York: Columbia University Press, 1992); Cynthia Enloe, *Bananas, Beaches and Bases: Making Feminist Sense of International Politics* (Berkeley, CA: University of California Press, 1990); Spike Peterson, ed., *Gendered States: Feminist (Re)visions of International Relations Theory* (Boulder, CO: Lynne Rienner, 1992). See also Valerie M. Hudson, Donna Lee Bowen and Perpetua Lynne Nielsen, *The First Political Order* (New York: Columbia University Press, 2020); Sara E. Davies and Jacqui True, eds, *The Oxford Handbook of Women, Peace and Security* (Oxford: Oxford University Press, 2019); Swati Parashar, J. Ann Tickner and Jacqui True, eds., *Revisiting Gendered States* (Oxford: Oxford University Press, 2018); Caron E. Gentry, Laura Shepherd and Laura Sjoberg, eds., *Routledge Handbook on Gender and Security* (London: Routledge, 2018); Fionnuala Ni Aolain et al., eds., *The Oxford Handbook of Gender and Conflict* (Oxford: Oxford University Press, 2018); Laura Sjoberg, *Gendering Global Conflict* (New York: Columbia University Press, 2013); Cynthia Cockburn, "War and Security, Women and Gender: An Overview of the Issues," *Gender and Development*, Vol. 21, No. 3 (2013), pp. 443–452; Valerie M. Hudson et al., *Sex and World Peace* (New York: Columbia University Press, 2012); Nicole Detraz, *International Security and Gender* (Cambridge, MA: Polity Press, 2012); Laura Sjoberg and Sandra Via, eds., *Gender, War and Militarism: Feminist Perspectives* (Santa Barbara, CA: Praeger, 2010).

42 Nadia Crevecoeur and Maya Whitney, *Gender and Security: A Survey of International Security Journals*, Women In International Security (WIIS) Policy Brief (Washington, DC: WIIS, May 2020).

43 *Charter of the United Nations*, Preamble.

44 *Universal Declaration of Human Rights*, Article 2.

45 See Sanam Anderlini, *Women Building Peace: What They Do and Why It Matters* (Boulder, CO: Lynne Rienner, 2007), pp. 33–41; Ali Mari Tripp, "Women's Organizations and Peace Initiatives," in Fionnuala Ni Aolain et al., eds., *The Oxford Handbook of Gender and Conflict* (Oxford: Oxford University Press, 2018), pp. 430–441.

46 See *Beijing Platform for Action*, Chapter E: Women and Armed Conflict (1995).

47 ECOSOC, *Agreed Conclusions 1997/2*.

48 See Felicity Hill, Mikele Aboitiz and Sara Poehlman-Doumbaya, "Non-Governmental Organizations' Role in the Buildup and Implementation of Security Council Resolution 1325," *Signs*, Vol. 28, No. 4 (Summer 2003), pp. 1255–1269; Sanam Anderlini, "The Civil Society Story of Adopting Resolution 1325," in *Oxford Handbook of Women, Peace and Security*, pp. 38–53.

49 See *UN Security Council Press Release*, SC/6816 (March 8, 2000).

50 See *UN Security Council Presidential Statements*, S/PRST/2004/40 (October 28, 2004) and S/PRST/2005/52 (October 27, 2005).

51 See Anne Marie Goetz and Rob Jenkins, "Participation and Protection: Security Council Dynamics, Bureaucratic Politics, and the Evolution of the Women, Peace and Security Agenda," in *Oxford Handbook of Gender and Conflict*, pp. 119–131, especially p. 121.

52 See Kerry Crawford, *Wartime Sexual Violence: From Silence to Condemnation of a Weapon of War* (Washington, DC: Georgetown University Press, 2017), p. 15. See also chapter 2 in this book.

53 Ibid. See also Goetz and Jenkins, "Participation and Protection."

54 The framework was based on UNSCR 1325 (2000), 1820 (2008), 1888 (2008), and 1889 (2009).

55 This pillar framework was inspired by the 2008–09 UN System-Wide Action Plan on implementing UNSCR 1325 and the comprehensive set of indicators developed by the United Nations in 2010 to measure implementation of the WPS agenda. See the *Reports of the UN Secretary-General on Women and Peace and Security*, S/2010/173 (April 6,

2010) and S/2010/498 (September 28, 2010). The 2015 review of the implementation of UNSCR 1325 refers to the fourth pillar as the peacebuilding and recovery pillar. See UN Women, *Preventing Conflict, Transforming Justice, Securing the Peace: A Global Study on the Implementation of UN Security Council Resolution 1325* (New York: UN Women, 2015); cited hereafter as *Global Study*.

56 See Hilary Charlesworth and Christine Chinkin, *The Creation of UN Women*, RegNet Research Paper Series, 2013/7 (Canberra: Regulatory Institutions Network, 2013).

57 See Goetz and Jenkins, "Participation and Protection," p. 126.

58 UNSCR 2122 (2013), which called for a study on the implementation of UNSCR 1325, was an exception and a victory for UN Women. In October 2013, the CEDAW Committee adopted a General Recommendation on women in conflict prevention, conflict and post-conflict situations (GR 30). This created greater synergies between the CEDAW and the WPS agendas.

59 See UNSCR 2122 (2013). Radhika Coomaraswamy of Sri Lanka was appointed as the lead author of the study. UN Women served as the secretariat for the study.

60 See *Report of the High-Level Independent Panel on Peace Operations: On Uniting Our Strengths for Peace: Politics, Partnerships and People*, A/70/95 and S/2015/446 (2015); *The Challenges of Sustaining Peace: A Report of the Advisory Group of Experts for the 2015 Review of the United Nations Peacebuilding Architecture* (June 29, 2015).

61 See *Global Study*, p. 5. See also Davies and True, *Oxford Handbook of Women, Peace and Security*.

62 See Security Council Report, *Women, Peace and Security: Closing the Security Council's Implementation Gap*, Research Report No. 2 (New York: Security Council Report, February 24, 2017).

63 See chapter 4 in this book.

64 See Security Council Report, *In Hindsight, Negotiations on Resolution 2467 on Sexual Violence in Conflict* and *In Hindsight Negotiations on Resolution 2493 on Women, Peace and Security* (New York: Security Council Report, May 2, 2019 and November 27, 2019); Heinrich Boll Stiftung, *German Government Treading on Dangerous Ground in the UN Security Council* (Berlin: Heinrich Boll Stiftung, March 7, 2019); Louise Allen and Laura J. Shepherd, *The Complex Politics of Resolution 2467* (London: London School of Economics, April 25, 2019, @ LSE blog).

65 For a comprehensive assessment of the WPS agenda, see Davies and True, *Oxford Handbook of Women, Peace and Security*.

66 See UNSCR 1820 (2008) and 1888 (2009).

67 See Crawford, *Wartime Sexual Violence*, p. 160.

68 See Jasmine Kim K. Westerdorf, "WPS and SEA in Peacekeeping Operations," in *Oxford Handbook of Women, Peace and Security*, pp. 222–236.

69 See Sanam Anderlini, *UN Peacekeepers' Sexual Assault Problem*, Foreign Affairs Snapshot (New York: CFR, June 9, 2017).

70 Sabine Lee and Susan Bartels, "They Put a Few Coins in Your Hand to Drop a Baby in You," *The Conversation* (December 17, 2019, @theconversation.com).

71 See Robert Ulrich Nagel, *The Known Knowns and Known Unknows in Data on Women, Peace and Security*, Working Paper No. 19 (London: London School of Economics, 2019).

72 *Report of the UN Secretary-General on Conflict Related Sexual Violence*, S/2019/280.

73 See *Global Study*, chapter 4.

74 CFR, *Women's Participation in Peace Processes*.

75 See the *Statement of the Executive Director of UN Women, Phumzile Mlambo-Ngcuka*, at the 2017 UN Security Council Open Debate on Women, Peace and Security, S/PV8079 (New York: United Nations, October 27, 2017).

76 *Report of the UN Secretary-General on Women, Peace and Security*, S/2019/800 (New York: United Nations, October 2019), p. 6.

77 Ibid.

78 See *UN Security Council Presidential Statements*, S/PRST/2004/40 and S/PRST/2005/52.

79 Norway, Sweden, Switzerland and the United Kingdom published NAPs in 2006. Austria, the Netherlands, and Spain published NAPs in 2007. Cote d'Ivoire, Finland, Iceland, and Uganda published NAPs in 2008.

80 See *Report of the UN Secretary-General on Women, Peace and Security*, S/2019/800, pp. 23–24.

81 See Barbara Miller, Milad Pournik and Aisling Swaine, *Women in Peace and Security Through United Nations Security Council Resolution 1325* (Washington, DC: George Washington University Elliott School of International Affairs, 2014); Christin Ormhaug, *OSCE Study on National Action Plans on the Implementation of the United Nations Security Council Resolution 1325* (Vienna: OSCE, 2014). See also *Global Study*; Jacqui True, "Explaining the Global Diffusion of the Women, Peace and Security Agenda," *International Political Science Review*, Vol. 37, No. 3 (June 2016), pp. 307–323; London School of Economics and University of Sydney, *WPS National Action Plans* (database @ wpsnaps. org).

82 See *Report of the UN Secretary-General on Women, Peace and Security*, S/2019/800, p. 3.

83 See *Global Study*.

84 See Laura J. Shepherd, "Making War Safe for Women? National Action Plans and the Militarisation of the Women, Peace and Security Agenda," *International Political Science Review*, Vol. 37, No. 3 (2016), pp. 324–335.

85 Cora Weiss, "We Must Not Make War Safe for Women," *Open Democracy-50.50* (May 24, 2011).

86 Sanam Anderlini, "Rise of Feminism and the Renewed Battle for Women's Rights," *InterPress Service* (March 5, 2018.) See also Swati Parashar, "The WPS Agenda: A Postcolonial Critique," in *Oxford Handbook of Women, Peace and Security*, pp. 829–839.

2

GENDER AND ARMED CONFLICT

Kathleen Kuehnast

A large scholarly literature exists about the causes and dynamics of armed conflict. Regrettably, the mainstream security studies literature has given little attention to the role of gender in the onset, practice and impacts of armed conflict. Nor has it listened to the voices of activists – notably community-based women activists – signaling impending armed conflict in their communities, countries and regions. As a result, the scholarly literature on armed conflict is both massive and incomplete as is the policy-focused literature on conflict prevention and conflict resolution.

In the traditional security studies literature, inter-state war is generally defined as an armed conflict between two or more states. Intra-state war is defined as an armed conflict between two or more political groups, one of which may or may not be a recognized government. Today, intra-state conflicts are the predominant form of armed conflict. However, most of these conflicts also involve external actors – including state actors, which blur the distinction between inter-state and intra-state armed conflicts. One-sided conflicts – deliberate attacks on civilians by governments and militias – are another deadly type of armed conflict.[1] In traditional security studies, armed conflicts are generally seen as distinct events with a beginning and an end. Mainstream security scholars analyze the onset of armed conflicts at the level of the individual (leaders and groups), the level of the state (decisionmaking processes within a state and economic, cultural and political dynamics) and the systemic level (the distribution of power among states in the international system).

Feminist and gender scholars have questioned these conceptions and explanations of armed conflict.[2] First, many feminist and gender scholars have contested the notion that armed conflict should be viewed as a distinct event, with a beginning and an end. Instead, they argue that violence is an ongoing problem in societies and that it should be viewed as a continuum. They note that many armed conflicts straddle the divide between the international and the domestic, the public and the private spheres and the collective and the individual. Sexual violence and interpersonal violence are often symptomatic and linked to broader conflict dynamics in societies.

Second, feminist and gender scholars have argued that different levels of analysis are difficult to disaggregate because they are often interdependent. These scholars have lamented the lack of attention to gender and gender hierarchies as factors in explaining armed conflicts. In addition, many scholars have questioned the assumption that the state is a unitary and genderless actor. They argue that more emphasis should be placed on the gendered nature of institutions and relationships within and between states.[3]

This chapter explores the relationship between gender and armed conflict. It focuses on three main issues. First, it examines the role of gender and gender inequalities in the onset of armed conflict. Second, the chapter considers how gender is used and manipulated during conflict. It gives particular attention to the tactical use of sexual violence in conflict. Third, the chapter concludes by identifying drivers of progress as well as the obstacles to integrating gender into analyses of and policy responses to armed conflict. It closes by proposing strategies for advancing progress in the future.

This chapter is premised on the idea that "war (and armed conflict) is a profoundly gendered practice" in theory and practice.[4] Unequal gender power relationships within societies are driving forces in the onset of armed conflict. In addition, war is a human activity in which both men and women participate, even if the roles and impacts of armed conflict are usually very different for men and women due to the different expectations and positions men and women occupy in the societies in which they live.

Gender and the onset of armed conflict

Since the mid-1980s, feminist and gender scholars have explored the multidimensional relationships between gender and armed conflict. The end of the Cold War and the 1995 Fourth World Conference on Women in Beijing brought the issue of women (and gender) to the fore in international debates on peace and security. The Beijing Conference galvanized discussion about the representation of women and their experiences during war. It also spurred local, national and international activism by women's groups. While many women's groups and policymakers have initially focused on the experiences of women during war and armed conflict, they have also emphasized the importance of preventing armed conflict. This has meant calling attention to the causes of armed conflict, including the role of gender and gender inequalities in the onset of violence.

In the public imagination, war and armed conflict are often seen as the results of innate male aggressiveness – too much testosterone and toxic masculinities. Many popularized renderings of war and armed conflict follow prescribed (stereotypical) gender roles, with men as soldiers and protectors and women as victims and spectators. This image of war and armed conflict has been perpetuated through eons of literature, from Homer's Iliad to present-day films. It is also fairly consistent across cultures. In many societies, the masculine is associated with physical strength, competitiveness, courage and ambition. The feminine is often associated with nurturing and caring. Stereotypical gender norms associate men with competition and war, and women with cooperation and peace. In his study on war and gender, Joshua Goldstein posits that "cultures develop gender roles that equate 'manhood' with toughness under fire." He argues that "across cultures and through time, the selection of men as potential combatants (and of women for feminine support roles) has helped shape the war system" and this, in turn, has helped shape gender norms and societal expectations.[5]

In explaining war, feminist scholars have pointed to the fact that the global political system is characterized by a patriarchal structure of privilege and control. Cynthia Cockburn has argued that "patriarchal gender relations are among the 'root causes' of militarisms and war."[6] She notes that, to explain and understand war and militarization, three dimensions of power are key: economic power; ethnic and national power; and gender power. For Cockburn, any theory of war and its causation is flawed if it lacks a gender dimension: "The gender drama is never absent: the male as subject, the female as alien, the alien as effeminate (both the one a man perceives out there, and the one he fears in himself)."[7]

Feminist scholars such as J. Ann Tickner have redefined and broadened core concepts in international relations theories. Tickner has argued that many mainstream theories have been based on rational actors in a state-centric world and masculine views of human nature.[8] She has contended that conceptions of national security should be expanded to include non-military considerations, including human security frameworks and environmental factors. Power should be redefined to include more than domination and control; it should also encompass cooperation and collective empowerment. She has encouraged scholars and experts to study the relationship between gender inequalities and structural violence and examine how militaristic practices of states are legitimated in the name of masculinity.[9]

Laura Sjoberg has engaged mainstream security studies and argued that gender hierarchies operate, not only at the individual level, but also at the state and systemic levels. She has argued that the international system is characterized by anarchy as well as a gender hierarchy. She posits,

> If gender hierarchy is a structural feature of the international system and a key organizing principle in dictating state identity, interaction, and relative position, then conflicts between states can be characterized as conflicts within/about the gendered order of the international structure . . . as gendered posturing between actors jockeying for a higher position along the gendered sociopolitical hierarchy among states. Conflict is not, as realists argue, a competition for survival. . . . Instead, it is a competition where states, as gendered actors in a gendered system, are out to dominate rather than survive. . . . States do not look to continue to exist or to end other's existence; they look to affirm their masculinity (and protect their feminine elements) while feminizing others.[10]

In the 1990s, scholars started to investigate the relationship between gender inequalities and the propensity for conflict. Mary Caprioli examined the relationship between state militarism and gender equality, showing how intra-state gender equality has a pacifying effect on state behavior at the international level. She concluded that states with higher levels of gender equality were less likely to rely on military force to settle international disputes.[11] She also observed how gender inequality and violence against women fuels intra-state conflict and how gender equality reduces the occurrence of intra-state violence. She contended that gender discrimination and structural gender violence are important in nationalist calls for mobilization. She concluded that "states characterized by gender inequality are more likely to experience intrastate conflict."[12]

Building on Caprioli's research about the relationship between gender equality and the onset of intra-state war, Erik Melander extended the analysis to examine changes in the level of intra-state conflict – that is, whether intra-state conflicts remain minor armed conflicts (with 25–999 battle deaths) or escalate into wars (with 1,000 or more battle deaths).[13] He found that countries with higher levels of female participation in political life – measured in terms of women in parliament and higher education – are more likely to keep armed conflicts from escalating to higher levels of lethality. Like Caprioli, Melander observed that gender equality has pacifying effects on countries and their conflicts. In a subsequent study, Elin Bjarnegard and Melander examined the relationship between democracy, gender equality and political violence. They found that there is no positive relationship between democracy and the percentage of women in politics or democracy and peace. The latter only shows a positive relationship when gender equality is introduced in the equation.[14] At an individual level, public attitudes toward gender equality (held by either men or women) also correlate with greater tolerance and less hostile views of other countries and minority groups.[15]

Valerie Hudson and her colleagues have developed a powerful "women and peace thesis" that links the treatment of women with the behavior of states. They found a high correlation between the physical security of women in a country – that is, protection from domestic violence and rape – and the overall peace of that country.[16] According to Hudson and her colleagues, "gender inequality is a form of violence that creates a generalized context of violence and exploitation at the societal level."[17] They have also developed an open-access database (WomenStats) that includes cross-national data, statistics and maps on the status of women.

Jeni Klugman and Mariana Viollaz confirm these findings in their study of the relationship between violent conflict and gender inequality. They conclude that "improvements in the level of women's education, increases in women's political participation, reductions in adolescent fertility rates, declines in informal forms of discrimination, and reductions in intimate partner violence are all associated with lower levels of organized violence."[18]

Some scholars have raised concerns about this line of empirical and quantitative research. They have questioned the ways gender equality and inequality are operationalized.[19] They have also noted that the use of aggregate data and aggregate indicators cannot capture the complex social phenomena that give and do not give power to women at the individual level. For example, the number of women in parliament is not a perfect indicator of female empowerment, participation, autonomy and leadership in the political arena. Although quantitative research in the social sciences has always faced challenges, this body of research has developed pathbreaking insights into the connections between gender equality and peace.

Scholars have also examined the relationship between demographics – gender imbalances, in particular – and security. Valerie Hudson and Andrea den Boer have argued that the deficits of women in China, India and Pakistan are likely to have an array of negative social and national security consequences, including increases in drug use, crime rates, prostitution, human trafficking and organized crime activity. Gender imbalances are likely to lead to social instability, which could lead governments to adopt increasingly harsh and authoritarian approaches to internal governance. These gender imbalances will generate large pools of unmarried men who might be conscripted into military service to keep them off the streets. The emergence of larger armies might make governments more inclined to start armed conflicts – perhaps to deflect attention from social instabilities at home. It will certainly make other countries more wary. In short, gender imbalances are likely to generate both intra-state and inter-state stability and security problems.[20]

Contrary to what one might expect, situations in which there is a surplus of men and a scarcity of women do not make the latter more valuable. On the contrary, powerful men will act to control women even more tightly under these circumstances. Women are also more likely to be kidnapped and sold. Rose McDermott, Valerie Hudson and Hilary Matfess have shown how marital systems including polygyny (where a man has more than one wife) and patrilineal practices such as bride prices (the price to be paid for men to marry) and dowries (the price to be paid for women to marry), which are practiced by approximately 75 percent of the world's population, can be early indicators of social instability and violent conflict.[21]

Feminist and gender scholars have emphasized that war and armed conflict should be viewed as existing on a continuum of violence. Many countries that are generally considered to be "at peace" (such as El Salvador, the Philippines or South Africa) are extremely violent societies that are subject to gang violence or terrorism.[22] In these violent places, the organization and activities of criminal, terrorist and paramilitary groups, including the use of violence, is highly gendered. The members of these groups are overwhelmingly male, and they subscribe to highly masculine and militarized values. Violence is often highly sexualized.[23]

Gender roles reflect the power dynamics within societies and are continuously redefined and renegotiated, particularly on the continuum of war and peace. In her essay, *On Violence*, Hannah Arendt questioned the perspective that political violence is the "most flagrant manifestation of power," and instead argued that violence is the failure of power.[24]

Anthropologists Nancy Scheper-Hughes and Philippe Bourgois use Arendt's hypothesis to challenge the war and peace dichotomy.[25] They blur these categories and the distinctions between violence in wartime and violence during peacetime.

Contending that violence as a social process is reproduced in everyday structures, they reject the idea that violence is biologically predetermined or "hard wired" in human beings. Instead, they argue that violence is socially constructed at the intersection of the individual, the communal and the political. They argue that the public version of violence in war is part of the same continuum of the private version of violence in the household. As feminist scholars Carol Cohn and Sara Ruddick describe it, war "is a continuum of violence running from bedroom to boardroom, factories, stadiums, classroom and battlefield, 'traversing our bodies and sense of self.'"[26]

In recent decades, scholars have made great contributions to our understanding of the relationship between gender and the onset of armed conflict. In particular, they have identified gender inequality as a major precursor to armed conflict and violence. Unfortunately, these insights have not been well-integrated into mainstream studies on war and peace. They have also not led to major changes in policies. Indeed, most conflict analyses in the security studies field are devoid of gender analysis. Gender perspectives and gender analyses have not been seriously integrated into conflict analyses in the academic world, think tanks and most governments.

Gender in armed conflict

Armed conflict may significantly alter gender norms and practices as well as expectations for men and women. Policymakers often reduce gender to a binary equation of men as violent perpetrators and women as powerless victims. This oversimplification of how gender is conceptualized as biological sex instead of as a social construct (a construct that is malleable and that can be manipulated) is seldom considered by international security scholars or by policymakers, whether they hail from diplomacy, defense or development.

Beyond identity, gender is a social, institutional and symbolic structure that intersects with economic and political power relations. At its core, gender is about the structural relations of power. Like race, slavery, class, caste and colonialization, gender is a primary component in the orchestration of power relations.[27] Armed conflict and even the threat of armed conflict amplifies these power relations and affects everyone.

The question is whether and how armed conflict offers opportunities to advance gender equality in the economic, political and social arenas. For example, wars have drawn more women into the workforce and created opportunities for more women to have public roles, allowing for economic, social and political gains.[28] These temporary advances have generally not led to a "new normal" nor to enduring changes in gender relations once wars come to an end. And at the same time, wars place additional responsibilities and heavy burdens on women's shoulders.

The threat of armed conflict (including pre-conflict and post-conflict insecurities) may also intensify hypermasculinity and masculinity nostalgia in societies – that is, a growing emphasis on stereotypical male behaviors, such as strength and a yearning for "a time of patriarchal power, authority and gender certainty."[29]

Marie Berry has examined the position of women before and after the wars in Bosnia and Rwanda.[30] She documents how these wars brought about increased mobilizations of women in the economic, political and cultural spheres. However, in both cases, underlying patriarchal structures remained intact and bounced back once the wars ended – thereby reducing women's power. Gender hierarchies are robust and difficult to change. Indeed, even if wars and armed conflicts change social and political orders and even out some gender inequalities, gains in gender equality are often temporary.[31]

Gender and its complex dynamics are at the core of many ideological and political debates in societies. The opportunities and challenges in the aftermath of armed conflicts often amplify the social binary of men and women, and they reduce the multiple and overlapping roles that men and women normally play into social silos where roles often become more highly restricted. War is a violent process that alters societies and changes behaviors. Yet, policymakers and other stakeholders rarely take advantage of these circumstances to transform social contracts and promote gender equality outside and inside the home. More research is needed on the impact of armed conflict (and the threat of armed conflict) on gender norms and gender roles.

Conflict-related sexual violence

Armed conflict affects men and women differently. The impact of sexual violence on civilian populations, particularly women, is one of the most gender-defining aspects of violence in war. Conflict-related sexual violence involves not just acts of rape, as defined in the Rome Statute of the International Criminal Court; it also includes a continuum of violent acts – sexual slavery, forced marriage, forced prostitution, forced pregnancy, forced abortion, enforced sterilization, torture, humiliation and other forms of sexualized violence.

Conservative estimates indicate that between 20,000 to 60,000 women were raped during the war and genocide in Bosnia and Herzegovina between 1992 and 1995.[32] Sexual violence has also been rampant in other conflicts. In Sierra Leone, between 50,000 and 64,000 women in camps for Internally Displaced Persons (IDPs) were sexually assaulted by combatants between 1991 and 2002. In the 1994 Rwanda genocide, between 250,000 and 500,000 people (mostly women) experienced some form of sexual violence. After two rounds of war in the Democratic Republic of the Congo in the 1990s and early 2000s, there were more than 400,000 victims and survivors of sexual violence, mostly women and girls.[33] The United Nations (UN) Human Rights Council has reported that sexual and gender-based violence has been used by the Syrian government as a systematic strategy to abuse prisoners in detention centers, to extract confessions, during house-to-house searches and at check-points following the Arab Spring uprising in 2011 and during the subsequent civil war.[34] ISIS used sexual violence as a component of its genocidal campaign against the Yazidis of Iraq and Syria. The Myanmar military used sexual violence, including rape and gang rape, in its campaign of forced expulsion and genocide against the Rohingya in 2016–17.

While the exact extent of conflict-related sexual violence is difficult to determine, the United Nations reported in 2019 that 19 countries were currently affected by conflict-related sexual violence and 50 parties (mostly non-state actors) were being listed as committing or being responsible for conflict-related sexual violence.[35] In addition, peacekeepers and humanitarian workers have also subjected populations under their protection to Sexual Exploitation and Abuse (SEA).[36]

Scholarship on conflict-related sexual violence

The scholarship on conflict-related sexual violence has expanded substantially in the 21st century.[37] Five strands of research can be distinguished. One strand of research situates and examines conflict-related sexual violence at a structural level and as symptomatic of gender inequality. It is connected to research on the role of gender inequalities and the onset of war, as well as research on the continuum of violence. A second strand of research examines the motivations behind and the roles and functions of sexual violence in war. A third strand of research focuses on the legal regimes of conflict-related sexual violence and issues related to prosecution. A fourth strand of research focuses on masculinity issues. The fifth strand of research analyzes the psycho-social consequences of conflict-related sexual violence.

For the first strand of research, sexual violence – including conflict-related sexual violence – is a symptom of gender inequality and a particular form of political violence. Sara Davies and Jacqui True have examined the relationship between gendered inequalities in countries and the prevalence of sexual and gender-based violence by comparing the UN's list of countries affected by sexual violence with the Social Institutions and Gender Index (SIGI) of the Organization for Economic Co-operation and Development (OECD) and the conflict data sets of Uppsala University. They observed that countries on the UN list of places affected by sexual violence are also countries that have a higher than average score on the SIGI gender inequality index. They found that there is a "strong association between countries with documented sexual violence and women's limited access to public spaces [which] suggests that [Sexual and Gender-Based Violence] SGBV is indeed a strategy of political domination and violence."[38] They noted that the countries on the UN list also included countries in non-conflict situations. They argued that the extent of SGBV in these countries may be an indicator for potential future conflict.

Davies and True have also examined the preexisting patterns of gender inequality prior to violence.[39] Connecting the preexisting conditions that allow for wartime rape allows for a deeper analysis of ways in which sexual violence is normalized in both war and peace. Preventative strategies to deal with sexual violence need to address the root causes of gender inequality and end the impunity of sexual violence during peacetime. This approach would take wartime rape out of the realm of the "exceptional" and conceptualize it as a part of a continuum of violence in general – and sexual violence in particular – where the common variable is gender inequality.[40]

Elisabeth Wood has contested the claims that conflict-related sexual violence is the result of gender inequality and part of a continuum of violence. She has argued that, if this was the case, we would not see much variation across conflicts and across armed groups.[41] In a study of eight conflict cases, Wood also challenged the notion that sexual violence is a common tactic or strategy of war, noting that sexual violence is not found in every conflict.[42] The most consistent explanation in the eight cases she studied was a combination of individual opportunity (which is enabled by the lack of command structure) along with explicit deterrents and shared values to prevent sexual violence. Wood argued that the lack of sexual violence by the Tamil Tigers in the Sri Lankan civil war, for example, was the result of strong internal hierarchies and communication systems. She also stressed that it is important to distinguish between different forms of sexual violence – such as sexual violence by intimate partners and multiple-perpetrator rape carried out by military organizations.[43] In addition, Wood has introduced the idea that wartime sexual violence should be seen as a practice – "a form of violence driven from 'below' and tolerated from 'above,' rather than purposefully adopted as policy."[44]

Wood's work has been pivotal in inspiring a new generation of scholars to explore the problem of conflict-related sexual violence and focus on the variation in conflict-related sexual violence across conflicts and across armed groups and organizations. Dara Kay Cohen has examined the role sexual violence plays in group behavior, especially in forming bonds among unlikely cohorts of rebel groups and soldiers. She found that groups using abduction as a recruiting practice were more likely to resort to sexual violence.[45] Amelia Hoover Green has shown how rebels in El Salvador worked to limit the use of sexual violence by emphasizing connections between civilian protection and long-term group goals.[46] Much of this research draws on quantitative datasets and the Sexual Violence in Armed Conflict (SVAC) dataset developed by Dara Kay Cohen and Ragnhild Nordas of the Peace Research Institute Oslo (PRIO).[47]

This quantitative research has increased our understanding of the possible roles and functions of conflict-related sexual violence. It has also confronted persistent myths related to conflict-related sexual violence, particularly that rape in war is ubiquitous and inevitable.[48] That said, as Kristen Campbell has argued, this strand of research "does not sufficiently address crucial questions of how wars are gendered (who fights, how, and why); how sexual violence is gendered (who does what to whom); and why sexual violence occurs before, during, and after conflict (why *sexual* violence)."[49] By ignoring how gender structures societies it underestimates the political nature (and functions) of sexual violence.

A third strand of research has focused on the legal regimes of conflict-related sexual violence and accountability for such crimes as war crimes, crimes against humanity and genocide. The inclusion of rape in the International Criminal Tribunal for Yugoslavia (ICTY) and the International Criminal Tribunal for Rwanda (ICTR) as a crime against humanity was intended to serve as a deterrent and a contribution to peace and reconciliation. However, there has been very little evidence of a link between the two. Prosecution of crimes has also been problematic due to the difficulty of reporting – including the stigma associated with sexual violence – the collection of data, the gathering of evidence and access to witnesses.[50] Research has also focused on the issue of reparations – that is, victim-oriented measures to recognize harms that have been suffered. In addition, a number of scholars have connected research and policies on sexual violence to a broader notion of gender justice – whereby justice has "the potential for transforming social relations of domination and oppression, and not only providing redress for wrongs."[51]

A fourth strand of research on sexual violence has focused on the issue of masculinities and how social constructions of masculinities shape ideas and practices of sexual violence perpetrated not only against women and girls, but also against men and boys.[52] This line of research posits that men are not inherently violent, but are made so by society. Ideas of what makes a man and the perceived inability for men to attain this ideal – due to economic dependence, early exposure to violence, traumatic indoctrination or militarization – all contribute to violent masculinities. This research also examines the particular challenges men may face in post-conflict situations and how to bring about changes in gender norms.

In this context, it is important to underscore that women also play a role in shaping the narratives of violent masculinities. Not only is there a hierarchy among men that yields unequal masculinities in their social circles, but these identities are also significantly reinforced by women in their multiple roles as wives, mothers, grandmothers, daughters, sisters, mothers-in-law and so on.[53] Masculinities are not inherent only to males; masculinities act as institutionalized and socialized understandings that both men and women utilize to navigate their societies.

The growing, critical scholarship on men and masculinities has built on the work of early feminist masculinities theory.[54] In addition, the field of social psychology has contributed important research about men, male issues and masculinities.[55] Research efforts such as the International Masculinity and Gender Equality Survey (IMAGES) provide insights on the relational dynamics between men and women in war and peace and the structural contexts that amplify or reinforce these power relations. This study has created a virtual roadmap of ways to engage men and help to solve the global gender equality gap.[56] In the 2010s, an expanded lens on men and their gender issues and dilemmas has become increasingly recognized as pertinent to the advancement of women's equality.[57]

A fifth strand of research on sexual violence has focused on the psychological and social impact of wartime sexual violence.[58] Most of this research has focused on individuals; relatively little research has been done on the societal impacts of widespread rape and sexual violence.[59]

Research on wartime sexual violence has expanded enormously in the 21st century. This research has been undertaken across many different disciplines. As a result, this research is characterized by different approaches, definitions and methodologies. There is a quantitative versus qualitative divide, a victim versus perpetrator divide and a structural versus individual divide – where conflict-related sexual violence is seen as part of a continuum or as separate and specific. While these different approaches are not necessarily in contradiction with one another and may be complementary, they do lead to different policy actions.

Policy responses

For a long time, policymakers saw rape as a collateral side effect of war. It was also seen as an individual act, rather than a weapon, tactic or strategy in war. Sexual violence and rape, while prevalent in World War II, were not a focus of the postwar Nuremberg trials nor were they initially included in the postwar definition of a crime against humanity.[60]

The wars in the Balkans in the 1990s and the deliberate use of sexual violence by Serb combatants as well as press reports about numerous rape camps in Bosnia shocked political elites and citizens in Europe and the United States and led to a number of policy initiatives on wartime sexual violence, most notably in terms of prosecution and legal actions.

Prosecution of rape and sexual violence was one of the justifications for the establishment of the ICTY in May 1993 and the ICTR in November 1994. The 1998 Rome Statute – establishing the International Criminal Court (ICC) – criminalized sexual violence as an act of genocide, a war crime and a crime against humanity.[61] Protection from rape (and other forms of sexual violence) in armed conflict was a main agenda item for the 1993 2nd World Conference on Human Rights held in Vienna; the 1995 4th World Conference on Women in Beijing; and the Women, Peace and Security (WPS) agenda launched with UNSCR 1325 (2000).

Although women's participation in decision-making was a top priority for the activists pushing the WPS agenda, UN member states preferred to focus on protection – that is, protecting women from sexual violence. The notion of sexual violence and rape as a threat to international peace and security and a weapon of war became a powerful political narrative (and framework) that allowed the UN Security Council to focus on and address these issues. Conflict-related sexual violence came to be seen as specific to armed conflict and punishable by national and international actors. The "rape as a weapon of war" framework also allowed sexual violence to be seen as different from sexual violence during peacetime.[62]

UN Security Council Resolution 1820 (2008) was the second UN Security Council Resolution adopted within the WPS framework and the first Council resolution to acknowledge that sexual violence and rape should be considered a tactic of war. It called on UN member states to end sexual violence against women and girls and acknowledged the responsibility of the international community to respond and prevent wartime sexual violence. The Security Council directed the UN Secretary-General to improve the UN's prevention and protection responses to sexual violence, including training of peacekeeping personnel and regular reporting on progress within the UN system. In 2008, the UN Security Council also agreed to include sexual violence against women as an explicit criterion for considering sanctions.[63] The Council later established a Special Representative on Sexual

Violence in Armed Conflict and called for annual reporting on these issues. In addition, the Council created new staff positions – Women Protection Advisors – to be deployed in UN peacekeeping and political operations.[64]

The United Kingdom became a powerful advocate at the UN Security Council for the prevention of conflict-related sexual violence. In 2012, it launched a major initiative to end impunity for perpetrators of sexual violence in conflict settings. Enlisting the help of noted actress Angelina Jolie, the United Kingdom held its first international forum on the Preventing Sexual Violence Initiative in London in June 2014. Representatives from more than 150 countries attended the summit, which also involved the launch of the International Protocol on the Documentation and Investigation of Sexual Violence in Conflict.

Although the issue has received increased international attention, the use of sexual violence in conflict as a tactic of war, terrorism, torture and repression has not diminished. While the international narrative in recent years has broadened and now includes recognition of the structural roots of sexual violence, including "deeply entrenched gender inequality and discriminatory perceptions of gender roles," international actions to address the structural and underlying causes of sexual violence in conflict remain lacking.[65]

Following pressure from civil society groups, accountability and survivor-centered approaches have become more prominent in international discussions and were at the heart of the open debate in the UN Security Council on the WPS agenda in April 2019. Regrettably, little progress has been made on either of these fronts, due to lack of concrete national commitments and actions.

Drivers, obstacles and strategies for progress

This chapter has focused on the gender dimensions of armed conflict, especially gender and the onset of armed conflict and gender in armed conflict. What have been the main drivers of progress and the main obstacles to progress to date? Given this track record, what are the most promising strategies for advancing the integration of gender perspectives in analyses of armed conflicts and, even more importantly, for enhancing the effectiveness of policy actions to prevent conflict-related sexual violence?

Drivers of progress

The changing international political environment – most notably, the end of the Cold War and the changing nature of armed conflict from mainly inter-state to predominantly intra-state conflict – contributed to a shift in focus from national, state-level security to a framework that also included community-level and individual-level security. This provided an opening for an increased focus on gender in security and conflict matters.

At the same time, civil society organizations, including women's organizations, became increasingly important actors at the national and international levels starting in the 1990s. Civil society organizations have been the key drivers leading to the adoption of gender-inclusive language in international commitments and the WPS agenda.

The efforts of these civil society actors culminated in the adoption of United Nations Security Council Resolution (UNSCR) 1325 (2000). It was the first UN Security Council resolution to address issues related to women, peace and security. Despite its shortcomings, UNSCR 1325 (2000) is a significant and unprecedented global commitment that not only recognized the disproportionate negative impact of armed conflict on women, but also highlighted the imperative of incorporating gender perspectives in conflict prevention, peacekeeping and reconciliation efforts. More importantly, UNSCR 1325 acknowledged the untapped potential of women as effective decisionmakers and negotiators, and it urged member states to intensify their efforts for equal representation and participation of women in all endeavors related to the maintenance and promotion of peace and security. This was a significant step in strengthening the nexus between sustainable peace and women's participation in decision-making. Between 2000 and 2019, the UN Security Council adopted nine additional WPS resolutions.[66]

The WPS framework – including National Action Plans (NAPs) and Regional Action Plans (RAPs) – has been critical in keeping the issue of women, peace and security on national and regional policy agendas. It has also provided civil society actors with instruments to hold national governments accountable. Although the WPS framework at the international political level has often been narrowly interpreted and has focused on protection from sexual violence, at local levels the WPS framework has mostly been interpreted as being about women's participation in decision-making structures.[67]

International organizations – such as the United Nations (UN), the African Union (AU), the European Union (EU) and the North Atlantic Treaty Organization (NATO) – have been important in increasing understanding and awareness of the role of gender in armed conflict. Through their resolutions, policies and reports, gender became part of the vernacular of international discussions around armed conflict. The creation of UN Women in 2010 (consolidating the UN's offices working on women's issues) and the creation of special representatives for WPS and sexual violence helped to institutionalize and elevate these issues within these organizations. The efforts of multilateral organizations have been supported by a small number of national governments. Multilateral organizations have also encouraged and supported additional research on gender and armed conflict issues.

Research on gender, including gender and armed conflict, has expanded and advanced impressively in the 21st century. This growing body of research is powerful and wide-ranging; it has led to new, important insights; and it has helped to make gender more visible in security and conflict studies. Quantitative and qualitative research has also been valued by multilateral institutions, in particular. Policymakers want evidence-based research and data to guide policy development and assess policy actions. In short, scholars and analysts have been major drivers of progress on gender and security issues – not just in the realm of ideas and knowledge but in the realm of policy and action.

Obstacles to progress

The obstacles to integrating gender into international and national analyses of armed conflict and taking concrete policy actions have been enormous. These obstacles are both conceptual and political in nature.

At a conceptual level, much of the discussion on gender and armed conflict has been centered around UNSCR 1325 (2000), which framed the problem as "women need protection" and "women should participate in peace processes." Equating "gender" with "women" and not including men (except as perpetrators of wartime sexual violence) has limited the lens for viewing and thinking about these complex problems at the UN and international level as well as the national level. As a result, opportunities have been lost for addressing the gender and conflict problems, including conflict-related sexual violence. The value of "gender" as a robust analytical approach has been poorly understood by most institutions of diplomacy, development and defense, and the goal of "gender mainstreaming" has consequently fallen short almost everywhere. Instead of developing sophisticated gender perspectives on these issues and mainstreaming these perspectives in national and international policy analyses, the prevailing approach has been to "add women and stir," and this usually involves adding very few women to the equation. This approach has not delivered in theatres of war nor in arenas of peace.

In addition, while research on gender and armed conflict has blossomed since the 1990s, this research has been carried out across many disciplines. As a result, no overarching theory has emerged on gender and conflict or conflict-related sexual violence. Although much progress has been made, there is still much that scholars and policymakers do not understand. For example, how and under which conditions does the threat of armed conflict affect gender norms and relations? In addition, scholarship on gender and armed conflict has not been integrated into mainstream security studies. Part of the problem is that some feminist and security studies scholars have fundamentally different epistemological, theoretical and methodological views. But even when feminist scholars have adopted a positivist, empirical approach, they have had a hard time connecting with the traditional security community. The latter has been slow to recognize the central importance of gender in conflict and security issues.

Although many rhetorical commitments have been made in favor of gender equality at the national and international political levels, there has been a lack of political will to follow through. Policy implementation has been poor with respect to gender inequalities in general as well as engaging women in decision-making processes related to international peace and security issues, including conflict resolution processes. Significant gender imbalances and gender inequalities consequently persist at the national and international political levels. Research on gender norms before, during and after conflict has shown the resilience of patriarchies – in interpersonal relations, institutions and national and international structures. This has led to poor implementation of the global WPS framework at the national level, including a lack of resources.

The lack of progress on preventing sexual violence in conflict, despite receiving considerable political attention, is due to a range of factors: a failure to commit sufficient resources to this priority; a widespread inability to develop and utilize proper gender analyses; data problems that interfere with policy development and assessment, as well as the collection of evidence for criminal prosecutions; continuing impunity for these crimes; and lack of political will to prosecute these crimes against humanity. As former UN Secretary-General's Special Representative on Sexual Violence in Armed Conflict, Zainab Hawa Bangura, recounted: "in many places perpetrators of conflict-related sexual violence walk the streets freely, run for political office, and then end up policing the same communities they violated."[68]

Strategies for progress

The dynamic relationship between men and women in armed conflict is often examined through the binary of war and peace. However, defining when an armed conflict is over and when peace begins is not as easy as it sounds. This widely held binary view is a simplistic way to think about the many problems associated with gender and armed conflict. A better way to understand gender and armed conflict is to expand upon the relationship between gender equality and peace.

Progress has to start with greater integration of gender into analyses of armed conflict. An inclusive analytical framework needs to consider both the biological sex of victims and armed actors as well as the socio-cultural roles men and women play in their societies. Continuing to analyze armed conflict without a gender lens perpetrates the idea that gender and sexual violence is a normal aspect of armed conflict, it perpetuates a normalization of hyper-masculinities and it perpetuates the expectation that this violence is a "rite of passage" for young men and women.

Societal fragility and gendered ideas about masculinity need far more scrutiny in conflict analyses. In countries where more than 50 percent of the population is between the ages of 16 and 35 years and where jobs are scarce, social and economic conditions pose almost impossible hurdles to existing status markers about manhood. When men who hold hyper-masculine views are faced with the prospect of social, economic and personal failure, violence and attempts to obtain power through violence may be more likely. IMAGES survey data from the Democratic Republic of the Congo demonstrates how wars confound the ability of men to fulfill societal expectations.[69]

Similarly, the pervasive problems of sexual and gender-based violence will not be solved until our approaches are inclusive of the whole of society. In societies in which violence has occurred over decades, it is critical to consider the socialized norms of violence through which young males reach adulthood. Research has found only limited evidence that men are more inherently violent than women, and neurobiologists suggests that violence is not necessarily "hardwired" into our species.[70] Research like this will help to re-write existing social narratives that men are by nature violent. Neuroscience is driving a research stream on how humans learn and reinforce violence in boys as a part of their male identity. Indeed, if violence is not hardwired, new possibilities open up for societies to solve individual and communal problems without resorting to violence.

The creation of international and national policy frameworks and institutionalization of these frameworks at the global and national levels have been important in keeping gender on the agenda with respect to international peace and security issues. In the decades ahead, it will be important to continue to support these frameworks and take care that they are not hollowed out. Even more important in the decades ahead is supporting civil society actors – women's organizations, in particular. Without their action, progress on the gender equality and the WPS agenda will be difficult to achieve. Their continued engagement will remain critical for the future.

Notes

1   For an early examination of conflict types and problems, see Harry Eckstein, ed., *Internal War: Problems and Approaches* (New York: Free Press, 1964). For sophisticated assessments of current conflict types and trends, see the reports of the Uppsala Conflict Data Program (UCDP), including Thérése Pettersson, Stina Högbladh and Magnus Öberg, "Organized Violence, 1989–2018," *Journal of Peace Research*, Vol. 56, No. 4 (June 2019), pp. 589–603.

2   See J. Ann Tickner, *A Feminist Voyage Through International Relations* (Oxford: Oxford University Press, 2014); J. Ann Tickner, *Gender in International Relations: Feminist Perspectives on Achieving Global Security* (New York: Columbia University Press, 1992); Spike Peterson, *Gendered States: Feminist (Re)visions of International Relations Theory* (Boulder, CO: Lynne Rienner, 1992); Cynthia Enloe, *Bananas, Beaches and Bases: Making Feminist Sense of International Politics* (Berkeley, CA: University of California Press, 1990). See also Laura Sjoberg, *Gendering Global Conflict: Toward a Feminist Theory of War* (New York: Columbia University Press, 2013).

3   See ibid. See also Swati Parashar, J. Ann Tickner and Jacqui True, eds., *Revisiting Gendered States* (Oxford: Oxford University Press, 2018).

4   Carol Cohn, "Women and Wars: Toward a Conceptual Framework," in Carol Cohn, ed., *Women and Wars* (Cambridge: Polity Press, 2013), p. 22.

5   Joshua S. Goldstein, *War and Gender: How Gender Shapes the War System and Vice Versa* (Cambridge: Cambridge University Press, 2001), p. 9.

6   Cynthia Cockburn, "Gender Relations as Causal in Militarization and War," in Annica Kronsell and Erika Svedberg, eds., *Making Gender, Making War: Violence, Military and Peacekeeping Practices* (London: Routledge, 2012), p. 30.

7   Ibid.

8   See J. Ann Tickner, "Hans Morgenthau's Principles of Political Realism: A Feminist Reformulation," in *A Feminist Voyage Through International Relations*, pp. 5–19.

9   See Tickner, *A Feminist Voyage*.

10 See Laura Sjoberg, "Gender, Structure and War: What Waltz Couldn't See," *International Theory*, Vol. 4, No. 1 (March 2012), pp. 1–38. See also Sjoberg, *Gendering Global Conflict*; Laura Sjoberg, *Gender, War and Conflict* (Cambridge: Polity Press, 2014), p. 105.

11 Mary Caprioli, "Gendered Conflict," *Journal of Peace Research*, Vol. 37, No. 1 (January 2000), pp. 53–68.

12 See Mary Caprioli, "Primed for Violence: The Role of Gender Inequality in Predicting Internal Conflict," *International Studies Quarterly*, Vol. 49, No. 2 (June 2005), p. 161.

13 Erik Melander, "Gender Equality and Intrastate Armed Conflict," *International Studies Quarterly*, Vol. 49, No. 4 (December 2005), p. 696.

14 Elin Bjarnegard and Erik Melander, "Disentangling Gender, Peace and Democratization: The Negative Effects of Militarized Masculinity," *Journal of Gender Studies*, Vol. 20, No. 2 (June 2011), pp. 139–154.

15 Elin Bjarnegard and Erik Melander, "Pacific Men: How the Feminist Gap Explains Hostility," *The Pacific Review*, Vol. 30, No. 4 (January 2017), pp. 478–493.

16 Valerie M. Hudson et al., "The Heart of the Matter: The Security of Women and the Security of States," *International Security*, Vol. 33, No. 3 (Winter 2008/09), pp. 7–45. See also Valerie M. Hudson et al., *Sex and World Peace* (New York: Columbia University Press, 2012).

17 Hudson et al., *Sex and World Peace*, p. 5.

18 Jeni Klugman and Mariana Viollaz, *Gender Inequality and Violent Conflict: A New Look*, Unpublished Manuscript (2017).

19 See Danny Hill and Sabrina Karim, "Conceptualizing and Measuring Gender Equality," Paper presented at the International Studies Association Meeting in Baltimore, MD (February 2017).

20 Valerie M. Hudson and Andrea M. den Boer, *Bare Branches: The Security Implications of Asia's Surplus Male Population* (Cambridge, MA: MIT Press, 2002).

21 See Rose McDermott, *The Evils of Polygyny: Evidence of its Harm to Women, Men and Society* (Ithaca, NY: Cornell University Press, 2018); Valerie Hudson and Hilary Matfess, "In Plain Sight: The Neglected Linkage Between Brideprice and Violent Conflict," *International Security*, Vol. 42, No. 1 (Summer 2017), pp. 7–40. See also Dan Reiter, "The Positivist Study of Gender and International Relations," *Journal of Conflict Resolution*, Vol. 59, No. 1 (December 2014), pp. 1301–1326.

22 See Mariana Viollaz and Jeni Klugman, *Gang Violence as Organized Violence: Investigating the Implications for the Women, Peace and Security Index* (Washington, DC: Georgetown Institute for Women, Peace and Security, 2018).

23 See Anne Applebaum and Briana Mawby, "Women and 'New Wars' in El Salvador," *Stability: International Journal of Security and Development*, Vol. 7, No. 1 (November 2018), pp. 1–15. See also David Duriesmith, "Hybrid Warriors and the Formation of New War Masculinities: A Case Study of Indonesian Foreign Fighters," *Stability: International Journal of Security and Development*, Vol. 7, No. 1 (August 2018), pp. 1–16.

24 Hannah Arendt, *On Violence* (Orlando: Harcourt, 1970).

25 Nancy Scheper-Hughes and Philippe Bourgois, eds., *Violence in War and Peace* (Hoboken, NJ: Wiley-Blackwell, 2003), p. 18.

26 Cited in Sjoberg, *Gender, War and Conflict*, p. 133.

27 See Cohn, "Women and Wars."

28 Melanie Hughes, "Armed Conflict, International Linkages, and Women's Parliamentary Representation in Developing Nations," *Social Forces*, Vol. 93, No. 4 (February 2009), pp. 1513–1540.

29 See Megan MacKenzie and Alana Foster, "Masculinity Nostalgia: How War and Occupation Inspire a Yearning for Gender Order," *Security Dialogue*, Vol. 48, No. 3 (2017), pp. 206–223.

30 Marie E. Berry, *War, Women, and Power: From Violence to Mobilization in Rwanda and Bosnia-Herzegovina* (Cambridge: Cambridge University Press, 2018).

31 See Kaitlyn Webster, Chong Chen and Kyle Beardsley, "Conflict, Peace and the Evolution of Women's Empowerment," *International Organization*, Vol. 73, No. 2 (Spring 2019), pp. 255–289.

32 Inger Skjelsbaek, "Sexual Violence in the Post-Yugoslav Wars," in Kathleen Kuehnast, Chantal de Jonge Oudraat and Helga Hernes, eds., *Women and War: Power and Protection in the 21st Century* (Washington, DC: US Institute of Peace, 2010), pp. 65–84.

33 See Kerry F. Crawford, *Wartime Sexual Violence: From Silence to Condemnation of a Weapon of War* (Washington, DC: Georgetown University Press, 2017), p. 15.

34 *UN Human Rights Council*, 37th Session (Geneva: United Nations, February–March 2018).

35 *Report of the UN Secretary-General on Conflict-Related Sexual Violence*, S/2019/280 (New York: United Nations, March 2019).

36 See Jasmine-Kim Westendorf and Louise Searle, "Sexual Exploitation and Abuse in Peace Operations: Trends, Policy Responses and Future Directions," *International Affairs*, Vol. 93, No. 2 (March 2017), pp. 365–387. See also Alicia Luedke, Chloe Lewis and Marisella Rodriguez, *Sexual Violence, Exploitation, and Abuse: Improving Prevention Across Conflicts and Crises*, Special Report No. 415 (Washington, DC: US Institute of Peace, November 2017).

37 See Social Politics, "Special Issue: Revisiting Methods and Approaches in Researching Sexual Violence in Conflict," *Social Politics*, Vol. 25, No. 4 (Winter 2018). See also Carlo Koos, "Sexual Violence in Armed Conflicts: Research Progress and Remaining Gaps," *Third World Quarterly*, Vol. 38, No. 9 (May 2017), pp. 1935–1951.

38 Sara E. Davies and Jacqui True, "Reframing Conflict-Related Sexual and Gender-Based Violence: Bringing Gender Analysis Back in," *Security Dialogue*, Vol. 46, No. 6 (October 2015), p. 505.

39 Sara E. Davies and Jacqui True, "Connecting the Dots: Pre-existing Patterns of Gender Inequality and the Likelihood of Widespread and Systematic Sexual Violence," *Global Responsibility to Protect*, Vol. 9, No. 1 (January 2017), pp. 65–85.

40 Maria Eriksson Baaz and Maria Stern contend that the framing of wartime sexual violence only as an act of power treats sexual violence as an inevitable form of violence in war. See Maria Eriksson Baaz and Maria Stern, "Curious Erasures: The Sexual in Wartime Sexual Violence," *International Feminist Journal of Politics*, Vol. 20, No. 3 (May 2018), pp. 295–314.

41 Elisabeth J. Wood, "Conflict-Related Sexual Violence and the Policy Implications of Recent Research," *International Review of the Red Cross*, Vol. 96, No. 894 (2014), pp. 457–478.

42 See Elisabeth J. Wood, "Variation in Sexual Violence During War," *Politics and Society*, Vol. 34, No. 3 (September 2006), pp. 307–341; Elisabeth J. Wood, "Armed Groups and Sexual Violence: When Is Wartime Rape Rare?" *Politics and Society*, Vol. 37, No. 1 (March 2009), pp. 131–161.

43 Elisabeth J. Wood, "Rape as a Practice of War: Toward a Typology of Political Violence," *Politics and Society*, Vol. 46, No. 4 (May 2018), pp. 513–537.

44 Ibid., pp. 514–515.

45 See Dara K. Cohen, *Rape During Civil War* (Ithaca, NY: Cornell University Press, 2016); Dara Kay Cohen, "Explaining Rape During Civil War: Cross-National Evidence (1980–2009)," *American Political Science Review*, Vol. 107, No. 3 (August 2013), pp. 461–477.

46 Amelia Hoover Green, "Armed Group Institutions and Combat Socialization: Evidence from El Salvador," *Journal of Peace Research*, Vol. 54, No. 5 (September 2017), pp. 687–700. See also Amelia Hoover Green, *The Commander's Dilemma: Violence and Restraint in War* (Ithaca, NY: Cornell University Press, 2018); Dara Kay Cohen, Amelia Hoover Green and Elisabeth Jean Wood, *Wartime Sexual Violence: Misconceptions, Implications, and Ways Forward*, Special Report No. 323 (Washington, DC: US Institute of Peace, February 2013).

47 See Dara Kay Cohen and Ragnhild Nordas, "Sexual Violence in Armed Conflict: Introducing the SVAC Dataset, 1989–2009," *Journal of Peace Research*, Vol. 51, No. 3 (May 2014), pp. 418–428.

48 See Cohen, Green, and Wood, *Wartime Sexual Violence*.

49 Kristen Campbell, "Producing Knowledge in the Field of Sexual Violence in Armed Conflict Research: Objects, Methods, Politics, and Gender Justice Methodology," *Social Politics*, Vol. 25, No. 4 (Winter 2018), p. 475.

50 See Kim Thuy Seelinger and Julie Freccero, *The Long Road: Accountability for Sexual Violence in Conflict and Post-Conflict Settings* (Berkeley, CA: University of California Berkeley School of Law, Human Rights Center, 2015); Anette Bringedal Houge, *Preventing Sexual Violence in War: Is Fighting Impunity the Only Game in Town?* Report of the Missing Peace Initiative Symposium (Oslo: Peace Research Institute Oslo, 2018).

51 Campbell, "Producing Knowledge in the Field of Sexual Violence in Conflict," p. 485.
52 See Joseph Vess, Gary Barker, Sanam Naraghi-Anderlini and Alexa Hassink, *The Other Side of Gender: Men as Critical Agents of Change*, Special Report No. 340 (Washington, DC: US Institute of Peace, December 2013).
53 A provocative discussion of the role of women in shaping male hegemony is found in Cynthia Cockburn, "The Gendered Dynamics of Armed Conflict and Political Violence," in Caroline N.O. Moser and Fiona Clark, eds., *Victims, Perpetrators or Actors? Gender, Armed Conflict and Political Violence* (Chicago: University of Chicago Press, 2001).
54 Tim Carrigan, Bob Connell and John Lee, "Towards a New Sociology of Masculinity," *Theory and Society*, Vol. 14, No. 5 (September 1985), pp. 551–604; R.W. Connell, *Masculinities* (Cambridge: Polity Press, 1995); Michael Kimmel, J. Hearn and R.W. Connell, eds., *Handbook of Studies on Men and Masculinities* (Los Angeles, CA: Sage, 2005).
55 See David D. Gilmore, *Manhood in the Making: Cultural Concepts of Masculinity* (New Haven: Yale University Press, 1990).
56 IMAGES surveys are carried out by Promundo, which was founded in 1997 in Brazil.
57 See Kimberly Theidon, "Reconstructing Masculinities: The Disarmament, Demobilization, and Reintegration of Former Combatants in Colombia," *Human Rights Quarterly*, Vol. 31, No. 1 (February 2009), pp. 1–34; Marc Sommers, *Stuck: Rwandan Youth and the Struggle for Adulthood* (Athens, GA: University of Georgia Press, 2012); Phillippe Bourgois, *In Search of Respect: Selling Crack in El Barrio* (Cambridge: Cambridge University Press, 2003).
58 See Koos, "Sexual Violence in Armed Conflicts." See also Carlo Koos, "Decay or Resilience? The Long-Term Social Consequences of Conflict Related Sexual Violence in Sierra Leone," *World Politics*, Vol. 70, No. 2 (April 2018), pp. 194–238.
59 See Inger Skjelsbaek, "Victim and Survivor: Narrated Social Identities of Women Who Experienced Rape During the War in Bosnia-Herzegovina," *Feminism & Psychology*, Vol. 16, No. 4 (November 2006), pp. 373–403; Marie E. Berry, "When 'Bright Futures' Fade: Paradoxes of Women's Empowerment in Rwanda," *Signs*, Vol. 41, No. 1 (Autumn 2015), pp. 1–27.
60 See Kas Wachala, "The Tools to Combat the War on Women's Bodies: Rape and Sexual Violence Against Women in Armed Conflict," *The International Journal on Human Rights*, Vol. 16, No. 3 (August 2011), p. 534.
61 Davies and True, "Reframing Conflict-Related Sexual and Gender-Based Violence."
62 See Crawford, *Wartime Sexual Violence*.
63 See Sophie Huve, *The Use of UN Sanctions to Address Conflict-Related Sexual Violence* (Washington, DC: Georgetown Institute for Women, Peace and Security, 2018).
64 See UNSCR 1888 (2009) and UNSCR 1960 (2010).
65 See *High-Level Open Debate on Sexual Violence in Conflict*, UN Security Council (April 2019); and UNSCR 2467 (2019). See also *Report of the UN Secretary-General on Conflict-Related Sexual Violence*, S/2019/280.
66 For a list and summaries of the WPS resolutions, see chapter 1 in this book.
67 See also Anne-Kathrin Kreft, *Sexual Violence in Armed Conflict: Threat, Mobilization and Gender Norms*, Doctoral Dissertation (Gothenburg: University of Gothenburg, 2019).
68 Address at the Missing Peace Symposium (Washington, DC: US Institute of Peace, February 2013).
69 Henny Slegh, Gary Barker, Benoit Ruratotoye, and Tim Shand, *Gender Relations, Sexual and Gender-Based Violence and the Effects of Conflict on Women and Men in North Kivu, Eastern Democratic Republic of Congo*, International Men and Gender Equality Survey (Washington, DC and Cape Town: Promundo-US and Sonke Gender Justice Network, 2014).
70 Deborah Niehoff, *The Biology of Violence: How Understanding the Brain, Behavior and Environment Can Break the Vicious Circle of Aggression* (New York: Free Press, 1999).

3

GENDER AND PEACEBUILDING

Anne Marie Goetz and Rob Jenkins

Since the end of the Cold War, the international community has supported a liberal peacebuilding paradigm in which human rights (including women's rights), democratic institutions, accountable governance and the delivery of justice are seen as keys to lasting peace in conflict-torn societies.[1]

The power and influence of affluent liberal democratic states have been indispensable in mainstreaming gender issues within the field of post-conflict peacebuilding. The financial contributions and operational capacities of these states in both the security and development fields has afforded them a leading role in shaping United Nations (UN) peacebuilding doctrine – that is, the conceptual framework underpinning the organization's efforts to prevent the recurrence of armed conflict. Three key western providers of development assistance (France, the United Kingdom (UK) and the United States (US)) are also permanent members of the United Nations (UN) Security Council.

The push to ensure gender sensitivity in peacebuilding is not, of course, solely a Western preoccupation, nor do the affluent democracies always prioritize gender issues when other diplomatic interests are at stake.

We argue that successful implementation of "gender-responsive peacebuilding" and the future of the Women, Peace and Security (WPS) agenda will depend largely on three trends in the international system: the backlash against liberal norms in the affluent democracies; the increasing tendency for influential regional powers in the developing world to adopt "authoritarian modes of conflict-management" when addressing insurgencies, terrorism and other forms of persistent insecurity within their borders; and the growing role of China as a provider of foreign assistance and purveyor of development models.

This chapter is organized as follows. Part I reviews perennial obstacles to implementing gender-responsive peacebuilding, including failures among external actors to provide adequate financing. Part II examines shifts in the international political environment that appear likely to influence the fate of the WPS agenda over the next decade. Part III concludes by examining the factors that might hamper the capacity of WPS advocates to respond to the international political shifts that are taking place, as well as some countervailing forces that may help to produce better outcomes.

Obstacles to gender-responsive peacebuilding

Studies of several African cases show how war's erosion of traditional gender roles, combined with women's mobilization and the international diffusion of gender-equality norms, can enable dramatic gains in constitutionally secured rights.[2] The most substantial cases of women's engagement in post-conflict peacebuilding have occurred in countries such as Colombia, East Timor, Nepal, the Philippines and South Africa, where strong women's movements built alliances with feminists within government, cultivated coalitions with other civil society groups working on human rights and engaged with supportive international actors and Non-Governmental Organizations (NGOs).

Despite these successes, in the two decades since the passage of United Nations Security Council Resolution (UNSCR) 1325 in 2000, efforts to involve women directly in post-conflict peacebuilding have faced perennial obstacles. Many of these obstacles stem from preexisting structures that reinforce gender inequality and war-induced constraints on women's capacities to demand responses to their needs. For instance, when women lack personal title to property or even personal identity documents, their chances of re-establishing livelihoods upon resettlement, engaging in collective action or participating in public decision-making – even voting – are compromised. These effects are compounded by women's economic vulnerability, which also tends to increase during and after conflict. Women also face intense social pressures to surrender to men any leadership and employment ground they may have gained during conflict.

Many post-conflict challenges facing women can be traced to their exclusion from conflict resolution processes and the terms of political settlements, which rarely if ever prioritize women's rights, economic autonomy or public participation. Even when women's voices are heard, few of their demands are met. Unlike an ethnic militia, even the largest national women's coalition is not seen as a potential "spoiler" that needs to be accommodated. Women's peace groups are in no position to disrupt the implementation of peace agreements that do not address their interests. Negotiating delegations on government and opposition sides are overwhelmingly male, and they represent armed actors and established elites. They rarely see gender issues as priorities, focusing instead on proposals for security guarantees and power-sharing mechanisms.

Since key obstacles to women's participation in peacebuilding stem from hostility among domestic actors to proposed legal and institutional changes that challenge patriarchal norms, women peace activists often appeal for normative reinforcement from external actors, including bilateral donors and multilateral institutions, notably the United Nations. Although a broad cross-section of member states has supported the Security Council resolutions on WPS, the largest Organization for Economic Co-operation and Development (OECD) aid donors have responded unevenly in terms of providing the technical, financial and diplomatic help needed for gender-responsive peacebuilding.

International efforts to promote women's participation and gender equality in post-conflict situations should include actions on a wide range of fronts: providing support for the formation of women's Civil Society Organizations (CSOs), devising consultative mechanisms and representative structures to bring women's policy priorities into national planning processes, supporting women's access to sustainable livelihoods and ensuring that transitional justice mechanisms address war crimes against women and enable their access as witnesses. Many of these interventions can be supported through peacebuilding assistance, but neither bilateral nor multilateral post-conflict spending has matched the rhetoric on gender-responsive peacebuilding with adequate financial assistance.

In 2010, the United Nations committed to increasing gender equality focused spending to at least 15 percent of post-conflict financing. However, the Secretary General's 2019 annual report to the Security Council on WPS stated that just 7 percent of UNDP's peacebuilding expenditure had gender equality as a "principal objective."[3] The only part of the United Nations to have met the 15 percent target is the multi-donor Peacebuilding Fund (PBF), operated by the UN Secretariat.

Donors consistently fail to disburse financial and technical assistance that local women's coalitions require to participate meaningfully in formal and informal peace talks and post-conflict planning processes. In 2015, UN Women established a "Women's Peace and Humanitarian Fund" to provide fast-disbursing funds to allow women's peace organizations to participate in conflict resolution and post-conflict planning processes. But tepid donor response and UN Women's capacity constraints have limited the reach of the program.[4]

Perhaps much more significant than funding, however, is the lack of leadership opportunities for women from the start of peacemaking efforts. Informal and preliminary talks, including track two talks (unofficial, non-governmental diplomacy) by international actors, remain male-dominated processes. The domestic elites who forge political settlements are mostly men, as are their primary external interlocutors.[5] Even women leaders who have been instrumental in sustaining communities, mediating between opposing groups and reintegrating combatants (notably child soldiers) have been ignored by international mediators as well as state and non-state negotiators.[6]

Unfortunately, there are no sanctions for failing to include women in peace talks or in post-conflict donor conferences. Women's exclusion from conflict resolution and transition-planning remains the norm. In 2018, neither the Stockholm talks on Yemen nor the Palermo meeting on Libya included women in any substantive capacity. These were both internationally supported peace processes whose managers were aware of UNSCR 1325 but chose to ignore its provisions. In the Libya case, neither the Italian sponsors nor the UN Department of Political and

Peacebuilding Affairs informed national women peace leaders of the content of discussions or invited them to participate.

International politics in transition

Three interrelated trends in international politics are likely to influence the future of gender-focused post-conflict reconstruction and state-building efforts: (1) the "illiberal drift" in the established democracies that have sponsored the liberal peacebuilding paradigm;[7] (2) the increasing tendency for emerging and regional powers to respond to insurgencies and other threats to state power with "authoritarian modes of conflict management";[8] and (3) the rising influence of China – and its development model – among post-conflict governments.

The backlash against liberalism and multilateralism is taking place at a moment when the pace of change in reaching gender equality globally is slowing. A 2020 World Economic Forum report found that large gender gaps remain in both economic participation and political empowerment. There has been a stalling or even reversal in the pace of improvement in these areas.[9]

The erosion of liberal and internationalist norms in affluent democracies

The first trend is the erosion of liberal norms and institutions in the established democracies of the Global North – most notably, the United States, which in 2016 elected a president with a demonstrated aversion to norms of institutional accountability, and the UK, whose citizens voted the same year to begin seceding from the EU. The wave of democracy that followed the end of the Cold War began crashing after the turn of the century. In 2019, Freedom House declared that democracy was in crisis, and it recorded net declines in civil and political liberties for the 13th year.[10] The trend extends, to greater or lesser degrees, to political developments in Australia, Austria, Germany, Italy, the Netherlands, Sweden and Switzerland.

Attacks on women's rights and increasingly virulent misogyny have accompanied the rise of illiberalism. In 2019 the UN's Special Rapporteur on the situation of human rights defenders documented an increase globally in violence against women journalists, politicians and civil society leaders. His report suggested state responsibility for some of this violence, tracing attacks on feminist activists to misogynist language used by populist leaders.[11] Yet, none of the three most widely discussed books on the rise of authoritarianism and populism in the west, all published in 2018, addressed the gender dimensions of these contemporary phenomena.[12]

Some of the affluent democracies drifting toward illiberalism are the same countries that have largely funded, provided diplomatic support for and constructed institutions to implement the array of international peacebuilding efforts undertaken in the decades since the Cold War ended. They have promoted liberal peacebuilding, a paradigm that identifies inclusive political institutions, human rights and the rule of law as preconditions for securing lasting peace after conflict. Through the use of diplomatic leverage, aid programs and cultural hegemony, the affluent democracies have been instrumental in transforming how gender is addressed in the humanitarian, security and development dimensions of post-conflict reconstruction. This is not to minimize the role of local women peacemakers, whose initiative and commitment remain irreplaceable. But any diminution in the international community's commitment to a rights-based understanding of peacebuilding poses threats to the agenda-setting capacities of local and national WPS advocates.

Among the indicators of the United States' flagging commitment to liberal principles are the tonal and substantive changes to its diplomacy on women's rights. To focus on the gender dimensions of American foreign policy is not to ignore the larger dynamic at work, which includes weaker reactions to domestic and international human rights abuses and a dismissive attitude toward international institutions, notably the United Nations. An assault on gender equality policies is a core feature of the agenda of the US administration of president Donald Trump.

On his first day in office in January 2017, President Trump signed an executive order reinstating a rule that prohibits US government funding for international women's health programs that mention abortion. This made it harder for international actors reliant on US funding to address women's health needs in fragile states and post-conflict situations. In 2019, researchers blamed this rule change for increases in teenage and unwanted pregnancies in several developing and conflict-affected countries.[13] These and related demographic phenomena have been associated with instability.[14]

Other US foreign policy decisions affecting women include the 2018 removal of domestic violence as grounds for asylum.[15] The administration also eliminated the "reproductive rights" section of the State Department's 2018 annual "Country Reports on Human Rights Practices."[16] This was replaced by a section titled "Coercion in Population Control," which reported on what the authors called "forced abortions," but not on the forced pregnancies caused by conflict-related sexual violence in the Democratic Republic of the Congo, Nigeria, South Sudan, Syria and elsewhere.

The US administration's hostility to abortion nearly scuttled passage in April 2019 of UNSCR 2467. A draft resolution introduced by Germany, the Council president that month, proposed improved services for rape survivors. The US delegation opposed language that called for providing "non-discriminatory and comprehensive health services, including sexual and reproductive health."[17] This wording, US negotiators argued, implied that abortion services would be made available for rape victims. They threatened the first-ever veto of a WPS resolution if any reference to sexual and reproductive health services remained.[18] Germany removed the offending language; the weakened resolution (UNSCR 2467) passed. This reversed normative advances on reproductive rights for rape survivors that had been achieved in UNSCR 2106 (2013) and 2122 (2013).

This experience was repeated in October 2019, when South Africa proposed a resolution calling for the "full" implementation of the WPS agenda and added a new component: protection of women human rights defenders. The United States objected to the word *full*, saying it was not committed to all aspects of all previous resolutions. This offered Russia and China an opportunity to push for the withdrawal of the term *human rights defenders*, as both countries have long considered human rights defenders to be agents of foreign influence. A statement by the Chinese delegation contended that NGOs should "play a constructive role by observing the laws of the countries concerned, respecting the ownership of the host Government and fully consulting with them."[19]

By allowing culturally conservative and religious groups to undermine international gender equality goals, the Trump administration is engaging in what one political scientist calls "norm-spoiling."[20] US-based evangelical Christian networks, such as C-Fam (Center for Family and Human Rights) and the World Congress of Families, became, under the Trump administration, an established presence in the US delegations to bodies such as the UN Commission on the Status of Women and the Commission on Population and Development.[21] After successfully lobbying to block the reproductive rights language in the Security Council's April 2019 WPS resolution, one C-Fam financial backer boasted, "Not even George W. Bush would have considered a veto threat in the Security Council over the question of reproductive health, especially in a resolution on rape in war."[22]

Ethnographic studies of western democracies find intimate links between the rise of populist authoritarianism and misogyny, particularly where globalized production systems have led to economic insecurity among working-class men, and thus the erosion of a key component of male identity.[23] Weronika Grzebalska, Easzter Kovats and Andrea Peto argue that gender serves as "symbolic glue" for right-wing populists, performing three vital functions.[24] First, it ties together disparate grievances that are unrelated to gender equality: the failure of democratic representation, the detachment of social and political elites and the influence of international economic forces on nation states. Second, opposition to gender helps to entrench a new "common sense" version of community, centered on family values. Third, a focus on gender fosters alliances between groups that would not normally cooperate.[25]

An example of the way this culture war is generating improbable alliances is the 27-country "Group of Friends of the Family" at the UN. Founded by Belarus and Russia in 2015, it includes many former socialist states in Eastern Europe and Central Asia, a few small Central American states, several Muslim-majority countries, a number of southern African states as well as Nigeria. It also has the support of the Vatican.[26] The United States is not a member, but Trump administration officials who spearheaded attacks on reproductive rights have participated in meetings of the Group.[27] The common denominator among this diverse coalition of countries is opposition to any policy proposal, agenda item, or reporting procedure that seems to grant equal rights to people of all gender identities and sexual orientations or that might call into question the norm of the heterosexual, patriarchal family.[28] They oppose abortion rights, adolescent sex education and the right to access contraceptives – positions that resonate strongly with countries experiencing declining fertility rates, some of which have introduced incentives for women to bear more children.

WPS advocates have expressed growing concerns that right-wing populism in OECD countries threatens the ability of international actors to press for women's empowerment in developing and post-conflict contexts.[29] In early 2019, one European diplomat described "an unholy alliance of the United States, the Russians, the Holy See, the Saudis and the Bahrainis, chipping away at the progress that has been made" on women's rights. This was, "at its heart, an attack on the progressive normative framework established over the past 25 years."[30]

"Pro-family" groups have lobbied transnationally to remove the term *gender* from UN human rights documents. In 2019, the US delegation came to their aid, attempting to replace *gender* with *women* or *women and girls* in resolutions under consideration by the UN General Assembly committee that deals with human rights issues. Domestically, they have pushed the US Health and Human Services Department to entrench a definition of gender as equivalent to biological sex.[31] This aligns the United States with longstanding calls from the Vatican and other conservative forces to oppose what they call "gender ideology" – the idea that gender is not binary and that gendered attributes and behaviors are not innate, but a social construction.

Some key donors have sought to counter this trend. Canada, France, Mexico and Sweden claim to practice feminist foreign policies. They are vocal in protesting abuses of women's rights – for instance, Canada and Sweden spoke out in early 2018 against the jailing of feminist activists in Saudi Arabia. No other OECD country joined them, and they were isolated in criticizing the Saudi leadership until the exceptionally grisly murder of government critic Jamal Khashoggi in Istanbul on October 2, 2018, pushed other states to condemn Saudi Arabia's blatant abuse of human rights. Although some OECD countries have sought to mitigate the impact of reduced US support for gender equality – for instance, a Dutch-led initiative in 2017 to establish an international safe-abortion fund – this has been a rearguard action incommensurate with the challenge from illiberal actors in both the established democracies and among other key international players.

Illiberal peacebuilding among influential regional powers

The second trend of relevance to the future scope, direction and effectiveness of WPS advocacy in post-conflict peacebuilding stems from a parallel rightward shift in the politics of many regionally important powers in the Global South. These include Brazil, India, Nigeria, Pakistan, the Philippines and Turkey. These countries are of strategic or diplomatic importance to the international community, as well as within their regions. This makes them influential actors, both in terms of the example set by their behavior and the positions they articulate in international settings. These countries also have large women's movements. Some have, in the past, been effective promoters of both democracy and gender equality goals in multilateral forums, helping to demonstrate that the gender equality project is universally valued, not a western preoccupation. Because the international community regards these increasingly illiberal middle and emerging powers as strategically important and because of their regional significance, the approaches taken by these states to conflict and its aftermath are closely watched in countries where conflict looms, is underway or threatens to recur. There is thus an outsize effect when governments of such countries engage in systematic human rights violations, including attacks on women human rights defenders, use or encourage forms of hate speech or politicize security and justice institutions.

In addition to experiencing a turn toward the political right, all but one of these countries (Brazil) are conflict-affected. Pakistan is engaged with both separatist movements and cross-border terror networks. Turkey faces a long-running Kurdish insurgency, which ebbs and flows in strength and is linked to events across the border in war-torn Syria. The Philippines faces a leftist insurgency as well as a separatist movement (in the province of Mindanao) that has had links to Islamist extremists. Nigeria must cope with the terror campaign waged by Boko Haram, but it is also engaged in a persistent low-level conflict with radical separatists in the oil-producing Niger Delta region.[32]

That states of this size and importance – all but Turkey have population over 100 million – systematically violate domestic civil rights and the laws of armed conflict, without substantial international sanction, provides powerful incentives for other governments to follow suit. A significant contagion effect is already evident. In January 2019, former Sri Lankan President Maithripala Sirisena declared his intention to emulate Philippine President Rodrigo Duterte's approach to prosecuting the country's "war on drugs," which has involved many thousands of extra-judicial killings. Perceived threats from terrorism are invoked to justify the disproportionate use of force, while also shifting the discussion to a topic of global concern. The "success" of such strategies has led some countries to suggest their approaches be given due consideration alongside the softer strategies that generally characterize international peacebuilding. The idea of drawing on the experiences of recent conflict-affected countries when developing best practices for preventing the outbreak, intensification, spread or recurrence of conflict – that is, peacebuilding policy – would ordinarily be a welcome development in a field where northern countries dominate the discussion. What links these countries, however, is their governments' common belief that challengers to the state must be pursued ruthlessly, without reference to international human rights standards.

In the early 2010s, Turkey had been seen by some observers as a potential model for integrating democracy and a moderate form of political Islam.[33] They believed it might become an ally for those seeking a gender-responsive (and otherwise largely liberal) approach to peacebuilding, notably with respect to the government's relations with the country's Kurdish minority. This did not take place. The Turkish government did little to involve women or address gender issues in its engagement with Kurdish-majority regions, and it has adopted a more aggressive tone in general.[34] Despite occasional rhetorical support by the government to WPS priorities, the government has not adopted a National Action Plan (NAP) on the implementation of UNSCR 1325. The hope that Turkey would help to promote gender-responsive peacebuilding internationally has been supplanted by a far grimmer reality domestically. One critic has characterized this as "women's authoritarian inclusion," in which women's rights laws and institutions have been weakened and ruling-party-linked organizations mediate women's access to public institutions and their ability to collectively challenge state practices.[35]

In 2011, President Recep Tayyip Erdoğan eliminated the Ministry of Women and Family Affairs. According to one scholar, this "means that women policies are being erased from the state's agenda."[36] Repeated attempts have been made to weaken women's rights protections. Erdogan has since 2012 repeatedly introduced legislation to restrict abortion (which is currently legal up to ten weeks). Levels of sexual and domestic violence and femicide have been on the rise in the country, but the government has preferred family "reconciliation" over prosecutions. In 2016, Erdogan backed a bill (which eventually failed) to pardon rapists who married their victims instead of creating shelters for victims of domestic violence, as the government committed to do under the Council of Europe Convention on Preventing and Combating Violence Against Women and Domestic Violence. Ironically, this Convention is known internationally as the Istanbul Convention because it was signed there in 2011.

The Philippines has long been seen as an international leader on gender equality approaches to conflict resolution and development, with large national women's peace coalitions. In 2010, it became the first country in Asia to formulate a NAP on UNSCR 1325, and the first to promote women's engagement in local conflict prevention and recovery in remote areas.[37] Under former president Benigno Aquino, the Office of the Presidential Advisor on the Peace Process (OPAPP) received international recognition for promoting women's participation and attention to gender issues in its efforts to resolve the conflict with the Moro Islamic Liberation Front (MILF) in 2014.[38]

This aspect of the country's peace work faded with the election of President Rodrigo Duterte in 2016. Among his first acts was to dismiss the OPAPP's feminist chief. Since then, Duterte has ignored international criticism of the extrajudicial killings that have characterized his war on drugs and the brutality of his approach to the multiple conflicts in which his government has been engaged. The country's armed forces all but destroyed the southern city of Marawi through a prolonged siege and bombardment in 2017.

Duterte presents almost a caricature of a misogynist "strongman." He appears to relish issuing public statements with exceptionally coarse language, such as, in 2017, expressing regret that he did not get to participate in the 1989 rape of an Australian missionary, or calling on soldiers in the Marawi siege to rape women and shoot them in the vagina.[39] This type of rhetoric is intended to outrage liberal sensibilities and may normalize and encourage misogyny and acts of violence. In 2018, Duterte was criticized by the UN Special Rapporteur on Human Rights Defenders for the way his "promotion and reinforcement of misogynistic and hetero-patriarchal norms" had contributed to an increase in threats to and attacks on women and feminist human rights defenders.[40] Among those who have been targeted are high-ranking feminist leaders. These include Duterte's own vice president (who he repeatedly and publicly mocked), the head of the Supreme Court (who he had impeached), a Senator and former Justice secretary (who he jailed) and the editor of a news site that reports on state abuses (who he arrested).[41] Both domestically and internationally, Duterte's misogyny is increasingly seen as integral, rather than incidental, to what has been called his "macho-fascist" brand of politics.

Duterte departs from other misogynist populists in the area of reproductive rights, however. He has liberalized access to contraceptives in defiance of the Catholic Church and the conservatives on the Supreme Court and in the legislature.[42] His law-and-order approach and support for reproductive rights earned him support from many women, even some feminists. During the 2016 election, a women's political party called "Gabriela" backed Duterte, despite serious concerns about his attitude toward gender issues.[43] It provided support in exchange for access, positions and the promise that jailed comrades would be released.[44] Gabriela also cited Duterte's reputation of having effected pro-women reforms during his long tenure as mayor of Davao City.[45] Ultimately, Gabriela withdrew its support, joining with other feminist and human rights movements in a growing pro-democracy resistance.[46]

Nigeria's military and security services have confronted domestic armed groups with a ruthlessness that has attracted international condemnation. The government has engaged in arbitrary arrests, mass detentions and questionable fast-track trials of suspected insurgents.[47] Not only do its actions set bad examples for other states, but because Nigeria is a regional and international provider of both development assistance and uniformed peacekeepers through the Economic Community of West African States, the African Union and the United Nations, its violations of international norms could have adverse demonstration globally effects.

Nigeria has embraced almost none of the social inclusion, group reconciliation or institutional reform agendas that are at the heart of liberal peacebuilding and that can provide entry points for addressing gender issues.[48] Security forces have been criticized for their slow responses to the kidnapping of almost 300 schoolgirls by Boko Haram in 2014 and for failing to respond to warnings about impending attacks on schoolgirls since then.[49] In international forums, Nigerian officials have a mixed record on gender issues. In 2018, Nigerian authorities were reportedly responsive to a suggestion (made by a visiting mission of Security Council ambassadors) that international actors should help to address women's lack of access to and underrepresentation in local government institutions in conflict-affected areas of the Lake Chad Basin. But in other arenas, such as the annual meeting of the Commission on Population and Development at the United Nations, Nigeria has for years collaborated with other states hostile to reproductive rights to prevent the Commission from reaching consensus. Nigeria has objected strongly to the inclusion of LGBTQ issues and adolescent sexuality education.[50]

Nigeria has adopted a NAP on Resolution 1325, though the plan has been criticized for its "cookie-cutter format."[51] There is little evidence that Nigeria has carried out any of the plan's operational measures in its engagement with armed groups or the communities where they are active. As one analyst put in, "[i]n

Nigeria, the absence of a UN mission means that there is little external pressure for NAP implementation."[52]

Although it is not a conflict country, Brazil has experienced extremely high rates of violence, particularly in urban areas where organized crime and local politicians are closely intertwined. For at least a decade, Brazil's police have engaged in pitched battles with criminal groups in the country's favelas. Even before Jair Bolsonaro was elected president in October 2018, Brazilian authorities had increasingly militarized the state's approach to re-asserting public safety and security – with heavily armed neighborhood sweeps, helicopter patrols and frequent curfews. The March 2018 assassination of the lesbian feminist and Rio de Janeiro city councillor Marielle Franco, a fierce critic of police killings, was widely seen as an indicator of growing authoritarianism and the impunity of security forces.[53]

President Bolsonaro wants the military directly involved in executing an even more aggressive strategy.[54] Poor women, in both urban and rural areas, face extremely high rates of violence – including at the hands of state security forces in regions where violence has already skyrocketed.[55] Addressing the gender dimensions of insecurity, not least by reforming the security services, has not been part of the government's militarized approach. Bolsonaro has signaled an intention to confine the discussion of women's rights to matters related to their traditional family roles. Immediately after his inauguration in January 2019, he converted the Human Rights Ministry into the Ministry of Women, Family and Human Rights, appointed a pro-abstinence evangelical pastor as its head and eliminated LGBTQ protections in its mandate.[56] This was in keeping with Bolsonaro's virulently homophobic rhetoric, which helped to make Brazil the world leader in homicides of LGBTQ individuals in 2019.[57] In his inaugural address to Congress, Bolsonaro checked off some of the misogynist themes uniting new right-wing populists, vowing to "value the family, respect . . . our Judeo-Christian tradition, combat the ideology of gender."[58] His statement was praised for its "exemplary leadership" by the evangelical International Organization for the Family.[59]

When Bolsonaro referenced "the ideology of gender," he was tapping into the same anti-feminist discourse that, as we have seen, has been promulgated by right-wing populists in the affluent democracies. The effectiveness of this discourse stems from its framing as part of a wider movement to combat the influence of globalizing elites. Pope Francis describes it as "the new ideological colonization that tries to destroy the family."[60] Bardou has identified examples of international coordination among conservative opponents of gender equality.[61] In Latin America, the Catholic right protested the mention of the word *gender* in Paraguay's 2011 national education plan, and this was followed in many countries in the region with campaigns against same-sex marriage and adolescent sex. Perhaps the strongest indication of a meeting of populist minds on the meaning of "gender" could be found in a speech delivered by Bolsonaro on a state visit to the United States soon after his inauguration: "Brazil and the United States stand side by side in their efforts to ensure liberties and respect to traditional family lifestyles, respect to God our creator, and stand against gender ideologies and politically incorrect attitudes and against fake news"[62] Invoking "gender ideology" signified a wholesale rejection of cosmopolitan and liberal perspectives on social and family life.[63]

Right-wing populists in both affluent democracies and emerging powers have employed similar tactics to erode gender-equality protections. National bureaucracies on women's rights have either been dismantled or repurposed to encourage motherhood; sexual and reproductive rights have been curbed; women human rights defenders and feminist politicians have come under attack. What this means for the gender-equality components of liberal peacebuilding, either domestically or in foreign policy, is not entirely clear. But an indication may be found in the fate of the 2016 Colombia peace accord with the Revolutionary Armed Forces of Columbia (FARC), narrowly rejected in a national referendum thanks to an intense conservative campaign against the accord's feminist content, particularly its commitment to prevent discrimination on the basis of "diverse gender identity" and "diverse sexual orientation." The conservative campaign, backed, according to the Brazilian feminist Sonia Correa, by the Catholic Church and funded by Brazilian Pentecostals, called the accord's gender language "a form of ideological colonization," precisely following the Pope's description of gender equality advocacy.[64] A revised version of the accord that replaced language on gender diversity with "equity between women and men" was agreed upon in late 2016. By 2019, few of the accord's gender-equality provisions had been implemented.[65]

Bolsonaro, Duterte, Erdogan and others represent a significant challenge to the liberal consensus on which decades of international peacebuilding have been predicated. Central to their approach are draconian actions against internal threats, justified as necessary to defeat the enemies of peace. The rise of "illiberal hegemony" has brought with it a normalizing of "illiberal peacebuilding" or "authoritarian modes of conflict management."[66] The new focus is on stabilization by force instead of through dialogue, with construction and infrastructure-based strategies prioritized over reconciliation, transitional justice or more inclusive governance. Although liberal peacebuilding has not always delivered for women, it nevertheless provided space, resources and opportunities for gender-equality advocates to influence policy. For post-conflict assistance to prioritize women's rights, including those that advance their economic and political participation, it must be rooted in a form of governance where rights are respected, whether this is called "liberal" or by some other name.

Further amplifying the effects of this trend toward illiberal governance and peacebuilding among regionally influential powers is that some of these countries are themselves donors in conflict-affected countries. Turkey's aid program has grown in recent years, with a particular focus on humanitarian contributions in conflict situations.[67] Turkish foreign assistance has stretched to involvement in the broader field of peacebuilding as well. By 2013, Turkey had "taken on a major post-conflict reconstruction role in Somalia," where it engaged "directly with the new Federal Government of Somalia, in contrast to most of the traditional donors, which prefer to engage with Somalia via multilateral institutions like the UN and EU."[68] According to critics, Turkey's bypassing of multilateral institutions was partly a means of accommodating Somali authorities, who felt "unduly imposed upon by the human rights and other requirements of traditional donors."[69] There were, moreover, no indications of gender-awareness in Turkey's Somalia program, much less a prioritization of women's participation in post-conflict politics or economic recovery.

This pattern extends beyond Turkey. While rising and regional powers generally regard peacekeeping "as a crucial international tool in a rule-based international system," they are "less enthusiastic about peacebuilding, because they perceive it to have been abused by the West as a tool to impose neoliberal values on weak states."[70] Rising powers generally seek to "check the transplanting of values and models from one region to another."[71] The revived nationalism propelling right-wing autocrats in this group of regional powers also contributes to the framing of liberal values – including gender equality – as neo-colonial.

The marked misogyny of emerging regional "strongmen" is in part a sign of their rejection of the liberal constraints on national sovereignty that come with international human rights norms. Over time, the influence of such states may "result in UN peacekeeping and peacebuilding becoming more sensitive to respect for sovereignty and national ownership."[72] In a post-conflict context, this typically means reduced external scrutiny of government performance in fulfilling international commitments, including those contained in UNSCR 1325 and other norms relating to women, peace and security.

The rising influence of China and its development model

The third broad trend of relevance to the future of gender-responsive peacebuilding is the unmistakable shift in the distribution of power in the international system due to the rise of China. This is evidenced in military terms – in its approach to regional maritime disputes, for instance – but also in how China uses its economic leverage and the power of its development model to win support among a broad range of governments.

In 2012, Emma Mawdsley called China's expanding program of external assistance the primary force behind "the changing developmental landscape."[73] The size of its operations in fragile and conflict-affected countries has now made China's foreign assistance program a de facto component of the international peacebuilding landscape as well. China will have considerable influence on WPS doctrine and practices.

China's approach to foreign assistance consists of a core set of principles: a focus on productive economic infrastructure such as ports, roads and pipelines; assistance via loans rather than grants; and direct, planned involvement by Chinese firms, public and private. China conceives of its approach to recipient governments as providing an alternative foreign-assistance paradigm based on explicit reciprocity, rather than charity. In theory, China also refrains from interfering in domestic social and political affairs.[74] This appeals to aid-recipient governments, particularly those in post-conflict settings, who fear that not only does aid from traditional sources come with policy strings attached, but that adherence to a western model of governance and development – the liberal peacebuilding framework – will also need to be embraced to ensure the continued flow of post-conflict assistance.[75]

China's development finance is not necessarily focused on undermining demo-cratic government.[76] Still, its programs are free of requirements to conduct social impact assessments – a major drawback from a WPS perspective.[77] China imposed no such requirements on its post-conflict assistance to Angola, a paradigmatic case of illiberal peacebuilding, where the absence of women in the process of post-conflict economic and political reconstruction was also notable.[78] The financial institutions China has helped to create do not prioritize gender issues. Activists, economists and international officials called on the management of the Beijing-backed Asian Infrastructure Investment Bank (AIIB) to adopt a more gender-responsive approach to project financing.[79] The AIIB's management considered a gender policy too prescriptive, though it framed its opposition to gender proposals as a plea against excessive bureaucracy, rather than a rejection of gender equality as a policy objective.[80] One can reject the simplistic "rogue donor" critique of China's aid policy while accepting that it has no obvious commitment to gender-responsive peacebuilding.[81] Project guidelines ensuring women's equal entitlement to resettle-ment allowances, or technical assistance to help countries facing refugee and Inter-nally Displaced Person (IDP) crises to improve women's land rights, do not figure in China's aid programs.[82] Chinese development assistance thus provides an alterna-tive to conventional (and often conditionality-laden) aid modalities, which typically include actions to promote women's rights. Women may in some cases stand to benefit from Chinese investments, but there is little evidence of serious attention being paid to addressing gender issues in the implementation of these programs.

China routinely highlights its state-led strategy for achieving rapid economic growth as an alternative to the Washington Consensus. James Millward notes that economic orthodoxy long imposed by the US-dominated World Bank and Inter-national Monetary Fund on developing countries in crisis has enjoyed a mixed record at best.[83] However, Millward ignores the other pillar of the western develop-ment agenda over the past quarter century – governance reforms designed to make institutions more transparent and accountable. The absence of these objectives, much less support for multiparty democracy, in China's development programming is notable. This is important, since governance programs have been a frequent entry point for donor-government initiatives to mainstream gender equality in post-con-flict situations.[84] This is partly, as Paul Chaney argues, because almost every aspect of a comprehensive peacebuilding agenda, such as designing a post-war country's institutions of justice, "presents an opportunity to redraft structures and processes of governance to embed gender equality."[85] To the extent that China's governance-free model of peacebuilding assistance influences international doctrine and prac-tice, it deprives gender-equality advocates of a potentially useful channel through which to institutionalize women's participation in post-conflict contexts.

China is also aggressively seeking to enhance its leverage within the UN system.[86] China is using its status as a major contributor to UN peacekeeping – it provides more peacekeepers than the other four permanent members of the Security Council combined – to press for changes in how peace and security are conceived.[87] For instance, China emphasizes post-conflict economic development as the key to sustaining peace. China has increasingly sought more significant roles in conflict resolution at the United Nations, strongly and successfully lobbying for the appointment in 2019 of a Chinese diplomat to the position of UN Envoy to the Great Lakes region in Africa.

In UN development institutions, China's rhetoric has not excluded attention to women's issues, in part because of a sense of national ownership of the Beijing Platform for Action, negotiated at the fourth World Conference on Women in 1995. In 2015, while commemorating the 20th anniversary of the Beijing conference in New York, President Xi Jinping announced a $10 million grant to UN Women to implement the Platform for Action.[88] China's 2015 white paper on development "added a new chapter on strengthening international cooperation on women's empowerment with the UN system," while also advocating "regional cooperation on women's empowerment at multilateral platforms, such as the G-20 and the Asia-Pacific Economic Cooperation (APEC)" Forum.[89] In early 2016, China's UN ambassador briefed a dialogue forum linked to the UN Commission on the Status of Women (CSW) on the country's commitment to advancing gender equality through strategies such as its "international cooperation" programs in developing and fragile states, which stress overseas technical training for women and girls.[90]

China's rhetoric on women's empowerment is mostly not matched in reality. In 2016, China assumed the rotating chair of the G-20. As chair of the G-20, China pledged to push for a focus on gender equality.[91] Yet, the chair's summit memorandum included only a couple of perfunctory references to women.[92]

This was consistent with China's approach to development assistance, which does not stress the promotion of social equality. The existence of this alternative aid channel, and China's hands-off approach, enhances the capacity of post-conflict authorities to resist donors advocating for equal rights and social justice-oriented peacebuilding processes. China seeks "direct" developmental impacts through support for infrastructure and extractive industries, in contrast to "the 'indirect'" western donor predilections for improvements in gender equality, human rights, transparency and empowerment."[93] The existence of an alternative aid channel that imposes no human rights standards enhances the leverage of post-conflict authorities that seek to resist external pressures to adopt liberal peacebuilding approaches.

Despite claims to the contrary, Chinese assistance may not only fail to consolidate peace; it may foster conditions conducive to the outbreak or resumption of armed conflict.[94] Chinese aid and investment have been linked to increases in the use of violence against citizens by state authorities in African countries.[95] In African countries where China is a large donor, resources flow disproportionately to the home regions of the country's political leaders.[96] Two key authoritarian tendencies that are seen to drive conflict – state repression and corruption – are therefore associated with Chinese economic engagement.

China is well-positioned to reinforce the turn toward illiberal peacebuilding under way in countries such as Nigeria, Pakistan, the Philippines and Turkey. The China-Pakistan Economic Corridor (CPEC), a tributary of China's Belt and Road Initiative (BRI), is influencing Pakistan's development strategy. Some fear that China is enticing Pakistan into a debt trap that could allow China to convert the sizable debt it will be owed on CPEC road and power projects into enhanced equity stakes. In any event, the result is likely to be reduced western influence.[97] This is not welcome news for WPS advocates, who have relied on the leverage of western donors to ensure that gender issues are not neglected in the process of, for instance, integrating Pakistan's Federally Administered Tribal Areas into the country's civilian governance structures.[98]

In the Philippines, President Duterte began seeking Chinese patronage soon after his election in 2016.[99] This has been expressed in a variety of ways, including various (debt-funded) investments and the use of Chinese contractors in several post-conflict reconstruction projects.[100] This process shows no signs of comporting with international human rights (or even basic financial transparency) standards, let alone fulfilling the commitments found in the Philippines' NAP on implementing UNSCR 1325.[101]

China's influence, in terms of its development model and through conditionality-free aid, is felt across Asia. It has an outsized influence in smaller and often poorer countries that are engaged in or recovering from conflict, such as Myanmar, Nepal and Sri Lanka. All three countries are part of the BRI. The government that ruled in Sri Lanka from 2004 through 2015 – a period that included the brutal end of the civil war in 2009 – had forged close links with Beijing.[102] The purpose, then as now, was to avoid the intensified human rights scrutiny that accompanies increased western aid. When president Mahinda Rajapaksa was elected in 2005, he immediately retreated from the liberal peacebuilding approach his predecessor had pursued, including negotiations supported by western powers and experiments with limited autonomy for the country's rebel-governed north. As Rajapaksa gravitated toward a military solution, he increasingly turned to China. In 2007–2008, China provided fighter jets, anti-aircraft artillery and advanced radar systems that enhanced the Sri Lankan military's battlefield advantage. This aided its decisive victory in 2009, during which tens of thousands of civilians were killed.

Sri Lanka's subsequent engagement with the United Nations shows what Chinese support can offer. The UN Security Council did not pass any resolutions on Sri Lanka thanks to the threat of a Chinese veto. Efforts in the Human Rights Council (HRC) were a slightly different matter: China was not a member, and no member possesses a veto in any case. By early 2015, pressure in the HRC for post-conflict accountability in Sri Lanka had grown strong enough to persuade the country's newly elected government to co-sponsor an HRC resolution that committed Sri Lanka to prosecuting war crimes and addressing the marginalization of the country's Tamil minority. The resolution included provisions for ensuring women's participation in post-conflict reconciliation and reconstruction. Since 2015, however, the Sri Lankan government has backtracked on the scope of its commitments. Sri Lanka's western aid donors failed to take action in response to the government's double flouting of international law – first, through the mass atrocities of 2009 and second, through the post-2015 government's failure to abide by the terms of the HRC resolution. The most compelling explanation for this reluctance is fear by western donors that alienating Colombo will enhance China's influence in the region.

In addition to the role China plays as a check on the ability of western powers to enforce international human rights standards, it has direct influence as a creditor.[103] Barely two percent of the $5 billion in loans issued by Chinese state entities to Sri Lanka between 2005 and 2012 were outright grants. By 2015, one-third of Sri Lankan government revenue went to servicing debt to China. When Sri Lanka could no longer meet its financial commitment to a joint port-development venture, the project reverted to China's control on a 99-year lease.[104]

China's support for illiberal peacebuilding can also be seen in Myanmar, a conflict-affected country where issues of women's protection and participation loom particularly large. Besides the extensive use of sexual violence by Myanmar's army in many of its ongoing ethnic conflicts and its expulsions of the Muslim Rohingya community, a eugenics policy was plainly behind three of the four 2015 laws known collectively as the Race and Religion Protection Laws. These were barely disguised efforts to reduce the fertility rate amongst Muslims and to prevent Muslim men from marrying Buddhist women.[105] Conflict-related sexual violence against Rohingya people during their expulsion from Rakhine state in 2017–2018 was on an unprecedented scale, not only by the standards of this conflict, but in comparison with other ethnic conflicts. China's response has been to portray the "humanitarian situation" in Rakhine state as driven by underlying economic problems, signaling its focus on ensuring the continuation of pipeline projects linking China to ports on the Bay of Bengal.[106] This is part of a larger pattern involving major Chinese-backed infrastructure projects in conflict-affected areas such as Kachin state.[107]

Conclusion

How can WPS advocates navigate the threat posed by authoritarian governments and populist political forces to the promotion of gender-responsive peacebuilding? Which additional obstacles are most likely to hamper the capacities of WPS advocates to respond effectively? What are the enabling factors that might help to drive the achievement of better outcomes?

Obstacles to progress

A major roadblock that WPS advocates will continue to face is the unwillingness of the most powerful non-western democracies to fill the void vacated by the traditional defenders of liberal values, including gender equality. Some of these states seek a more active role in international institutions, including peacebuilding operations.[108] Even South Korea, which has given rhetorical support to WPS concerns, particularly on efforts to address conflict-related sexual violence, has failed to make its development cooperation programs more systematically attuned to gender issues.[109] Its funding patterns and institutional practices in both developing and conflict-affected countries do not reflect its rhetorical commitments.[110]

It is difficult to pin down a consistent peacebuilding doctrine on the part of democratic emerging powers.[111] Their foreign assistance and diplomatic engagement efforts are not particularly liberal, and there is little reason to expect even the established democracies in this camp to stand up for human rights in forums where peacebuilding priorities are discussed.[112] As a member of the UN Peacebuilding Commission, for instance, India maintained its usual reticence about anything resembling democracy promotion, or in fact anything that had the appearance of external imposition.[113] India's diplomats worked overtime to ensure that projects financed by the UN Democracy Fund, which India helped to establish in 2006, were governed by eligibility requirements and operational regulations that would make them as unthreatening as possible to host governments in both conflict and non-conflict countries. India's political analysts have been uncharacteristically unanimous in discounting the possibility that any foreseeable Indian government would revert to a foreign policy platform that stressed democracy and human rights or indeed any other set of ethical principles.[114]

In fact, India reflects all three of the trends outlined in this chapter. First, while India has sustained democracy continuously since 1947, it faces some of the same threats to its liberal order as the United States and European democracies – targeted attacks on the press, the politicization of independent institutions and the demonization of minorities. And like the regional and emerging powers at the center of the second trend, India's BJP government, in power since 2014, has pursued a much more militarized, less accommodating approach to dealing with the many insurgencies facing the country. Draconian anti-terror laws that undercut accountability for actions undertaken by the military are increasingly employed not only in the disputed region of Kashmir, but in India's northeast and in areas dominated by Maoist-inspired rebels in the country's interior. India's government has drawn closer in policy and diplomacy to other illiberal peacebuilders such as the Philippines.[115] India's experience also resonates with the third trend: the redistribution of power in the international system. India, like China, seeks to use its development cooperation programs (which have been in existence since the 1960s) to advance its strategic interests. Indian strategic analysts have for years been closely monitoring China's growing influence in South Asia, including through BRI projects in Pakistan and Sri Lanka.[116] In the 2010s, India did not join forces with other developing-world democracies, such as South Africa, in supporting the creation of a more rights-respecting vision of development.

Drivers of progress

The shrinking space for liberal peacebuilding in the face of growing illiberalism has elevated the significance of multilateral institutions and individual liberal states in sustaining support for gender-responsive peacebuilding. International organizations have committed themselves to inclusive post-conflict governance reforms (including legal reforms and transitional justice) and funding for women's organizations. Inadequate as international approaches to peacebuilding may have been from a gender equality perspective, they have nonetheless provided space for recognizing the importance of women's peace movements and incorporating gender analysis into policymaking.

The most significant driver of progress in implementing the WPS agenda has always been women's peace movements in conflict-affected countries. But women's peace organizations face serious basic capacity constraints in conflict situations. Even when women are provided opportunities to engage in peace processes or post-conflict planning, they continue to face huge challenges in seeking to influence policy agendas. They must often forge temporary alliances across political, ethnic and other divides. In conflict-torn countries, women's movements are often underfunded, their members focused on survival, their leadership dispersed. Recovering organizational strength, let alone achieving unity and demonstrating constituency support, is a challenge.

Despite these obstacles, women's movements have significantly influenced peace processes. One of the most encouraging examples was the process by which Colombia ended its half-century of civil war in 2016. Colombia's peace accord was called "an international example for women's involvement."[117] Women's organizations pressured the government to include women in the peace talks, through high-visibility protests and by demonstrating solidarity across the lines of conflict. By 2015, women comprised 20 percent of the government delegation and 43 percent of the rebels' delegation. A gender sub-committee of peace negotiators – which heard testimony from victims, policy advocates and community mediators – fed gender-equality proposals directly into the peace talks. The resulting agreement ensured that the land-restitution processes would include the issuing of titles to displaced and indigenous women, that transitional justice arrangements would provide reparation for crimes against women and that female combatants would benefit equally from disarmament and rehabilitation programs.

A second potential driver of progress is a subtle yet important initiative to institutionalize WPS principles within the workings of the Security Council. The Council has received well-deserved criticism for failing to operationalize its WPS resolutions in the context of country-specific deliberations. But since 2015, the Security Council has brought gender issues more firmly into its work through the creation of a new forum within the Council – the Informal Experts Group (IEG) on WPS. The IEG provides a mechanism for bringing information and analysis on gender-related issues to the attention of member state delegations. This could shape their deliberations on country specific situations on the Council's agenda. Because the Security Council develops instructions for the UN's peace operations – in the form of detailed resolutions mandating each field mission's activities – the IEG is a helpful mechanism for ensuring that peace operation leadership prioritizes women's involvement in all aspects of post-conflict peacebuilding. This has produced positive results in some cases. Perhaps not surprisingly, the successes have tended to involve close collaboration between the UN Secretariat (which coordinates the information supplied to the IEG) and women's peace organizations working on the ground. By specifying and documenting specific gaps in women's representation, protection, access to justice and other aspects of gender-responsive peacebuilding, CSOs that work in conjunction with the IEG's Secretariat – which is housed UN Women – are able to effectively use the IEG to amplify the voices of local women peacebuilders.

In light of the challenging international peacebuilding landscape outlined in this chapter, one particularly hopeful development is the important role being played by the Security Council's non-permanent members – the so-called Elected Ten. A significant number of elected members – including some not necessarily associated with a strong commitment to gender equality – have nevertheless been vigorous in questioning field-mission leaders about failures to fulfill Council mandates on gender issues in the peace operations over which these UN officials have authority. This reflects in part a desire by Council members to play a more active role in supervising officials who are often effectively controlled by a small coterie of powerful states. But it is the IEG process – which requires field missions to subject themselves to closer scrutiny by Council members – that makes this possible. The underlying urge toward institutional innovation that the IEG represents may turn out to be a significant driver of progress on WPS issues in the future, even if the wider international peacebuilding landscape continues to present clear and present dangers.

Notes

1 Edward Newman, "'Liberal' Peacebuilding Debates," in Edward Newman, Roland Paris and Oliver P. Richmond, eds., *New Perspectives on Liberal Peacebuilding* (New York: United Nations University Press, 2009).
2 Jane Freedman, *Gender, Violence and Politics in the Democratic Republic of Congo* (Surrey: Ashgate, 2015); Rirhandu Mageza-Barthel, *Mobilizing Transnational Gender Politics in Post-Genocide Rwanda* (Surrey: Ashgate, 2015); Aili Mari Tripp, *Women and Power in Post-Conflict Africa* (Cambridge: Cambridge University Press, 2015).
3 *Report of the Secretary-General on Women and Peace and Security*, S/2019/800 (New York: United Nations, 2019), p. 31.
4 Ibid. See also UN Women, *Women's Peace and Humanitarian Fund*, Annual Report January–December 2018 (New York: UN Women, 2019).
5 Fionnuala Ní Aoláin, "The Relationship of Political Settlement Analysis to Peacebuilding from a Feminist Perspective," *Peacebuilding*, Vol. 4, No. 2 (June 2016), p. 157.
6 Ibid.
7 Barry R. Posen, "The Rise of Illiberal Hegemony," *Foreign Affairs*, Vol. 97, No. 2 (March–April 2018), pp. 20–27.
8 David Lewis, John Heathershaw and Nick Megoran, "Illiberal Peace? Authoritarian Modes of Conflict Management," *Cooperation and Conflict*, Vol. 53, No. 4 (December 2018), pp. 486–506.
9 World Economic Forum (WEF), *The Global Gender Gap Report 2020* (Geneva: WEF, December 2019).
10 Freedom House, *Democracy in Retreat: Freedom in the World 2019* (Washington, DC: Freedom House, 2019).
11 See *Report of the Special Rapporteur on the Situation of Human Rights Defenders: Women Human Rights Defenders*, A/HRC/40/60 (Geneva: United Nations, January 10, 2019); Janvich Mateo, "Philippines Urged to End Attacks vs Human Rights Defenders," *Philstar* (December 20, 2018).

12 Timothy Snyder, *The Road to Unfreedom: Russia, Europe, America* (New York: Tim Duggan Books, 2018); Yascha Mounk, *The People vs. Democracy: Why Our Freedom Is in Danger and How to Save It* (Cambridge, MA: Harvard University Press, 2018); Steven Levitsky and Daniel Ziblatt, *How Democracies Die* (New York: Crown, 2018).

13 Henry J. Kaiser Family Foundation (KFF), *The Mexico City Policy: An Explainer* (San Francisco: KFF, January 2019); Anne Marie Goetz, "Will Reactionary Delegations Torpedo UN Talks on Rural Women?" *OpenDemocracy* (March 12, 2018).

14 Rebecca Ratcliffe, "'People Will End Up Dying': Trump's Cuts Devastate Clinics in Zambia," *The Guardian* (January 25, 2019).

15 Natasha Lennard, "The Misogynistic Logic of Jeff Sessions's Horrifying New Asylum Policy for Domestic Violence Victims," *The Intercept* (June 15, 2018).

16 US State Department, *Country Reports on Human Rights Practices* (Washington, DC: US State Department, April 20, 2018).

17 From the April 20 draft of what would become UNSCR 2467.

18 Dulcie Leimbach, "At the UN, the US Darkens Women's Right to Abortion," *PassBlue* (April 23, 2019).

19 Cited in Security Council Report, *In Hindsight: Negotiations on Resolution 2493 on Women, Peace and Security*, December 2019 Monthly Forecast (New York: Security Council Report, November 27, 2019).

20 Rebecca Saunders, "Norm Spoiling: Undermining the International Women's Rights Agenda," *International Affairs*, Vol. 94, No. 2 (March–April 2018), pp. 271–291.

21 Goetz, "Will Reactionary Delegations Torpedo UN Talks on Rural Women?"

22 Stefano Gennarini, "For the First Time Ever, the U.S. Threatened Pro-Life Veto at UN Security Council," *C-Fam: Center for Family and Human Rights* (April 25, 2019).

23 Ulrike M. Vieten, "Far Right Populism and Women: The Normalisation of Gendered Anti-Muslim Racism and Gendered Culturalism in the Netherlands," *Journal of Intercultural Studies*, Vol. 37, No. 6 (November 1, 2016), pp. 621–636; Aida A. Hozic and Jacqui True, *Scandalous Economics: The Politics of Gender and Financial Crises* (Oxford: Oxford University Press, 2018).

24 Weronika Grzebalska, Easzter Kováts and Andrea Peto, "Gender as Symbolic Glue: How 'Gender' Became an Umbrella Term for the Rejection of the (Neo)Liberal Order," *Krytyka Polityczna & European Alternatives* (January 13, 2017).

25 Ibid.

26 C-Fam, Family Watch International and Group of the Friends of the Family, *Uniting Nations for a Family-Friendly World*, UN Event (New York: United Nations, May 16, 2016).

27 C-Fam, "It Takes a Family," *Friday Fax* (May 15, 2019).

28 See UN Women, *Progress of the World's Women: Families in a Changing World* (New York: UN Women, 2019).

29 Community of Democracies (CD), *World Forum for Democracy Side-Event: Gender Equality and Political Empowerment of Women: A Populist Reaction?* (Strasburg: CD, 2017).

30 See Julian Borger, "US Threatens to Veto UN Resolution on Rape as Weapon of War," *The Guardian* (April 22, 2019).

31 Julian Borger, "Trump Administration Wants to Remove 'Gender' from UN Human Rights Documents," *The Guardian* (October 25, 2018).

32 Terry Hallmark, "Oil and Violence in the Niger Delta Isn't Talked About Much," *Forbes* (February 13, 2017).

33 See *The Foreign Policies of Emerging-Market Democracies: What Role for Human Rights and Democracy?* (Washington, DC: Brookings Institution, 2001).

34 Vanessa Tinker, *Women, Peace, and Security: The Case of Turkey* (Rome: International Institute of Social and Economic Sciences, April 2015).

35 Canan Aslan Akman, *The Rising Tide of Populism and Women's Authoritarian Inclusion in Turkey Under the Justice and Development Party Governance*, Paper Presented at the 5th European Conference on Politics and Gender (Lausanne: University of Lausanne, June 3–10, 2017).

36 See Burcin Belge, "Women Policies Erased from Political Agenda," *Bianet* (June 9, 2011).

37 Government of the Philippines, *PAyapa at MAsaganang PamayaNAn* (Manila: OPAPP).

38 José Alvarado Cóbar, Emma Bjertén-Günther and Yeonju Jung, "Assessing Gender Perspectives in Peace Processes with Application to the Cases of Colombia and Mindanao," *SIPRI Insights on Peace and Security*, No. 6 (November 2018), pp. 20–24.

39 Hannah Ellis-Petersen, "Philippines: Rodrigo Duterte Orders Soldiers to Shoot Female Rebels 'in the vagina'," *The Guardian* (February 12, 2018).

40 "UN Special Rapporteur: End Attacks, Stigmatization vs. Human Rights Defenders in PH," *CNN Philippine* (December 19, 2018).

41 Clare Baldwin and Andrew R.C. Marshall, "All the President's Women: Duterte's Fiercest Critics and a Surly Political Heir," *Reuters* (September 14, 2017); Anne Marie Goetz, "The Silencing of Lila De Lima, Duterte's First Political Prisoner'," *OpenDemocracy* (July 7, 2017); Aika Ray, "Rappler CEO Maria Ressa Arrested for Cyber Libel," *Rappler* (February 13, 2019).

42 Jonathan Abbamonte, *Duterte Ignores Supreme Court, Orders Action on Controversial Reproductive Health Law* (Manila: Population Research Institute, January 17, 2017).

43 Andrei Medina, "Gabriela Supports Duterte, Asks Voters to Look Beyond Womanizing Ways," *Cosmopolitan* (February 29, 2016).

44 Gabriela USA, *Gabriela USA Welcomes President Duterte Joining Millions of Women Calling for Change*, (San Francisco, CA: Filipina Women's Network, July 13, 2016); A. Salaverria, "Duterte Names Former Gabriela Rep DSDW USEC," *Inquirer News* (September 15, 2017).

45 "Gabriela Clarifies Stand: Catcalling 'Demeans Women'," *Rappler* (June 5, 2016).

46 MindaNews, "Gabriela on Duterte: 'We Were Mistaken'," *Edge Davao*, blog (November 15, 2018); Suyin Haynes, "Women in the Philippines Have Had Enough of President Duterte's 'Macho' Leadership," *Time* (July 23, 2018).

47 Saskia Brechenmacher, *Achieving Peace in Northeast Nigeria: The Reintegration Challenge* (Washington, DC: Carnegie Endowment for International Peace, September 5, 2018).

48 Susanna P. Campbell, David Chandler and Meera Sabaratnam, *A Liberal Peace? The Problems and Practices of Peacebuilding* (London: Zed Books, 2011).

49 Amnesty International, *Nigeria: Security Forces Failed to Act on Warnings About Boko Haram Attack Hours Before Abduction of Schoolgirls* (London: Amnesty International, March 20, 2018).

50 Anne Marie Goetz, *A New Cold War on Women's Rights?* (Geneva: UNRISD, June 22, 2015).

51 Heidi Hudson, "The Power of Mixed Messages: Women, Peace and Security Language in National Action Plans from Africa," *Africa Spectrum*, Vol. 52, No. 3 (December 2017), p. 17.

52 Ibid.

53 Dom Phillips, "Marielle Franco Murder: Amnesty Urges Independent Monitor of Police Inquiry," *The Guardian* (July 12, 2018).

54 Maria Carolina Marcello, "Brazil's Bolsonaro Says He Intends to Use Armed Forces to Fight...," *Reuters* (October 21, 2018).

55 Lulu Garcia-Navarro, "For Brazil's Women, Laws Are Not Enough to Deter Rampant Violence," *NPR.Org* (July 24, 2016).

56 Frida Ghitis, "Bolsonaro Could Realize His Critics' Worst Fears-and His Supporters' High Hopes," *World Politics Review* (January 10, 2019).

57 Anthony Faiola and Marina Lopes, "LGBT Rights Threatened in Brazil Under New Far-Right President," *Washington Post* (February 18, 2019).

58 ProFamOrg Admin, "Exemplary Leadership in Brazil," *International Organization for the Family* (January 2019).

59 Ibid.

60 Floyd Whaley, "As Pope Francis Visits Philippines, Tensions Between Church and Government Surface," *The New York Times* (January 16, 2015).

61 Florian Bardou, "Théorie du genre, Doctrina Diabolicum," *Libération* (October 18, 2017).

62 Jen Kirby, "Jair Bolsonaro Says Brazil and the US Stand Side by Side 'Against Fake News'," *Vox* (March 19, 2019).

63 Grzebalska, Kováts and Peto, "Gender as Symbolic Glue."

64 Sonia Correa, David Paternotte and Roman Kuhar, "The Globalisation of Anti-Gender Campaigns," *International Politics and Society* (May 31, 2018).

65 Silvia Rojas-Castro, *Gender in Peace Agreements: Lessons from Colombia*, Polis Brief No. 6 (Berlin: Polis 180, January 2019).

66 Posen, "The Rise of Illiberal Hegemony"; Oliver P. Richmond, *After Liberal Peace: The Changing Concept of Peacebuilding*, RSIS Commentary No. 272 (Singapore: S. Rajaratnam School of International Studies, 2015); Lewis, Heathershaw and Megoran, "Illiberal Peace?"

67 Mehmet Evren Eken, *Turkey's Foreign Aid: Who Is the Target Audience?* (Los Angeles, CA: USC Center for Public Diplomacy, November 2016).

68 Benjamin Carvalho and Cedric De Coning, *Rising Powers and the Future of Peacekeeping and Peacebuilding* (Oslo: NOREF, 2013), p. 5.

69 Theodore Baird, "The Geopolitics of Turkey's 'Humanitarian Diplomacy' in Somalia: A Critique," *Review of African Political Economy*, Vol. 43, No. 149 (July 2, 2016), pp. 470–477.

70 Carvalho and De Coning, *Rising Powers*, p. 4.

71 Ibid., p. 5.

72 Ibid., p. 1.

73 Emma Mawdsley, *From Recipients to Donors: Emerging Powers and the Changing Development Landscape* (London and New York: Zed Books, 2012).

74 Rick Waterford, "Chinese Investment Strategies Towards Developing Countries," *The Centre for Chinese Studies*, blog (September 26, 2017); David Shinn, "Africa Test's China's Non-Interference Policy," *China-US Focus*, blog (May 15, 2014).

75 Ron Matthews, Xiaojuan Ping and Li Ling, "Learning from China's Foreign Aid Model," *The Diplomat* (August 25, 2016).

76 David Dollar, "Where Is China's Development Finance Really Going?" *Brookings*, blog (October 12, 2017).

77 AidData, *China's Global Development Footprint* (Williamsburg, VA: AidData, 2018).

78 Ricardo Soares de Oliveira, "Illiberal Peacebuilding in Angola," *The Journal of Modern African Studies*, Vol. 49, No. 2 (June 2011), pp. 287–314; Stein Eriksen, "The Liberal Peace Is Neither: Peacebuilding, Statebuilding and the Reproduction of Conflict in the Democratic Republic of the Congo," *International Peacekeeping*, Vol. 16, No. 5 (November 2009), pp. 652–666.

79 "Gender-Inclusive Infrastructure Is Need of the Hour, Says AIIB," *ChinaDaily.com* (June 27, 2018).

80 "AIIB's Approach to Gender Might Not Involve a Gender Policy," *Devex* (June 29, 2018).

81 Moisés Naím, "Help Not Wanted," *The New York Times* (February 15, 2007).

82 Claire Provost, "China Publishes First Report on Foreign Aid Policy," *The Guardian* (April 28, 2011).

83 James A. Millward, "Is China a Colonial Power?" *The New York Times* (August 7, 2018).

84 UNDP and Government of the Philippines, *Mainstreaming Gender and Women's Rights into Governance Reform Initiatives* (Manila: Miriam College, November 15, 2006).

85 Paul Chaney, "Civil Society and Gender Mainstreaming: Empirical Evidence and Theory-Building from Twelve Post-Conflict Countries 2005–15," *World Development*, Vol. 83 (July 2016), pp. 280–294.

86 Stephanie Fillion, "China's Priorities in the UN Security Council: Peacekeeping," *PassBlue* (November 4, 2018).

87 Robbie Gramer and Colym Lynch, "Haley Tried to Block Appointment of Chinese Diplomat to Key UN Post. He Got the Job Anyway," *Foreign Policy* (February 14, 2019).

88 CGTN America, "China to Donate $10 Million to UN for Women's Rights," *CGTN America* (September 27, 2015).

89 Zhibo Qiu, "Why China Is So Interested in Gender Equality," *The Diplomat* (March 10, 2016).

90 UN Women, *Stakeholders Tackle How to Make the SDGs a Reality for Women and Girls* (New York: UN Women, January 22, 2016).

91 Qiu, "Why China Is So Interested in Gender Equality."

92 "G-20: 2016-China," Pre-Summit Chair's Statement, Beijing (December 1, 2015), pp. 13, 16.

93 Matthews, Ping and Ling, "Learning from China's Foreign Aid Model."

94 Dorothy Guererro and Firoze Manji, eds., *China's New Role in Africa and the South: A Search for a New Perspective* (Cape Town: Fahamu Books, 2008).

95 See Roudabeh Kishi and Raleigh Clionadh, *Chinese Aid and Africa's Pariah States* (Brighton: University of Sussex, 2015); Huan-Kai Tseng and Ryan Krog, *No Strings Attached: Chinese Foreign Aid and Regime Stability in Resource-Rich Recipient Countries*, Working Paper (Washington, DC: George Washington University, 2016).

96 Axel Dreher et al., *Aid on Demand: African Leaders and the Geography of China's Foreign Assistance*, Working Paper No. 3 (Williamsburg, VA: AidData, November 2014).

97 Panos Mourdoukoutas, "What Is China Doing to Pakistan? The Same Thing It Did to Sri Lanka," *Forbes* (April 15, 2018).

98 Zeenia Faraz, *Women, Peace, and Security in Pakistan*, Peace Brief No. 218 (Washington, DC: US Institute of Peace, February 16, 2017).

99 Jeff M. Smith, "Why Duterte's Deals with China May Be Security Concerns," *The Diplomat* (November 2, 2016).

100 "Philippines Publishes $15bn Shopping List of Chinese Investment Projects," *Global Construction Review* (October 24, 2016).

101 John Reed and Grace Ramos, "Philippines Revamp of Battle-Scarred Marawi Turns to China," *Financial Times* (October 8, 2018).

102 Neil DeVotta, "China's Influence in Sri Lanka: Negotiating Development, Authoritarianism, and Regional Transformation," in Evelyn Goh, ed., *Rising China's Influence in Developing Asia* (Oxford: Oxford University Press, 2016).

103 Haley J. Swedlund, "Is China Eroding the Bargaining Power of Traditional Donors in Africa?" *International Affairs*, Vol. 93, No. 2 (March 1, 2017), pp. 389–408.

104 Maria Abi-Habib, "How China Got Sri Lanka to Cough Up a Port," *The New York Times* (October 8, 2018).

105 Human Rights Watch, *Burma: Discriminatory Laws Could Stoke Communal Tensions* (Washington, DC: Human Rights Watch, August 23, 2015).

106 Adrienne Joy, *Understanding China's Response to the Rakhine Crisis* (Washington, DC: US Institute of Peace, February 8, 2016).

107 Isabel Hilton, *China in Myanmar: Implications for the Future* (Oslo: NOREF, 2013).

108 Rob Jenkins and Emma Mawdsley, *Democratic Emerging Powers and the International Human Rights System* (New York: Friedrich Ebert Stiftung, 2013).

109 Jisun Song and Eun Mee Kim, "A Critical Review of Gender in South Korea's Official Development Assistance," *Asian Journal of Women's Studies*, Vol. 19, No. 3 (January 1, 2013), pp. 72–96.

110 See Kim Sook, *Open Debate on Women, Peace and Security* (New York: Permanent Mission of the Republic of Korea to the UN, 24 June 2013).

111 Oliver Richmond and Ioannis Tellidis, *The Brics and International Peacebuilding and State-building* (Oslo: NOREF, 2013).

112 Bruce Jones, ed., *Shaping the Emerging World: India and the Multilateral Order* (Washington, DC: Brookings Institution Press, 2013).

113 Rob Jenkins, *Peacebuilding: From Concept to Commission* (London: Routledge, 2013).

114 Pratap B. Mehta, "Reluctant India," *Journal of Democracy*, Vol. 22, No. 4 (October 2011), pp. 101–113.

115 Dharel Placido, "Duterte, Modi Meet in India," *ABS-CBN News* (January 25, 2018); Makoi Popioco and V.J. Bacungan, "Duterte Assures Support, Protection for Indian Businessmen," *CNN Philippines* (February 21, 2018).

116 Amit Bhandari and Chandni Jindal, *Chinese Investments in India's Neighbourhood* (Mumbai: Gateway House, Indian Council on Global Relations, March 12, 2018).

117 Jamille Bigio and Rachel Voglestein, *Women's Participation in Peace Processes: Colombia* (New York: Council on Foreign Relations, December 15, 2017).

4

GENDER AND TERRORISM

Jeannette Gaudry Haynie

On August 29, 1969, a flight from Rome to Tel Aviv was hijacked by members of the Popular Front for the Liberation of Palestine (PFLP). The pilots were forced to land the aircraft in Syria, where the hijackers, Leila Khaled and Salim Issawi, were subsequently arrested.[1] In the months that followed, Khaled's involvement attracted widespread international attention because as a 25-year-old woman, she defied the commonly accepted image of a terrorist.

What kept the media spotlight on Khaled was her sex and the gender-based stereotypes and expectations that accompany her sex. Conventional wisdom holds that a terrorist is a man, alienated by political, economic and societal inequalities, who has been radicalized and uses violence toward political means.[2] Khaled fascinates because society does not expect women to hijack planes, threaten pilots with hand grenades and proudly pose with an automatic weapon and a smile.

Khaled's actions reinvigorated a debate about the factors that cause terrorism and how communities, states and international bodies address terrorist threats. The 9/11 attacks and subsequent high-profile terrorist attacks further spurred scholars and policymakers to search for factors to explain what drives people to terrorism.[3] Unfortunately, despite decades of research, the terrorism literature remains muddled on these issues. Each new attack demonstrates that questions remain about how people become radicalized, how they operate and what can be done to predict or counter terrorist activity. Current knowledge does not sufficiently explain why terrorist attacks occur, nor does it guide policymakers to develop programs that successfully address the threats.[4]

As scholars and policymakers struggle to understand and address terrorism, the impacts of gender inequality and – less frequently – the role of gender itself are increasingly considered as contributing or permissive factors that help to explain terrorism.[5] The Women, Peace and Security (WPS) agenda has contributed to this discussion, as it highlights the gender dimensions of conflict in its many forms, including terrorism. As the WPS agenda has grown, counter-terrorism (CT) programs that focus on gender inequality and women's empowerment have developed.[6]

The growing attention to gender in terrorism is long overdue. While the majority of terrorists are men, women have historically been significant actors in terrorist organizations.[7] Research has also linked the incidence of gender inequality to higher rates of terrorism.[8] Unfortunately, current research and policies do not go far enough. To understand the role of gender in terrorism, it is not enough to focus on female terrorists and gender inequality; researchers and policymakers also need to focus on the identities, norms, structures and ideologies that constitute masculinities and femininities around the world.[9]

Like all political phenomena, terrorism is complex. There are no clear formulas to predict radicalization, group formation or terrorist behavior, just as there are no policy responses that are guaranteed to work. Gender is similarly complex, and the concepts that inform discussions on gender fall apart when applied to a difficult problem such as terrorism.

The gender dimensions of terrorism are many, and they include terrorist recruitment and radicalization, the support terrorists draw from their wider communities, the structure of terrorist organizations, terrorist operations, as well as myriad local, state and international responses to terrorism. Women and men occupy specific roles and are used by terrorist organizations in distinct capacities.[10] Male and female stereotypes are also exploited by terrorists within their operations. Gender identities, norms, structures and ideologies shape pathways to radicalization, recruitment strategies and terrorist activity. CT programs often use female stereotypes to counter terrorism while remaining blind to the way masculinities can shape terrorist narratives.[11] Contemporary considerations of the gender dimensions of terrorism are inadequate. Progress has certainly been made, but this progress remains limited and incomplete.

To get to the next level, policy and research communities must consider *all* of the gender dimensions of terrorism and significantly broaden the scope of future research. This will require action in five areas. First, more inclusive leadership in academia, advocacy and policymaking must be prioritized. Diversity and representativeness will drive the search for more creative solutions. Second, the experience and knowledge of local practitioners should be incorporated in policy and research. Third, a more robust and coherent research agenda must be pursued to better understand how gender shapes terrorism. Fourth, policymakers must learn lessons from both policy successes and policy failures. Policy lessons should be actively pursued and effectively communicated in order to drive progress. And finally, CT programs must be based on respect for human rights and civil liberties.

If policy communities fail to do a better job of understanding the complex connections between gender and terrorism, opportunities will be wasted and practitioners who place their lives on the line to counter terrorism will be at risk around the globe.

In this chapter, I analyze the gender dimensions of terrorism and assess how they are considered from research and policy perspectives. Second, I discuss the track record of how gender is considered in CT discussions, programs and policies.

Third, I identify obstacles and drivers to progress. Fourth, using the 9/11 hijacker Mohamed Atta and the phenomenon of Incel terrorism as a case study, I offer a brief analysis of how exploring the gender dimensions of terrorism can inform research and policy. Finally, I discuss strategies for progress.

This chapter is not comprehensive. It does not capture every aspect of gender and terrorism. Because of space considerations, I do not address the growing field of research into violent extremism and Preventing and Countering Violent Extremism (PVE/CVE). *Violent extremism* is a relatively new term, and the PVE field is rapidly changing; there exists no broad agreement on where violent extremism overlaps with terrorism and where it does not, since extremism is not well-defined and the phenomenon covers a broader swath of activity and beliefs than terrorism.[12] While violence can be identified, its links to extreme beliefs and ideologies is less clear.

To make the chapter more digestible for readers who are new to the concepts of gender and terrorism, I also limited the discussion of gender to women and men instead of exploring a more expansive, non-binary gender spectrum. Much more research is needed on the latter.

Defining terrorism and gender

Terrorism emerged as a major field of study in the 1970s, when scholars sought to understand a phenomenon that had captured global attention yet was poorly understood. These scholars developed groundbreaking arguments linking terrorism to factors such as power disparities, oppression, disaffection and fragmented populations.[13] Defining terrorism was – and remains – a major challenge. Scholars initially defined terrorism as a form of political violence, describing differences between permissive, or contributing, causes of terrorism and precipitant causes – the more immediate factors that sparked specific incidents or campaigns.[14] David Rapoport, identified four waves of terrorism, each lasting a generation: anarchic terrorism, anti-colonial terrorism, the new leftists and religious terrorism.[15] Scholars also analyzed the levels of violence displayed by different groups, and they studied differences between terrorism and other kinds of warfare at every level from the tactical to the strategic.[16] For this chapter, I employ the definition of terrorism used by the University of Maryland's Global Terrorism Database: "the threatened or actual use of illegal force and violence by a non-state actor to attain a political, economic, religious, or social goal through fear, coercion, or intimidation."[17]

Terrorist attacks tend to be premeditated and politically motivated; terrorists can also seek specific goals: media attention, publicity and/or fear; and terrorists' targets are often distinct from their victims.

The causes of terrorism similarly can be complex. Immediately after 9/11, observers listed poverty, lack of education and nondemocratic regimes as primary causes of terrorism. These answers reflected widely held beliefs that states experiencing these problems were more likely to suffer terrorist attacks and that individuals impacted by socio-economic stress were more likely to become terrorists.

Policymakers have often advocated for increased funding to regions facing these problems as a way to combat terrorism.[18]

However, research shows anything but a direct line from poverty or lack of education to terrorism; these relationships vary widely.[19] Some scholars find no direct connection between socio-economic factors and terrorism, while others find that any link is conditioned by cultural or geographical factors.[20] Overall, terrorists seem no more likely to come from poorer or less educated backgrounds, and when holding factors such as civil liberties and ongoing conflict constant, socio-economic factors do not have consistent effects on rates of terrorism.[21]

Regime type is another factor that has been identified as a cause of terrorism. Some researchers hold that democratic ideals and the methods for conflict resolution that are present in democracies allow grievances to be addressed without violence.[22] Contemporary research, however, does not consistently support this proposition: while some scholars have observed a negative relationship between regime openness and terrorism, others have observed greater rates of terrorism in democracies than in autocracies (possibly due to the increased ease of communications and the level of openness in democracies).[23] Democratic stability also seems to be a factor: newer democracies experience more terrorist attacks than autocracies and older, more stable democracies.[24]

There is broader agreement among scholars on the effects of factors such as state stability, civil liberties and human rights on the making of terrorists and the likelihood of terrorism.[25] Unstable and weak states might not have the capacity to prevent terrorist organizations from growing. Insecure leaders add to these instabilities.[26] Discrimination against minorities and human rights violations, combined with a lack of civil liberties, can facilitate terrorist recruitment and spark more terrorist attacks. Instabilities can exacerbate these conditions, and the status of human rights within a state could be used as a predictor of terrorist activity.[27] Despite agreement on some of these issues, the state of the literature remains inconclusive.

Gender is also complex and only partially understood. Gender runs deeper than sex, carrying with it the weight of "socially constructed characteristics" that have deep structural and hierarchical implications.[28] Gender has an identity, usually male or female, and sets of expectations and norms that follow. Gender structures exist, which enable hierarchical relationships to emerge and exert private and public pressures on men and women – shaping pathways taken, options available and individual or group responses.[29] The social construction of gender varies over time and across countries and cultures.

Most importantly, gender does not mean female alone: it also means the norms, ideologies and structures associated with femininities; gender also means male and the norms, ideologies and structures accompanying masculinities. Just as critical for the study of gender and terrorism is the understanding of how masculinity is connected to warfighting, dominance and power.[30]

The intersection of gender and terrorism

When most people think about gender and terrorism, a common image is that of a female terrorist. This is only one small dimension of gender and terrorism, and it is a simplistic image. It is the one that attracts the most attention.[31] There are more complex, multifaceted dimensions to the intersection of gender and terrorism than "terrorists who happen to be women." These dimensions can be organized into three broad categories.

The first category is the terrorist's gender. While female terrorists attract a disproportionate amount of attention – which some terrorist organizations attempt to capitalize on – male terrorists have a gender, too.[32] This category encompasses the roles that men and women occupy in terrorist organizations and why they select (or are forced into) those roles.

The second category is the gender dynamic at work in the broader population from which terrorist organizations draw support. Understanding the population within which terrorists operate is critical; without community support, terrorists cannot function. Understanding this, terrorist organizations often embrace specific norms and select specific targets to differentiate themselves from other groups and exploit community characteristics.[33]

The third and most complex category includes how gender – gender hierarchies, gender structures, gender norms and gender expectations – shapes terrorist behavior and activity. Social and cultural identification and the different (and changing) values ascribed to masculinity and femininity shape propensity for violence, acceptance and normalization of violence and individual perpetrator actions.

Considering the intersections of gender and terrorism in three categories helps to clarify this complicated and dynamic relationship. The effects of this relationship play out in everything from terrorist recruitment and radicalization, support from the wider population, organization structure and terrorist operations to local, state and international CT responses. With these categories in mind, I assess the track record of how the policy community and scholars consider gender in policy and research.

Individual terrorists – male or female?

Research into gender and terrorism has overwhelmingly focused on female terrorists. As a result, a significant amount of information is known about women who belong to terrorist organizations.

Women have long played critical roles in terrorist organizations. As far back as the first wave of terrorism, which included anarchist groups such as Narodnaya Volya in Russia and the third-wave Baader-Meinhof group in Germany, women have acted as supporters, fundraisers and leaders in terrorist organizations. Throughout every wave of terrorism and in nearly every type of terrorist organization, women have been involved.[34] The conventional image of a female member of a terrorist organization is that of a mother, wife, or other family member who supports the organization through fundraising; performing stereotypically female tasks such as child-raising, cleaning and cooking; passing down cultural expectations to her children in ways that support the group; providing logistical support; and in modern times, using social media to spread the group's message. This image is not inaccurate, since women have performed these tasks in organizations as diverse as the Ku Klux Klan and the Islamic State in Iraq and Syria (ISIS), and they have done so in significant numbers.[35]

However, women have also acted as operatives, committing violence along-side their male counterparts, in groups that span the ideological spectrum from the Kurdistan Workers' Party and the Liberation Tigers of Tamil Eelam to Boko Haram and ISIS. Increasingly, women have carried out suicide attacks with devastating effectiveness.[36] Boko Haram, in particular, has used female suicide bombers at unprecedented levels; approximately 54 percent of Boko Haram's suicide attacks have been perpetrated by women, with the youngest being approximately nine years old.[37]

Female terrorists attract a disproportionate amount of attention because conventional wisdom, based on stereotypes, holds that women are not violent. Thus, when women do commit terrorist acts, scholars and policymakers want to understand why. Today, far more is known about female radicalization and roles within organizations than before. However, gender-based stereotypes and beliefs run deep. As a result, even though research into female terrorists is growing, myths about terrorism and gender hold fast.[38]

For example, over the years, scholars have found support for the idea that terrorist organizations employ women not only when they lack manpower but also strategically – to draw media attention, to differentiate themselves from other groups and to exploit existing gender norms and stereotypes in order to attack specific targets or avoid CT efforts. However, CT policies remain relatively uninformed about these terrorist calculations, and governments are regularly caught flat-footed by terrorists' exploitation of gender norms.[39] ISIS and al Qaeda in Iraq were both willing to ignore existing norms when doing so would advance their ambitions.[40] Little research has been done in this area, and few CT policies are informed by the knowledge that terrorist groups will innovate to exploit gender-based norms and beliefs, regardless of their underlying ideology. Further, CT programs that focus on women primarily address them in their roles as mothers, wives and keepers of culture.[41]

CT programs that stick to gendered myths about who terrorists are and how they radicalize minimize female agency and limit the application of lessons learned from earlier research.[42]

Male terrorism is also misunderstood.[43] Lessons learned about female terrorists are not applied to increase understanding of male radicalization. Gender-based stereotypes continue to inform the assumption that men are simply more likely to resort to violence and aggression and are therefore less interesting to study. Male stereotypes prevail, and male agency is also assumed away.

Broader community support

The second area of interest in the intersection of gender and terrorism is the composition of the broader society within which terrorists operate and from which they draw support. Researchers increasingly consider gender inequality to be an explanatory factor for terrorism.[44] A society's mistreatment of women often provides an indication of likely violence and extremism; organizations such as the Pakistan Taliban and Boko Haram have exploited and altered existing gender norms to restrict women's dress and behavior while ramping up extremist activity.[45]

Research has also shown that terrorism is correlated with various forms of gender inequality at the aggregate level.[46] Unfortunately, the implications of these findings are unclear. Studies tend to apply different definitions and operationalizations of terrorism and gender, and they do not agree on which forms of terrorism matter and how to measure gender.[47] These problems are exacerbated by the lack of rich, reliable sources of data on gender rights and equality levels around the world and by researchers having to rely on basic indicators that leave out important local contexts.[48]

Although it is important to analyze the many inequalities women and girls endure around the world, it is also essential to consider the role played by male privilege and masculinities in the overall equation[49] – including the ways that gender norms, structures and hierarchies shape the behavior of men – the 50 percent that commit most terrorist violence.[50] The idea that gender and gender perspectives refer only to women and women's perspectives remains widely accepted in societies and policy circles. Terrorism analyses that focus on women's inequality, capture only part of the puzzle.[51]

Gender norms, hierarchies, structures and expectations

Gender norms define social rules of behavior for those identified as men and women. These norms can encourage aggression and violence on the part of men while urging passivity and silence for women. Gender hierarchies take the social constructs of gender and arrange them in dominant and subordinate roles, adding power and force to masculine behavior and attributes – and the opposite to feminine ones. Gendered structures emerge throughout government and society, including terrorist organizations, further enabling and reinforcing certain behaviors while deepening the hierarchies that exist.

Gender shapes and limits the range of acceptable behaviors. Yet little research exists on how cultural applications of masculinity shape violence. For example, there is no research how Latin American machismo encourages violent behavior.[52] Studies on how American masculinity feeds violent white supremacist narratives do not inform US policy.[53] And while research demonstrates how ISIS has exploited gender norms to further its own goals, it is not clear that CT policy has taken these findings into account.[54]

The gender dimensions of terrorism are not widely understood or accepted in research and policy. In mainstream scholarship, few substantive assessments of how terrorist groups exploit gender norms and structures in their internal operations exist. Research into the role of gender hierarchies and structures in shaping violence, how groups exploit gender to recruit members and the interaction between gender norms and terrorism at the local and state level is rare, as is substantive research into how gender dynamics affect and enable radicalization of women and men.[55]

US government entities such as the United States Agency for International Development (USAID), the US Departments of State and Justice and various Non-Governmental Organizations (NGOs) have created and sponsored programs that target gender inequalities as way of combating terrorism. Similarly, governments as diverse as the United Kingdom, Pakistan, Sri Lanka and Saudi Arabia have sponsored programs that target women as potential CT agents.[56]

Women should be included in the development and implementation of CT policy, but simply including women is by no means enough. Programs should be developed to target hypermasculinity and norms that feed the violent strains of masculinity in Boko Haram or the offshoots of the Provisional Irish Republican Army (PIRA), for example.[57] Attacks on targets such as a gay nightclub in Orlando, Florida, also demonstrate the need for programs that focus on how violent and nationalist masculinity can be threats.[58]

Policy implementation

In 2015, the United Nations (UN) Security Council made countering terrorism part of the WPS agenda. Adopting United Nations Security Council Resolution (UNSCR) 2242, the Security Council stressed the importance of the participation of civil society organizations and the integration of gender perspectives in all CVE policies and programs. The Council urged member states to expand research and data collection on the gendered impacts and effects of CVE policies and programs. The Council also called on members states to ensure the participation and leadership of women and women's organizations in developing strategies to counter terrorism and violent extremism.

The rhetoric is ambitious, but the practice has fallen short. Three main issues plague policy implementation. First, by focusing primarily on women, women's inequality and female stereotypes and roles, women and men alike are assigned one-dimensional, unchallenged stereotypes and experiences. This deprives people of agency, motivations and intent beyond what stereotypes describe. It also ignores structural factors, such as the role of the patriarchy.[59]

This perspective limits understanding of motivations, recruitment methods, organizational structure and operations.[60] Not surprisingly, the policies meant to address the issues are ineffective. Programs that aim to reintegrate former female terrorists by offering them the means to begin stereotypically female businesses – such as the pastry carts or chickens offered by the government of Sri Lanka to reintegrating female members of the Tamil Tigers – or programs that push former terrorists to get married and settle down force women into one-dimensional roles and could even make them more vulnerable.[61]

Second, these trends threaten the independence and wider acceptance of the WPS agenda. When programs that include women or target gender inequality as a way of countering terrorism struggle or fail, the goals of the WPS agenda are placed at risk. If the WPS agenda is viewed as merely an instrument of CT policy, it could weaken an agenda that is critical in its own right. The inclusion of women should inform terrorism scholarship and CT policy development, but the WPS agenda itself must remain distinct.[62]

Finally, masculinity remains neglected. As a result, research and policy remain underinformed about how men and boys are exploited by terrorist organizations. Policies and strategies will therefore continue to fall short of their intended goals.[63]

Case studies: Mohammed Atta and Incel terrorism

Mohamed Atta was one of the 9/11 hijackers and probably the pilot of American Airlines Flight 11, which crashed into one of the World Trade Center towers in New York City. Atta's story – as presented by most sources – appears to fit the conventional wisdom about male radicalization. Born into a modern Muslim family and raised in a suburb of Cairo, the youngest child of a domineering and discipline-heavy lawyer, as a boy Atta appeared to be overwhelmed by the personalities of his father and well-educated sisters. His father considered him spoiled by his mother, and Atta was seen by his peers as shy.[64]

Although his family was not particularly religious, Atta began praying regularly in his pre-teen years.[65] Despite earning an engineering degree, he caved into pressure from his father and traveled to Germany to pursue a master's degree. In Germany, he slowly became radicalized.[66] His generation faced significant social, economic and political strife in Egypt over the course of his younger years. The government had cracked down on fundamentalists while the population grew divided by fundamentalism and Western influences. College degrees did not guarantee good jobs, and Atta was exposed to growing unrest and anger in Egyptian Muslim society – anger that proliferated in communities in Europe as well.[67]

During 1997–98, Atta disappeared into al Qaeda training camps in Afghanistan; the timing of his disappearance suggests that he was in the al Qaeda camps when Osama bin Laden's followers attacked the US embassies in Kenya and Tanzania. Upon his return to Germany, he affiliated with an al Qaeda cell in Hamburg. He also travelled to the United States and earned his pilot license in Florida.[68] On September 11, 2001, he and his fellow hijackers attacked.

Atta's story seems straightforward. Grievances against the Egyptian government and Western influences seem to have shaped his life. Exposure to al Qaeda in his early adult years undoubtedly influenced him. But other factors – including the weight of societal expectations of a man of his class – might also have contributed significantly to his radicalization.

He is remembered by classmates as being introverted and sensitive – and of having idealistic and unrealistic expectations of women.[69] Those who met him in college, during his graduate work in Hamburg, and in flight school remember him as cold, sullen and disrespectful to women.[70] Family dynamics could have introduced and reinforced personality characteristics that made him vulnerable to radicalization. Shy and pampered by his mother, Atta seems to have spent his life overshadowed by his father, who considered him timid – a "virgin girl in his politeness and shyness" – descriptions that could have festered.[71] Emotional abuse from his father and social awkwardness – given a push by toxic beliefs – could turn into hatred.

Atta seems to have developed a growing misogyny over time. Three separate women developed concerns about his behavior; each came forward after the 9/11 attacks. An academic adviser of Atta's in Hamburg noticed signs of increasing fundamentalism in his dress and behavior. She noted that Atta began to avoid working physically close to her and seemed uncomfortable talking with her – even refusing to shake a female professor's hand at graduation. A female flight school classmate of Atta in Florida felt that he was consistently dismissive and rude to her and tried to avoid contact with her. Finally, a businesswoman found herself sitting near Atta at Boston's Logan Airport two days before 9/11. She described his stare as cold and penetrating. She recognized his face two days later on the news.[72]

Atta's misogyny also emerged in his own words. In a will found in his luggage after 9/11, Atta stated, "I don't want a pregnant woman or a person who is not clean to come and say good-bye to me because I don't approve it. . . . I don't want any women to go to my grave at all during my funeral or on any occasion thereafter."[73]

Misogyny alone does not appear to have driven Atta to terrorism, but his growing aversion to women seems significant. If a young man growing up in a culture with strict gender roles is abused or neglected when he fails to conform to the masculine ideal, he could be vulnerable to radicalization. Dissatisfaction, grievances and internalized anger can increase susceptibility to the ideas of terrorist groups.[74] There are parallels between Atta's case and the stories of other terrorists – in particular, Incel terrorists.

In 2014, a young man named Elliot Rodger killed six people and wounded 13 others in Isla Vista, California, before killing himself. Moments before his attack began, he published a video and a 137-page manifesto.[75] Angry because he was a virgin and because he felt that women had consistently rejected him, he blamed women – and men with active sex lives – for his lack of a sex life. He swore revenge. After his death, Rodger's video and manifesto were hailed and he was idolized by the "Incel" community – an online community of young men who are "involuntarily celibate."[76] These young men link up online to vent their frustrations with society and women; their community displays elements of misogyny intertwined with violent fantasies. Rodger's work has spawned at least one copycat: in 2018, Alek Minassian drove his van onto the sidewalk in Toronto, Canada, killing ten. He was linked to the Incel community: in Internet posts he saluted Rodger and promised to continue the violence.[77]

Both Rodger and Minassian displayed elements of misogyny in their online presence and violent actions – a misogyny linked to social gender norms and expectations about the masculine ideal. Both men had been socialized to expect attention and sexual favors from women by virtue of their manhood; when none were forthcoming, both resorted to violence to exact revenge. There are parallels between their anger, growing misogyny and eventual radicalization and Atta's anger, growing misogyny and radicalization. All three men fell short of a masculine ideal, all three men were aware of that shortcoming and all three turned to violence and terrorism.

When considering the intersection between gender and terrorism, beyond looking simply at physiological sex, what should be questioned is far more complex. The policy community should study how Rodger's and Atta's gender shaped their actions. Borrowing from Pearson's conceptualization of how gender shapes society, scholars and policymakers should study how gender identity, societal gender structures, cultural gender norms and deeply held gender ideologies shaped choices and actions for each man. These communities can study female terrorists in the same way – to understand how Leila Khaled's actions (and those of the greater PFLP leadership) were shaped by gender.

Obstacles, drivers and strategies for the future

Five main obstacles to the development of more creative, pragmatic and gender-inclusive research and policies can be identified.

First, stereotypes run deep and myths hold fast where gender is concerned. Gender remains ignored or underestimated in terrorism research and policy development. It is common to find mainstream policymakers and established scholars who remain ignorant about how gender shapes security discourses.[78] The tight hold that stereotypes have is fed by a lack of diversity in policy circles, where those with different perspectives are often marginalized or cut out entirely. This lack of diversity allows stereotypes to remain unchallenged and unseen.

Second, even when gender is considered, analysis is often limited and simplistic. Scholars and policymakers who are open-minded enough to consider gender overwhelmingly equate gender with the feminine and disregard the masculine. Adding women to the equation is necessary but not sufficient. Looking at only half of the equation will inevitably lead to uninformed and misguided policies.[79]

Third, incorporation of local actors into CT programs remains poorly implemented. Civil society remains largely decoupled from the programs meant to operate in its midst, and research often neglects the role of local actors. This decoupling is a major obstacle to progress. It is worsened by a lack of relationships between external organizations and the local practitioners doing the work. This problem can be exacerbated by racism or colonial aspirations. This problem is also enabled by a lack of diversity in decisionmaking and policymaking circles.[80]

Fourth, the tradition of having separate categories and fields of study for terrorism and gender is an obstacle to integration of the two.[81] The lines between microaggression, domestic violence, violent extremism, support for terrorist operations and full-scale conflict are rarely clear. Likewise, gender norms, gender structures and gender expectations are not easily quantifiable; rough indicators are often employed, presenting an obstacle to the development of nuanced policies and research.[82] Related is a lack of empirical evidence on women's involvement in terrorist organizations and group gender dynamics. Collecting this data could be dangerous, if it is doable at all, and this of course impedes analysis of these issues.[83]

Finally, these obstacles are exacerbated when a gender perspective is applied without local or cultural understanding of the situation. Even good intentions can lead processes astray. The peace negotiations between the communist New People's Army (NPA) and the government of the Philippines – a process that has lasted decades – exemplifies this idea. External actors – including government leaders within the Philippines and the NPA negotiators, who were disconnected from the fighters themselves – pushed for the inclusion of women in the negotiations.[84] However, the women they selected had no local credibility and no experience with or understanding of the conditions that needed to be addressed in the negotiations.[85]

Far from being a simple pattern that can transfer from situation to situation, consideration of gender dimensions requires an understanding of local contexts. Developing textured understandings is both necessary and exceedingly difficult, particularly for bureaucracies and external actors. It runs counter to the desire by policymakers for simple, concrete, measurable research and programs.

I have also identified five drivers of progress in the track record. First, scholarly research and local, state and international CT responses suggest that practical experiences drive progress. Non-Governmental Organizations and small pilot programs, as well as hands-on experiences, demonstrate that gender matters – that women are not simply victims but also can be agents of change.[86] As actors at every level gain diverse experiences studying and fighting terrorism, their awareness of the role that gender plays in shaping terrorism grows as well. This progress is spurred by the WPS agenda and its push for inclusive leadership.

Second, civil society actors are often on the front lines during times of conflict and disaster, and they repeatedly demonstrate the important role they play in understanding and dealing with terrorism.[87] Civil society activism drives from the bottom up a push for more diverse leadership and perspectives.

Third, failures also drive progress. Since 9/11, in particular, the failures of traditional CT programs to stop terrorist attacks and the failures of research to adequately explain terrorism have encouraged scholars to look for nontraditional factors outside of the traditional security sphere.[88] Failures can lead to major leaps forward; when policymakers and scholars are humbled by the failure to stop an attack or to understand the factors that enabled it, deeper and more critical analysis often follows.

Fourth, the stereotypical notion of gender that flooded early research and policy efforts is increasingly being questioned by researchers and civil society. The risks of framing women and men in limited, stereotypical roles are increasingly highlighted in current research.[89] As scholars accept that women are complicated, they can begin to think about men and masculinity being equally complicated and important. This can lead to more sophisticated ways of thinking about agency.[90]

Finally, increasing diversity in government, academia and in all kinds of leadership positions contributes to more open minds, more creative responses and a broader range of perspectives. Diversity in leadership demographics leads to diversity in analytical perspectives. Diversity of thought drives progress at every level.

These drivers demonstrate the potential for change and offer ways to overcome established obstacles to progress. Developing the minds and the mechanisms for understanding the gender dimensions of terrorism will not be easy, but the risks of inaction are greater.

Drawing on this analysis of ongoing obstacles to progress and proven drivers of progress, I will suggest five viable strategies for enhancing the prospects for progress in the future.

First, a more diverse cohort of leaders should be recruited at all levels of government and academia. Diverse leadership groups better understand the roles that everyone plays in enabling or countering terrorism. Diverse leadership teams bring broader sets of perspectives to the table, supporting a wider range and higher quality of research and policy responses. Leadership is key and homogeneity in leadership is a major obstacle to progress. By recruiting leaders with a range of perspectives and experiences, gender is less likely to be ignored, underestimated or misunderstood. Gender is more likely to be analyzed as the complex factor that it is.

Second, local practitioners should be intentionally and directly included at every possible stage in the development of research and policy. The exclusion of civil society actors, in particular, is an enormous mistake. Drawing on the knowledge and experience of the people immersed in the conflict at hand is key. Local actors are best positioned to understand and act in the surrounding culture. This integration can happen organically, as it has in some peace processes – such as the peace process in Northern Ireland during the 1990s – but inclusion should not be left to chance or existing power structures.[91] This should be a conscious, prominent, permanent priority.[92]

Third, policymakers and leaders in academia should support a more creative and critical research agenda that examines the reasons why terrorist organizations promote female operatives and how those groups exploit gender dynamics.[93] Research should consider normative aspects of gender and culture to include any cultural associations of gender with violence. It should examine gender stereotypes and expectations more systematically. Research should also analyze the ways that cultural and structural factors encourage broader civil society engagement and growth. As part of this process, scholars should develop frameworks for considering gender perspectives that include a deeper set of questions that challenge assumptions and internal biases.[94]

Fourth, policymakers and academics should put more effort into thoroughly and effectively learning lessons from policy successes and failures. Failure can be a critical tool for learning; lessons learned from failures should be developed and disseminated throughout academic and governmental communities. Existing networks that seek to develop and communicate lessons learned – such as the RESOLVE network hosted at the US Institute of Peace – should be better funded and better supported in their outreach efforts.

Fifth, CT programs should be based on respect for human rights and civil liberties. The state responses to terrorism that ignore the basic rights of citizens and engage in torture or other serious human rights abuses fuel resentment and radicalization. Law enforcement and military responses to terrorism in Pakistan in the late 2000s are examples of how human rights were discarded by the government in its responses to terrorism.[95] CT programs should also recognize that people can be both victims and perpetrators, regardless of gender. The example of Boko Haram again proves instructive here. Its strategic use of hostages – including women and children – to execute terror attacks represents a situation where both victim and perpetrator can be one and the same. If governments and practitioners commit to more nuanced and creative CT programs that include measures of rehabilitation and reintegration, flexibility in defining victim and perpetrator will be needed.

All of these strategies will require patience, open-mindedness and commitment. The complexity of the subject matter demands it. Research findings are not guaranteed to transfer from one group or culture to another, nor will program observations and lessons learned easily apply outside of specific conditions and environments. A systemic commitment to press forward will be critical if we want to make progress in countering terrorism.

Notes

1 Thomas D. Boyatt, "The Hijacking of TWA Flight 840," *Foreign Service Journal* (December 1969), pp. 4–8.
2 Jessica Davis, *Women in Modern Terrorism* (Lanham, MD: Rowman and Littlefield, 2017).
3 See William McCants, "Why Did ISIS Attack Paris?" *The Atlantic* (November 16, 2015).
4 See Joseph Young and Michael Findlay, "The Promise and Pitfalls of Terrorism Research," *International Studies Review*, Vol. 13, No. 3 (2011), pp. 411–431; Todd Sandler, "The Analytical Study of Terrorism: Taking Stock," *Journal of Peace Research*, Vol. 51, No. 2 (2014), pp. 257–271; Naureen Chowdhury Fink, Sara Zeiger and Rafia Bhulai, eds., *A Man's World? Exploring the Roles of Women in Countering Terrorism and Violent Extremism* (Abu Dhabi and New York: Hedayah and Global Center on Cooperative Security, 2016), p. 7.
5 Fink, Zeiger and Bhulai, *A Man's World?* p. 7.
6 Ibid.
7 Davis, *Women in Modern Terrorism*.
8 Kristopher Robison, "Unpacking the Social Origins of Terrorism: The Role of Women's Empowerment in Reducing Terrorism," *Studies in Conflict and Terrorism*, Vol. 33, No. 8 (2010), pp. 735–756.
9 Elizabeth Pearson, "The Case of Roshonara Choudhry: Implications for Theory on Online Radicalization, ISIS Women, and the Gendered Jihad," *Policy and Internet*, Vol. 8, No. 1 (September 2015), p. 13.
10 Erin Marie Saltman and Ross Frenett, "Female Radicalization to ISIS and the Role of Women in CVE," in *A Man's World?* pp. 142–163.
11 Chantal de Jonge Oudraat, "Preventing and Countering Violent Extremism: The Role of Women and Women's Organizations" and Sahana Dharmapuri, "UNSCR 1325 and CVE: Using a Gender Perspective to Enhance Operational Effectiveness," both in *A Man's World?* pp. 18–21, 36–38.
12 See Stockholm Forum on Security and Development, *Reframing the 'Counterterrorism' Debate: What 'Violent Extremism' and 'Radicalization' Mean for Development*, Forum Policy Brief No. 11 (Stockholm: SIPRI, May 2016).
13 See Ted Robert Gurr, "Why Terrorism Subsides: A Comparative Study of Canada and the United States," *Comparative Politics*, Vol. 21, No. 4 (1989), pp. 405–426.

14 Martha Crenshaw, "The Causes of Terrorism," *Comparative Politics*, Vol. 13, No. 4 (1981), pp. 379–399.

15 David Rapoport, "The Four Waves of Modern Terrorism," in Audrey Kurth Cronin and James M. Ludes, eds., *Attacking Terrorism: Elements of a Grand Strategy* (Washington, DC: Georgetown University Press, 2004), pp. 49–62.

16 Brian Jenkins, "Statements About Terrorism," *Annals of the American Academy of Political and Social Science* (1982), pp. 11–23.

17 *Global Terrorism Database*, National Consortium for the Study of Terrorism and Responses to Terrorism, University of Maryland.

18 Paul R. Ehrlich and Jianguo Liu, "Some Roots of Terrorism," *Population and Environment*, Vol. 24, No. 2 (2002), pp. 183–192; Alan B. Krueger and Jitka Maleckova, "Education, Poverty and Terrorism: Is there a Causal Connection?" *The Journal of Economic Perspectives*, Vol. 17, No. 4 (2003), pp. 119–144; Tim Krieger and Daniel Meierricks, "What Causes Terrorism?" *Public Choice*, Vol. 147 (2011), pp. 3–27; Bruce Hoffman, *Inside Terrorism* (New York: Columbia University Press, 2006); James Piazza, "Poverty, Minority Economic Discrimination, and Domestic Terrorism," *Journal of Peace Research*, Vol. 48, No. 3 (2011), pp. 339–353; Sandler, "The Analytical Study of Terrorism," p. 263.

19 Krueger and Maleckova, "Education, Poverty and Terrorism"; Javed Younas and Todd Sandler, "Gender Imbalance and Terrorism in Developing Countries," *Journal of Conflict Resolution*, Vol. 61, No. 3 (2017), pp. 483–510; Sandler, "The Analytical Study of Terrorism."

20 Alan B. Krueger, *What Makes a Terrorist* (Princeton, NJ: Princeton University Press, 2018); Piazza, "Poverty, Minority Economic Discrimination."

21 Younas and Sandler, "Gender Imbalance and Terrorism"; Sandler, "The Analytical Study of Terrorism," p. 263.

22 Erica Chenoweth, "Democratic Competition and Terrorist Activity," *The Journal of Politics*, Vol. 72, No. 1 (2010), pp. 16–30; W. Eubank and L. Weinberg, "Terrorism and Democracy: Perpetrators and Victims," *Terrorism and Political Violence*, Vol. 13, No. 1 (2010), pp. 155–164.

23 Q. Li, "Does Democracy Promote or Reduce Transnational Terrorist Incidents?" *The Journal of Conflict Resolution*, Vol. 49, No. 2 (2006), pp. 278–297; Brian Lai, "'Draining the Swamp': An Empirical Examination of the Production of International Terrorism, 1968–1998," *Conflict Management and Peace Science*, Vol. 24, No. 4 (2007), pp. 297–310; Chenoweth, "Democratic Competition."

24 Chenoweth, "Democratic Competition;" James A. Piazza, "Regime Age and Terrorism: Are New Democracies Prone to Terrorism?" *International Interactions*, Vol. 39, No. 2 (2013), pp. 246–263.

25 Sandler, "The Analytical Study of Terrorism," p. 263.

26 Alberto Abadie, "Poverty, Political Freedom," *The American Economic Review*, Vol. 96, No. 2 (2006), pp. 50–56; Piazza, "Regime Age and Terrorism."

27 Abadie, "Poverty, Political Freedom"; James A. Piazza and James Igoe Walsh, "Physical Integrity Rights and Terrorism," *PS: Political Science and Politics*, Vol. 43, No. 3 (July 2010), pp. 411–414; Piazza, "Poverty, Minority Economic Discrimination."

28 J. Ann Tickner, "Feminist Perspectives on 9/11," *International Studies Perspectives*, Vol. 3, No. 4 (November 2002), p. 336.

29 Ibid.; Pearson, "The Case of Roshonara Choudhry," p. 13.

30 Tickner, "Feminist Perspectives on 9/11," p. 338.

31 Davis, *Women in Modern Terrorism*.

32 Ibid., p. 135.

33 Jacqui True and Sri Eddyono, *Preventing Violent Extremism: Gender Perspectives and Women's Roles* (Melbourne: Centre for Gender, Peace and Security, Monash University, 2018), pp. 6–35; Davis, *Women in Modern Terrorism*, p. 135.

34 Mia Bloom, "Women and Terrorism," in *Oxford Research Encyclopedia of Politics* (Online Publication, January 2017), pp. 1–3.

35 Ibid., pp. 1–12; Karla Cunningham, "Cross-Regional Trends in Female Terrorism," *Studies in Conflict and Terrorism*, Vol. 26, No. 3 (May 2003), pp. 171–180. See also Davis, *Women in Modern Terrorism*, p. 138.

36 Benjamin Maiangha and Olumuyiwa Babatunde Amao, "'Daughters, Brides, and Supporters of the Jihad': Revisiting the Gender-Based Atrocities of Boko Haram in Nigeria," *African Renaissance*, Vol. 12, No. 2 (2015), pp. 117–120; Davis, *Women in Modern Terrorism*, pp. 4–11.

37 Davis, *Women in Modern Terrorism*, pp. 107–110.

38 Ibid., pp. 5–13.

39 Ibid., p. 135; Heather Hurlburt and Jacqueline O'Neill, "We Need to Think Harder About Terrorism and Gender: ISIS Already Is," *Vox* (June 1, 2017).

40 Davis, *Women in Modern Terrorism*, pp. 121–127.

41 Cunningham, "Cross-Regional Trends in Female Terrorism," pp. 171–176; True and Eddyono, *Preventing Violent Extremism*, pp. 12–14.

42 Cunningham, "Cross-Regional Trends in Female Terrorism," pp. 171–175.

43 Fidelma Ashe, "Gendering War and Peace: Militarized Masculinities in Northern Ireland," *Men and Masculinities*, Vol. 15, No. 3 (2012), pp. 232–233.

44 See Nilay Saiya, Tasneem Zaihra and Joshua Fidler, "Testing the Hillary Doctrine: Women's Rights and Anti-American Terrorism," *Political Research Quarterly*, Vol. 70, No. 2 (2017), pp. 421–432; Valerie M. Hudson et al., *Sex and World Peace* (New York: Columbia University Press, 2012); Krista London Couture, *A Gendered Approach to Countering Violent Extremism* (Washington, DC: Brookings Institution, July 2014), p. 18.

45 True and Eddyono, *Preventing Violent Extremism*, pp. 6, 35.

46 See Jeannette Gaudry Haynie, *They Give Peace a Chance*, Ph.D. Dissertation (Washington, DC: The George Washington University, 2017); Robison, "Unpacking the Social Origins of Terrorism."

47 See Madiha Afzal, *Are the Better Educated Less Likely to Support Militancy and Terrorism? Women Are: Evidence from a Public Opinion Survey in Pakistan* (College Park, MD: Center for International and Security Studies at Maryland, University at Maryland, 2012); Robison, "Unpacking the Social Origins of Terrorism."

48 Hudson et al., *Sex and World Peace*.

49 R.W. Connell, "Studying Men and Masculinity," *Resources for Feminist Research*, Vol. 29, Nos. 1–2 (2002), pp. 43–55.

50 Ibid.

51 Chona Echavez, Sayed Mahdi Mosawi, Leah Wilfreda and R.E. Pilongo, *The Other Side of Gender Inequality: Men and Masculinities in Afghanistan* (Kabul: Afghanistan Research and Evaluation Unit, 2016); Kathleen Kuehnast and Nina Sudhakar, *The Other Side of Gender: Including Masculinity Concerns in Conflict and Peacebuilding*, Peace Brief No. 75 (Washington, DC: US Institute of Peace, January 2011).

52 Cunningham, "Cross-Regional Trends in Female Terrorism," p. 179.

53 Jonathan Greenblatt, "The Resurgent Threat of White-Supremacist Violence," *The Atlantic* (January 17, 2018).

54 Hurlburt and O'Neill, "We Need to Think Harder About Terrorism and Gender."

55 See Alan Bairner, "Soccer, Masculinity, and Violence in Northern Ireland: Between Hooliganism and Terrorism," *Men and Masculinities*, Vol. 1, No. 3 (1999), pp. 284–301; Syed Haider, "The Shooting in Orlando, Terrorism or Toxic Masculinity (or both?)," *Men and Masculinities*, Vol. 19, No. 5 (2016), pp. 555–565; Collin D. Barnes, Ryan P. Brown and Lindsey L. Osterman, "Don't Tread on Me: Masculine Honor Ideology in the US and Militant Responses to Terrorism," *Personality and Social Psychology Bulletin*, Vol. 38, No. 8 (2012), pp. 1018–1029.

56 William McCants and Clint Watts, *US Strategy for Countering Violent Extremism: An Assessment* (Philadelphia, PA: Foreign Policy Research Institute, December 2012); Couture, *A Gendered Approach to Countering Violent Extremism*; Council on Foreign Relations (CFR), *Global Governance Monitor: Terrorism* (New York: CFR, 2017); UN Women, *Setting the*

Scene for Preventing Violent Extremism in South East and South Asia: A Way Forward for Women's Engagement in Indonesia and Bangladesh, Policy Brief (New York: UN Women, 2018).

57 See Jacob Zenn and Elizabeth Pearson, "Women, Gender, and the Evolving Tactics of Boko Haram," *Journal of Terrorism Research*, Vol. 5, No. 1 (February 2014), pp. 46–57; Bairner, "Soccer, Masculinity, and Violence in Northern Ireland."

58 See Haider, "The Shooting in Orlando"; Barnes, Brown and Osterman, "Don't Tread on Me."

59 Dharmapuri, "UNSCR 1325 and CVE," pp. 37–42; Jessica Auchter, "Gendering Terror," *International Feminist Journal of Politics*, Vol. 14, No. 1 (2012), pp. 121–139.

60 See Lori Poloni-Staudinger and Candice Ortbals, "Gendering Abbottabad: Agency and Hegemonic Masculinity in an Age of Global Terrorism," *Gender Issues*, Vol. 31, No. 1 (2014), pp. 34–57; Royal United Services Institute (RUSI), *Strive: Lessons Learned, Horn of Africa – Strengthening Resilience to Violence and Extremism* (London: RUSI, 2017), pp. 9–11.

61 See Nimmi Gowrinathan and Kate Cronin-Furman, *The Forever Victims? Tamil Women in Post-War Sri Lanka*, White Paper (New York: City College of New York, 2015).

62 Jayne Huckerby, "The Complexities of Women, Peace, Security and Countering Violent Extremism," *Just Security* (September 24, 2015); de Jonge Oudraat, "Preventing and Countering Violent Extremism," pp. 24–26.

63 See de Jonge Oudraat, "Preventing and Countering Violent Extremism," pp. 20–22.

64 Public Broadcasting System (PBS), *Frontline: Inside the Terror Network – Who Were They?* (@ pbs.org); Amany Radwan, "Portrait of the Terrorist as a Young Man," *Time* (October 6, 2001).

65 PBS, *Frontline: Inside the Terror Network*.

66 Ibid. See also Mary Sisson, "Mohammed Atta: Egyptian Militant," *Encyclopedia Britannica* (September 30, 2019).

67 Neil MacFarquhar, Jim Yardley and Paul Zielbauer, "A Nation Challenged: The Mastermind; A Portrait of the Terrorist: From Shy Child to Single-Minded Killer," *The New York Times* (October 10, 2001).

68 PBS, *Frontline: Inside the Terror Network: Chronology of the Sept. 11 Terror Plot* (@ pbs.org).

69 Radwan, "Portrait of the Terrorist as a Young Man."

70 Robert Smith and Dina Temple-Raston, "'The Banality of Evil': Following the Steps to September 11," *National Public Radio (NPR)* (September 9, 2011, @ npr.org).

71 Ibid.

72 Jane Corbin, "A Premonition of Evil," *The Guardian* (July 4, 2002).

73 PBS, *Frontline: Inside the Terror Network: Mohamed Atta's Last Will and Testament* (@ pbs.org).

74 Crenshaw, "The Causes of Terrorism," pp. 383–385.

75 Joseph Serna, "Elliot Rodger Meticulously Planned Isla Vista Rampage, Report Says," *The Los Angeles Times* (February 19, 2015).

76 British Broadcasting Company, "Elliot Rodger: How Misogynist Killer Became 'Incel Hero'," *British Broadcasting Company News* (April 26, 2018).

77 Lulu Garcia-Navarro, "What's an 'Incel'? The Online Community Behind the Toronto Van Attack," *NPR* (April 29, 2018, @ npr.org).

78 Richard Jackson et al., *Terrorism: A Critical Introduction* (London: Palgrave MacMillan, 2011); Martin Scheinin, "Foreword: Gender and Counter-Terrorism – Reflections by a Former United Nations Special Rapporteur," in Margaret Satterthwaite and Jayne Huckerby, eds., *Gender, National Security, and Counter-Terrorism: Human Rights Perspectives* (London: Routledge, 2013), pp. xi–xiv.

79 de Jonge Oudraat, "Preventing and Countering Violent Extremism"; Haider, "The Shooting in Orlando."

80 See Robert McKenzie, *Countering Violent Extremism in America: Recommendations for the Next President* (Washington, DC: Brookings Institution, 2016); Couture, *A Gendered Approach to Countering Violent Extremism*; Sean Bex and Stef Craps, "Humanitarianism, Testimony, and the White Savior Industrial Complex: What Is the What Versus Kony 2012," *Cultural Critique*, Vol. 92 (2016), pp. 32–56.

81 Hoffman, *Inside Terrorism*.
82 Sarah V. Marsden and Alex P. Schmid, "Typologies of Terrorism and Political Violence," in Alex Schmid, ed., *The Routledge Handbook of Terrorism Research* (London: Routledge, 2011).
83 Davis, *Women in Modern Terrorism*, pp. 2–3.
84 Patty Chang et al., *Women Leading Peace: A Close Examination of Women's Political Participation in Peace Processes in Northern Ireland, Guatemala, Kenya and the Philippines* (Washington, DC: Georgetown Institute for Women, Peace and Security, 2016).
85 Signs of Peace, *Interview with Peace Advocate Joeven Reyes* (Manila: Stiftung Asienhaus, September 2016).
86 Couture, *A Gendered Approach to Countering Violent Extremism*; Karima Bennoune, *Your Fatwa Does Not Apply Here: Untold Stories from the Fight Against Muslim Fundamentalism* (New York: Norton, 2015).
87 Marie O'Reilly, Andrea O Suilleabhain and Thania Paffenholz, *Reimagining Peacemaking: Women's Roles in Peace Processes* (New York: International Peace Institute, 2015).
88 Fink, Zeiger and Bhulai, *A Man's World?*; Sandler, "The Analytical Study of Terrorism."
89 de Jonge Oudraat, "Preventing and Countering Violent Extremism"; Nimmi Gowrinathan, "The Committed Female Fighter: The Political Identities of Tamil Women in the Liberation Tigers of Tamil Eelam," *International Feminist Journal of Politics*, Vol. 19, No. 3 (2017), pp. 327–341.
90 Auchter, "Gendering Terror."
91 Kate Fearon, *Women's Work: The Story of the Northern Ireland Women's Coalition* (Belfast: Blackstaff, 1999).
92 Fionnuala Ni Aolain and Jayne Huckerby, "Gendering Counterterrorism: How to, and How Not to – Part II," *Just Security* (May 3, 2018).
93 See Davis, *Women in Modern Terrorism*, pp. 135–136.
94 Ibid. See also True and Eddyono, *Preventing Violent Extremism*, pp. 12–13.
95 Naeem Ahmed, "Combating Terrorism: Pakistan's Anti-Terrorism Legislation in the Post-9/11 Scenario," *Journal of the Research Society of Pakistan*, Vol. 52, No. 2 (2015), pp. 115–133.

5

GENDER AND MILITARY ORGANIZATIONS

Ellen Haring

Military historian John Keegan argues that "warfare is . . . the one human activity from which women, with the most significant exceptions, have always and everywhere stood apart."[1] Joshua Goldstein maintains that there is no human endeavor that is more gendered than war and that despite a few mythical examples of women serving in Amazonian type units, the military is a striking example of cross-cultural consistency with respect to gender: men fight and women stay home.[2]

National military organizations are quintessentially masculine constructs that rely on notions of men as warrior-protectors and women as the protected. They are constructed along a patriarchal hierarchy with commanders ("old men") leading small to large units ("bands of brothers") whose mission is to protect the homeland in the name of "national defense." The prototypical warrior is a large, physically strong, stoic man who embodies notions of physical courage, honor and self-sacrifice and euphemistically stands as a protective barrier in front of the nation. The feminine identity exists in stark contrast and direct opposition to the masculine identity. National militaries are set up to optimize men's participation and rely on patriarchal social structures where women perform traditional family duties centered around caregiving while men go to war, raising the men's families and supporting the organization through the exploitation of their free labor. Within this conception, there is no room or accommodation for women who want to join national militaries. The result is that when women have joined, they have generally been confined to support roles, are rarely the focus of recruiting efforts, are not promoted at the same rate as men and suffer from marginalization, discrimination and harassment. Although many progressive-sounding political statements have been made, some by member states of the North Atlantic Treaty Organization (NATO) and NATO partners, recognizing the importance of increasing the number of women in national forces "to enhance operational effectiveness and success," most military organizations remain bastions of men who are highly resistant to the inclusion of women.[3]

As a result, opportunities to effectively address conflict and respond to crises by understanding and engaging the entire population are overlooked, making military responses less than optimal. This became glaringly obvious during the conflicts in Iraq and Afghanistan, when extreme gender-based cultural norms – on all sides – prevented international, male-dominated forces from interreacting with local women. Not only were the women of Iraq and Afghanistan prohibited from interacting with men from outside their family units, but international forces practices limited or outrightly prohibited women's participation in their formations; this made it nearly impossible to interact effectively with half of the population in the areas of operations. After several frustrating years, military adaptations occurred in these conflicts in the form of Lioness, Female Engagement and Cultural Support Teams. Military necessity drove changes to existing all-male combat units that required the presence of women in uniform.

Adaptation – driven by necessity – is one of the principal forces behind the evolution of military policy on the formal inclusion of women in the 20th and 21st centuries.

This chapter focuses on women's participation in state-sponsored national militaries. I do not examine women's involvement in other security forces and armed groups, including police, gendarmeries and guerilla and insurgent groups. In some instances, women's inclusion in non-traditional, insurgent groups has moved more quickly than in state-sponsored security forces. Perhaps the most comprehensive use of women in armed groups has occurred in insurgent groups such as the Revolutionary Armed Forces of Colombia (FARC), where women comprised an estimated 40 percent of insurgent forces.[4] But even in such instances, women are often assigned administrative, medical, communication and logistic duties. Many of the dynamics we see in national military organizations also apply to non-national military forces. I also do not address the issue of integrating gender perspectives into conflict analyses and military operations.[5] Military organizations around the globe have made little or no progress in adopting gender perspectives in their analyses and operations.

This chapter focuses on the integration of women soldiers in national military organizations and operations. I first provide an overview of women in the military globally. Second, through a case study of the United States (US) military, I examine drivers of progress that have helped to increase the number of women in the military and identify obstacles to the integration of women in the military. I conclude by identifying successful strategies for increasing women's participation in national military organizations.

Women's participation: the track record

Historically, if women wanted to be part of formal military organizations, they did so by disguising themselves as men. History is replete with examples. Rosalind Miles and Robin Cross have documented women warriors on ancient and modern battlefields. They report that, before 1840, there were at least 119 documented cases of women − disguised as men − serving in the Dutch military.[6] In the US Civil War (1861–1865), there were more than 400 documented cases of women serving while disguised as men.[7] Women who were not prepared to disguise themselves as men, but were committed to war efforts, did so informally and in the shadows as saboteurs, scouts, couriers and spies. Women who served openly performed traditional roles − as nurses and care givers, cooks and laundresses. When wars ended, women were often sent home; few were recognized for their service, and even fewer received any military compensation.

It is not until World War I that women were accepted "into uniform." The enormous loss and sheer demand for male recruits during World War I drove political leaders to consider using women in military roles. The United States began to enlist women in the Naval reserves, where they served as yeomen and performed a wide range of clerical, communications and recruiting duties. Eventually, more than 12,500 women served as "yeomanettes."[8] The US Army and US Navy created a Nurse Corps, where 34,000 women served by war's end.[9] Even larger demands on European forces resulted in 80,000 women serving in the British military as non-combatants.[10] The most extensive use of women in uniform occurred in Russia, where extreme casualty levels had exhausted the supply of male recruits. In addition to women serving in traditional roles, Russia took the unprecedented step of deploying approximately 6,000 women as combatants. These women served in sex-segregated battalions, the most famous of which was the Battalion of Death. These units were disbanded by the new Bolshevik government after the war.[11] Indeed, at the end of the war, women from all countries were universally discharged and expected to return to their homes and resume traditional family roles.

World War II was the second major milestone in the inclusion of women in military organizations in the 20th century. As in World War I, the demand for male recruits forced political and military leaders to look for additional sources of manpower. Fortuitously, many women were showing up at recruiting stations demanding to enlist to defend their homelands. In the United States, Great Britain and Germany, women were limited to non-combat duties with one exception: British women manned anti-aircraft batteries, where they performed every duty in the battery except one. They could spot, set the range and bearing dials, adjust the fuses and load the guns, but they were not allowed to "pull the trigger on a man, even if he was a Luftwaffe pilot."[12]

The only nation to use women as traditional combatants during World War II was the Soviet Union. More than 820,000 Soviet women served in both combatant and non-combatant roles in the war, and at least half of them served on the front lines.[13] Soviet women reported to recruiting stations early in the war and demanded to serve in military units. These women participated in extended combat operations, served in the infantry as machine gunners, mortarmen and snipers, as well as in other ground combat roles. The Soviet Union was the first country to allow women to fly combat missions, and by war's end, Soviet women had flown more than 30,000 combat sorties. In total, 90 Soviet women from across the military branches received the Hero of the Soviet Union award, the highest military honor given to any soldier during the war.[14] When the war was over, these women were largely pushed out of the military and told that their new duty was to return home to repopulate the homeland.[15]

The full scope of Soviet women's participation and their stories went unrecognized for decades. Only in the 21st century have researchers such as Svetlana Alexievich, Anna Krylova and Reina Pennington been able to conduct research in Soviet archives and publish their interviews with these hidden women combatants.[16]

After World War II, women began to make permanent inroads into military organizations. In the United States, women petitioned the government to remain in service, and in 1948, for the first time and by an act of Congress, women were allowed to serve in the peacetime military. Their numbers and the scope of their service were severely limited by laws and policies. They were capped at two percent of the total force; women officers could not be promoted beyond the rank of colonel, and they could not command men. If they married, their spouse was denied benefits, and if they had children they were discharged.[17] It was only in 1967 that the cap was lifted and women could be promoted to flag officer ranks.

Perhaps the most robust use of women in military organizations since World War II has been in Israel. During Israel's War of Independence and later in the newly formed Israeli Defense Force (IDF), single and married women without children were conscripted alongside men, although they were limited to non-combat jobs. Eventually, demand and legal challenges would open most combat occupations in the IDF to Israeli women, although some units have remained closed. Military service through conscription remains a civic duty in Israel, and it has resulted in Israel having the largest percentage of women serving in the military of any country in the world. Almost half of the IDF is comprised of women.[18]

The entry of women in military organizations has also been driven by the United Nations (UN). United Nations Security Council Resolution (UNSCR) 1325 (2000) and subsequent Women, Peace and Security (WPS) resolutions recognized the importance of women's equal participation in all efforts for the maintenance and promotion of international peace and security and called on UN member states to increase women's participation in security organizations and peace processes. Governments regularly make statements expressing support for gender equality and for increasing the number of women in peacekeeping operations. In 2017, Canada launched the Elsie Initiative on Women in Peace Operations to address the obstacles to deploying more women in peace operations. In 2018, the UN Secretary-General launched the Action for Peacekeeping (A4P) initiative, which included commitments, signed by the majority of UN member states, to increase "the number of civilian and uniformed women in peacekeeping at all levels and in key positions" and to "systematically integrate a gender perspective into all stages of analysis, planning, implementation and reporting."[19] In 2019, the UN Secretary-General issued a gender parity strategy for UN peacekeeping operations. This initiative sets a target of deploying 15 percent uniformed women in UN peace operations by 2028.[20] That would be an increase of more than 11 percent. In the

2010s, the number of deployed uniformed female peacekeepers in UN operations has hovered around three to four percent.

NATO has also recognized that "the integration of gender and the inclusion of women's voices in all aspects of NATO's work is an essential factor in the success of peace and security."[21] NATO has committed to increasing the number of women in its operations and has called on its member states and partners to increase the number of women in their national military organizations.[22] NATO was an early adopter of the WPS agenda and has released WPS policy and action plans since 2007.

Despite these commitments and calls for action, women remain a minority group in all national militaries. Only a few countries, including Canada, Norway, Denmark, Sweden, Australia and the United States, allow women equal access to all military occupations. Integration of women in the military most often occurs because of military and operational necessity. In addition, organizations are pressured by women who resent discrimination based on gender and challenge their exclusion through political and legal means.[23] In most instances, change is strongly resisted by military leadership.

TABLE 5.1 Women as a Percentage of the Total Force

Country	Percent Women	Conscription	Restrictions on Women's Participation
Israel[1]	40	Yes, men and women	Some restrictions
South Africa[2]	24	No	Some restrictions
Hungary*[3]	19	No	No restrictions
Moldova*	17	Yes, men only	No restrictions
Australia*	17	No	No restrictions
United States[4]	17	No	No restrictions
Canada*	16	No	No restrictions
France*	15	No	No restrictions
Norway*	12	Yes, men and women	No restrictions
Russia[5]	10	No	Restrictions
Sweden*	8	Yes, men and women	No restrictions
China[6]	5	Yes, men only	Restrictions

Sources: [1] Information received from the Public Diplomacy Office of the IDF (January 27, 2020). It may be noted that only 10 percent of officers in the rank of Colonel are women. [2] Nina Wilen and Lindy Heinecken, "Regendering the South African Army: Inclusion, Reversal and Displacement." Gender Work Organ (2018), pp. 1–17; [3] Hungary reports the highest percentage of women in the military of all NATO member and partner nations; [4] Service Women's Action Network (SWAN), Women in the Military: Where They Stand, 10th ed. (Washington, DC: SWAN, 2019); [5] International Institute for Strategic Studies (IISS), The Military Balance 2002–2003 (London: IISS); [6] Elsa Kania and Kenneth Allen, Holding Up Half the Sky?: The Evolution of Women's Roles in the PLA, Part 2 (Washington, DC: The Jamestown Foundation, October 26, 2016). * Data for NATO member and partner nations was drawn from the 2017 Summary of the National Reports of NATO Member and Partner Nations submitted to the NATO Committee on Gender Perspectives. (Research on women in the military is hampered by limited data. Many countries do not report sex-disaggregated demographic data on their military forces.)

Case study: women in the US military

In 1991, as the first Gulf War came to a close, US servicewomen's participation was noted by Congressional lawmakers. Approximately 41,000 women had been forward deployed, and despite policies that were designed to keep them out of combat, women were both killed and captured during the war.[24] In 1992, the US Congress eliminated the last law that limited women's military service to non-combat support roles. In 1993, then Secretary of Defense Les Aspin directed the military to open all combat aircraft and most combat ships to women. Women continued to be excluded from submarines. In 1994, in place of laws that had limited women's service, the US Department of Defense established an institution-wide policy that officially banned women from assignment to more than 300,000 "direct ground combat" positions.[25] Women could fight in the air and at sea but not on land. The policy further restricted women from being assigned to or co-located with all-male ground combat units even in supporting roles. The policy was put to a test less than ten years later.

In 2001, when the United States and allied countries invaded Afghanistan, women from support specialties were not allowed to be assigned to or co-located with all-male combat units. Although the US military had historically discriminated against women by limiting job and assignment opportunities, they had not violated laws or their own policies to do so. But by 2005, well into the conflicts in Afghanistan and Iraq, military necessity drove change. US commanders on the ground began violating the co-location prohibition by devising creative ways to circumvent polices that limited their ability to use servicewomen on the front lines. Quietly and creatively, they violated official policies because senior leaders refused to address the untenable and deeply gendered nature of the policies themselves.

Commanders engaged in a game of semantics by "attaching" rather than "assigning" women to ground combat units when they needed them. They "attached" servicewomen who were Arab linguists, engineers, medics and explosive ordinance specialists to infantry companies when they needed translators, construction and medical support or demolition experts; "assigning" women to all-male combat units was prohibited by US Department of Defense (DOD) policy.[26] Commanders sent small teams of servicewomen to work from forward operating bases and at combat outposts as Lionesses – servicewomen assigned to conduct searches of civilian women at checkpoints and during combat patrols – and as Female Engagement Teams – small teams of servicewomen (two to four women) assigned to combat units to interact with civilian women during military operations. Commanders intermittently shuttled servicewomen back to rear areas for short durations, sometimes just overnight, and returned them to forward-operating bases to avoid the appearance of violating co-location rules that prohibited women from being permanently co-located with combat units. But shuttling women to rear areas and "attaching" women to units were distinctions without practical differences that violated the intent of existing policies.

In 2006, two US Army colonels who were then students at the Army War College conducted a series of surveys and studies that documented the wide variations that commanders used in interpreting the restrictive policies. In one survey, 70 percent of their War College classmates agreed that the policy needed to be revised, and 74 percent agreed that "all soldiers regardless of gender should be assigned to positions for which they are qualified."[27] They found that the "Combat Exclusion Policy with its attendant 'co-location' restriction was incompatible with the nature of the war in which the US Army was engaged and the forms of conflict it was likely to encounter in the future."[28] But in 2006, no official steps were taken to eliminate or modify this policy.

In 2012, six years after the War College study, US servicewomen – two of whom had been wounded in combat and decorated – filed two lawsuits that challenged their exclusion on legal grounds. In January 2013, the exclusion policy was rescinded. It took the US military three more years to "study" the feasibility of integrating women into ground combat units, although extensive studies had already been conducted by Canada before it opened its combat units to women. Even after studies found no compelling reason to keep any occupation closed to *all* women,[29] the US Marine Corps requested an exemption to the new policy in order to continue to keep women out of its infantry formations.[30] The request was denied, and in 2016 the US military reluctantly opened all occupations and units to women. Although formal directives to include qualified women were issued, the process has been slow and challenged by ongoing efforts to resist women's inclusion.

Drivers of progress

The international track record and the US case study show that change is driven by a diverse set of factors, including national and international norm changes as expressed in national laws and policies and UN Security Council resolutions. In the case of the United States it is likely that it was a combination of changing social norms along with the extent and sustained use of women in combat operations in Iraq and Afghanistan that cleared the path for full integration into the US military.

That said, the most effective arguments for increasing women's participation in military organizations have not been based on notions of equality, fairness or merit – even in countries that hold these principles in high regard. For security professionals, the majority of whom are men, equality and fairness are secondary considerations when security is concerned. For them, the only legitimate reason for increasing women's participation is a functional one. Political and military leaders must be convinced that women's participation adds value by increasing military effectiveness.

UNSCR 1325 and subsequent resolutions have highlighted the role of women in peacekeeping operations. The United Nations (UN) has argued that participation of women in peace operations "contributes to the overall success of the mission by enhancing effectiveness, improving the mission's image, access and credibility vis-à-vis the affected population, including by making UN peacekeepers more approachable to women."[31] The UN Secretary-General has noted that the presence of women has led to more credible protection responses and that women's presence at checkpoints has promoted less-confrontational situations. The presence of women also led to higher reporting of sexual and gender-based violence in conflict zones and lower incidence rates of Sexual Exploitation and Abuse (SEA).[32]

Members of the US Special Operations Command Cultural Support Teams (CST) have argued that their participation enhanced mission effectiveness by 20 percent.[33] Established in 2012, the CST program recruits and trains all-women teams that are assigned to special forces and ranger teams for the specific purpose of gathering information and conducting searches. According to one cultural support team member, adding women to special operations teams ultimately "opened up 70 percent of the population in which we were operating."[34] Servicewomen assigned to special operations teams were able to engage men, women and children in local communities in ways that were different from their male counterparts. Indeed, CSTs often became favored interlocutors for Afghan men in rural villages. Local men saw US servicewomen as a sort of "third gender" – women who operated outside of Afghan traditional gender norms and were less threatening than male members of the international security forces. The mere presence of CSTs on missions had a calming effect on operations, including direct action raids. When women were found to be among the force, the culturally gendered assumption was that they were not there to fight.[35]

Increasing the number of women in the military can also be done through conscription and quotas. Many countries use conscription, but few countries conscript men and women equally. Israel – an early leader in conscripting women – does not apply the same conscription rules to men and women. Women have a shorter period of service and receive more exemptions then men. Despite the different rules for men and women, conscription in Israel has resulted in high levels of women's participation in the military. Only two countries – Norway in 2016 and Sweden in 2018 – have moved to gender-equal conscription. However, both Norway and Sweden begin by filling their ranks with volunteers, who are predominately men, and then use conscripts to round out their ranks. As a result, in both countries women remain a minority population. South Africa provides an example of how focused recruitment and quotas can raise women's participation levels in military organizations. When apartheid ended, the new South African government pledged to have public institutions reflect the demographic makeup of the general population. Although women have not achieved parity in South African military forces, they do represent one of the higher levels of women's participation in a national military at 24 percent of the force.[36]

In the absence of conscription, pay incentives that encourage countries to increase women's participation can have positive effects. Many UN troop-contributing countries provide peacekeepers because they are a source of national revenue and military training. Troop-contributing countries are paid $1,428 per month per UN peacekeeper, but in most cases, troops receive much lower salaries in accordance with their national standards.[37] The difference becomes revenue for the military. If the United Nations were to raise the pay for women peacekeepers, it is likely that troop-contributing countries would make greater efforts to recruit women into their armed forces.

Some countries use gender-neutral incentives that effectively increase the rates of women's participation in military organizations. In the United States men and women receive educational incentives to join the military. Women make up 57 percent of undergraduate college students in the country, and military education incentives help to increase the number of servicewomen.[38] As of 2017, women made up 28 percent of military scholarship recipients at US civilian universities; approximately 25 percent of US military academy student populations were women.[39] Women who enlist receive 36 months of educational benefits when they complete a four-year term of service. As a result, despite having an all-volunteer military, women's participation is expected to grow from 17 percent to 20 percent of the force by 2020.

It is not enough to attract women to military service if they do not stay for long. Most militaries have had trouble retaining women in their ranks. Policies must be established that make continued military service attractive and possible for women. Maternity and family leave policies must be offered so that women, like men, can have families. Cultures that allow women to be marginalized, harassed and abused must be eliminated. Training and equipping practices, designed for men, must be developed to reduce injuries and optimize women's performance. If military organizations remain male-centered, with few accommodations made for women, then women will remain a fractional minority in these organizations.

Obstacles to progress

There are many obstacles to women's participation in military organizations, the most significant of which are laws and policies that formally limit or forbid women's access to military occupations and units. However, even after laws and policies are changed, there has been and will be resistance that may take decades to overcome.

There are many cultural and structural challenges within military organizations that keep women's participation rates low. Even in countries that have fully opened their military organizations, such as Australia, Canada, Sweden and the United States, women face marginalization, sexual harassment and assault and lower promotion rates. In the 2010s, the pervasive problem of sexual harassment and assault in even the most inclusive military organizations has received widespread attention. In 2017, Sweden – long considered to be one of the most gender-equal countries in the world – had a high-profile scandal when women in the Swedish military reported widespread sexual harassment.[40] This problem is also widespread in other countries, including the United States.[41]

In addition to problems of harassment and assault, women often leave the military for family reasons. Most militaries lack adequate family policies that support women who want both military careers and families. A few militaries, including Canada and Sweden, offer women and men extended maternity and paternity leave options. In the Canadian Armed Forces, women receive 26 weeks of paid maternity leave (which can be shared by both parents). In Sweden, paid maternity/paternity leave is extended to 18 months.

Women are also less likely to keep pace in terms of promotions, and as a result there are very few women at the most senior levels in any military organization. Even in Israel, where women are conscripted and serve in large numbers, promotions for women lag behind men, and few women become senior military leaders. Although women in the IDF are only excluded from eight percent of available positions, these exclusions are major obstacles for career advancement; the positions women are excluded from are the ones that lead to the military's senior ranks. Fifty-one percent of IDF officers are women, but they tend to be junior officers. This suggests that while including women in drafts and opening up combat positions helps increase the percentage of women in military organizations, these steps are not enough to ensure equal treatment. Changes in promotion policies and elimination of structural barriers are key.

Even when women do rise to high ranks, they rarely receive prestigious operational assignments. In 2014, Major General Kristin Lund of Norway was celebrated for being the first woman to command a UN peacekeeping force. In 2017, Major Nina Raduha of Slovenia was celebrated as the first woman to command a UN military contingent.

Changing military organizations

According to organizational change theorists, resistance to change occurs at multiple levels – at the individual, group and organizational level.[42] Efforts to increase women's participation in military organizations activates resistance at all these levels.

Individual resistance comes in three forms: blind resistance, political resistance and ideological resistance. Blind resistance comes from individuals who are uncomfortable with any type of change. Change requires learning new things, operating in new environments and potentially failing at new challenges: it can be destabilizing. Political resistance is about power, and it comes from those who believe they stand to lose something in the change process. They fear their position, authority and ultimately their identity might be diminished in some way. Ideological resistance is based on specific beliefs – that the change is wrong for the organization because it is ill-fated or not in line with the organization's principles.

In military organizations, blind resistance is often reflected in the "band of brothers" argument and cloaked as an issue of cohesion. Captain Lauren Serrano, a Marine Corps officer, argued in 2014 that men should be able to maintain a space where they can "tell raunchy jokes, walk around naked, swap sex stories, wrestle, and simply be young men together."[43] According to this line of reasoning, if women were introduced into units, men would have to change their behavior due to existing social norms that frown upon certain kinds of behavior in mixed-gender groups. Some men do not want to change their behavior and be forced to operate according to another paradigm. Changing behavior creates uncertainty and anxiety for many people; this can generate blind resistance to change.

Individual resistance to changing roles is also motivated by fear of losing the prestige that is automatically accrued by men who serve in the role of protector.

This type of resistance is even harder to reveal since most men will not explicitly say they do not want women to diminish their status by joining their ranks. According to one military observer, men from the combat specialties feel superior as long as women are kept in what are considered inferior positions in the military. This allows men to maintain a position of "unearned recognition."[44] Carol Cohn examined men's objections to women's inclusion by interviewing more than 80 US military officers. She found that objections often fell in "the PT protest" category. The PT (physical training) protest is an objection to the creation of different physical fitness standards allowed for women – a complaint that is not leveled against older men whose fitness requirements are lowered as they age. Cohn found that the standards argument is a more acceptable way to say that women do not belong because it is grounded in a "fairness" argument. Cohn argued that the PT protest is "a means of constructing and reinforcing gender difference, a way of asserting male superiority, a form of expressing anger about competition from women, and rage and grief about the loss of the military as a male sanctum."[45]

Ideological resistance is perhaps the easiest form of resistance to identify because the arguments against women are based on military effectiveness. According to this line of reasoning, women do not belong because their presence will harm fighting units. The claim is that combat units' capabilities rest on vital unit cohesion that can only exist in all-male units. Retired Major General Robert Scales argued that "the precious and indefinable band of brothers effect so essential to winning in close combat would be irreparably compromised within mixed-gender infantry squads."[46] This line of argument was also used to keep black soldiers in segregated units and homosexual men closeted, but it is no longer accepted today, nor was it ever validated after integration occurred in the past.

Group resistance draws on many of the objections raised by individuals. Group resistance includes turf protection, closing ranks, changing allegiances and making demands for new leadership.[47] "Turf protection" is a group behavior that protects existing functions and practices. "Closing ranks" is behavior that pulls group members into a close-knit team that refuses to adapt to changing requirements. "Changing allegiances" means engaging in tactics to align with another, less threatening, group. "Demanding new leadership" is a form of revolt by members who refuse to accept change or disagree with change for ideological reasons.

Turf protection is common in the combat branches. As soon as it appeared likely that women might be allowed to join the ground combat branches in the US military, barriers were erected to keep women out. The most prominent examples occurred in the US Marine Corps. The Marines changed entrance standards to their infantry officer course in order to make it nearly impossible for women to gain entry. Specifically, they changed the Day-1 Combat Endurance Test from a test that male officers who did not pass on Day-1 could retake until they passed to a test that women had to pass on the first day with no option to retake.[48] Of the 29 women who attempted the course in 2014, only four passed the screening test. Later in the course, the four were all eliminated for other reasons. Some women have called attention to these structural and discriminatory barriers and have forced the Marine Corps to adjust their practices.

Closing ranks was evident shortly after the US Secretary of Defense lifted the exclusionary policy in 2013. Then Commandant of the Marine Corps said that the Marines would not let enlisted women even attempt to join the infantry until there were "enough" women infantry officers in the ranks to make it "worth" it.[49] But as noted previously, a structural barrier had been erected to keep women officers from completing the infantry officer course. Interestingly, in an effort to protect the infantry while conceding some ground, the Commandant acknowledged that it might be possible to include women in most of the other combat branches. This is an example of diversionary tactics or changing allegiances. The Commandant was willing to sacrifice some of the combat specialties in order to preserve the sanctity of the most honored and most masculine branch of the Corps – the infantry.

Many Marines objected to the Commandant's position on women in combat units, calling it too soft and accusing him of making politically motivated concessions. In the comments sections of many blogs, some called for his resignation. One article questioned his ability to lead the Marine Corps at all because, as an aviator, he did not come from one of the ground-combat branches.[50] This is an example of group resistance that demands new leadership in an effort to avoid organizational change.

Although, the terms *institution* and *organization* are often used interchangeably, they are different. Institutions are enduring entities that become a "way of organizing relationships that is widely familiar and routinely practiced" and are "defined by the unwritten rules that everyone understands about some kind of organized behavior."[51] Marriage is considered an institution because it is a widely followed, organized human behavior. Similarly, higher education is a widely followed institution of learning, and the military is an institution of national defense. All of these institutions are comprised of many organizations that are deeply gendered, with clear roles assigned to men and women. Over time, values, beliefs and practices become so ingrained that there is little questioning of the normative beliefs and behaviors upon which institutions, and the organizations that comprise them, rest. Institutions are long-lasting, resilient and stable. While they are subject to change processes, change is typically incremental and often discontinuous.[52]

Organizations provide stable, routinized structures in which humans operate cooperatively. They are comprised of varying levels and degrees of human social systems that, ideally, work harmoniously toward common goals. As organizations are established, these social systems are structured according to the functional needs and requirements of the organization. According to systems theorists, systems are self-organized (we create them), hierarchical and very resilient.[53] Over time, organizations develop a degree of equilibrium that makes them particularly stable and resistant to change. Not only does the hierarchical nature of the structure – perhaps epitomized in the military – contribute to stability, but multiple social-psychological factors also work to stabilize organizations. At the organizational level, resistance is systemic. That is, the system inherently resists being altered.

Most militaries are long-standing institutions composed of multiple subordinate organizations. These subordinate organizations may include an army, an air force, a navy, a maritime corps or a coast guard. They are well-established entities whose long-lasting, hierarchical structures are perhaps prototypically stable, making them highly resistant to change. Although the US military claims it has been ahead of other national organizations in terms of social inclusion, the reality is that the US military has been forced to make changes. Most of the important changes instituted in the US military in the 20th and 21st centuries have come about because of operational imperatives or civilian orders, not because the military embraced progressive policies or organizational change.

As military organizations move forward with the inclusion of women, organizational change theory explains not just likely sources of resistance but how to overcome resistance in implementing positive and effective change. Many theorists and practitioners have found that the more control and input individuals have in the change process, the more likely they are to adapt to the changing environment.[54] While many have advocated for participative change processes that give individuals a greater sense of control, others have determined that specific conditions determine whether or not participative change is better than directive change. Directive change may be necessary in situations where external forces, such as new laws or policies, require an organization to adopt new behaviors, resulting in individuals having less control over the impending change.

Strategies for progress

Increasing women's participation in military organizations is inherently about organizational and cultural change since military units are masculine constructs that have been developed and optimized for men. As countries have approached this issue, they have rarely done so in a holistic manner that recognizes the need for large-scale systemic change. Instead, women have been expected to assimilate into the existing male model while the model remains largely unchanged. Introducing or increasing women's participation beyond token representation requires systemic change.

The "Eight-Stage Change Process" is an organizational change model that is part of the curriculum at the US Army's two professional military schools – the Command and General Staff College and the Army War College. This model lays out a step-by-step process for bringing about large-scale, systemic change. It identifies priorities and specific steps for leaders who are embarking on systemic change. I use it here to assess how the US military implemented the decision to allow women in ground combat positions. More generally, this model provides a set of strategies and guidelines for advocates of change relative to the inclusion of women in national militaries.

Establishing a sense of urgency

In order to mobilize human capital and resources, organizational leadership must overcome not just active resistance but a multitude of sources that contribute to complacency and impede change efforts. Creating urgency and momentum for change requires bold and even risky action. When the senior leadership of the US military announced its plan to allow women to serve in all previously closed specialties, it did so in a way that created a sense of urgency. First, the change was *directive* in nature. It stated that the 1994 Direct Ground Combat Definition and Assignment Rule "is rescinded effective immediately."[55] Second, although the new policy opened positions and units "immediately," the leadership gave the military services three years to implement the change, allowing them some time to adjust. Finally, it established planning and implementation milestones to ensure the services met the targeted goal of full integration within three years.

Creating a guiding coalition

Effective change must be steered by a guiding coalition that includes people who have power, expertise, credibility, good leadership skills and commitment to the change.[56] When the US Secretary of Defense and the Chairman of the Joint Chiefs of Staff announced their decision to rescind the previous policy, they placed responsibility for implementing this change on the military service chiefs, and they designated the personnel and readiness office within the staff of the Office of the Secretary of Defense (OSD) to oversee implementation.[57] Unfortunately, their actions violated some of the key principles for creating a good guiding coalition. First, the overseeing organization – OSD – was (and is) an administrative staff that has no authority to direct the actions of the military departments. Second, the OSD staff lacked credibility for understanding the nature of the integration challenges faced by the different services. Finally, OSD staff had little expertise in overseeing an integration effort of this magnitude, and it was not within the office's core mission or competencies.[58]

Despite the fact that the OSD staff was not well-suited to leading a guiding coalition, each of the military departments assumed responsibility for implementation within its own organizations. Each of the departments took different approaches toward establishing an internal guiding coalition. Some created robust guiding coalitions, while others engaged in ad hoc efforts. For example, the US Army designated a specific command to take the lead on the integration effort, while the US Marine Corps doled out responsibility to numerous subordinate agencies and staffs. After a year, the Marine Corps had made little progress and was forced to develop a new plan that included a well-defined guiding coalition.[59] Unfortunately and most damaging was that some senior military leaders continued to express reservations over the wisdom of the directed change.[60]

Developing a vision and a strategy

Vision guides people where the organization needs to go and explains why it needs to go there. Strategy defines a way to get there.[61] The best organizational visions and strategies include some degree of member participation. In this case, the US military had a mixed approach that failed to incorporate best practices. When the Secretary of Defense made the announcement to rescind the old policy, he told the services where they needed to go but he failed to explain why it was in the best interest of the organizations to get there. However, he did give the services a limited chance to influence the final outcome. He told them that if they determined that areas of their organizations could not be fully integrated, then they could request an exception to the new policy. Any exception would have to be "narrowly tailored" and based on a "rigorous analysis of the factual data regarding the knowledge, skills, and abilities needed for the position."[62] Therefore, while this change was directive in nature, it allowed for some degree of participatory decisionmaking relative to the final outcome. Interestingly, the services took different approaches to this guidance depending upon how they interpreted the language of the guidance. As for strategy, the Secretary of Defense largely left that up to the services. He provided some guiding principles as well as benchmarked dates, but how they reached the end state was up to the organizations themselves.

Communicating the change vision

To bring about major organizational change, one scholar observes that a "shared sense of a desirable future can help motivate and coordinate the kinds of actions that create transformations."[63] In the US case, insufficient communication and mixed messages led to confusion about the desired future state. When the Secretary of Defense and the Chairman of the Joint Chiefs of Staff announced the policy change (and in subsequent statements), they used qualifying language such as "we must open up service possibilities for women as fully as possible." This created ambiguity about the end state.[64]

The individual services interpreted this vague vision in various ways. The Marine Corps' professional journal, *The Gazette*, engaged in a public debate about the merits of opening up all combat occupations to women. It published numerous articles challenging the efficacy of allowing women into its core combat specialty, the infantry. Most of the critiques argued that, for a myriad of reasons, it was not "possible" to open the infantry to women.[65] At the same time that the Marine Corps was debating whether women should be allowed into combat specialties, the Army made a deliberate effort to figure out how women would be integrated.[66] These different approaches reflect widely differing interpretations of what should have been a clearly communicated vision and strategy for bringing about organizational change.

Empowering employees for broad-based action

Structural impediments, recalcitrant leaders, and a lack of training are all potential barriers to organizational change.[67] Removing these barriers gives organizational staff both the power and resources to effect change. In the US military, many of these barriers have hindered the change process. One of the structural barriers lies in the joint nature of the US military services. All of the services support each other in various ways and to varying degrees, and all of the services provide personnel to Special Operations Command. As the services moved forward on this directive, they found themselves blocked by slower-moving services. For example, the Army trains Armor Officers for both the Army and the Marine Corps. The Marines said that they could not move forward on gender integration until the Army opened its armor school to women. Similarly, all of the services said that, until Special Operations Command began accepting women, they could not open their elite specialty training programs to women because women's assignment and promotion opportunities would be limited.

Another barrier was senior military leaders who made public statements that impeded full integration. For example, Marine Corps Commandant General James Amos said that if there were not *enough* women officers who were interested or who qualified for the Marine Corps infantry, then it would not worth the effort to allow *any* of them to serve in the infantry.[68] The Commandant never defined what would be "enough" women officers; he only indicated a lack of senior leadership support for this change. The Commandant later changed his tone and his level of support for this initiative.[69]

Throughout 2014, the Marine Corps made a concerted effort to overcome organizational resistance and barriers by holding a series of town hall meetings at units and installations around the world to address the integration concerns of Marines. These events were open to all Marines and to the public. These meetings were designed to reassure Marines that standards would remain unchanged and units would not be weakened by the introduction of women. The meetings were conducted by senior Marine men who were themselves infantry officers.[70] The speakers emphasized that standards would be maintained and that only women who met existing high standards would be admitted to combat jobs. But these leaders never explained how units and capabilities might be improved by the presence of women.

Generating short-term wins

As an organization begins to change, it is important that members see and understand how the change is benefiting the organization. If short-term successes are not highlighted, then skeptics will begin to challenge the value of the change.[71] As the US military moved forward with this integration initiative, it highlighted and celebrated some early successes. Both the Army and the Marine Corps allowed women from historically open specialties – such as communications, logistics and intelligence – to serve in previously closed combat units. Both services noted that women were well received in the newly opened units. Also, when the first enlisted women graduated from infantry training during a trial period, the Marine Corps celebrated its success by allowing the media to cover the training.

However, others have noted that some of the early statements designed to celebrate this change were less successful. One observer pointed out that the US military made a number of statements to sell this change as one that would not "harm" the identity of the combat arms community rather than celebrate it as a step forward. Robert Egnell noted, "The issue of women in combat should not be approached through the lens of damage control, but rather with an emphasis on maximizing the effectiveness of military organizations in the contemporary strategic context."[72] The vision and the reasons for change should have been articulated more powerfully at the outset of the process.

Consolidating gains and producing more change

As one scholar observed, resistance to change is "always waiting to reassert itself."[73] Hardcore resisters continue to look for opportunities to undermine the change process, and short-term gains are not enough to transform the entire system. The interdependent nature of complex social systems means that change must be widespread throughout the system before long-term change and transformation is realized. When the US military was in the early stages of this change process, it identified mid-term and long-term challenges to fully realizing this change. For example, in order to accommodate women in the Navy, Navy officials believed that submarines would have to be modified to provide separate berthing for men and women. Some of the Navy's older ships could not be retrofitted without incurring prohibitive expenses. The Navy decided to allow some of these older ships to be decommissioned rather than modified to accommodate women.[74] The continued existence of some male-only ships allows pockets of resistance to persevere.

Anchoring new approaches in culture

Culture is arguably "the most difficult element to change in an organization" and should not be the focus of the change.[75] According to Kotter, "culture changes only after you have successfully altered people's actions, after the new behavior produces some group benefit for a period of time."[76] Kotter's rule of thumb is that any organization that sets out to change culture as a first step is doomed to failure. Regardless of how cultural change is tackled, it is clear that culture develops slowly and is hard to see and understand, even for those who are imbedded in the culture. Some aspects of culture are visible, while others are hidden deep within the subconscious of the organization. Most definitions of organizational culture refer to an organization's shared values, norms, rituals, stories and expectations.[77] Culture is sometimes referred to as the software that invisibly guides all aspects of an organization's functioning.[78]

National military organizations stand out as being especially steeped in tradition with enduring cultures. These cultures rest on centuries of "the universal gendering of war," where women have served in support roles and rarely as combatants.[79] For full integration and increased participation to take root, organizational change will require sustained efforts on the part of leaders and change activists to highlight improved capabilities and to cement new beliefs and normative behaviors in the organizations. Changes of this magnitude take decades.

Best practices or common approaches?

In 2019, NATO hosted a two-day workshop intended to "identify and share research and best practices" for integrating women into NATO member and partner nation militaries.[80] Much is made of identifying and implementing "best practices" for women's increased inclusion, as if there is a magical set of discrete actions that should be taken. However, although women have been slowly integrating into military organizations for decades, there is little research on the most effective strategies for successful integration or for increasing participation and retention. Monitoring and evaluation often ends abruptly after the first few years of integration, and there is limited information on how women may or may not have affected operational capabilities.[81]

While many countries appear to follow similar strategies and practices for integrating and increasing women's participation, little attention has been paid to whether these strategies and practices are or should be considered best practices. For example, the US military recently implemented a "Leaders First" policy that requires the presence of at least two women leaders (officers or non-commissioned officers) in a combat unit before junior enlisted women can be assigned. It was meant to ease the introduction of enlisted women. This was touted as a best practice, but subsequent research found that it may be harming efforts to integrate women. It might not be a "best practice" that other countries should follow.[82]

An approach adopted by many countries is to tout the increased capabilities of diverse teams. Linking women's participation to increased capabilities is a strategic communications strategy being used to overcome organizational resistance, but it might not be having the intended effects. A growing body of research shows that training based on this line of reasoning may be counterproductive and may actually reduce acceptance of diverse teams.[83]

The best way to overcome resistance to women's inclusion might be the creation of gender-neutral job standards that are applied to men and women equally.[84] Many arguments against women center on their physical differences; the assumption is that women cannot perform the most physically demanding jobs. When the US Army opened ground-combat jobs to women, many members of the military were certain that women would never qualify for elite units such as the Army's 75th Ranger Regiment. However, in 2015 three women soldiers successfully completed the grueling Ranger course, and they qualified using the same standards as men. The school's commanding officer publicly stated that the women had been held to the exact same standards as the men.[85] Women have continued to graduate from this course, (although in much smaller numbers than the men), and they have been selected to serve in the 75th Ranger Regiment.

There is an almost myopic focus in many NATO countries on establishing "gender-free" or "gender-neutral" occupational standards as a way of garnering acceptance of women in traditionally masculine jobs, but there are no established best practices for setting these standards. The result is that there are no two countries with the same standards for what are inherently identical jobs such as "tanker" or "infanteer." Common approaches to women's inclusion have included:

- Reviewing occupational standards to ensure that they are job-based, gender-neutral and applied to men and women equally.
- Pledging not to set quotas for women, to avoid creating the appearance that standards are being lowered.
- Engaging in messaging that touts the benefits of increased capabilities brought about by a larger recruiting pool and more diverse teams.
- Examining organizational policies to identify those that are gendered and have a disproportionately negative impact on women, including recruitment, promotion and retention policies.
- Identifying equipping and training needs that optimize women's performance, reduce injuries and increase participation.

Conclusion

Despite the assertion by John Keegan that "women do not fight," it is clear that the historical record is less about women's capabilities and desires and more about what women have been allowed to do in military organizations. Not only have women shown interest and aptitude, but as cultural norms have changed women are increasingly joining military organizations. The quickest way to increasing women's participation is through conscription, targeted recruitment and incentive programs that treat men and women as citizens with the same responsibilities for national defense.

Ultimately, though, military organizations will have to make military service attractive to all genders, including women. Organizational cultures that allow discrimination and harassment must be eliminated. Training and equipment have to be adapted to allow for a more diverse force. If military organizations remain male-centered, with few accommodations made for women, then women will remain a fractional minority.

The record to date reveals a series of mixed approaches to this organizational and cultural change process. Mixed messages from senior leaders and outright challenges to a modified military identity, evident in professional journals, do not bode well for a smooth transformation to reconstructed individual, group and organizational identities. However, military organizations in many countries will have to adapt to the new strategic and technological challenges of the 21st century. Today and in the future, militaries need personnel with a much broader range of skills than those typically associated with armies of the past. The final push to integrate women in the military is coinciding with a reconstructed, high-tech, post-modern soldier identity that embraces the contributions and inclusion of new capabilities.

Women's greater inclusion in military organizations is and will be a function of changing cultural norms that can be advanced through a series of mutually supporting efforts. UN Security Council resolutions, demands for women on the ground and legal challenges will all serve to push change, but it is possible that women may never serve in military organizations at the same rate as men. Even as adaptation occurs, organizational cultures evolve and reconstructed identities emerge. How long this process takes will depend on the change methods that each country employs. Women's acceptance into support-based occupations has been slow but steady in many militaries. As national militaries open combat positions to women, the path to changing cultures and adapting individual, group and organizational identities within combat sub-communities is likely to be even slower – but it is not impossible. A hundred years ago, it would have been unthinkable to envision a woman sailor on a Navy ship, but today, women command Navy combat ships.

Notes

1 John Keegan, *A History of Warfare* (New York: Knopf, 1993), p. 76.
2 Joshua Goldstein, *War and Gender* (New York: Cambridge University Press, 2001).
3 See UN Security Council Resolution 1325 and Subsequent Women, Peace and Security Resolutions. See also NATO/EAPC, *Women, Peace and Security Policy and Action Plan* (Brussels: NATO, 2018).
4 Megan Alpert, "To Be a Guerrilla, and a Woman, in Colombia," *The Atlantic* (September 28, 2016).
5 See *Integrating UNSCR 1325 and Gender Perspective into NATO Command Structure*, Bi-SC Directive 40-1 (Brussels: NATO, October 17, 2017).
6 Rosalind Miles and Robin Cross, *Hell Hath No Fury: True Stories of Women at War from Antiquity to Iraq* (New York: Random House, 2008), p. 68.
7 US Army, *Women in the Army, History: The Civil War* (@ www.army.mil).
8 Jeanne Holm, *Women in the Military* (Novato, CA: Presidio Press, 1992).
9 Ibid.
10 Joanna Bourke, "Women and the Military during World War One," *BBC History* (March 3, 2011).
11 Laurie Stoff, "They Fought for Russia: Female Soldiers of the First World War," in Gerard J. De Groot and Corinna Peniston-Bird, eds., *A Soldier and a Woman: Sexual Integration in the Military* (London: Longman Pearson, 2000), pp. 66–82.
12 D'Anne Campbell, "Women in Combat: The World War II Experience in the United States, Great Britain, Germany, and the Soviet Union," *The Journal of Military History*, Vol. 57, No. 2 (April 1993), pp. 301–323.
13 Anna Krylova, *Soviet Women in Combat* (New York: Cambridge University Press, 2010).
14 Reina Pennington, *Wings, Women & War: Soviet Women in World War II Combat* (Lawrence: University Press of Kansas, 2001).
15 Ibid.
16 See above. Svetlana Alexievich, *The Unwomanly Face of War: An Oral History of Women in World War II* (New York: Random House, 2017).
17 Lory Manning, *Women in the Military: Where They Stand*, 10th ed. (Washington, DC: Service Women's Action Network, 2019).
18 Paul Caukill et al., *Women in Ground Close Combat Roles: The Experiences of Other Nations and a Review of the Academic Literature* (Porton Down: UK Defence Science and Technology Laboratory, September 29, 2009), p. 24.
19 United Nations, *Action for Peacekeeping, Declaration of Shared Commitments on UN Peacekeeping Operations* (New York: United Nations, September 2018), para. 8.

20 UN Department of Peace Operations (UNDPO), *Uniformed Gender Parity Strategy 2018–2028* (New York: UNDPO, 2018). See also UN Secretary-General, *Letter to the President of the UN Security Council*, S/2019/275 (New York: United Nations, March 28, 2019).

21 NATO/EAPC, *Women, Peace and Security Policy and Action Plan*.

22 Ibid., p. 7.

23 Ibid.

24 Manning, *Women in the Military*, p. 3.

25 See General Accounting Office (GAO), *Gender Issues: Information on DOD's Assignment Policy and Direct Ground Combat Definition* (Washington, DC: GAO, October 1998).

26 Attaching soldiers for short duration to make use of specialized skills is common practice in the US military. However, in situations where the need is enduring, like the requirement for a medic to support an infantry company during extended periods, women were being temporarily attached while a male medic would be permanently assigned.

27 US Army War College, *Women in Combat Compendium* (Carlisle, PA: US Army War College, 2008), p. 2.

28 Ibid., p. viii.

29 See US Department of Defense, *Women in Service Studies* (Washington, DC: US Department of Defense, @ dod.defense.gov).

30 Lolita Baldor, "Officials: Marine Commandant Recommends Women Be Banned from Some Combat Jobs," *Marine Corps Times* (September 18, 2015).

31 UNDPO, *UN Peacekeeping: Women, Peace and Security* (New York: UNDPO, 2019).

32 See *Remarks of the UN Secretary-General in the Security Council Open Debate on Women in Peacekeeping*, Meetings Coverage SC/13773 (April 11, 2019).

33 Ellen Haring, Megan H. MacKenzie and Chantal de Jonge Oudraat, *Women in Combat: Learning from Cultural Support Teams*, Policy Brief (Washington, DC: Women In International Security (WIIS), 2015).

34 Ibid., p. 3.

35 Ibid.

36 Nina Wilen and Lindy Heinecken, "Regendering the South African Army: Inclusion, Reversal and Displacement," *Gender Work Organ* (2018), p. 2.

37 As of July 2019. See UN Peacekeeping, *How We Are Funded* (@ peacekeeping.un.org).

38 Statista, *Number of Bachelor's Degrees by Gender Since 1950* (New York: Statista, @ statista.com).

39 Claudia Grisales, "As Women Make Strides in Military, Battle Remains to Address Recruitment, Retention Gaps," *Stars and Stripes* (March 20, 2018).

40 DN Debatt, "1,768 Kvinnor i Försvaret: Alla Anmälningar Måste Tas På Alvar (1,768 Women in the Defense: All Notifications Must Be Taken Seriously)," *DN Debatt* (December 2, 2017).

41 Andrew R. Morral, Kristie L. Gore and Terry L. Schell, eds., *Sexual Assault and Sexual Harassment in the U.S. Military*, Vols. I–IV (Santa Monica, CA: RAND, 2014–2016).

42 W. Warner Burke, *Organization Change: Theory and Practice*, 4th ed. (Los Angeles, CA: Sage, 2014).

43 Lauren R. Serrano, "Why Women Do Not Belong in the US Infantry," *Marine Corps Gazette*, Vol. 98, No. 9 (September 2014), pp. 38–39.

44 Rosemary Bryant Mariner, "A Soldier Is a Soldier," *Joint Force Quarterly*, No. 3 (Winter 1993–1994), p. 56.

45 Carol Cohn, "How Can She Claim Equal Rights When She Doesn't Have to Do as Many Push-Ups as I Do? The Framing of Men's Opposition to Women's Equality in the Military," *Men and Masculinities*, Vol. 3, No. 2 (October 2000), p. 147.

46 Robert Scales, "Not Yet Time for Women to Serve in the Infantry," *The Washington Post* (December 6, 2012).

47 Burke, *Organization Change*, pp. 120–121.

48 Sage Santangelo, "Fourteen Women Have Tried, and Failed, the Marines' Infantry Officer Course. Here's Why," *The Washington Post* (March 28, 2014).

49 James Dao, "In Arduous Officer Course, Women Offer Clues to Their Future in Infantry," *The New York Times* (February 17, 2013).

50 Hope Hodge Seck, "The Amos Legacy: How the First Aviator Commandant Will Be Remembered," *The Marine Corps Times* (October 14, 2014).

51 Howard Lune, *Understanding Organizations* (Cambridge: Polity Press, 2010), p. 2.

52 W. Richard Scott, *Institutions and Organizations*, 2nd ed. (Los Angeles, CA: Sage, 2001), pp. 48–49.

53 Donna H. Meadows, *Thinking in Systems* (White River Junction, VT: Chelsea Green, 2008), p. 75.

54 See Burke, *Organization Change*; Jeanenne LaMarsh, *Change Better: How to Survive and Thrive During Change at Work and in Life* (Chicago: Agate, 2010).

55 Martin Dempsey and Leon Panetta, *Elimination of the 1994 Direct Ground Combat Definition and Assignment Rule* (Washington, DC: Department of Defense, January 24, 2013).

56 John P. Kotter, *Leading Change* (Cambridge, MA: Harvard Business School Press, August 1, 1996), chapter 4.

57 Dempsey and Panetta, *Elimination of the 1994 Direct Ground Combat Definition*, p. 3.

58 WIIS, *A Review of the Implementation Plans for the Elimination of the Direct Ground Combat Assignment Rule* (Washington, DC: WIIS, October 2013).

59 James Amos, *Integrating Female Marines Within the Ground Combat Element* (Washington, DC: Department of the Navy, March 12, 2014).

60 Melanie Sisson, "Mattis Is Poisoning the Well on Women in Combat," *The Hill* (September 9, 2018).

61 Kotter, *Leading Change*, chapter 4.

62 Dempsey and Panetta, *Elimination of the 1994 Direct Ground Combat Definition*, p. 2.

63 Kotter, *Leading Change*, chapter 6.

64 *Press Briefing – Panetta, Dempsey on the Women in Service Implementation Plan* (Washington, DC: Department of Defense, January 24, 2013).

65 John Keenan, "An Open Letter to the Secretary of Defense," *Marine Corps Gazette* (July 2014); Katie Petronio, "Get Over It! We Are Not All Created Equal," *Marine Corps Gazette* (March 2013); Serrano, "Why Women Do Not Belong in the US Infantry."

66 Amy Robinson, *TRADOC Leads Review of MOS Standards, Gender Integration* (US Army, July 2, 2013, @ army.mil).

67 Kotter, *Leading Change*, chapter 7.

68 Julie Watson, "James Amos, Marine Corps Commandant, Voices Skepticism About Women in Combat," *Huffington Post* (February 1, 2013).

69 See Amos, *Integrating Female Marines*.

70 Ellen Haring, "Deck Stacked Against Women in Experimental Task Force," *Marine Corps Times* (July 6, 2014).

71 Kotter, *Leading Change*, chapter. 8.

72 Robert Egnell, "Gender Perspectives and Fighting," *US Army War College Quarterly Parameters*, Vol. 43, No. 2 (Summer 2013), p. 41.

73 Kotter, *Leading Change*, chapter 9.

74 Jacqueline Klimas, "Navy Opening More Jobs to Women, but Some Might Stay Closed," *Navy Times* (June 26, 2013).

75 Aspa Sarris and Neil Kirby, eds., *Organisational Psychology: Research and Professional Practice* (Prahran, VIC: Tilde University Press, 2013), p. 335.

76 Kotter, *Leading Change*, p. 156.

77 Burke, *Organization Change*, pp. 14–18.

78 Edgar H. Schein, *Organizational Culture and Leadership* (San Francisco, CA: Jossey-Bass, 2010), pp. 7–22.

79 Goldstein, *War and Gender*, p. 10.

80 Ellen Haring, Karen Davis and Laura Chewning, *Technical Evaluation Report SAS-137 Research Symposium on Integration of Women into Ground Combat Units* (Brussels: NATO Science and Technology Organization, February 2019).

81 Karen Davis, *Socio-Cultural Change in Gender and Military Context: Measuring Value*, Paper Presented at the NATO Research Symposium: Integration of Women into Ground Combat Units (Quantico: Marine Corps Base, February 7, 2019).

82 Antonietta Rico, *Understanding Differences in Experiences Between Enlisted Women and Officers*, Paper Presented at the NATO Research Symposium: Integration of Women into Ground Combat Units (Quantico: Marine Corps Base, February 7, 2019).

83 Peter Bregman, "Diversity Training Doesn't Work," *Harvard Business Review* (March 12, 2012); Glen Llopis, "5 Reasons Diversity and Inclusion Fails," *Forbes* (January 16, 2017).

84 Meghann Myers, "The Army Turns to Functional Fitness Testing, Is the End of Gender Standards Near?" *The Army Times* (March 26, 2018).

85 ABC News, "First Females to Graduate from Army's Ranger School," *ABC News* (August 8, 2015).

6

GENDER AND POPULATION MOVEMENTS

Jane Freedman

In the 21st century, many political leaders and national security establishments have focused on what they characterize as the security "threat" posed by population movements. This has been accompanied by ever more restrictive policies to control who crosses borders. The increasing securitization of migration has prioritized state security over human security. The measures put in place to close borders and to prevent population movements have had highly negative impacts on the security of women and men who are attempting to migrate. The causes and forms of insecurity are often specific for women migrants. Because of their social, economic or political status they may find it more difficult to move. They are also in greater danger of becoming victims of sexual and gender-related violence during their migration and on arrival in their country of destination.

In this chapter, I consider the various forms of migration and the ways in which they are gendered before going on to examine how and why women migrants may be particularly affected by the insecurities of migration. I focus on the specific issues of trafficking and of gender-related asylum claims. Finally, I examine the case of the European Union (EU), which provides a good example of the ways in which policies to restrict migration and to "secure" borders can result in increasing insecurities for migrants. I analyze, in particular, the gendered nature of these insecurities. I argue that the growing concern with the supposed threats to state security from migration acts as an obstacle to progress in advancing measures for reinforcing the human security of migrants themselves.

Why gender matters in population movements

Population movements – whether of migrants, refugees or Internally Displaced Persons (IDPs) – are a major global phenomenon. People move for different reasons: to flee persecution and war, escape natural disasters, find work or a better way or life, study abroad, migrate for marriage or reunite with family members in other countries. In 2019, the number of international migrants – people residing in a country other than their country of birth – was estimated at 272 million worldwide.[1] Added to these international migrants are an estimated 41.3 million IDPs, who have not crossed borders but have been forced to move from their homes due to disaster or conflict.[2] In an attempt to "manage" migration, national governments and international organizations have created categories of migrants with different statuses and rights under national and international law.

There is no formal definition of a migrant in international law. In its 2019 Glossary on Migration, the International Organization for Migration (IOM) defines an international migrant as "any person who is outside a state of which he or she is a citizen or national, or, in the case of a stateless person, his or her state of birth or habitual residence. The term includes migrants who intend to move permanently or temporarily, and those who move in a regular or documented manners as well as migrants in irregular situations."[3] A refugee has a specific status under international law based on the 1951 Convention Relating to the Status of Refugees, which defines a refugee as a person who "owing to well-founded fear of being persecuted for reasons of race, religion, nationality, membership of a particular social group or political opinion, is outside the country of his nationality and is unable or, owing to such fear, is unwilling to avail himself of the protection of that country."[4] Those who seek protection from the government of another country after being forced to flee are classified as asylum seekers. They must apply for refugee status in that country, proving their well-founded fear of persecution in order to be granted refugee status and a legal right to stay in the country. Many people who are forced to flee never cross an international border and remain internally displaced within their own country.

All of these legal definitions and classifications are increasingly difficult to map onto the reality of population movements. The causes of migration are rarely simple, and people move for a variety of intermingled reasons with journeys that are not straightforward but may involve many stops (sometimes lengthy) in various countries of "transit" before onward migration to a final "destination." People may be forced to migrate because of poverty, for example, but they may also be victims of violence and persecution on their journeys, which force them to move onward to another destination. In addition, newer causes of migration such as climate change and environmental disasters are increasing the migratory pressure in many regions of the world. These complexities are exacerbated by the fact that individual countries and regional entities, such as the EU, have put in place varying immigration and visa regimes to regulate who can enter their territory, who can stay there and who can legally access different rights and services. The interplay between these regimes and international conventions and laws creates situations in which migrants may become "illegal" not because of any of their own actions, but because of the legal and political systems within which they are caught up.

Migration is increasingly regarded as a security issue, as population movements are seen to be linked to threats to state security – such as terrorism – and threats to political stability, including questions related to national identity, culture and economic burdens. There has also been a spread of anti-immigrant and xenophobic discourses which feed into and are in turn reinforced by the rise of far-right political parties in various countries.[5] These discourses advocate for stricter migration controls to prevent the "uncontrolled" entry of migrants and the deportation of "illegal" migrants from national territories. The belief in widespread anti-immigrant sentiment has been used to justify actions by national governments and regional and international organizations to control or restrict migration.[6] But whilst the securitization of migration has prioritized state security, much less attention has been paid to the ways in which laws and policies regulating migration can lead to increasing insecurities for those who are on the move.

Gender is an important factor in population movements. The causes of migration are often gendered. Gendered structures of power and inequality affect women's and men's opportunities for migration. Gendered inequalities also shape migrants' strategies, routes and journeys in countries of origin, transit and destination. The gender-migration nexus can be seen as a circular relationship whereby gender influences who migrates, how and why they migrate and their experiences during migration. Women often find migration more difficult because they have fewer economic resources to pay for their journeys or because they have primary responsibilities for childcare, which restrict their opportunities for movement. Restrictive gender norms or discriminatory legal contexts may limit women's mobility and access to public spaces. Fear of sexual and gender-based violence on the migration routes may also act as a brake on women's migration. Research has shown that in many situations, the decision to migrate is not made as an individual, but rather as a family. Families may choose to privilege migration of their men, given the perceived risks for women.[7] In some cases, however, families choose to send women to work abroad because they believe that women are more reliable in sending remittances home.

Migration in turn reshapes gender relations – either entrenching traditional gender roles and inequalities or challenging them and forging new constructions and relations of gender. Whilst women migrants might face increased insecurities because of the prevalence of gender-based forms of violence, they may also in some cases have better opportunities for integration into host societies, and they may be able to take on new roles that were not possible for them before migrating. Women migrants may also gain new forms of economic independence, and with this economic independence they may have more opportunities to exercise their rights. The experiences of women migrants are mediated by other intersecting social identities, such as sexual orientation, class, race, nationality and age. It is therefore impossible to talk about a general experience or reality for women in migration. In this chapter, I discuss some of the major issues relating to the ways in which gender relations shape the security dangers faced by women and men in various types and situations of migration and mobility.

Until recently, the typical image of a migrant was a man, and many policies are still based on this image of the male migrant worker or refugee, or on models of "family" migration that prioritize the model of a male-headed family. Only more recently have research and policy begun to consider issues of gender. In the early 21st century, women make up half of migrants worldwide, and many women are now migrating not as part of a couple or family, but on their own, with their own autonomous migratory projects. It is important to examine how global gender inequalities – in intersection with other forms of inequality based on race, class, ethnicity and sexual orientation – impact population movements. We also need to analyze how policies and legislation at international, regional and national levels have gendered impacts and how they affect the security of migrants. Whilst there has been some recognition at the policy level that women may be more vulnerable during migration, there has been little policy effort to reduce the gendered insecurities of migration.

Despite the increases in women's migration (which date from the 1960s) mainstream migration research has been slow to incorporate women and gender into its analyses.[8] One of the primary reasons for the invisibility of women in migration research is that the primary models for analyzing migration were based on labor migration, where the migrant worker was assumed to be a man, and women were presumed to be economically inactive.[9] In 1993, Stephen Castles and Mark Miller wrote about "feminization" as one of the new characteristics of global migration.[10] This was perhaps the first time that the idea of feminization entered mainstream academic discourse on migration research. Unfortunately, there is still relatively little research that focuses on the gendered politics of migration.[11] In addition, whilst there is more awareness that population movements are not comprised solely of men, policies and laws on migration have been slow to integrate a gendered approach that takes full account of the different situations of individual migrants based on gender, race, nationality, class, age and other factors.

Population movements have taken place throughout history, with people moving across the globe for a wide variety of reasons. It is only more recently, however, that these population movements have been seen as security issues and that states seek to close borders and restrict access to their territory. The contemporary period is described by Castles and Miller as the "Age of Migration," characterized by an increasing scale, globalization, feminization and politicization of migration.[12] The politicization is demonstrated by the salience of migration in political debates, party manifestos and election campaigns around the world, with promises to limit migration and to build walls (either metaphorical or real). The politicization of migration as an issue has also led to more significance being placed on migratory categories, as organizations and governments attempting to "manage" migration seek to impose common understandings and definitions of who should be allowed to cross borders and who should be expelled or rejected.[13] They seek to determine who is a "desirable" or "deserving" refugee in need of protection and who is an "undesirable," "underserving" or "illegal" economic migrant who poses a threat and should be expelled or excluded.

In reality, the determination is difficult and perhaps even impossible to make. The reasons that people flee their countries of origin are multiple and diverse.

They may flee because of a particular incident of violence or oppression, an arrest, torture or death threats. It may also be that the general circumstances in which they are living make it impossible for them to remain. Economic and political causes of migration are not opposites but form part of a continuum. Political conflict is often the expression or result of a failure to bring about economic or social development or to safeguard human rights.[14] Further, political conflict may be the cause of economic crises and may push people into untenable conditions of poverty. It is nearly impossible to classify migrations either as the result of political or economic circumstances or as "forced" or "voluntary." In addition, these artificial categorizations are highly gendered and racialized, with women more often being represented as "vulnerable" or "victims," whilst male migrants – and especially those of Muslim origin – are viewed as dangers or threats.[15]

Borders, gender and violence

The scale of international migration – together with attempts to control or manage migration by many countries in the Global North – has reinforced a focus on borders, physical and virtual. Borders have become sites both of symbolic deterrence and of material reinforcement of mechanisms of control – sites for the filtering of "undesirable" individuals.[16] The attempts to secure borders and to prevent migrants from crossing have largely failed, as none of the attempts at reinforcing border controls have actually managed to stop flows of migrants. Despite the ineffectiveness and inefficiency of these securitization measures, states continue to try and make it more difficult for migrants to cross borders and enter their territories. In fact, the securitization of borders – through increased border controls and harsher visa regimes – acts to increase the insecurities of those trying to cross them, making journeys longer, more dangerous and more expensive. Securitization also acts to increase the role and involvement of trafficking and smuggling networks, as migrants can no longer cross borders on their own. And whilst many governments have attempted to blame smugglers or traffickers for encouraging migration, in fact, it is restrictive migration regimes that push migrants into the hands of these smugglers.[17]

Migrant journeys are becoming increasingly violent and insecure. Violence is an element of many migrant journeys, but women who migrate face particular threats including heightened risks of sexual and gender-based violence. The interconnections between gender, migration, violence and insecurity have been highlighted by research in regions around the world.[18] Different push and pull factors, migration control regimes, as well as social and economic conditions in countries of origin, transit and destination create varying types of insecurity and violence for men and women, depending on their social and economic positions and power relations between them. As Marianne Marchand argues: "It goes without saying that the migration-violence nexus is gendered. Men and women are affected in different ways and the violence to which they are exposed is related to their position with respect to the migration-violence nexus."[19]

Violence against women migrants comes from multiple sources including border guards and police, immigration officials, smugglers and traffickers, but also other migrants and members of their own families. During the European migration crisis in the 2010s, there were multiple reports of sexual and gender-based forms of violence committed by border guards against women on the routes through Turkey, Greece and the Balkans to the EU. There are reports that as many as 80 percent of Central American women travelling through Mexico to the United States have been victims of rape.[20] Gender-based forms of violence are also widespread in migrant detention centers. Some smugglers perpetrate rape and sexual violence against women migrants. A lack of economic resources to pay smugglers often forces women into transactional sexual relations in return for their passage. Transactional sex is commonplace around migrant and refugee routes and camps, and it is often a survival strategy for migrant women. Transactional sex as an income-generating or survival strategy for women migrants links to debates on trafficking and prostitution, but policymakers rarely address the gendered insecurities that result in women being forced into transactional sexual relations as their only means of survival.

Inadequate reception conditions for migrants also pose security problems for women, including a lack of safe and sanitary accommodation as well as access to health services or psychological support. The poor reception conditions in destination countries puts strains on family relations and leads to increasing incidences of domestic violence amongst migrant and refugee families. Women who are victims of domestic violence in these circumstances have little chance of obtaining legal or social support. Moreover, the prevailing models of family migration still often recognize a man as the head of family who will protect his wife; it is assumed that women travelling with their husbands or other male companions will be protected by their male partners. Incidents of violence and domination within family groups are thus often overlooked.

Recent research has also highlighted the physical risks of border crossing for women and higher rates of mortality at borders for women than for men.[21] For those attempting to reach the United States from Mexico, women are more likely to die in the desert. For migration to Europe and Australia, women are more likely to drown during sea crossings because they may not know how to swim, be unsuitably dressed, have less access to life jackets or because they may attempt to save their children. The Non-Governmental Organization (NGO) Watch the Med Alarmphone reports on the situation of women taking the Central Mediterranean route from Libya to Italy: "In the Central Mediterranean, they are often seated in the middle of rubber boats intended to keep them as far as possible from the water and thereby 'safe.'" However, it is in the middle of the boats where sea water and fuel gather the most, creating a toxic mix that burns the skin and often causes grave injuries. There women are also most at risk of being trampled and suffocated when panic breaks out on board. In some of the larger wooden boats, women often sit in the vessel's hold, where suffocation due to the accumulation of dangerous fumes occurs more quickly, and where, in situations of capsizing, escaping is more difficult.

Many women wear longer and heavier clothes than men, making it more difficult to stay above water when they fall into the sea.[22]

Trafficking

Governments and international organizations have been quick to point to trafficking networks as responsible for the increasing violence and insecurity of migration. However, the increase in trafficking is the result of restrictive migration policies that prevent people from taking legal routes to migrate. Trafficking cannot be considered as a security problem in isolation from more general considerations of the roots of the insecurities of migration. The framing of trafficking as a border security problem obscures the realities of those who are trafficked, with a simplified focus on women as innocent victims who are kidnapped and forced into prostitution in countries of destination. As Rutivica Andrijasevic and Nicola Mai argue, "The stereotypical image of the victim is of a young, innocent, foreign woman tricked into prostitution abroad. She is battered and kept under continuous surveillance so that her only hope is police rescue."[23]

Trafficking is a highly gendered phenomenon. It is estimated that 72 percent of trafficking victims worldwide are women.[24] The fact the majority of trafficking victims are women may hide other realities that are not so readily understood, such as the fact that men are also trafficked. Also overlooked is the fact that in some cases, women are also involved as traffickers. Trafficking is often understood as forced migration for the purposes of sexual exploitation and prostitution, but migrants are also trafficked for many other forms of labor exploitation such as agricultural, domestic or construction work. The United Nations Office on Drugs and Crime (UNODC) admits that its statistics may be biased toward an overrepresentation of trafficking of women for sexual exploitation, as this is the most visible form of trafficking. Other forms of trafficking and exploitation are underreported: forced or bonded labor; domestic servitude and forced marriage; organ removal; and the exploitation of children in begging, the sex trade and warfare.[25]

The simplified representations that dominate the trafficking debates nationally and internationally fail to take into account the structural inequalities – gender inequalities but also inequalities of race, class and age – that underlie trafficking and make some people more vulnerable to trafficking.[26] Young women have been found to be the most vulnerable to trafficking because they often have lower levels of education, less access to information about migration and fewer opportunities for legal migration.[27] Their vulnerability is tied to structural inequalities within their countries of origin but also to the migration policies within countries of destination. Reports from Libya suggest that the majority of African women attempting to transit through Libya to reach the EU are under the control of traffickers. The process by which these women become dependent and controlled by traffickers is not simple. Most set out independently on their migratory journeys, but find that through lack of knowledge, information or resources, they become dependent on trafficking networks. Some women may know that they are migrating to work in the sex industry, but they may not be aware of the conditions of this work and the control that traffickers will have over their income.

Anti-trafficking policies that focus on the criminalization of prostitution and sex work, with the objective of "saving" the innocent victims, are problematic. These policies ignore the agency of many of these "victims" and that, for some migrants, working in the sex industry may provide an income-generating activity and an opportunity to achieve geographical and social mobility. Policies that are merely repressive do not address the inequalities that make sex work a means of making money. The repression of "illegal" migration may mean that women and men who are victims of trafficking may feel that they are unable to go to the police in their country of destination for fear of being deported.[28]

Sex work is just one of the exploitative forms of labor in which migrant women are engaged worldwide. Women are increasingly migrating alone, often to seek employment in a richer country. In some cases, such as migrants from the Philippines, women are now the large majority of migrants going to work in another country to earn money for themselves and their families. Although women's skilled labor migration should not be ignored, it remains true that for many migrant women the types of jobs into which they are recruited are largely unskilled, low-paid and insecure in terms of having little social or legal protection.[29]

Incidents of violence against women in domestic employment are frequent.[30] Violence against migrant women workers can be seen as a consequence of state violence in that the strict application of immigration laws renders women increasingly vulnerable and at risk. The fact that many of these women are working illegally – because they do not have the requisite work permits – makes their work conditions even more insecure and makes it harder for them to mobilize because they may be afraid to make themselves visible in the public space. The type of work in which migrant women are involved often means that they remain isolated and cannot access support either from other migrant women or from outside sources such as trade unions. Women migrant workers are thus treated as workers not worthy of protection.[31] In some cases, states benefit from structural violence by granting their national citizens unlimited control over migrant domestic workers, who are relegated to the private sphere of the home.[32]

Gender and international refugee protection

One of the reasons that women migrate is to flee gender-based violence and persecution and to seek international protection as refugees. The United Nations High Commissioner for Refugees (UNHCR) reported that there are 70.8 million forcibly displaced people worldwide.[33] Contrary to some perceptions in the Global North, the majority of the world's refugees remain in the South, most often in neighboring countries. Most of the refugees from Syria, for example, are located in Lebanon, Turkey and Jordan. The largest refugee camp in the world is in Uganda. Forced displacement presents particular challenges for women.

Refugee camps can be envisaged as zones of protection for the populations within them (places where they are safe from the conflicts they have fled), but these camps are often also zones of conflict.[34] Specific problems arise for women within these camps both because of material factors, such as the lack of essential resources, and the gendered political and power structures that exist within the camps. The spatial organization of the camp structures the way women manage their time and shapes their social routines and income-earning strategies. Access to health care, food and other services is often concentrated within one area in the camp, which facilitates the work of the international staff but can be inconvenient and dangerous for those who live in the camp – especially women.[35] Refugee camps are designed to facilitate the administrative tasks of UNHCR and other aid agencies that run the camps or work in them, rather than to make life easier for the refugees who live there. This puts women at risk of violence – for example, when they have to go outside of the camp to look for firewood. Gathering firewood is generally designated as a task for women since women are responsible for cooking and they usually have no choice in the type of fuel they can use for cooking. In addition to the dangers of violence incurred whilst collecting firewood or water, women are also faced with a lack of resources for their basic needs. Women are often principally responsible for feeding their families and thus bear the brunt of the problems involved in managing the very scarce resources they receive.[36] Facilities for sanitation and washing are frequently also inadequate. The violence and insecurities of life in refugee camps also lead to increasing familial restriction and control on girls' and young women's mobility. For example, among some Syrian and Rohingya refugees, displaced families in refugee camps have chosen early or forced marriage for their daughters as a strategy to cope with economic hardship or perceived risks of sexual violence.

Adjusting to life within a camp can also be a process of realignment and redefinition of gender roles and relationships. These processes of change can benefit women as they are empowered to take on roles not previously open to them, but they can also have negative impacts. Some studies have shown that changes in gendered divisions of labor are at the expense of women – for example, when women have to take on extra tasks that are not economically rewarding or income-generating.[37] Other studies have pointed to a reinforcement of the gender roles that existed in countries of origin within the new setting of a refugee camp. Studies have also shown increasing violence by men in refugee camp settings as a result of their feeling unable to fill their roles as breadwinners and heads of family.[38]

Above all, refugee camps are sites of violence – much of this violence is clearly gendered in nature. This violence stems from the disruption of family and community structures during forced migration and the continuation and reproduction of previously experienced violence whilst in exile. Although UNHCR and NGOs have made commitments to protect women within camps, in practice, the organization of camps, the political structures within them and the representations and conceptualizations of women and men within these camps mean that this protection is often not effective.

Most refugees remain in camps or in situations of urban displacement in countries of the South, but a minority do travel to countries of the North to claim asylum. Around 30 percent of asylum claims in these countries are made by women – and these numbers are growing. Claims for asylum are increasingly being made on the grounds of gender-based persecutions such as female genital mutilation, forced marriage, domestic violence or rape and sexual violence in conflict.

Such claims have been difficult to process because neither gender nor sex is included as one of the grounds of persecution for which persons can claim asylum under the 1951 Convention on the Status of Refugees. As with other international human rights conventions, the 1951 Refugee Convention was written from the male perspective, which overlooks infringements of the human rights of women. Human rights laws and conventions have been elaborated in terms of the violation of *existing* rights; they offer only limited redress in cases where there is pervasive and structural *denial* of rights, such as those cases where rights are denied because of pervasive and structural gender inequalities. During the negotiations that led to the drafting of the 1951 Convention, the relevance of gender was discussed only once, and it was quickly rejected.[39] These views were typical of the time in which the Convention was written, when the questions of gender, sexuality and women's rights were far from the center stage of international politics.

The lack of attention to gender in the 1951 Convention has led some to argue that the Convention itself should be re-written to add gender as a sixth ground of persecution in addition to the existing five of race, religion, nationality, political opinion and membership of a particular social group.[40] Others argue that it might be dangerous to open up discussion on the re-drafting of the 1951 Convention given the level of anti-immigrant sentiment that exists globally and the fact that gender-based forms of persecution can be treated under the terms of the Convention if the victims of this type of persecution are considered as members of a "particular social group."[41]

It is clear that there are still multiple barriers for those claiming asylum on the basis of gender-related forms of persecution. While the right of asylum is enshrined in international law, states have increasingly rejected asylum claims on the grounds that they are not genuine asylum claims but false claims made by migrants to enable them to gain a legal residence status. The rejection of asylum claims takes the form of denying the existence of persecution or increasing demands for proof of persecution, which is often impossible for asylum seekers to provide. These developments have particular negative impacts on women who are victims of gender-related persecution, which might not be recognized as a legitimate motive for seeking asylum under the Refugee Convention. Many women also have their asylum claims rejected because their stories are judged not to be credible.[42]

In theory, gender-related forms of persecution should allow many women to be accorded refugee status; the practices in place discourage this because of the underlying fear of a huge influx of new women asylum seekers. Although there have been some advances in terms of women receiving refugee status on the grounds of gender-specific persecution, these have only been in individual cases; judges have been careful to frame their decisions in ways that limit the generalization of such decisions to other women in similar situations. The asylum process – which involves women recounting their experiences of persecution over and over again in front of various officials, judges and often members of NGOs as well – also poses a barrier as it requires women to relive and recount experiences that may have been highly traumatic and might seem shameful to them. These processes tend to reinforce gendered stereotypes of women as passive and apolitical victims and to reinforce the notion of the illegitimacy of asylum claims based on the grounds of gender-related persecutions that are not "political." Further, restrictions on access to housing and welfare services for asylum seekers – introduced as a deterrent by many governments – have a profoundly negative impact on women asylum seekers, reinforcing gendered inequalities in capital and resources.

Gender, climate change and migration

As climate change causes increasingly perilous conditions for millions of people across the globe, the question of those who are forced to move due to flood, tsunami, drought, rising sea levels or other natural causes is becoming more and more contentious. States increasingly argue about who should bear the responsibility for protecting and finding new homes for these refugees. Even the term *refugee* is contentious when applied to these populations, with some arguing that these people should be protected under the existing Refugee Convention, others arguing that a new convention needs to be developed and some arguing that this is not a question that should be addressed within any kind of refugee framework.[43]

The question is also a gendered one. Many studies have shown that women and men are affected differently by climate change and natural disasters, with women in many cases being more vulnerable to climate change because of preexisting social and economic inequalities.[44] Women and men affected by natural disasters face different sources of insecurity and have varied strategies for survival and mitigation to deal with the impacts of such disaster. Such disasters are called "natural," but they are in fact inherently social phenomena in that their consequences (and in some cases their causes) are linked to "who we are, how we live and how we structure and maintain our society."[45] This means that existing social, economic and political inequalities in societies determine who is most at risk from natural hazards and disasters. Further, men and women respond differently to risk because of their location in social structures.[46] As Hunter and David argue, gendered insecurities as a result of natural disasters are linked to "inequalities such as poverty, limited access to resources and mobility, as well as culturally constructed expectations that shape work patterns, household divisions of labor and caretaking responsibilities."[47]

Displacement following disasters also has gendered dimensions. When people are displaced and forced to migrate because of disasters, they may find refuge in the homes of family or friends, but many are forced into shelters provided by governments, NGOs or international organizations. Within these shelters, many of the same issues arise as in refugee camps, as these temporary shelters are not designed to cater to the needs of women. Women face lack of privacy and lack of adequate facilities for childcare, cooking or laundry. They are vulnerable to violence within the shelters both from intimate partners and other men.[48] Those who migrate further and seek protection in another country may not find it easy to voice their claims for protection or to gain a legal status within that country. As several scholars have pointed out, the securitized and state-centric reactions to climate change migration have focused on the threats to state security from influxes of large numbers of climate change migrants.[49] These state security discourses have highlighted the same types of fears as those that are prominent in political and media discourses on asylum seekers, highlighting the threats that climate change refugees could pose to resources, services, social cohesion and political stability. Both the United States and the EU have issued policy documents that encourage policymakers to take into account the potential threats to security from climate change refugees and the need to take these threats seriously in policies for management of migration.[50] These state-centric discourses do little or nothing, however, to address the insecurities of those forced to migrate because of climate change.

Gendered representations

The idea that migrants are a threat to the security of countries of transit and destination has become commonplace globally, evidenced by the growing popularity and acceptability of right-wing and xenophobic, anti-immigrant discourses and policies. These representations of migrants as security threats are constructed in gendered and racialized terms which build on stereotypical dichotomies whereby women are "vulnerable" or "victims" and men "dangerous."[51] These stereotypical gendered representations have been strengthened since 9/11 and subsequent terrorist attacks in Europe and the United States.

Migrant men, and in particular young Muslim migrant men, are increasingly portrayed as potential terrorists and subjected to restrictive policing and surveillance practices. The rumor that some of the terrorists involved in the attack on the Bataclan in Paris in 2015 had followed the refugee route through Turkey and Greece, for example, led to calls to impose further restrictions on the movement of young men along this route. Representations of male migrants as a specific threat to women have also emerged, with the idea that men from "other cultures" may pose a sexual threat to European or American women. They are represented as hypersexualized and dangerous, unaware of the more "civilized" gender norms prevalent in Western societies. These types of representation were clearly in evidence in Germany after the report of sexual violence against women in Cologne on December 31, 2015 – incidents of violence which were immediately blamed on refugees. This type of representation has led some countries to set up special education courses for migrant men to "teach" them about women's rights and gender equality.

Migrant women, on the other hand, are stereotyped as vulnerable or victims – representations which could be considered as perhaps less harmful than those of migrant men, but which act to deny their agency and autonomy. Thus, although women might be offered some extra protection (because of their supposed vulnerability), they are also treated as dependent, and their independent migratory strategies and wishes are ignored. Even well-meaning charitable or humanitarian interventions tend to classify women as vulnerable victims, objects of pity. These women are then targeted for interventions in ways that foreclose their agency.[52] These representations of women (and particularly Muslim women) as "vulnerable" or "victims" devoid of agency, combine a racialized and gendered discourse which reduces their ability to express and make heard their own needs, wishes and opinions.

Policy frameworks

Policies to manage or control migration – even when supposedly "gender neutral" – do have gendered impacts because of the gendered inequalities and hierarchies of power outlined in this text. There have been some attempts to integrate gendered considerations into migration policies at national, regional and international levels. Unfortunately, the continued prioritization of state sovereignty and national security over the security of migrants has meant that the impacts of the integration of gender into migration policies has been limited in terms of positive effects for women. Migration policies in Australia, Europe or North America are based on the premise that the number of migrants entering the national territory of these countries can be limited, and that it is possible to select the "good" migrants and allow them to enter and stay legally whilst keeping out or expelling others. These efforts are based on a false belief that it is possible to establish clear categories of migrants with easily identifiable boundaries and characteristics. The reality is far more complex and messier, and the reductive nature of many policies do nothing to reduce the insecurities of migrant women or to promote their agency.

There are some international policy frameworks for integrating gender into policies on migration and refugees. These policy frameworks advance the security of women migrants, but they are also problematic because of a reliance on stereotypical visions of women's vulnerability. In reaction to widespread criticism from feminist groups at the lack of specific guidance on protection for women asylum-seekers and refugees, UNHCR has issued guidelines on the protection of women, victims of sexual violence and victims of trafficking.[53] These guidelines integrated an assumed notion of vulnerability of these groups and their need for added protection in the face of this vulnerability. The criteria used by UNHCR for selecting refugees for resettlement to third countries rely almost entirely on the notion of vulnerability. Any refugees who wish to be candidates for resettlement need to prove that they are indeed vulnerable in order to gain a place on the list. This insistence on the notion of women's vulnerability to justify their protection undercuts any recognition of their independent status and agency. Unfortunately, despite a commitment to gender mainstreaming, to the prevention of gender-based violence and to greater protection for women refugees, in practice, many refugee situations gender-based insecurities remain.

Some countries have integrated UNHCR's guidelines into national asylum and refugee policies. In 1993, the Canadian Immigration and Refugee Board issued Guidelines on Women Refugee Claimants Fearing Gender-Related Persecution. These guidelines affirmed that the definition of a refugee should be interpreted so as to protect women who demonstrate a well-founded fear of gender-related persecution. They also sought to provide principles that would lead those making decisions on asylum claims to more fully account for the particularities of women's experiences of persecution. In 1995, the US Department of Justice issued a memorandum that directed immigration officers to consider that women may face specific types of persecution and to treat these persecutions seriously when adjudicating asylum claims. In 1996, the Australian Department of Immigration and Multicultural Affairs issued Guidelines on Gender Issues for Decision Makers. Audrey Macklin argues that Canada's adoption of international norms in this area provided an example for the other two states, so that "demonstrating what could be achieved – politically and legally – in one jurisdiction, made it politically feasible to follow suit."[54] Several EU countries as well as countries such as South Africa have also adopted the UNHCR guidelines. However, research has shown that the impacts of this adoption have been limited by the continued actions of states to limit migration. Asylum seekers are viewed with suspicion and often their stories are simply deemed "not credible." As Debra Singer argues, despite the national frameworks for integrating gender into national refugee status determination systems, many women's claims fail because they are judged to lack credibility or because women do not have enough proof to back up their claims.[55]

Policy frameworks on labor migration have also failed to fully integrate gendered concerns and may thus penalize women migrants. In the EU the Policy Plan on Legal Migration sets out regulations for the entry and stay of four categories of migrants: highly qualified workers, seasonal workers, intra-corporate transferees and remunerated trainees.[56] No gender differences are mentioned in any of these categories. The categories of domestic work and care work (within which women are the majority) are not mentioned. Indeed, domestic work remains largely unregulated and is not the subject of any EU directives.[57] Neither does the EU plan make any mention of the problems of de-skilling or non-recognition of qualifications obtained in third countries, which disproportionately affect migrant women. The plan does little "to mitigate inequalities already inherent in labor migration, namely the extent to which skilled females are disproportionately subject to de-qualified, part-time or insecure service work upon arrival."[58]

Gender in the EU common asylum system

The case of the EU is illustrative of many of the issues relating to gender, migration and security. It shows that whilst there are strategies for progress in integrating gender issues into immigration and asylum laws and policies, the primacy of discourses on the threat of migration and the need to reinforce state security through closing borders has rendered the progress irrelevant. This reflects what has been happening globally, where drivers of progress (in recognizing the gendered insecurities of migration and in trying to combat these insecurities) have been halted or reversed by the securitization of migration, closure of borders and repressive policies against migrants.

On paper, the EU can be seen as an example of good practices in integrating gender concerns into asylum and refugee policies. Under the Common European Asylum System, there has been some progress toward recognition of gender-based violence as a motive for claiming refugee protection, and in the acknowledgement that victims of such violence may have specific needs during their asylum claims. The 2004 Qualification Directive explicitly recognized that gender-related persecution should be considered under the terms of the 1951 Refugee Convention, and not merely as grounds for subsidiary forms of protection.[59] The Directive also recognized that non-state actors could be agents of persecution. This improved the recognition of gender-related persecution by overcoming the distinction between public and private, which has undermined attempts to establish recognition of various forms of persecution specific to women. Pressured by the European Women's Lobby, Asylum Aid and other groups – who made proposals for a more gender-sensitive text – the EU adopted a new Qualification Directive in 2011.[60] The 2011 Directive obliges member states to take into account the "specific situation of vulnerable persons such as victims of human trafficking . . . and persons who have been subjected to rape or other serious forms of psychological, physical or sexual violence." There are, however, still gaps in the protection offered to victims of gender-based persecution under the Directive. For example, the Directive still recognizes non-state agents as actors of protection, which is problematic in cases of gender-based violence where non-state agents may be unreliable in their desire or ability to protect women. The fact that the 2011 Directive does little to improve the gender sensitivity of the asylum determination process means that "inconsistencies in the interpretation and application of the Directive at domestic level are likely to persist."[61]

The EU's Asylum Procedure and Reception Directives have also been recast and have included some measures to increase gender sensitivity.[62] They now call for an assessment of vulnerabilities of persons who have been subject to rape or other serious forms of violence to be carried out within the asylum reception systems. Member states are required to submit information concerning the procedures that they have put in place for reception of asylum seekers with special vulnerabilities. Officials interviewing asylum seekers are required to be trained and competent to take account of vulnerabilities; they should, wherever possible, be of the same sex as the applicant. Finally, the Reception Directive places an obligation on member states to prevent assault and gender-based violence in reception and accommodation centers. This progress should be welcomed, but there remain significant gaps in implementation.

All of this progress in integrating gender concerns into the EU's asylum and refugee policies has been undermined by the reactions to the latest refugee "crisis" and the way in which increasing restrictions and border controls have placed migrants and refugees in situations of extreme insecurity and danger. Since the arrival of more than one million refugees in Europe in 2015, national governments and EU institutions have closed borders and implemented policies to keep refugees from arriving in Europe. The EU-Turkey Agreement of March 2016 allows for the immediate return of any refugee arriving by boat in Greece from Turkey, based on the underlying assumption that Turkey is a "safe country" and that refugees can seek asylum there.

The practical implications of this Agreement have led to thousands of refugees being stuck in temporary camps on Greek islands in rapidly deteriorating sanitary and security conditions. Women and girls have been particularly affected, with reports of rape and sexual violence, harassment, lack of medical attention, access to sexual and reproductive health services or to psychological support for victims of violence and trauma. Although there are many women stuck in Greece who have made claims to be relocated to another EU country under the rules on family reunification, this right is being blocked because of the reluctance of other EU member states to accept more refugees.

Refugees trying to reach the EU via Libya are also subject to restrictive border controls and migration policies that push them into dangerous sea crossings or place them at risk of violence from smuggling and trafficking networks operating in Libya. In 2017, Italy signed a Memorandum of Understanding with the Libyan government to combat illegal immigration, human trafficking and contraband and to reinforce the border security between the Libya State and the Italian Republic. This agreement promises funding for Libya's coast guard, to enable it to intercept more migrant boats, and for the improvement of conditions in Libya's migrant detention centers. These policies – which are justified by the need to save the lives of migrants by preventing them from undertaking dangerous sea crossings – will in fact reinforce the insecurities for these men and women in a country where their rights are not respected. As UNHCR points out, "Years of armed conflict and political divisions have weakened Libyan institutions, including the judiciary, which have been unable, if not unwilling, to address the plethora of abuses and violations committed against migrants and refugees by smugglers, traffickers, members of armed groups and State officials, with near total impunity."[63]

Thus, while the EU claims that it is mainstreaming gender considerations into its asylum and immigration policies and seeking to protect the rights of women, it is clear that the imperative of preventing the arrival of migrants on its shores is taking precedence over any real concern about the violence and insecurities faced by migrant women.

Strategies for progress

This chapter has examined the ways in which progress in integrating gender concerns into migration policies globally has been hampered by increasingly securitized and restrictive management of migration. One of the major obstacles to progress is the rise of a dominant discourse amongst political leaders and in the media that migration is a threat that needs to be addressed and that restricting migration will increase the security of states. Many political parties have put the policy of limiting or even stopping migration at the center of their manifestos. In some cases, they have enjoyed electoral success, which they have attributed to this policy direction. It has thus become more difficult for those supporting migrants' rights and arguing for the protection of individual migrants and refugees. There is a general assumption that public opinion is becoming more favorable to the restriction of migration and hostile to migrants; this view is also a major obstacle to progress in ensuring the security of migrants. Given the dominance of the "anti-migration" discourses in politics and the media globally, it is challenging to advance strategies to re-assert the importance of protecting migrants and refugees.

However, research has pointed to the fact that public attitudes toward migrants are measured on the basis of "imagined immigration" rather than actual immigration.[64] Much anti-migrant sentiment is built on the basis, not of real knowledge of migrants or migration policies, but on imaginary fears about the threats of migration. These representations and imaginations are highly gendered and racialized. These types of findings may provide encouragement, in that they seem to indicate that a more comprehensive understanding of migration might encourage more tolerant and open attitudes amongst the public. Thus, in order to help support migrants' rights and protect migrants and refugees, those supporting migrant rights need to start educating, informing and dispelling myths about the threats posed by migration to national security.

One of the major drivers of progress is the growing organization of migrants themselves to defend their rights and to lobby citizens and governments for changes that would increase their security.[65] Migrant women's associations are at the forefront of this movement, and many have recently sprung up in addition to older networks and organizations. In Greece, which has been at the center of the European refugee "crisis," many migrant women's associations have been created to provide mutual support and aid. These associations and networks – as well as providing support in relation to legal procedures, domestic issues, child care and work – can also act to give migrant women a visible political presence.[66] These types of organizations can also encourage solidarity with local citizens, thus acting to modify public opinion and gain popular support for migrants and refugees.

One strategy for progress is to further integrate concerns relating to gender and migration into existing international frameworks on gender and security. The Women, Peace and Security (WPS) agenda could be mobilized to consider issues relating to migration. Although migration is often closely linked to violence and conflict, there has been a general failure to incorporate questions of migration into the WPS agenda. There has been some consideration of women displaced within their countries of origin, but far less attention has been paid to women who undertake international migration as a result of this violence and conflict. Concern for protection of these women seems too often to be limited to zones of conflict and not extended to migrant women.

A number of WPS National Action Plans (NAP) have incorporated references to refugees.[67] The United Kingdom (UK) NAP, for example, mentions refugees in conflict-affected areas, through provisions for "safe spaces" programming to protect adolescent girls from violence in conflict and post-conflict settings, including projects in refugee settings. Fewer NAPs however, make specific reference to asylum seekers who have arrived in their countries. France's NAP mentions the need to protect women within the French asylum system but does not specify how this should be done. More specific guidelines within NAPs are some of the ways in which the insecurity of women migrants could be incorporated into wider international frameworks on WPS. In recognizing the gendered insecurities of refugees and putting in place measures to protect them – such as gender-sensitive refugee status determination procedures, separate accommodation and reception centers for women and men and appropriate medical and psychological support for women and men refugees – states could do more to improve the security of all refugees.

Gender concerns should also be integrated into future international policies and conventions on migration. Following the 2016 New York Declaration for Refugees and Migrants of September 2016 – a set of commitments adopted by the UN General Assembly to enhance the protection of migrants and refugees – two new global compacts have been adopted by the UN General Assembly: the Global Compact for Safe, Orderly and Regular Migration and the Global Compact on Refugees. The negotiation of these new Compacts should have been an opportune moment for states to commit to policies that offer real protection to migrants and refugees, whatever their status or category. However, despite the gender-responsive language within both Global Compacts, there have been criticisms of the failure to move beyond normative perceptions of "gender" and of women, and of the continuing prioritization of the interests of states over those of migrants and refugees.[68] To go further, it will be necessary to adopt an intersectional analysis that examines the multiple ways in which migrants and refugees may be rendered insecure by existing policies and how policies that are assumed to be neutral may have highly gendered impacts. A starting basis would be to consider all migrants and refugees as persons with rights that must be protected and to end the categorizations that lead to the construction of differences between "good" and "bad" migrants. The representations of migrants and refugees as security threats for states – which have become so widespread – can only be combatted if governments take the lead in providing fairer migration policies and adequate reception and integration procedures for migrants. Investing in language lessons for arriving migrants, for example, or recognizing their skills and qualifications would help them integrate into national labor markets.

Policymakers must consider ways of reducing insecurities and vulnerabilities of migrants, both men and women, through consideration of individual rights to mobility and the ways in which these rights have been obstructed through the securitization and control of migration. Creating safe, legal routes for migration would contribute to reducing the gender-specific vulnerabilities of migrant women. These legal routes could be created through expanded availability of work permits, including permits for work that has traditionally been done by women. Family reunification rules could be clarified and applied more fairly to ensure that women and men can be reunited with family members in different countries more quickly and safely. There is also scope for the expansion of private sponsorship programs for refugees, as pioneered by Canada. These efforts can provide a safe and legal route for refugees and help them integrate into host societies.

Listening to women's and men's needs and considering them as rights-bearing people with their own strategies and projects is also vital if policies are to offer effective protection. Too often, gender is not fully considered in relation to population movement. The inequalities that create the need to migrate are overlooked, and policies to regulate migration are made without consideration for their gendered aspects. States are trying to reinforce their security through better control of migration, but this exacerbates insecurities for individual migrants. Some policies have attempted to protect the "vulnerable," but women should not automatically be considered as vulnerable victims. Women migrants have agency and independent strategies. To protect their rights and increase their security, policymakers need to consider the specific situations women face and respond to these challenges by listening to the migrants themselves.

Notes

1 International Organization for Migration (IOM), *World Migration Report 2020* (Geneva: IOM, 2019, @ iom.int).
2 Ibid.
3 IOM, *Glossary on Migration*, IML Series No. 34 (Geneva: IOM, 2019), p. 110.
4 The 1951 Convention was negotiated to deal with the millions of refugees and displaced persons in Europe after World War II. In 1967, an additional protocol extended the reach of the Convention to deal with other situations of forced displacement. UN General Assembly, *Convention Relating to the Status of Refugees*, Article 1(A)2, United Nations, Treaty Series, Vol. 189 (New York: United Nations, July 28, 1951), p. 137.
5 Ronald Inglehart and Pippa Norris, *Trump, Brexit, and the Rise of Populism: Economic Have-Nots and Cultural Backlash* (Rochester, NY: Social Science Research Network, July 29, 2016); Christopher Cochrane and Neil Nevitte, "Scapegoating: Unemployment, Far-Right Parties and Anti-Immigrant Sentiment," *Comparative European Politics*, Vol. 12, No. 1 (January 1, 2014), pp. 1–32.
6 Dietrich Thränhardt, "The Political Uses of Xenophobia in England, France and Germany," *Party Politics*, Vol. 1, No. 3 (July 1, 1995), pp. 323–345.
7 Brenda S.A. Yeoh, "Postcolonial Geographies of Place and Migration," in Kay Anderson, et al., eds., *Handbook of Cultural Geography* (Thousand Oaks, CA: SAGE, 2003), pp. 369–380.
8 Hania Zlotnik, *The Global Dimensions of Female Migration* (Washington, DC: Migration Policy Institute, March 1, 2003).
9 Eleonore Kofman et al., *Gender and International Migration in Europe* (London: Routledge, 2001).
10 Stephen Castles and Mark J. Miller, *The Age of Migration: International Population Movements in the Modern World* (London: Macmillan, 1993).
11 Jane Freedman, *Gendering the International Asylum and Refugee Debate*, 2nd ed. (Basingstoke: Palgrave Macmillan, 2015); Nicola Piper, "Gendering the Politics of Migration," *International Migration Review*, Vol. 40, No. 1 (2006), pp. 133–164.

12 Castles and Miller, *The Age of Migration*.
13 Heaven Crawley and Dimitris Skleparis, "Refugees, Migrants, Neither, both: Categorical Fetishism and the Politics of Bounding in Europe's 'Migration Crisis'," *Journal of Ethnic and Migration Studies*, Vol. 44, No. 1 (January 2018), pp. 48–64.
14 Ibid.; Stephen Castles and Sean Loughna, "Trends in Asylum Migration to Industrialized Countries, 1990–2001," in George J. Borjas and Jeff Crisp, eds., *Poverty, International Migration and Asylum* (London: Palgrave Macmillan, 2005), pp. 39–69.
15 Jennifer Allsopp, "Aggressor, Victim, Soldier: Intersecting Masculinities in the European Refugee Crisis," in Jane Freedman, et al., eds., *A Gendered Analysis of the Syrian Refugee Crisis* (London: Routledge, 2017), pp. 155–175; Marcus Herz, "'Becoming' a Possible Threat: Masculinity, Culture and Questioning Among Unaccompanied Young Men in Sweden," *Identities*, Vol. 26, No. 4 (March 7, 2018), pp. 1–19.
16 Marie Bassi and Shoshana Fine, "La gouvernance des flux migratoires 'indésirables' – Cas d'étude de Calais et Lampedusa," *Hommes & Migrations, Revue française de référence sur les dynamiques migratoires*, No. 1304 (October 2013), pp. 77–83.
17 Rutvica Andrijasevic, "Beautiful Dead Bodies: Gender, Migration and Representation in Anti-Trafficking Campaigns," *Feminist Review*, Vol. 86, No. 1 (July 2007), pp. 24–44.
18 Marianne H. Marchand, "The Violence of Development and the Migration/Insecurities Nexus: Labour Migration in a North American Context," *Third World Quarterly*, Vol. 29, No. 7 (October 2008), pp. 1375–1388; Jane Freedman, "Analysing the Gendered Insecurities of Migration," *International Feminist Journal of Politics*, Vol. 14, No. 1 (March 2012), pp. 36–55.
19 Marchand, "*The Violence of Development*," p. 1387.
20 Amnesty International, *Invisible Victims: Migrants on the Move in Mexico* (London: Amnesty International, 2010).
21 Sharon Pickering and Brandy Cochrane, "Irregular Border-Crossing Deaths and Gender: Where, How and Why Women Die Crossing Borders," *Theoretical Criminology*, Vol. 17, No. 1 (February 2013), pp. 27–48.
22 Alarm Phone, "The Struggle of Women Across the Sea," *Alarm Phone* (March 22, 2018).
23 Rutvica Andrijasevic and Nicola Mai, "Trafficking (in) Representations: Understanding the Recurring Appeal of Victimhood and Slavery in Neoliberal Times," *Anti-Trafficking Review*, Special Issue, No. 7 (September 2016).
24 UN Office for Drugs and Crime (UNODC), *Global Report on Trafficking in Persons* (New York: UNODC, 2018).
25 Ibid.
26 Laura María Agustín, "Migrants in the Mistress's House: Other Voices in the 'Trafficking' Debate," *Social Politics: International Studies in Gender, State and Society*, Vol. 12, No. 1 (March 2005), pp. 96–117.
27 Jyoti Sanghera, "Unpacking the Trafficking Discourse," in Kamal Kempadoo, ed., *Trafficking and Prostitution Reconsidered* (Boulder, CO: Paradigm, 2005), pp. 3–24.
28 Askola Heli, "Violence Against Women, Trafficking, and Migration in the European Union," *European Law Journal*, Vol. 13, No. 2 (March 2007), pp. 204–217.
29 Lin Lean Lim and Nana Oishi, "International Labor Migration of Asian Women: Distinctive Characteristics and Policy Concerns," *Asian and Pacific Migration Journal*, Vol. 5, No. 1 (March 1996), pp. 85–116.
30 Nicola Piper, "Feminization of Labor Migration as Violence Against Women: International, Regional, and Local Nongovernmental Organization Responses in Asia," *Violence Against Women*, Vol. 9, No. 6 (June 2003), pp. 723–745.
31 Christine B.N. Chin, "Walls of Silence and Late Twentieth Century Representations of the Foreign Female Domestic Worker: The Case of Filipina and Indonesian Female Servants in Malaysia," *The International Migration Review*, Vol. 31, No. 2 (1997), pp. 353–385.
32 Mark Johnson and Christoph Wilcke, "Caged in and Breaking Loose: Intimate Labor, the State, and Migrant Domestic Workers in Saudi Arabia and Other Arab Countries," in Sara L. Friedman and Pardis Mahdavi, eds., *Migrant Encounters: Intimate Labor, the*

Sate, and Mobility Across Asia (Philadelphia, PA: University of Pennsylvania Press, 2015), pp. 135–159.

33 UN High Commissioner for Refugees (UNHCR), *Figures at a Glance* (Geneva: UNHCR, @ unhcr.org).

34 Wenona Giles and Jennifer Hyndman, *Sites of Violence: Gender and Conflict Zones* (Berkeley, CA: University of California Press, 2004).

35 Jennifer Hyndman, *Managing Displacement: Refugees and the Politics of Humanitarianism* (Minneapolis: University of Minnesota Press, 2000); Awa Mohamed Abdi, "Refugees, Gender-Based Violence and Resistance: A Case Study of Somali Refugee Women in Kenya," in Evangelia Tastsoglou and Alexandra Dobrowolsky, eds., *Women, Migration and Citizenship* (London: Routledge, 2016), pp. 245–266.

36 Linda Kreitzer, "Liberian Refugee Women: A Qualitative Study of Their Participation in Planning Camp Programmes," *International Social Work*, Vol. 45, No. 1 (January 2002), pp. 45–58.

37 Alastair Ager, Wendy Ager and Lynellyn Long, "The Differential Experience of Mozambican Refugee Women and Men," *Journal of Refugee Studies*, Vol. 8, No. 3 (January 1995), pp. 265–287; Agnes Callamard, "Flour Is Power: The Gendered Division of Labour in Lisongwe Camp," in Wenona Giles, Helene Moussa and Penny Van Esterik, eds., *Development and Diaspora: Gender and the Refugee Experience* (Dundas, ON: Artemis, 1996).

38 Simon Turner, "Angry Young Men in Camps: Gender, Age and Class Relations Among Burundian Refugees in Tanzania," *New Issues in Refugee Research* (June 1999), pp. 1–15.

39 See Thomas Spijkerboer, *Gender and Refugee Status* (London: Routledge, 2017).

40 Mattie L. Stevens, "Reorganizing Gender-Specific Persecution: A Proposal to Add Gender as a Sixth Refugee Category," *Cornell Journal of Law and Public Policy*, Vol. 3, No. 1 (1993), p. 179.

41 Andrea Binder, "Gender and the Membership in a Particular Social Group Category of the 1951 Refugee Convention," *Columbia Journal of Gender and Law*, Vol. 10, No. 1 (2001), p. 167.

42 Debora Singer, "Falling at Each Hurdle: Assessing the Credibility of Women's Asylum Claims in Europe," in Efrat Arbel et al., eds., *Gender in Refugee Law: From the Margins to the Centre* (London: Routledge, 2014).

43 Susan Martin, "Climate Change, Migration, and Governance," *Global Governance*, Vol. 16, No. 3 (July–September 2010), pp. 397–414.

44 See chapter 8 in this book.

45 Alice Fothergill, "Gender, Risk, and Disaster," *International Journal of Mass Emergencies and Disasters*, Vol. 14, No. 1 (1996), pp. 33–56. See also chapter 9 in this book.

46 Fothergill, "Gender, Risk, and Disaster."

47 Lori M. Hunter and Emmanuel David, "Climate Change and Migration: Considering the Gender Dimensions," in Etienne Piguet, Paul de Guchteneire and Antoine Pecoud, eds., *Climate Change and Migration* (Paris: UNESCO, November 2009), p. 318.

48 Jane Freedman, *Gendering the International Asylum and Refugee Debate* (Basingstoke: Palgrave Macmillan, 2015), p. 213.

49 Ibid.

50 Nicole Detraz and Leah Windsor, "Evaluating Climate Migration," *International Feminist Journal of Politics*, Vol. 16, No. 1 (January 2014), pp. 127–146.

51 Allsopp, "Aggressor, Victim, Soldier, Dad"; Herz, "'Becoming' a Possible Threat."

52 Annastiina Kallius, Daniel Monterescu and Prem Kumar Rajaram, "Immobilizing Mobility: Border Ethnography, Illiberal Democracy, and the Politics of the 'Refugee Crisis' in Hungary," *American Ethnologist*, Vol. 43, No. 1 (February 2016), pp. 25–37.

53 See UNHCR, *Guidelines on International Protection* (Geneva: UNHCR, April 7, 2006).

54 Audrey Macklin, "Cross-Border Shopping for Ideas: A Critical Review of United States, Canadian, and Australian Approaches to Gender-Related Asylum Claims," *Georgetown Immigration Law Journal*, Vol. 13 (1998), p. 25.

55 Singer, "Falling at Each Hurdle."

56 European Commission (EC), *Policy Plan on Legal Migration* (Brussels: European Union, 2005).

57 Anja K. Franck and Andrea Spehar, *Women's Labour Migration in the Context of Globalisation* (Brussels: WIDE, 2010).

58 Gabriele Abels and Joyce Marie Mushaben, eds., *Gendering the European Union: New Approaches to Old Democratic Deficits* (London: Springer, 2012).

59 EC, *Common European Asylum System* (Brussels: EC, @ ec.europa.eu).

60 Ibid.

61 Ruth Rubio-Marín, *Human Rights and Immigration* (Oxford: Oxford University Press, 2014).

62 EC, *Common European Asylum System*.

63 UNHCR, *Desperate and Dangerous: Report on the Human Rights Situation of Migrants and Refugees in Libya* (Geneva: UNHCR, December 20, 2018), p. 4.

64 Scott Blinder, "Imagined Immigration: The Impact of Different Meanings of 'Immigrants' in Public Opinion and Policy Debates in Britain," *Political Studies*, Vol. 63, No. 1 (March 2015), pp. 80–100.

65 Ilse Lenz and Helen Schwenken, "Feminist and Migrant Networking in a Globalising World Migration, Gender and Globalisation," in Ilse Lenz et al., eds., *Crossing Borders and Shifting Boundaries* (Wiesbaden: Verlag für Sozialwissenschaften, 2002), pp. 147–178.

66 Nadina Christopoulou and Mary Leontsini, "Weaving Solidarity: Migrant Women's Organisations in Athens," *Journal of Intercultural Studies*, Vol. 38, No. 5 (September 3, 2017), pp. 514–529.

67 See London School of Economics and University of Sydney, *WPS National Action Plans* (database @ wpsnaps.org).

68 Jenna L. Hennebry and Allison J. Petrozziello, "Closing the Gap? Gender and the Global Compacts for Migration and Refugees," *International Migration*, Vol. 57, No. 6 (December 2019), pp. 115–138.

7

GENDER, DEVELOPMENT AND SECURITY

Jeni Klugman

This chapter analyzes a range of development challenges – from economic opportunities to education and health to voice and representation – with a gender and security lens. It will present an array of evidence about the gender dimensions of these challenges, the underlying constraints and what works to advance gender equality, development and security.

A multidimensional framework is applied to explore the obstacles, drivers and strategies influencing key development outcomes and gender equality. The dimensions of this analysis include but are not limited to: justice (such as formal laws and informal discrimination), inclusion (economic, social and political) and security (at the household, community and societal levels).[1]

I argue that the challenges underlying gender inequality vary greatly across countries. For example, fragile and conflict-affected states face different challenges in promoting women's security and empowerment than stable democracies. Similarly, while some governments have both the willingness and capacity to advance gender equality, others do not. Finally, a range of stakeholders – including states, inter-governmental organizations, Non-Governmental Organizations (NGOs) and civil society – play critical roles in development, gender and security outcomes.

Evolution of international development discourse

In exploring the layers of gender equality, security and development, it is helpful to understand the evolution of the international community's perspective on women's empowerment over the past 50 years. During this time, the focus has shifted from "Women and Development" to a broader understanding of "Gender and Development."

The Women in Development (WID) approach originated in the 1970s as policy-makers became increasingly aware that "trickle down" development interventions were gender blind, and women often failed to benefit from these programs in the same way as men. The WID approach emphasized the economic inefficiency of women's exclusion from the market sphere, suggesting more growth could be achieved if women had more control over resources.[2] The WID approach thus embodied concerns about both gender equity and economic efficiency.[3]

By the mid-1980s, the WID approach drew criticism for failing to address the underlying structural problems leading to women's discrimination in the first place. It was argued that gender equality could not be achieved solely by seeking to integrate women into the development process; gender relations must also change.[4] The Gender and Development (GAD) approach recognized that a holistic approach to gender relations was needed to empower women in the long term. Under the GAD framework, policies seek to tackle the underlying sources of women's subordination, while considering the power dynamics between women and men.[5] The GAD approach has brought an added focus on eliminating institutional forms of gender discrimination through, for example, strengthening legislation on domestic violence and improving women's land rights,[6] alongside concerns about equity and parity in participation in development programs from education to agriculture and entrepreneurship. For many development partners – multi-lateral, bilateral and Non-Governmental Organizations – GAD is now institutionalized in the notion of gender mainstreaming – the process of ensuring gender implications and norms are central to the planning, implementation and monitoring of programs and projects.

This chapter is organized as follows. First, I outline the importance of gender for development and security by examining the links between gender equality and education, health and economic growth outcomes. Second, using the Women, Peace and Security (WPS) Index, I assess patterns of women's disadvantage worldwide through key indicators related to inclusion, justice and security. Third, I outline the key obstacles to gender equality, such as discriminatory norms and legal barriers. Finally, I assess the policy implications of gender discrimination and develop strategies for advancing equality and security in the development realm.

Why gender is important for development and security

Gender equality is central to the Sustainable Development Goals (SDGs) adopted by 193 governments at the United Nations (UN) in 2015. SDG 5 explicitly aims to eliminate gender inequality in all its forms. Gender equality is central to progress on the Sustainable Development agenda and is vital for sustaining peace. Gender equality has both intrinsic value – as a matter of basic human rights, as enshrined in international law – and instrumental benefits for human development and economic growth.[7] Figure 7.1 illustrates the positive relationship across countries between human development and women's well-being.

Alongside the growing prominence of gender equality in development discussions, the links between gender inequality and conflict have attained renewed importance on the global policy agenda. There is an emerging agenda around SDG 16 that highlights the links among the SDGs and emphasizes the integrated and

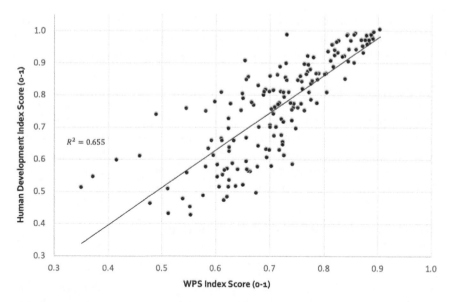

FIGURE 7.1   Gender Equality and Human Development

Source: Author estimates based on UNDP, *Human Development Report 2019* (New York: UNDP, 2019) and GIWPS and PRIO, *WPS Index 2019/20.*

cross-cutting nature of the peace and security agenda.[8] This agenda not only promotes the inclusion, peace and justice themes of the SDGs, but also is directly related to women's empowerment in the home, the community, the economy and political life. Several studies have found that the treatment of women in highly gender-unequal societies is associated with an increased risk of conflict.[9] The new global development goals underline the importance of tackling both gender inequality and reducing violent conflict.

The world, however, remains characterized by major manifestations of gender inequality. Economic, social and political gender gaps around the world remain large, pervasive and persistent. The most glaring manifestations of inequality include:

- Missing women: an estimated 1.4 million girls annually are not being born due to son preference.
- Death in childbirth: an estimated 800 women die in childbirth every day. Ninety-nine percent of these deaths are in developing countries, and most are preventable.
- Access to schooling: an estimated 31 million girls are out of school. Of those girls, half are unlikely to return to a classroom.
- Violence: 700 million women worldwide are subject to violence by their intimate partners.
- Unpaid work: women carry the bulk of unpaid work at home, even when working outside the home.

- Exclusion from power: there are only 22 women chief executive officers (CEOs) in Fortune 500 companies, about four percent of the total. In Australia's ASX200, there are more CEOs named Peter than women CEOs.

The disadvantages and inequalities are typically largest for women who are poor and marginalized in other ways. Gender is part of the broader socio-cultural context. Other important aspects include class, poverty, ethnic group and age. The United Nations Educational, Scientific and Cultural Organization (UNESCO) estimates that, at current rates of progress, all rich girls are expected to be completing secondary school in sub-Saharan Africa by 2051 (and rich boys by 2041), but the poorest girls will not have full access until well into the next century: 2111.[10]

The track record: patterns of disadvantage around the world

In assessing patterns of women's disadvantage around the world, it is important to note the challenges and limitations of gender data and statistics. The SDGs assert that "comprehensive, valid, unbiased gender data allows policymakers to better understand the needs and aspirations of women and girls" and to develop effective policies accordingly. Quality gender data strengthens evidence-based decisionmaking and improves transparency and accountability.[11]

The data collected on women's rights and gender equality has historically been limited, likely reflecting prevailing norms about government priorities.[12] However, it is now accepted that gender-sensitive data is needed on issues including poverty, education, health, violence, decisionmaking power and women's economic opportunities.[13] Unfortunately, data limitations persist – including a lack of sufficient resources and underdeveloped statistical units in line ministries.[14] Only 13 percent of the world's countries have a dedicated budget for collecting and analyzing gender statistics, and data is available for less than one-quarter of key gender indicators across the SDGs.[15]

Despite these data challenges, it is possible to construct a global picture of women's disadvantage. The WPS Index brings together the many dimensions of women's inclusion, justice and security into a single number and ranking.[16] It represents a major innovation in assessment of women's well-being by bringing achievements in, for example, schooling and access to cell phones together with data on violence against women.

The WPS Index aggregates three broad dimensions of well-being:

- *Inclusion* has multiple aspects – economic, social and political – with indicators ranging from employment and financial inclusion to cell-phone access and parliamentary representation.
- *Justice* is captured in both formal laws (drawing on the World Bank's Women, Business and the Law database) and informal discrimination (as reflected in lack of acceptance of women working and son bias).[17]
- *Security* is measured at the family, community and society levels.

Intimate partner violence is the most common form of violence experienced by women. Globally, 13 percent of women are subjected to intimate partner violence each year, with substantial variation across countries. Reported current rates of violence range as high as 47 percent in South Sudan and as low as 1 percent in Switzerland, Singapore, Georgia, and Canada. Outside the home, safety in the community is assessed by women's responses to the Gallup World Poll question, "Do you feel safe walking in your neighborhood at night?"

The measure of organized violence, which reflects general insecurity in society, relies on the widely-used Uppsala Conflict Data Program measure.[18] This measure is not perfect – deaths are not gender disaggregated, and the measure does not capture the broader negative repercussions of conflict, which differ by sex. It also does not account for sexual and gender-based violence.

WPS Index scores have been calculated for 167 countries, covering more than 98 percent of the world's population, using transparent and reliable data that is publicly available.

Figure 7.2 shows the top and bottom dozen countries on the WPS rankings. Norway currently leads the world rankings, and Yemen ranks in last place. The top dozen countries are experiencing hardly any conflict, while the bottom dozen countries are experiencing very high levels of armed conflicts. Looking behind these aggregate results reveals extensive unevenness in performance – only about 30 countries score in the top third for all three dimensions. This underlines the universality of the gender and security agenda.

While there are clear regional patterns in performance, there are also major differences within each region, which suggests that reaching the standards of neighbors should be feasible. There are countries in all regions that outperform the global average of .703, including Nepal in South Asia; Mauritius, Namibia, Rwanda, South Africa, Zimbabwe, Ghana and Tanzania in sub-Saharan Africa; and Jamaica, Costa Rica, Argentina, Chile and Peru in Latin America and the Caribbean.

However, it is striking that in many countries – even those that have made partial progress – women face serious justice and security constraints. In Afghanistan and Saudi Arabia, for example, there exists a raft of legal constraints and prejudices against women in paid work, restricting the expansion of their opportunities.

Echoing what the UNDP's Human Development Report has underlined for many years, money matters, but it is not the whole story.[19] Many countries do far better on the WPS Index – or far worse – than their per-capita income rank. Saudi Arabia plummets 108 places on the WPS Index relative to its income ranking; Kuwait drops 88 places and Iran drops 61 places, as shown in Figure 7.3.

While the WPS Index provides a valuable overview and enables useful comparisons, it is a snapshot in time. The obstacles to gender equality have deep roots.

Obstacles to progress

Gender inequality is multidimensional, and the obstacles vary across dimensions. The constraints on women vary enormously across individuals and communities, and they are shaped by overlapping disadvantages such as poverty, location and

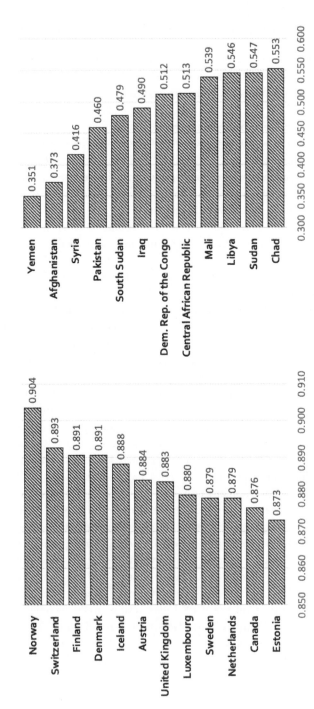

FIGURE 7.2 The Best and Worst Performers on the WPS Index

Source: GIWPS and PRIO, WPS Index 2019/20.

GDP rank
(GDP per capita 2017 PPP $)

Index rank

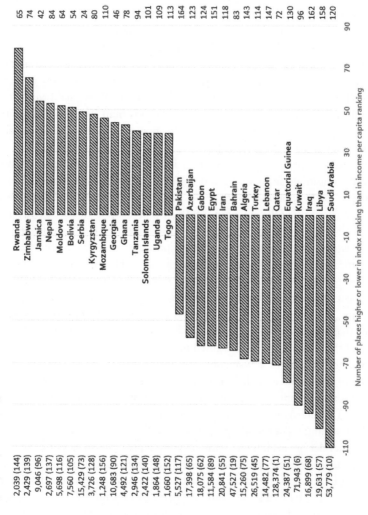

Number of places higher or lower in index ranking than in income per capita ranking

FIGURE 7.3 Gender Equality and GDP

Source: GIWPS and PRIO, *WPS Index 2019/20.*

ethnicity. For example, lack of access to affordable sexual and reproductive health services may undermine women's health outcomes in some places, whereas legal restrictions on women's pursuit of business opportunities may be limiting elsewhere.

At the same time, it is true that several overarching constraints face many women in all regions and at all development levels, such as: adverse social norms, restrictive and discriminatory laws, a lack of legal protections and unpaid household work and care.

Gender norms shape gender inequality in many ways. Violence against women may be accepted as normal, as in Niger, where more than seven out of ten women condone violence for trivial reasons such as burning dinner.[20] Society may expect that women do care work for free and may assess their paid work, such as teaching young children and offering personal care, as low skill and low value. Some of the most restrictive norms are those that require a woman to spend most of her life within her home. In many communities in South Asia and West Asia, a woman seen in public brings shame to the family. Adverse norms limit women's expectations about whether they should work outside the home and girls' aspirations about which occupations they should pursue.

Discriminatory norms vary across regions and even more widely across countries. The Social Institutions and Gender Index (SIGI), estimated and published by the Organization for Economic Co-operation and Development (OECD), provides a useful global overview of the extent of gender discrimination.[21] It covers five dimensions of discriminatory social institutions – discriminatory family code, restricted physical integrity, son bias, restricted resources and assets and restricted civil liberties – and quantifies such variables as unequal inheritance rights, early marriage, violence against women and unequal land and property rights across 180 countries. Figure 7.4 shows the patterns across countries, where higher values on the index are worse.

Changing discriminatory norms is central to addressing inequality, especially in countries that stand out for the extent of discrimination – as in Yemen, Pakistan, Guinea and the Philippines – highlighted in Figure 7.4.

For young women in low-income countries, social norms and household responsibilities, combined with lack of access to education and safety concerns, cause isolation and limit opportunities to develop aspirations, skills, networks and confidence. The alternative to economic advancement – early family formation – reduces opportunities later in life, perpetuating the cycle of limited choice.

Adverse gender norms interact with laws and regulations in ways that constrain women's independence. For example, norms are reflected in requirements that husbands cosign banking applications for their wives in some countries, limiting women's access to financial services and property ownership.

In many countries, discrimination under the formal legal system underpins gender inequality. The World Bank has documented the extent of discrimination in property, contract, inheritance and related legal domains in its biannual *Women, Business, and the Law* report, which tracks how women and men are treated differently under the law.

Empirical analysis has explored how legal discrimination limits women's economic opportunities.[22] In countries where husbands legally control marital property, women are less likely to have an account at a financial institution, and thus are even less likely to start a business due to lack of collateral and finance.[23] When men

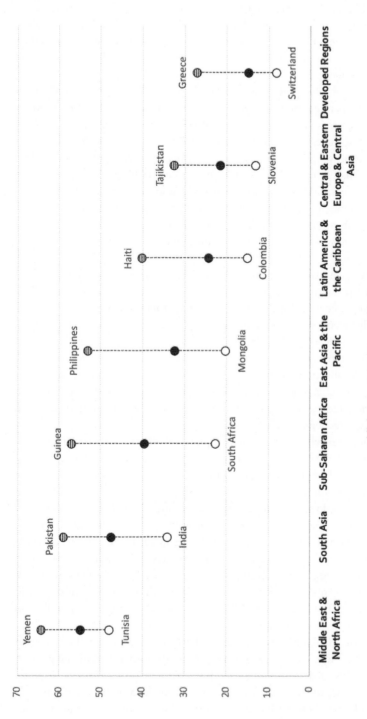

FIGURE 7.4 Gender Discrimination by Region

Source: Author estimates based on OECD, Social Institutions and Gender Index (SIGI), *Global Report: Transforming Challenges into Opportunities* (Paris: OECD, 2019).

and women have equal inheritance rights, women are more likely to have official bank accounts and credit.[24] Recent International Monetary Fund (IMF) analysis shows that lower gender equality in the law is associated with fewer girls attending secondary school relative to boys, fewer women working or running businesses and a wider gender wage gap.[25]

Legal barriers are also present in the health sphere. These restrictions – such as laws requiring parental notification of a minor's intended abortion or allowing husbands or partners to veto women's use of contraception – can delay or block access to essential maternal health services.[26] In 2013, two out of three countries permitted abortion when the physical or mental health of the mother was endangered, and only half in cases of rape, incest or fetal impairment. Legal grounds for abortion have expanded but remain much more restrictive in developing countries.[27] Governments in developing regions are more than four times as likely to have restrictive abortion policies: only one-fifth of developing countries permit abortion for economic or social reasons or on request, compared to four-fifths of industrial countries.

Legal reforms can play an important role in improving reproductive health outcomes, particularly with respect to access to abortion services. Nearly 22 million unsafe abortions occurred globally in 2008, many of them in developing countries. Over half of all abortions in developing countries are unsafe, compared with just six percent of those in developed countries.[28]

While highly restrictive abortion laws do not tend to lower abortion rates, they do typically make abortion unsafe. The 82 countries with the most restrictive abortion legislation are also those with the highest incidence of unsafe abortions and rates of abortion mortality.[29] By contrast, where abortion is permitted on broad legal grounds, it is generally safer.[30]

Even in countries where women have equal legal rights, weak implementation by the authorities, low awareness among women and constraints on women's access to legal resources all limit enforcement of existing laws and undermine effective legal protection for women.[31]

Globally, women do about three times as much unpaid work as men, and spend about half as much time in paid work.[32] At all development levels, and to varying degrees, women face challenges and limited choices in balancing unpaid care work, paid economic opportunities, education, leisure and rest.[33] Unpaid care constraints are especially severe for women from poor households who cannot afford to purchase child care to substitute for their unpaid labor. In a recent Latin American study, more than half of women age 20 to 24 said that their unpaid responsibilities at home were the main reason they could not look for paid work.[34]

Looking ahead, changing demographics indicate that eldercare will loom larger as societies age and fertility rates decline in many developed and developing countries.[35] Most countries do not provide any long-term support for eldercare, partly because of the failure to recognize the value of unpaid eldercare provided primarily by female family members.[36] Estimates from the United States, for example, indicate that daughters spend more than twice the number of hours that sons spend caring for elderly parents. A survey in China found that 95 percent of women have responsibilities for elderly relatives.[37]

The good news is that norms and laws are not fixed. Gender attributes, opportunities and relationships are socially constructed and are learned through socialization. Also, the pace of legal reform is accelerating. Norms and laws are changeable in ways that advance gender equality and security.

Drivers of change and strategies for progress

It is increasingly recognized that failures to address gender inequality will inhibit progress across all major international development goals and threaten security. The multidimensional and persistent nature of the challenge means that there is no single or easy way to effectively close gender gaps and that action needs to be undertaken on multiple fronts. Making progress involves governments at all levels working together with corporate actors and major influencers.

Given the breadth of the challenges and the diversity of circumstances, it is unwise to attempt to prescribe a grand global strategy. However, the evidence does reveal a range of development policy areas where concerted efforts have been made to close gender gaps and reduce discrimination against women. The focus here is limited to selected entry points, demonstrating how well-designed actions can make a difference. While governments play a central role, a range of actors need to participate in advancing this agenda, with women's groups playing an important role.

Legal reforms to address gender inequality

There is a range of fronts where legal reforms are needed, from ensuring protection against violence to eliminating discrimination that is enshrined in law. There are several promising avenues for reform explored here that appear to especially matter for women's well-being, though broader sets of legislative reforms are also important.

The SDGs include a specific target "focused on eliminating all forms of violence against women and girls."[38] A global review found that there has been major progress in establishing – in both international and national law – the rights of women to live free from violence; progress on both fronts was especially rapid in the 2010s.[39] Legislation that prohibits violence against women can play an important symbolic role by indicating that such behavior is socially unacceptable, and the associated sanctions may serve a deterrence function. Either or both of these levers may work in practice to reduce the incidence of violence. In addition, legislation can be responsive to victims by providing social protection and access to support services.

The pace of legislative reform across countries has been rapid since 1976, when only one country prohibited marital rape. Civil society mobilization and grassroots women's movements have been active in this sphere. The World Bank reports that this pace has accelerated: globally, the share of countries with laws on domestic violence rose from 71 to 76 percent between 2013 and 2017, with reforms in Algeria, Belarus, China, Kenya, Latvia, Lebanon, the Netherlands and Saudi Arabia.[40]

Can laws against domestic violence be expected to reduce the risk of violence in the home? Simply comparing countries with and without domestic violence laws in place reveals that average current rates of violence are indeed lower in countries with legislation prohibiting violence – ten versus 17 percent. At the same time, there is a large range in the rates of violence within both sets of countries. And the causality may run in the direction of countries with lower acceptability of violence being more likely to enact prohibitions against violence.

Li Li and I provide new insights about the correlates of rates of intimate partner violence against women and the potential role of laws to reduce the practice: systematic regression analysis for a diverse sample of 124 countries suggests that laws – more specifically, laws against violence – do matter.[41] On average, the existence of such legislation is associated with more than five percent less physical and/or sexual intimate partner violence.

Abortion policy liberalization – coupled with the implementation of safe abortion services and other reproductive health interventions – can lead to dramatic declines in abortion-related mortality, as the experiences of several countries show. In Romania, following policy reform in 1989, the abortion-related mortality ratio dropped from 148 deaths per 100,000 live births in 1989 to five deaths per 100,000 in 2006. In South Africa, the annual number of abortion-related deaths fell by 91 percent between 1994 and 2001, following the liberalization of the abortion law in 1996.[42]

Changing discriminatory property laws can also help to reduce domestic violence and address gender inequality. In India, land ownership reduces women's experience of domestic violence. Reforms to India's inheritance laws gave women greater economic power and resulted in delays in marriage for girls, an 11 to 25 percent increase in years of schooling and lower dowry payments.[43]

Changing norms

Changing norms requires understanding the constraints, identifying entry points for reform and, often, deliberately engaging men and boys in efforts for change.

The good news is that concerted efforts can change norms. Accumulating evidence suggests that these efforts are usually most successful when they work in multiple ways on different levels, rather than as simple, stand-alone interventions. The scope can cover schools, communities, workplaces, civil society and the media. Some of the most effective strategies for positive norm change involve working with children and adolescents, both boys and girls. This can take place in schools, through skill-based interventions, girls' clubs and other dedicated safe spaces, and community programs.

Schools are communities where respect and equality can be modeled, which helps shape positive attitudes and behaviors at an early stage and affect lifetime attitudes. An evaluation of the Gender Equity Movement in Schools program shows the potential for change. The program aims to help boys and girls adopt more gender-equitable norms through role-playing games, interactive extracurricular activities and lessons exploring topics around gender-based violence, marriage and sharing of household tasks. After running for two years in Mumbai, "participating students were more likely to support higher education for girls, openly express opposition to gender-based violence, and champion delaying marriage."[44]

Various types of programs fall under the heading of "girls' clubs," and these are becoming increasingly popular. The results are generally encouraging. These programs typically provide life skills and vocational skills (such financial literacy, livelihood skills and employment assistance) and may be based in formal centers or in the community.

A female empowerment program run by BRAC in Uganda (providing teenage girls with vocational training and information on sex and marriage) led to a 26 percent decline in teenage pregnancy rates, a 58 percent drop in early entry into marriage or cohabitation, and a 50 percent decrease in the share of girls reporting sex against their will – alongside substantial increases in income-generating activities.[45]

In Ethiopia and Kenya, a Youth-to-Youth club initiative aimed at building life skills and self-esteem helped female youth gain income-earning opportunities and increased men's acceptance of women's leadership.[46]

Community-based life skills programs run by the Population Council in Ethiopia and Iraq have reported positive results. In Ethiopia, the measured outcomes included delayed marriage, improved enrollment in school and increased use of family planning methods, especially among early adolescents.[47]

The World Bank has conducted several evaluations of programs to empower adolescent girls. The most effective programs were found to have the following characteristics:[48]

- Locally appropriate and deliberate recruitment strategies to reach marginalized girls
- Appropriate support and structures, including timing of training, transport and childcare
- Incentives for providers so they have a vested interest in success
- Links to the local labor market and economic opportunities

Overall, the most promising programs take place in girl-friendly settings and provide a combination of information about sexual and reproductive health and complementary training and assets. However, because programs usually combine skills training, mentoring, social support and other features, it is hard to know exactly which components contributed the most to successful outcomes and for whom. More research is needed to identify the most effective components of these programs and assess longer-term impacts.[49]

Small-group workshops and training can also engage men and change gender stereotypes and norms at a community level. A growing array of programs is working with men to promote more gender-equitable norms. Almost fifteen years ago, Promundo launched Program H, aimed at encouraging critical reflection of rigid norms related to manhood, and it has since been expanded to countries around the world. The MenCare campaign – designed for health workers, social activists, Non-Governmental Organizations, educators and other individuals and institutions – uses "men as caregivers" as a starting point to improve family well-being and gender equality. It engages men in active fatherhood from the start of pregnancies to children's early years. In Nicaragua, participating men reported greater sharing of household duties, dedicating more time to their children and partners and teaching their children values of respect and equality.[50] Similar results were reported in preliminary findings from randomized control trials in Rwanda, along with lower violence against children.

More programs are working with boys to change social norms, including the Rwanda Men's Resource Centre's Boys4Change club, the Equal Community Foundation in India and the Brave Men project in Bangladesh. These types of programs have been shown to improve men's and boys' attitudes toward gender equality.[51]

Community dialogue and mobilization engaging women and men can work to change norms.[52] Evidence is accumulating on how groups of people can be supported to prevent gender-based violence. These programs include Oxfam's We Can campaign across South Asia, Men's Action to Stop Violence Against Women in India, and Raising Voices' SASA! in Uganda.[53] SASA! is a community mobilization program that aims to prevent violence against women by changing community norms and behaviors that result in gender inequality, violence and increased HIV vulnerability for women. The program promotes critical discussions around power dynamics and mobilizes communities around norm, attitude and behavior change specifically regarding intimate partner violence. A randomized control trial of the SASA! intervention in Uganda found that the community mobilization component is key in preventing violence against women.[54]

Although popular images often reinforce negative stereotypes, television and radio can be allies in bringing about change by exposing people to different views, creating counter-narratives and challenging commonly held norms about what is acceptable and typical. One evaluation found that increased access to cable television in Indian villages (without any special programming) increased acceptance of women working outside the home and reduced tolerance for domestic violence. Launched in 1994 in South Africa, the popular *Soul City* television drama communicates health and development messages. It models healthy behavior through characters and scenarios with which local audiences can identify. It is supported by radio, print and advocacy campaigns. The show and the campaigns have been shown to generate positive changes in perceptions and behavior by men, particularly with respect to violence against women.[55]

Education for girls

Although there has been important progress on the education front, rates of girls' secondary enrollment are below 65 percent in low- and middle-income countries, and still below half in Sub-Saharan Africa.[56]

Education inequality is an important dimension of overall gender gaps, with repercussions for a whole range of outcomes, from economic opportunities to leadership. Increasing access to schooling is especially important where enrollment and completion remain far from universal and gender gaps are large. At the primary level, two-thirds of countries have achieved gender parity, but only one-fifth of low-income countries have. Of the eighteen countries with fewer than ninety girls for every one hundred boys enrolled, thirteen are in sub-Saharan Africa. Only half of all countries – and only ten percent of low-income countries – have achieved gender parity at lower secondary level.[57]

Evidence is accumulating about what works for girls' education. On the demand side, reducing costs – eliminating fees and subsidizing the costs of uniforms and textbooks – is important.[58] Increasing job opportunities – or awareness of job opportunities – for women can also help increase the demand for education. In India, an increase in call center jobs for women led to more young women enrolling in computer and English language courses. In areas with these jobs, girls ages 6 to 17 were 5 percent more likely to be enrolled in school.[59]

Increasing the supply of or access to quality education is also important. As Sarah Baird and Berk Özler highlight in their review, building "girl-friendly schools" is a highly effective way to increase access to schooling, whether by building schools within villages, building girls' secondary schools, building schools with girl-friendly amenities or providing safe transportation for girls.[60] In Afghanistan, reducing the average distance from home to school from 3 miles to less than half a mile increased enrollment for both boys and girls and improved girls' test scores.[61] A review of cash transfer programs (focusing on five- to 22-year-olds) indicates that cash transfers, even if not specifically targeted to girls, improve girls' school enrollment and attendance.[62]

Supporting leadership

Among the multitude of gender inequalities that persist are gaps in leadership, as revealed by observed rates of representation and leadership of women at all levels of government and in the private sector. This has also been a recurrent finding in studies about women's representation in peace negotiations.

Engaging adolescent girls in leadership activities is an important foundation for closing gender gaps in political representation and leadership. Studies have found that one of the characteristics of women leaders today is that they usually started early, participating in educational and leadership activities as girls.[63] External programs and positive role models, both in and out of school, can help level the playing field by building girls' self-esteem, skills and networks. Because family attitudes and behavior have a strong influence on girls' success, engaging families is also essential.[64]

An Overseas Development Institute review of the evidence highlights that mentorships, networks, experiential learning opportunities, smart deployment of technology and support from boys and men can all help build girls' and women's leadership skills and capabilities.[65] These experiences can expand girls' choices and their aspirations for the future. When a conditional cash transfer program in

Nicaragua added a component helping girls communicate with successful and motivated nearby leaders, the girls subsequently had higher aspirations and higher incomes.[66]

Education is critical. The evidence shows that women leaders are educated, particularly so beyond the community level. Women need education to access power.

Role models also play an important role. An influential study on the effect of female political leadership in India found that the presence of women on village councils, enabled by affirmative action, had a positive influence on girls' career aspirations and educational attainment.[67] This randomized experiment found that exposure to female leaders eliminated the gender gap in education and reduced the gender gap in aspirations by 20 percent in parents and 32 percent in adolescents.

Collective action

Feminist political activists and women's rights organizations have been working for decades to change discriminatory behavior and attitudes, while also mobilizing for legal and policy reform to address inequality. There are numerous examples of success, including the Self -Employed Women's Association in India, which has effectively lobbied for changes in laws and practices to enable poor women to more effectively pursue a range of livelihoods.

New technology and social media can support feminist collective action by facilitating communication between individuals and groups. Many of these initiatives appear promising. Social media and networking are the basis for campaigns such as Hollaback! (an international movement launched in 2005 to end harassment, spur public conversation and develop strategies for equal access to public spaces) and Stop Street Harassment (a nonprofit organization launched in 2012 that documents and addresses gender-based street harassment globally).[68]

Collective voice and action are critical not only to argue for reform, but also to hold decisionmakers accountable. This is apparent from the local to national level, where governments are being held to account for their international commitments. Three examples illustrate this phenomenon:

- In Nepal, women members of community committees were able to influence decisions affecting women's lives − for example, by lobbying for pumps to operate around mealtimes when water is most needed and for better access to maternal health care.[69]
- A review of the effectiveness of the Solidarity for African Women's Rights (SOAWR) coalition's campaign to compel African states to ratify and implement the Protocol to the African Charter on Human and Peoples' Rights on the Rights of Women in Africa found it to have been a key driving force behind Kenyan ratification.[70]
- In Uganda, members of SOAWR persuaded the two main political parties to address key articles of the protocol on reproductive health rights in their campaign manifestos.[71]

Conclusion

This chapter has framed a range of development challenges – from economic opportunities, to education and health, to voice and representation – with a gender and security lens. I analyzed the multidimensional obstacles to progress and the key drivers of progress in development outcomes and gender equality. This, in turn, suggests the most promising strategies for continued progress in the future.

The nature of constraints on women varies enormously across individuals and communities and is shaped by overlapping disadvantages such as poverty, location and ethnicity. At the same time, several overarching constraints that face many women in all regions and at all development levels have emerged, namely, adverse social norms, restrictive and discriminatory laws and a lack of legal protections and unpaid household work and care.

The chapter highlighted what works to close gaps and advance gender equality, development and security and illustrated the roles of a range of stakeholder – including states, inter-governmental organizations, NGOs and civil society – in advancing development, gender and security outcomes.

The author is grateful to Elena Ortiz and Haiwen Zou for research support.

Notes

1 Georgetown Institute for Women, Peace and Security (GIWPS) and Peace Research Institute Oslo (PRIO), *Women, Peace and Security Index, 2019–20* (Washington, DC: GIWPS and PRIO, 2019).

2 Sarah Bradshaw, *Women's Role in Economic Development: Overcoming the Constraints. Background Paper for the High-Level Panel of Eminent Persons on the Post-2015 Development Agenda* (London: Sustainable Development Solutions Network, 2013).

3 Shahrashoub Razavi and Carol Miller, *From WID to GAD: Conceptual Shifts in the Women and Development Discourse* (Geneva: UN Research Institute for Social Development, 1995).

4 Joanna Kerr, *From "WID" to "GAD" to Women's Rights: The First 20 Years of AWID* (Toronto: Association for Women's Rights in Development, 2002).

5 Ibid.

6 Bradshaw, *Women's Role in Economic Development.*

7 UN Secretary-General's High-Level Panel on Women's Economic Empowerment, *Leave No One Behind: A Call to Action for Gender Equality and Women's Economic Empowerment* (New York: United Nations, 2016); McKinsey Global Institute, *The Power of Parity: Advancing Women's Equality in the United States* (New York: McKinsey & Company, 2016).

8 Pathfinders for Peaceful, Just and Inclusive Societies, *Roadmap for Peaceful, Just and Inclusive Societies* (New York: Center on International Cooperation, 2017).

9 See Mary Caprioli, "Gendered Conflict," *Journal of Peace Research*, Vol. 37, No. 1 (January 2000), pp. 51–68; Mary Caprioli, "Primed for Violence: The Role of Gender Inequality in Predicting Internal Conflict," *International Studies Quarterly*, Vol. 49, No. 2 (June 2005), pp. 161–178; Mary Caprioli and Mark A. Boyer, "Gender, Violence, and International Crisis," *Journal of Conflict Resolution*, Vol. 45, No. 4 (August 2001), pp. 503–518; Theodora-Ismene Gizelis, "Gender Empowerment and United Nations Peacebuilding," *Journal of Peace Research*, Vol. 46, No. 4 (June 2009), pp. 505–523; Theodora-Ismene Gizelis, "A Country of Their Own: Women and Peacebuilding," *Conflict Management and Peace Science*, Vol. 28, No. 5 (November 2011), pp. 522–542; Valerie M. Hudson et al.,

"The Heart of the Matter: The Security of Women and the Security of States," *International Security*, Vol. 33, No. 3 (Winter 2008/2009), pp. 7–45; Erik Melander, "Gender Equality and Intrastate Armed Conflict," *International Studies Quarterly*, Vol. 49, No. 4 (December 2005), pp. 695–714.

10 UNESCO, *Education for All Global Monitoring Report 2013/14* (Paris: UNESCO, 2014).

11 Data2x.org, *Gender Data and the Sustainable Development Goals: Political Action Toward 2030* (Washington, DC: Data2x.org, 2017).

12 Organization for Economic Co-operation and Development (OECD) Development Centre, *Measuring Gender Equality – Taking Stock and Looking Forward* (Issy-les-Moulineaux, France: OECD Development Centre, 2007).

13 World Bank, *Developing Gender Statistics a Practical Tool: Module 1 – Gender Statistics and Gender Analysis* (Washington, DC: World Bank, 2010).

14 OECD Development Centre, *Improving Gender Sensitive Data Collection and Quality in Africa: Challenges and Opportunities* (Issy-les-Moulineaux, France: OECD Development Centre, 2007).

15 Data2x.org, *Gender Data.*

16 GIWPS and PRIO, *Women, Peace and Security Index, 2019–20.*

17 World Bank, *Women, Business and the Law* (@ wbl.worldbank.org).

18 Uppsala University, *Uppsala Conflict Data Program* (@ ucdp.uu.se).

19 UNDP, *Human Development Report 2019* (New York: UNDP, 2019).

20 Jeni Klugman et al., *Voice and Agency: Empowering Women and Girls for Shared Prosperity* (Washington, DC: World Bank, 2014).

21 OECD Development Centre, *Social Institutions and Gender Index* (@ genderindex.org).

22 Christian Gonzales et al., *Fair Play: More Equal Laws Boost Female Labor Force Participation*, Staff Discussion Note (Washington, DC: International Monetary Fund, 2015); Mary Hallward-Driemeier, Tazeen Hasan and Anca Bogdana Rusu, *Women's Legal Rights Over 50 Years: What Is the Impact of Reform?* Policy Research Working Paper No. 6617 (Washington, DC: World Bank, 2013).

23 See World Bank, *Women Business and the Law 2016: Getting to Equal* (Washington, DC: World Bank, 2016).

24 Asli Demirguc-Kunt et al., *The Global Findex Database 2014: Measuring Financial Inclusion Around the World*, Policy Research Working Paper No. 7255 (Washington, DC: World Bank, 2015).

25 Ibid.

26 Rodolfo Carvalho Pacagnella et al., "The Role of Delays in Severe Maternal Morbidity and Mortality: Expanding the Conceptual Framework," *Reproductive Health Matters*, Vol. 20, No. 39 (July 2012), pp. 155–163.

27 Department of Economic and Social Affairs, United Nations, *Abortion Policies and Reproductive Health Around the World* (New York: United Nations, 2014).

28 Department of Reproductive Health and Research, World Health Organization (WHO), *Unsafe Abortion: Global and Regional Estimates of the Incidence of Unsafe Abortion and Associated Mortality in 2008*, 6th ed. (Geneva: WHO, 2011).

29 Marge Berer, "National Laws and Unsafe Abortion: The Parameters of Change," *Reproductive Health Matters*, Vol. 12, No. Supplement 24 (November 2004), pp. 1–8.

30 Gilda Sedgh et al., "Induced Abortion: Incidence and Trends Worldwide from 1995 to 2008," *The Lancet*, Vol. 379, No. 9816 (February 2012), pp. 625–632.

31 Jeni Klugman and Sarah Twigg, *Gender at Work in Africa: Legal Constraints and Opportunities to Reform*, Working Paper No. 3 (Oxford: Oxford Human Rights Hub, 2015).

32 See UNDP, *Human Development Report 2015* (New York: UNDP, 2015), p. 118.

33 McKinsey Global Institute, *The Power of Parity.*

34 Rania Antonopoulos, *The Unpaid Care Work-Paid Work Connection*, Working Paper No. 541 (Annandale-on-Hudson, NY: Levy Economics Institute, 2008).

35 WHO, *World Report on Ageing and Health* (Geneva: WHO, 2015).

36 Xenia Scheil-Adlung, *Long-Term Care Protection for Older Persons: A Review of Coverage Deficits in 46 Countries*, Working Paper No. 50 (Geneva: International Labour Organization, 2015).

37 Rutil Levtov, *Men, Gender, and Inequality in Unpaid Care*, Background Paper for the UN Secretary-General's High-Level Panel on Women's Economic Empowerment (New York: United Nations, 2016); Sylvia Ann Hewlett, "Elderly Care, Child Care, and the Struggle of Chinese Women," *Harvard Business Review* (April 8, 2011).

38 United Nations, *Sustainable Development Goal 5: Achieve Gender Equality and Empower All Women and Girls* (New York, NY: United Nations, 2015).

39 Rangita de Silva de Alwis and Jeni Klugman, "Freedom from Violence and the Law: A Global Perspective in Light of Chinese Domestic Violence Law," *University of Pennsylvania Journal of International Law*, Vol. 37, No. 1 (2015), pp. 1–54.

40 Paula Tavares and Quentin Wodon, *Ending Violence Against Women and Girls: Global and Regional Trends in Women's Legal Protection Against Domestic Violence and Sexual Harassment* (Washington, DC: World Bank, 2018).

41 Jeni Klugman and Li Li, *Combatting Intimate Partner Violence: Do Laws Have a Role?* Unpublished Manuscript (2019).

42 Janie Benson, Kathryn Andersen and Ghazaleh Samandari, "Reductions in Abortion-Related Mortality Following Policy Reform: Evidence from Romania, South Africa and Bangladesh," *Reproductive Health*, Vol. 8, No. 39 (2011); Rachel Jewkes et al., "The Impact of Age on the Epidemiology of Incomplete Abortions in South Africa After Legislative Change," *BJOG*, Vol. 112, No. 3 (March 2005), pp. 355–359.

43 Pradeep Panda and Bina Agarwal, "Marital Violence, Human Development and Women's Property Status in India," *World Development*, Vol. 33, No. 5 (May 2005), pp. 823–850; Sanchari Roy, *Empowering Women: Inheritance Rights and Female Education in India*, Working Paper No. 46 (Coventry, UK: Centre for Competitive Advantage in the Global Economy and Department of Economics, University of Warwick, 2011).

44 International Center for Research on Women (ICRW), CORO and Tata Institute for Social Sciences, *Building Support for Gender Equality Among Young Adolescents in School: Findings from Mumbai, India* (Washington, DC: ICRW, 2011).

45 Oriana Bandiera et al., *Women's Empowerment in Action: Evidence from a Randomized Control Trial in Africa* (Washington, DC: World Bank, 2017).

46 Siegrid Tautz, *Youth to Youth Initiative: Assessment of Results in Ethiopia and Kenya* (Hannover, Germany: Deutsche Stiftung Weltbevoelkerung, 2011).

47 Annabel S. Erulkar and Eunice Muthengi, "Evaluation of Berhane Hewan: A Program to Delay Child Marriage in Rural Ethiopia," *International Perspectives on Sexual and Reproductive Health*, Vol. 35, No. 1 (March 2009).

48 Kelly Ann Cassaday et al., *The Spirit of Boldness: Lessons from the World Bank's Adolescent Girls Initiative* (Washington, DC: World Bank, 2015); Adolescent Girls Initiative, *Life Skills: What Are They, Why Do They Matter, and How Are They Taught?* (Washington, DC: World Bank, 2013).

49 Sarah Baird and Berk Özler, *Sustained Effects on Economic Empowerment of Interventions for Adolescent Girls: Existing Evidence and Knowledge Gaps* (Washington, DC: Center for Global Development, November 2016).

50 ECPAT Guatemala, Puntos de Encuentro, Red de Masculinidad por la Igualdad de Género and Promundo-US, *MenCare in the Public Health Sector in Central America* (Washington, DC: Promundo-US, 2015).

51 Julie Pulerwitz et al., *Promoting More Gender-Equitable Norms and Behaviors Among Young Men as an HIV/AIDS Prevention Strategy* (Washington, DC: Population Council, 2006); Gary Barker et al., *The Individual and the Political: Promundo's Evolving Approaches in Engaging Young Men in Transforming Masculinities*, Paper Presented at "Politicising Masculinities: Beyond the Personal" (Dakar, Senegal, October 15–18, 2007).

52 Rachel Marcus and Ella Page, *Changing Discriminatory Norms Affecting Adolescent Girls Through Communication Activities: A Review of Evidence* (London: Overseas Development Institute, 2014).

53 Emma Fulu, Alice Kerr-Wilson and James Lang, *What Works to Prevent Violence Against Women and Girls? Evidence Review of Interventions to Prevent Violence Against Women and Girls* (Pretoria: Medical Research Council, 2014).

54 Tanya Abramsky et al., "Findings from the SASA! Study: A Cluster Randomized Controlled Trial to Assess the Impact of a Community Mobilization Intervention to Prevent Violence Against Women and Reduce HIV Risk in Kampala, Uganda," *BMC Medicine*, Vol. 12, No. 122 (July 2014).

55 Soul City, *Soul City 4: Theory and Impact (Synopsis)* (Johannesburg: Soul City Institute for Health and Development Communication, 2001).

56 World Bank, *World Development Report 2018* (Washington, DC: World Bank, 2018).

57 UNESCO and United Nations Girls' Education Initiative, *Gender and EFA 2000–2015: Achievements and Challenges* (Paris: UNESCO, 2015).

58 See Katharine M. Conn, *Identifying Effective Education Interventions in Sub-Saharan Africa: A Meta-Analysis of Rigorous Impact Evaluations*, Ph.D. Dissertation (Columbia University Teacher's College, 2014); Alejandro J. Ganimian and Richard J. Murnane, *Improving Educational Outcomes in Developing Countries: Lessons from Rigorous Impact Evaluations*, Working Paper No. 20284 (Cambridge, MA: National Bureau of Economic Research, 2014); Elaine Unterhalter et al., *Interventions to Enhance Girls' Education and Gender Equality* (London: Department for International Development, 2014).

59 Robert Jensen, "Do Labor Market Opportunities Affect Young Women's Work and Family Decisions? Experimental Evidence from India," *The Quarterly Journal of Economics*, Vol. 127, No. 2 (2012), pp. 753–792.

60 Baird and Özler, *Sustained Effects on Economic Empowerment of Interventions for Adolescent Girls*.

61 Dana Burde and Leigh Linden, *The Effect of Village-Based Schools: Evidence from a Randomized Controlled Trial in Afghanistan*, Working Paper No. 18039 (Cambridge, MA: National Bureau of Economic Research, May 2012).

62 Sarah Baird, Craig McIntosh and Berk Özler, *When the Money Runs Out: Do Cash Transfers Have Sustained Effects on Human Capital Accumulation?* Policy Research Working Paper No. 7901 (Washington, DC: World Bank, 2016).

63 Tam O'Neil, Georgia Plank and Pilar Domingo, *Support to Women and Girls' Leadership: A Rapid Review of the Evidence* (London: Overseas Development Institute, 2015).

64 Duncan Green, *What Kinds of Women Become Leaders, and How Can We Support Them?* (Oxford: Oxfam, May 28, 2015).

65 O'Neil, Plank and Domingo, *Support to Women and Girls' Leadership*.

66 Karen Macours and Renos Vakis, *Changing Households' Investment and Aspiration Through Social Interactions: Evidence from a Randomized Transfer Program in a Low-Income Country*, Policy Research Working Paper No. 513 (Washington, DC: World Bank, 2008).

67 Lori Beaman et al., "Female Leadership Raises Aspirations and Educational Attainment for Girls: A Policy Experiment in India," *Science*, Vol. 335, No. 6068 (February 2012), pp. 582–586.

68 Alison Evans and Divya Nambiar, *Collective Action and Women's Agency: A Background Paper* (Washington, DC: World Bank, 2013); Estelle Loiseau and Keiko Nowacka, *Can Social Media Effectively Include Women's Voices in Decision-Making Processes?* (Paris: OECD Development Centre, 2015); Jessica Horn, *Gender and Social Movements: Overview Report* (Brighton, UK: BRIDGE, 2013).

69 Oxfam, *Programming on the Right to Be Heard: A Learning Companion* (Oxford: Oxfam, 2014).

70 Oxfam, *Promoting Women's Rights Across Africa: Raising Her Voice – Pan Africa Effectiveness Review* (Oxford: Oxfam, 2013).

71 Oxfam, *Programming on the Right to Be Heard*.

8

GENDER AND ENVIRONMENTAL SECURITY

Edward R. Carr

Environmental security is inherently multidimensional. It encompasses challenges related to land degradation, land use, access to land, food, water and the impacts of a changing climate on all of these vital resource issues.[1] While early work in environmental security tended to focus on one of these dimensions, more recent work explicitly looks across environmental sectors to better understand the relationship between the environment and security outcomes.[2] As Jon Barnett and Neil Adger note, "environmental change does not undermine human security in isolation from a broader range of social factors."[3] Factors such as income, state effectiveness and global economic processes shape the sensitivity of communities and individuals to environmental shocks and stresses, and they affect the ability of those impacted to adapt.

Environmental security therefore engages a wide range of sectors and challenges from a variety of perspectives. It is not surprising, then, that the field of environmental security is marked by disagreements over an equally wide range of issues, including whether or not there exists a causal connection between the environment and conflict, the character of that connection should it exist and what should be secured by environmental security policies. I argue that the persistence of these tensions and the resultant policy challenges they produce results from an uneven attention to and incorporation of gender and gender perspectives into the study of environmental security. The field of environmental security, strictly speaking, is marked by a near-absence of engagement with gender approaches and perspectives. This absence leads many working in this field to identify, understand and address environmental security without specifying whose security is under discussion. These approaches obscure different – often gendered – experiences of and engagement with the environment in particular places and populations. As a result, they often overlook identity-specific drivers and forms of environmental insecurity within populations, which limits their ability to address the root causes of the environmental and security outcomes they observe at more aggregated levels.

In the context of a changing global environment, this blindness to heterogeneous environmental and security experiences is concerning, as it hinders the development of understandings of the connections between the environment and security that could lead to clear, effective policy. However, this is not a problem inherent to environmental security studies. Through an examination of water security as well as climate change and security (two important subfields of environmental security), I argue for building on the parts of the environmental security literature that take gender seriously and have produced actionable, salient knowledge that advances policy development. The subfields of environmental security that have taken up questions of gender – and feminist approaches to the environment and security, more broadly – are developing nuanced understandings of environmental security that can lead to the design of inclusive, effective policies.

I begin with a review of the development of environmental security as a field – and the place of gender and women in the field – highlighting the broad inattention to gender and feminist thought in this literature and practice. To demonstrate the impact of this inattention on our understanding of environmental security and our ability to build effective environmental security policy, I analyze the very different approaches of water security and climate and security, both with gender lenses. These different engagements have produced very different understandings of environmental security and have resulted in policies, projects and programs with very different outcomes. Drawing on this discussion, I identify current drivers of policy progress related to the incorporation of gender lenses into environmental security discussions, examine obstacles to progress and suggest steps we can take to produce more effective policies that preserve human well-being at a time of considerable environmental change.

Environmental security: a brief introduction

Barnett argues that "security is a function of power. The more power a person or group has to shape social life to suit their ends, the more secure they will be."[4] Traditional approaches to security – in the form of challenges to the state posed by armed conflict – tend to focus on the material aspects of power relations. Environmental security has its roots in this view of security, but it rapidly evolved to embrace broader framings, such as human security, which extend this discussion beyond the state and violence. As a result, the field of environmental security has become extremely diverse. Some aspects of the contemporary literature, such as water security, take on broad human security framings that examine how different people gain or lose access to water and the ways in which access shapes well-being. Other parts of the literature, such as those debating the role of climate change in conflict, remain deeply preoccupied with narrower conceptions of security focused on armed conflict and state stability.

The concept of environmental security emerged in the context of the 1987 Brundtland Report.[5] The initial literature focused on understanding the ways in which environmental change – whether subtle or dramatic, slow-building or rapid-onset – might trigger or exacerbate armed conflict. This focus was closely aligned with conventional political and military studies of security, in that it concentrated on threats to the stability of social and political order, especially the stability of the state.[6] However, the field rapidly evolved to encompass a wider range of issues that have to do with the security of human social and biological needs. As part of this widening conceptualization, some argued that what needed to be secured was the environmental basis of human life and well-being (sometimes framed as ecological security).[7] Others argued that environmental security is about securing human well-being from conflict while providing the security to meet basic human needs.[8] At the same time, environmental security recognized that the environment is not a single, homogenous resource or set of services, but it is comprised of many different resources and services that impact human well-being in different ways. As a result, environmental security research is increasingly oriented toward particular resources, shocks and stresses, producing subfields that include food security, water security and, more recently, climate and security. In this way, the field of environmental security has come to serve as an umbrella for a wide and diverse conceptualization of security.

If the framing of what is to be secured through environmental security has shifted, so too has our understanding of the pathways from the environment to conflict. These pathways initially focused on questions of scarcity: assuming that where there are not enough environmental resources or services to meet the needs of those in a particular place, the distribution and use of those resources increases the risk of conflict. This could be scarcity created by human-induced degradation of the natural environment, scarcity induced by increases in human consumption (often described in neo-Malthusian terms) or scarcity for the poorest and most vulnerable created by concentrations of wealth that limit access to needed resources.[9]

Resource-specific literatures under the environmental security umbrella also took scarcity as their starting point. For example, early work on water security focused on the scarcity pathway.[10] More recently, studies of the relationship between climate variability and/or change and conflict rest on a similar scarcity pathway. Solomon Hsaing and his co-authors link scarcity of food resources to increases in conflict. They argue that the appearance of a relationship between extreme precipitation events and some forms of intergroup violence "is primarily documented in low-income settings, suggesting that reduced agricultural production may be an important mediating mechanism, although alternative explanations cannot be excluded."[11]

Although scarcity was initially posited as the principal pathway from environment to conflict, an extensive literature now complicates this pathway through its examination of environmental abundance and its connections to conflict, particularly civil conflict within a country.[12] Much of this literature can be placed under the heading of the "resource curse," which Paul Collier and Anke Hoeffler divided into two broad causal pathways – often characterized as "greed" and "grievance."[13] The greed proposition states that economic dependence on natural resources produces low rates of income growth, which in turn enables or encourages conflict by keeping the opportunity costs of rebellion or conflict low. The grievance proposition states that a resource-dependent state stunts the growth of strong institutions, instead fostering systems of patronage that benefit relatively few people, thus creating stresses that can lead to civil conflict.[14]

A large literature challenges the idea of a causal connection between the environment and conflict. The work of Thomas Homer-Dixon and other scarcity-focused scholars has been criticized due to the very weak empirical record of armed conflict over natural resources.[15] More recently, the climate change and conflict literature has been engaged in an intense debate over the degree of connection between climate change (which can produce shocks) and actual conflict. Some studies have claimed a clear connection between shifts in climatic conditions and conflict,[16] others have found more attenuated or specific pathways through which climate shifts might influence conflict,[17] while still others argue that the identified correlations are conceptually or methodologically problematic and therefore likely spurious.[18]

In reviewing the state of the climate-conflict literature, Sebastian Van Baalen and Malin Mobjörk ask two critical questions applicable to broader environmental security discussions: "why have scholars not found any results that remain robust across studies; and second, how can we move past these challenges?"[19] The answers include: a research focus on large-scale rather than small-scale violence, the absence of fine-grained and reliable data, a failure to account for contextual factors or intervening variables, the difficulties related to temporal and spatial scale and the complexity in linking actors and agency. These limitations arise at least in part from the high interdisciplinary nature of the field, the lack of adequate theoretical and analytical frameworks and the lack of interactions between quantitative and qualitative scholars.[20]

Another critique of environment and conflict research is that this focus has shifted attention away from the opportunities for cooperation that scarcity can present.[21] As the Human Security chapter of the Intergovernmental Panel on Climate Change (IPCC) Fifth Assessment report notes, "Research on bilateral and multilateral interactions between two or more states from 1948 to 2008 shows strong evidence of significant formal cooperation among river basin riparian states, and no cases of water causing two states to engage in war."[22] A growing literature on environmental peacebuilding reinforces this critical shortcoming of the mainstream environmental security literature.[23]

Efforts to generalize broad greed and grievance pathways from the environment to conflict have also been challenged. Some of these criticisms examine the specific ways in which these pathways represent the environment. For example, Katharina Wick and Erwin Bulte argue that we must consider the spatial distribution of the resource in question, as more spatially diffuse resources benefit a wider number of people and therefore reduce conflict potential.[24] Matthias Basedau and Jann Lay argue that the per capita income effects of resource extraction greatly shape conflict outcomes, with high incomes associated with lower levels of conflict.[25] Other critiques focus on the oversimplification of human decisionmaking often implicit in greed and grievance frameworks. For example, Macartan Humphreys argues that to understand the connection between resource abundance and conflict, one must engage with at least three variants of a greedy rebels mechanism, a greedy outsider's mechanism, four variants of the grievance mechanism, a feasibility mechanism (in which natural resources make financing a conflict possible), a weak states mechanism and a sparse networks mechanism.[26]

Therefore, the literature on environmental security, whether focused on scarcity or abundance, wrestles with the identification of appropriate framings of the relationship between the environment and conflict that align with empirically observable events in the world. The lack of conceptual and empirical clarity around the relationship between the environment and conflict is significant beyond academia, as it has led to confused and contradictory policy responses. For example, addressing scarcity (often presumed to be at the heart of environmental conflicts) requires securing critical environmental resources, though there is little clarity over the best way to secure these resources or who they should be secured from. For others, the focus has been on reducing population growth – a driver of consumption and degradation that produces scarcity. In either case, this narrow focus on scarcity as a pathway has not produced clear policy guidance to address environmental security threats.

In the absence of clear pathways from environmental stress to security outcomes, policy communities find themselves struggling to understand the relationship between the environment and security. For example, the part of the policy community engaged with climate and security issues has moved from causal framings of the relationship between environmental stress and conflict toward a "threat multiplier" approach, where environmental changes can exacerbate existing drivers of conflict.[27] The question of whether policy should focus on the climate (environment) versus other underlying conditions makes it difficult to identify appropriate intervention points. It leaves unclear *where* to intervene – a critical question as sites of climate impact may not be where those impacts are most acutely felt, such as a when a failed harvest in one part of the world drives food price increases in another.[28] This reflects a broader policy and conceptual challenge for environmental security: mobility. As Idean Saleyhan notes, "if there are reasons to believe that rural people affected by drought or other natural disasters will take their protests to the capital, migrate to urban areas, or join highly-mobile rebel organizations, then there is no reason to believe that local-level climatic variables will correlate with conflict in that same locality."[29] Thus, an aspect of the causal pathway between the environment and conflict identified by Homer-Dixon and others – mobility and migration – is also a source of uncertainty for policymakers, who need to know where problems are likely to develop.

These problems – and the persistence of debates over the character, importance and policy ramifications of environmental security – are compounded by a near-absence of serious attention to gender and gender perspectives in environmental security studies.

Gender and gender perspectives in environmental security

A striking feature of the environmental security literature is the near absence of gender perspectives in discussions of environmental security, strictly speaking. A few studies apply feminist approaches to environmental security, but they do not employ gender or a gender lens to environmental security policy.[30] As Nicole Detraz notes, there is a great deal of affinity between the broad definition of security encompassed by environmental security and feminist approaches to security.[31] It is therefore both surprising and troubling that most approaches to environmental security omit, as Detraz observes, "both the gendered nature of separating humans and environment as distinct entities and many of the gendered impacts of its key constitutive factors."[32] That is, environmental security studies fail to account for gendered framings of human relationships to the environment.

In this sense, environmental security is somewhat unusual in the broad field of human-environment relations. For example, numerous studies in the climate change adaptation literature point to the ways in which women mobilize their unique roles to develop unique, gendered adaptations to environmental shocks and stressors.[33] A contemporary gender lens on human relationships to the environment, however, rejects generalized statements about gendered relationships with the environment, such as claims that women have a closer relationship to nature than men and therefore are likely to be different, if not better, stewards.[34] A contemporary gender lens recognizes that different people interact with their environments differently, depending on their site and situation. This suggests that policies aimed at generic "women's" or "men's" environmental relationships will be highly problematic.[35]

If a gender lens on environmental security highlights the gendered impacts of the environmental shocks and stressors that might challenge human well-being and the gendered ways in which people secure themselves in the face of such challenges, this lens also reveals the gendered impacts of interventions aimed at producing environmental security. For example, a gender lens on the causes of insecurity reveals the ways in which a neo-Malthusian focus on population pressure and scarcity as causes of environmental insecurity make "women the potential target of policy solutions to environmental change because of their role as child bearers."[36] This targeting can become particularly problematic, Detraz notes, because pushing questions of environmental stress and human well-being into the security realm can frame otherwise-objectionable actions – such as population control measures – as justifiable or necessary.[37] These policies would have different implications for men and women (and indeed for different kinds of men and women).

Finally, a broadly feminist view of environmental security – which asks "security from what?" and "security for whom?" – highlights the ways in which efforts to address environmental insecurity might themselves produce conflict. The Environmental Change and Security Program at the Woodrow Wilson Center coined the term *backdraft* to describe the counterproductive effects of some climate adaptation and mitigation programs: the differential benefits from these efforts can become drivers of conflict in and of themselves.[38] Similarly, Julie Snorek and her co-authors describe divergent adaptation, where adaptation interventions produce positive adaptation outcomes for some in a place or population, while compromising the adaptive capacity and adaptation outcomes of others.[39] These inequities can lead to conflict.

Water security, climate and security

A focus on two dimensions of environmental security – water security, and climate and security – highlights the range of ways in which gender fits into environmental security studies. The literature on water security has taken up highly nuanced framings of gender. Work on climate and security, on the other hand, has paid little attention to gender or women. Comparing these two literatures shows how different engagements with gender produce very different views of security and its causes. This, in turn, allows us to examine how these differences influence policy.

Water security

Water security is one of the oldest domains in the environmental security field. The early literature on water security focused on inter-state water conflicts.[40] According to Tobias von Lossow, this issue is "a nearly exclusively masculine discipline" insofar as the issues it examined, including "dispute, conflict, confrontation, and warfare are very much connected with classic masculine clichés of virtue, strength and power."[41] Further, these conflicts "are located at the level of inter-state politics and diplomacy, which are traditionally perceived as masculine disciplines and highly dominated by male actors."[42] Finally, water management via hydro-engineering and building water infrastructure "is basically understood as dominating, controlling, and exploiting the natural water resources."[43]

While initially dominated by debates around the connection between water scarcity and inter-state conflict, such as in the work of Homer-Dixon, the field has since taken on a much wider view of this issue. In his review of debates in this field, Alex Loftus argues that the mainstream view of water security, such as seen in major Non-Governmental Organizations (NGOs) and government documents, is "a question of human security and emphasizes a concern for the most vulnerable in the world."[44] This conception of water security can be broadly defined as an "acceptable level of water-related risks to humans and ecosystems, coupled with the availability of water of sufficient quantity and quality to support livelihoods, national security, human health and ecosystem services."[45] The contemporary literature is marked by a significant engagement with gender lenses that has moved discussions in this field well beyond those in the mainstream of environmental security.

First, as suggested by the limited literature on gender and environmental security more broadly, the part of the water and security literature engaged with gender carefully considers questions of who is made insecure in the face of resource stress and conflict, and when and where these insecurities emerge.[46] This work takes a broadly feminist approach, recognizing the different uses and experiences of water not only between genders, but also among men and women.[47] In her examinations of gender, development and water in Bangladesh, Farhana Sultana argues against simplistic expectations about female exclusion from development projects broadly and water projects specifically. Instead, she notes that in the context of water management, the patterns of exclusion derive from both gender and wealth, with men excluding women in decisionmaking roles, and men and women of wealthier households excluding people of other households from accessing their safe water sources. It is not just women: many poor and marginalized men are also excluded.[48]

Some scholars have argued that water security is shaped by all forms of social difference that produce different types of resource insecurity.[49] These scholars argue that feminist framings have focused too much on women and gender at the expense of caste, class and age. In her work on gendered experiences of water, Sultana rejects a natural connection between women and emotion, arguing "both men and women speak about resource access and conflicts through the emotions they experience."[50] The work of Sultana and others advances understanding of the ways in which gender roles and other markers of identity produce various forms of insecurity for people in a community or society.[51]

Second, this work recognizes that a gender lens can help us understand cooperation and complementarity around water issues.[52] As Bakker and Morinville note, "social power is a key factor in explaining water insecurity. Yet the converse is equally true: social power is an enabling condition for water security."[53]

The nuanced framing of gender and water security in the academic literature is now reflected in donor policy as well. The United States Agency for International Development's (USAID) "Water and Conflict Toolkit" adopts a somewhat normative framing of gender roles, noting: "Women tend to have greater water needs due to their domestic responsibilities like washing family clothes, bathing children, and preparing meals."[54] However, it moves beyond this view to reject the construction of women as a priori more vulnerable to water-related conflict than men. The toolkit notes: "The humanitarian discussion of water access and violence generally focuses on women as victims. However, water resources are part of a system that affects and is affected by its entire population. In some contexts, men and boys access water for their households and face the same risks as females."[55] Further, the toolkit observes that the experiences of men and women are not consistent across time and culture. There is variation across gender experience based on social and community tradition, class structure, ethnic relations, urban vs. rural environments, livelihoods practices and other variables. Due to their different roles in their communities, women and men may have different information and perspectives about the causes and consequences of water-related problems. In addition, gender roles often change as a consequence of conflict and fragility. The toolkit concludes: "Water practitioners will therefore find it constructive to move their analysis beyond the limited focus on female vulnerabilities and to consider gender dynamics within the system as a whole."[56]

USAID's water and conflict guidance goes beyond binary gender categories to consider them as relational, having meaning in a local context and drawing importance from their intersection with other important aspects of identity such as class and ethnicity. This sophisticated view is not universally shared across the policy world. For example, the German Technical Cooperation Agency Gesellschaft für Technische Zusammenarbeit (GTZ), the institutional predecessor to Gesellschaft für Internationale Zusammenarbeit (GIZ), issued a 2010 concept paper on water security that did not mention gender or women.[57] However, the paper did refer to the role of asymmetrical power relations in increasing the potential for water-related conflicts.

Climate and security

Where the literature on water and security focuses intently and carefully on gender, the literature on climate change and security pays much less attention to gender – similar to that seen in the environmental security literature in general. While there is a vast literature on gender and women in the context of climate change (and a growing portion of that literature mirrors the interest in intersectionality and the contextual character of vulnerability found in the water security literature), the literature that focuses specifically on climate and security has not yet taken up gender as a significant issue.[58]

The climate and security literature focuses heavily on the connection between climate variability and conflict, and it generally relies on large-N studies to establish or refute causal connections.[59] Large samples obscure intra-sample variability, and they generally obfuscate an important question: when, and for whom, does climate variability and change contribute to conflict? As Janani Vivekananda and her co-authors note, these studies are of "limited use from a peacebuilding perspective as they provide no insights into why there may be a correlation between climatic and conflict variables."[60]

While the mainstream climate and security literature generally operates with large datasets and high levels of social aggregation – and while it appears to be preoccupied with the overarching question of whether there is a connection between climate variability and conflict – a few studies emphasize gender and social difference as key parts of the equation. In their study of the relationship between climate vulnerability and conflict in the Philippines, Alvin Chandra and his co-authors note that the literature on climate change and food security is aware of the importance of gender and social difference in determining food security outcomes. However, they also note that the ways in which these social differences intersect with climate and other vulnerabilities remains poorly understood. Their study demonstrates that the intersection of climate change effects and other drivers of vulnerability, when exacerbated by conflict, tends to marginalize women and their work. For example,

they found that women were particularly vulnerable to conflict and resource insecurity, in part because of their domestic and childcare responsibilities.[61]

Policy guidance on climate change and conflict also largely overlooks gender
and women. USAID's Office of Conflict Management and Mitigation issued a
review of problems related to climate change, adaptation and conflict in 2009,
long before climate change and conflict became a subject of intense attention.[62]
The USAID document provides a broad overview of the issues, but it makes no
mention of gender or women. Similarly, the report of a 2015 workshop on climate
change and peacebuilding, sponsored by USAID and the State Department, makes
almost no mention of women or gender.[63] However, there are signs of change in
this policy and programming area. A follow-up guidance document issued as an
annex to USAID's Climate Resilient Development Framework mentions gender
once, noting that it plays a role in vulnerabilities.[64] It also mentions women three
times. While all three references to women are brief, one mention in an illustrative scenario asks how changing rainfall patterns have "changed the distribution
of power in the community" and how the experience of those changing patterns
is "different for men and women."[65] This is perhaps the only mention in USAID
guidance and policy on climate change and conflict where a reference to women
or gender moves toward a more nuanced understanding of gender as a situational
expression of power dynamics that can produce different patterns of vulnerability
at the community and household levels.

A guide on "Conflict, Climate, and Environment," commissioned by the United
Kingdom's (UK) Department for International Development (DfID), treats gender
as a cross-cutting issue about which relatively little is known.[66] The authors note
that more work is needed on conflict, climate change, the environment and gender
relations, a phrasing which recognizes that a gender lens includes understanding
gender roles as processes that evolve over time. A GTZ document on "Climate
Change and Security" addresses gender once and women twice, all on the same
page.[67] These references come in a section that explicitly notes that climate change
tends to exacerbate existing patterns of marginalization in populations. In both
cases, however, the authors go on to make claims about women usually being more
vulnerable than men to things such as natural disasters.

The fields of water security and climate and security demonstrate the spectrum of ways in which gender has been taken up by parts of the environmental
security community. Currently, broad discussions of environmental security have
little engagement with gender, even in the academic literature. However, environmental security policy is more commonly framed around specific environmental
resources and stressors. At this level, we see that some fields of inquiry, such as
water security, employ a far more nuanced view of gender – in both the academic
and policy worlds. There is a recognition that gender shapes individual capacities
and decisions in specific places around specific resources. For other fields, such as
that of climate change and security, there is much less engagement with gender.
Even those policy documents that recognize that a focus on gender relations and
patterns of social marginalization is critical tend to revert to stereotypical framings

of gender, arguing that women (as a unified category) are more vulnerable or marginal than men.

Drivers of policy progress

Comparing the ways in which the different gender engagements of these two subfields play out in their respective literatures highlights how paying attention to gender can produce progress in the policy domain. Specifically, policy progress takes shape around research and analysis connecting security to particular aspects of the environment, where it is possible to increase the stock of empirical evidence around the different, locally-specific ways in which gender contributes to vulnerability or creates opportunities for new adaptations. By focusing on a specific resource or stressor, it is possible to understand how gendered vulnerabilities and opportunities emerge and how these situations play out for women. This is true even in the case of climate change – since climate change encompasses a range of environmental stressors, including the amount of precipitation, the timing of precipitation, temperature and the intensity and frequency of a wide range of extreme events. It is possible that one effect of climate change, such as changes in the timing of rainfall, could have gendered effects on security while others do not.

The rise of resilience as a key concept in the development and climate change communities offers another opportunity to advance the adoption of gender perspectives and approaches across the different dimensions of environmental security. Organizations such as USAID are focusing their resilience efforts on contexts where environmental insecurity is likely to be a challenge, such as "areas where chronic poverty intersects with shocks and stresses to produce recurrent crises and undermine development gains."[68] In many ways, the use of resilience in contemporary development policy characterizes it as a precondition for environmental security – one where increased adaptive capacity, improved ability to address and reduce risk and better social and economic conditions for vulnerable populations will address different drivers of insecurity.[69] In invoking the social and economic conditions of vulnerable populations, this framing of resilience explicitly calls out the role of social difference in the production of environmental insecurity. This is clear in USAID's resilience guidance, which explicitly recognizes the importance of a gender lens for addressing the causes of observed vulnerability and insecurity in populations:

> Despite the fact that women often face a range of unique challenges in areas of recurrent crisis and often bear the heaviest burden of shocks and stresses – they also possess enormous individual and collective capacity to help themselves, their families, and their communities. . . . Approaches that systematically and visibly reduce key gender gaps and ensure that women are given the tools, resources, and opportunities to lead and participate are critical to the success of our efforts to achieve sustainable change.[70]

While this view of women considers them as a single category, the fact that it moves beyond the assumption that women are inherently more vulnerable than men represents an important step forward in identifying the causes of insecurity and productive responses. The turn to resilience in development, humanitarianism and the climate change community offers an opportunity to drive the environmental security community toward a more serious engagement with gender and social difference.

Obstacles to policy progress

As Fröhlich and Gioli note, feminist insights into the relationship between people, the environment and conflict – such as the fact that women and men often have different relationships to the environment as a result of their different roles and responsibilities – tend to become generalized and oversimplified.[71] For example, a feminist examination of gendered agricultural practices in Ghana reveals the importance of both gender and livelihood strategies in shaping the differences between women's and men's agricultural activities.[72] If, however, this specific insight is then applied to project design in Sudan – where different social norms and agroecology prevail – it has been removed from the Ghanaian context that made the observation valid. This occurs because the oversimplification of complex identities that take their meaning in particular situations and through specific social relations "infuses an aura of science by universalizing partial truths grounded on real issues."[73]

As a result, observations that have cross-contextual value (for example, *in some places*, women's identity *can be* shaped by the livelihood strategies in which they are engaged) become universal, fixed truths (for example, women's identity *is always* shaped by livelihood strategies, and therefore all project design, implementation and evaluation should focus on this intersection). The GTZ report on "Climate Change and Security" notes that disasters tend to have effects that enhance the marginalization of sections of a population and that this is "particularly true for women, who in the aftermath of disasters, for example, often fall victim to attacks (as with the 2004 tsunami)."[74] In this case, the report draws on a concrete example where women became vulnerable to attacks after a disaster, removes the context within which these attacks occurred and then generates a general, broadly applicable lesson – that women are vulnerable to attack after disasters.

These oversimplifications and generalizations become embedded in institutions, policies and practices through repetition.[75] As Fröhlich and Gioli note, repetition replaces uncertainty and nuance with generic, decontextualized slogans.[76] For example, in a promotional document for the Japan International Cooperation Agency (JICA), an article on gender issues in conflict and disaster claims: "Whether in natural or man-made crises, women often face risks that men do not. Sexual assault on women has been a part of war everywhere in the world throughout history."[77] These two sentences conflate women's vulnerability in conflict and disaster settings, and they generalize across both domains. USAID repeats this narrative in a document outlining its implementation of the US National Action Plan on Women, Peace and Security (WPS).[78]

USAID works across the spectrum of crisis prevention, response, recovery and transitions. In these environments, it is a challenging but vital imperative to protect and empower women and girls: protection from abuses such as sexual and gender-based violence, which are often perpetrated as weapons of war or exacerbated by natural disasters, and empowerment that promotes women's substantive participation and leadership at the negotiating table, in rebuilding conflict and crisis-affected communities and in shaping the full range of important decisions confronting societies in critical transition periods.

While there is no question that natural disasters *might* result in both the disempowerment of women and greater risk of sexually-based violence, this framing implicitly links these two challenges and universalizes them, suggesting that women in post-disaster situations are uniformly at risk of violence and disempowerment. Repetition of this claim makes it ubiquitous and difficult to challenge.

Other significant barriers to policy progress are the Monitoring and Evaluation (M&E) frameworks employed by organizations – such as large development donors – that seek to build environmental security on the ground. While development donors are themselves few in number, their funds support the work of a wide array of organizations, all of which must respond to the M&E frameworks used by their donors. This generates two challenges to serious, sustained engagement with gender in the context of environmental security: what is measured and why it is measured. For example, USAID's guidance for the measurement of gender outcomes in its projects demands that sex disaggregated data be collected. The Agency offers ten standard performance indicators to assess progress toward "gender equality, women's empowerment, gender-based violence, and women, peace, and security."[79] However, both this requirement and these indicators rest on a definition of gender that allows its contractors and partners to treat women and men as undifferentiated categories.[80] Further, these indicators leave out critical contextual factors. For example, one indicator – the percentage of participants reporting increased agreement with the concept that males and females should have equal access to social, economic and political resources and opportunities – means different things in different contexts.[81] In some contexts, this might be a pathway to significant change in the roles and responsibilities of women, which can address underlying causes of environmental insecurity. In other contexts, however, the overt promotion of this idea can lead to increased social conflict as men seek to preserve their privileges. A higher level of conflict is likely to exacerbate women's insecurity and may create new sources of insecurity.

Of course, indicators are merely tools for understanding project performance and outcomes. The context in which they are applied determines why this data is gathered, and thus its ultimate value. In a context where M&E is aimed at learning about what works – and adjusting interventions, projects, programs and policies accordingly – even coarse indicators can be used to "revisit assumptions, check for any unintended negative consequences, make decisions, and manage any course corrections [to allow] for gender considerations to be addressed throughout the Program Cycle."[82] However, most development donors do not focus M&E on learning; they use M&E for performance monitoring – the achievement of specified targets. Further, despite their rhetoric about learning, many donors operate in cultures where failure is not an option. The collection of data is therefore aimed more at avoiding negative institutional consequences than learning about what does and does not work.[83] As long as project and program activities focus on performance monitoring that obscures project failures and lessons learned, the empirical basis for environmental security policy will lag.

Gender and environmental security: strategies for progress

These barriers to progress matter because they are likely to produce policies, programs and projects that are locally inappropriate and therefore ineffective. However, these poor outcomes are not inevitable. My analysis of these challenges suggests six recommendations for a more effective approach to environmental security that is enabled and enhanced by a gender lens.

First, organizations and institutions with an interest in environmental security should focus their work on specific environmental resources and stressors. Individuals and communities do not use "the environment" in a holistic manner. They access and influence parts of the environment in the course of their day-to-day activities, often in resource-specific ways.[84] While "environmental security" might be a useful conceptual umbrella for grouping policies and programs, projects and interventions with a more specific focus are more likely to identify and address specific causes of insecurity.

Second, organizations and institutions with an interest in environmental security must make place-specific and context-specific decisions about the people they are trying to help. Focusing on a specific resource will privilege some people over others. Rather than framing vulnerability and needs assessments around population-level efforts to secure the material basis of existence, environmental security programs should employ assessments that seek out gendered and other socially differentiated stresses for targeting.

Third, while an attention to gender is critical for productive work on environmental security, *gender* is not a synonym for *women*. An attention to gender requires that we recognize how the categories of men and women are defined in relation to one another, and through intersections with other important social differences. Further, these are not homogenous categories. Some women are wealthy, while others are poor. Some men are married, and others are not. The different economic and social positions of men and women in the same population may result in some experiencing significant insecurity from a shock or stressor, while others feel little impact.

Fourth, environmental security policy and programs should abandon the use of simple, universal framings of gendered environmental relationships in policy, program and project design and in monitoring and evaluation frameworks. These efforts require locally specific understandings of these relationships. Generic framings are more likely to obscure important local relationships than productively inform the design of effective projects and interventions. This recommendation mobilizes requirements for gender assessment that are already part of the policy and program design processes in many organizations but demands a different approach to the achievement of this requirement. Whatever institutional challenges might emerge will be more than compensated by improvements in policy and project effectiveness.

Fifth, in post-crisis settings, organizations should carefully consider gender and other forms of social difference as they assess who benefits from efforts to rebuild environmental security. Going forward, a central question for the environmental security field will be the desired outcome of a policy or intervention. As the literature on resilience has shown, interventions aimed at securing people in times of environmental stress must ask if the status quo (or a return to the status quo) is an appropriate goal. In many cases, returning to the status quo ante would re-create the conditions that led to the insecurity in the first place.[85]

At the same time, thinking about "building back better" without a critical evaluation of the perspective from which "better" is defined, leaves out key questions: what is secured and for whom? This could create new conditions of insecurity and vulnerability that might result in different crises in the future.[86] For example, the Global Framework for Disaster Risk Reduction advocates for humanitarian responses that not only address the speed of response and the need to repair infrastructure but also the need to ensure that the response is inclusive of the different needs of the society in question.[87] As important as inclusivity is for humanitarian responses, in this report inclusiveness is principally framed around socio-economic need. For example, the section of the report that discusses building back more inclusively frames difference around assets and income: poor people are not only more vulnerable to natural hazards, but they also tend to have less access to post-disaster support mechanisms such as insurance, borrowing or remittances, and they have fewer savings to draw on. As a consequence, they tend to experience higher losses relative to income, and they often have to resort to "negative coping mechanisms" – such as reducing food intake, cutting down on health care or reducing education spending.[88]

Gender only appears twice in the "Building Back Better" report: a passing mention in two case studies. Yet one's gender – and indeed one's identity more broadly – are often central to the ability to access assistance, secure assets and change one's situation. By focusing principally on material measures of status and well-being, the humanitarian policy community overlooks the ways in which gender and identity shape these fundamental causes of insecurity and vulnerability, reproducing them even as they attempt to deliver humanitarian responses in a more inclusive manner.

Sixth, environmental security projects and programs should assess the insecurities that might be caused by transformative environmental security efforts, at scales ranging from the household to the state and beyond. Transformative policies and interventions are difficult to develop and implement. As the gender-informed literature on environmental security shows, questions of vulnerability and security are inextricably intertwined with questions of identity and even questions of how to live in the world. Efforts to reduce vulnerability or address the sources of conflict emerging around environmental shocks and stressors, or to change the behaviors that lead to resource-based insecurity, often touch on fundamental ideas of who people think they are in the world.[89] Thus, efforts to secure the environment and the benefits that people obtain from it via environmentally or socially transformative efforts can call the fundamental organization of society into question, and with it the privileges of the powerful. These are privileges the powerful will undoubtedly try to protect.

Adaptation projects that do not account for these risks and insecurities may generate "backdraft" problems and conflict. For example, working in Mali, Carr and his co-authors identify situations in which climate change adaptation interventions might increase the risk of domestic violence and household conflict.[90] In another case, Snorek and her co-authors demonstrate how adaptation projects in Niger that focus on sedentary agriculture produce new stresses on pastoral populations that result in low-level conflicts over land access.[91] Without careful consideration of what is being transformed and for whom, programs might create as much conflict and insecurity as they address.

These recommendations have the potential to pivot our framing of environmental insecurity from assumptions about risk and vulnerability via scarcity toward a process of recognizing how risk and vulnerability emerge for different people in populations through specific pathways. We could then more accurately assess everything from the likelihood of future environmentally-related conflicts to the most effective interventions to facilitate peacebuilding and cooperation in times of environmental stress.

These recommendations also point the way to evidence-based policies that promote security, safety, cooperation and well-being in the context of environmental shocks and stressors. They highlight the inherently political nature of efforts to address environmental security. They force us to identify the goals of our interventions and who will be served by those goals. Even if the current state of knowledge does not allow these questions to be answered definitively for all people in all places, a policy community that can identify and ask these questions will be one that is more effective going forward.

Notes

1 Clionadh Raleigh and Henrik Urdal, "Climate Change, Environmental Degradation and Armed Conflict," *Political Geography*, Vol. 26, No. 6 (August 2007), pp. 674–694; Ane Cristina Figueiredo Pereira de Faria and Issa Ibrahim Berchin, "Understanding Food Security and International Security Links in the Context of Climate Change," *Third World Quarterly*, Vol. 37, No. 6 (2016), pp. 975–997; Emmy Simmons, "Harvesting Peace: Food Security, Conflict, and Cooperation," *Environmental Change and Security Program Report*, Vol. 14 (Washington, DC: Woodrow Wilson International Center for Scholars,

2013); Nina Von Uexkull et al., "Civil Conflict Sensitivity to Growing-Season Drought," Vol. 113, No. 134 (2016); Christina Cook and Karen Bakker, "Water Security: Debating an Emerging Paradigm," *Global Environmental Change*, Vol. 22, No. 1 (2012), pp. 94–102; Radoslav S. Dimitrov, "Water, Conflict, and Security: A Conceptual Minefield," *Society and Natural Resources*, Vol. 15 (2002), pp. 677–692; Peter H. Gleick, "Water and Conflict: Fresh Water Resources and International Security," *International Security*, Vol. 18, No. 1 (1993), pp. 79–112; Jon Barnett and W. Neil Adger, "Climate Change, Human Security and Violent Conflict," *Political Geography*, Vol. 26, No. 6 (August 2007), pp. 639–655; W. Neil Adger et al., "Human Security," in C.B. Field et al., eds., *Climate Change 2014: Impacts, Adaptation, and Vulnerability. Part A: Global and Sectoral Aspects. Contribution of Working Group II to the Fifth Assessment Report of the Intergovernmental Panel on Climate Change* (Cambridge: Cambridge University Press, 2014), pp. 755–791.

2   Malin Falkenmark, "The Greatest Water Problem: The Inability to Link Environmental Security, Water Security and Food Security," *International Journal of Water Resources Development*, Vol. 17, No. 4 (2001), pp. 539–554.

3   Barnett and Adger, "Climate Change, Human Security and Violent Conflict," pp. 641.

4   Jon Barnett, *The Meaning of Environmental Security: Ecological Politics and Policy in the New Security Era* (London: Zed Books, 2001), pp. 122–123.

5   World Commission on Environment and Development, *Our Common Future* (Oxford: Oxford University Press, 1987).

6   Nicole Detraz, "Environmental Security and Gender: Necessary Shifts in an Evolving Debate," *Security Studies*, Vol. 18, No. 2 (June 2009), pp. 345–369; Dennis Pirages, "Demographic Change and Ecological Security," *Environmental Change and Security Program*, Vol. 3 (1997), pp. 5–14; Steven Ney, "Environmental Security: A Critical Overview," *Innovation: The European Journal of Social Science Research*, Vol. 12, No. 1 (1999), pp. 7–30; Barnett, *The Meaning of Environmental Security*.

7   Barnett, *The Meaning of Environmental Security*.

8   Ney, "Environmental Security."

9   Thomas F. Homer-Dixon, *Environment, Scarcity and Violence* (Princeton, NJ: Princeton University Press, 1999); Thomas F. Homer-Dixon, "Environmental Scarcities and Violent Conflict: Evidence from Cases," *International Security*, Vol. 19, No. 1 (1994), pp. 5–40; Thomas F. Homer-Dixon, "On the Threshold: Environmental Changes as Causes of Acute Conflict," *International Security*, Vol. 16, No. 2 (1991), pp. 76–116.

10   Gleick, "Water and Conflict"; Joyce Starr, "Water Wars," *Foreign Policy*, Vol. 82 (1991), p. 19; Joyce Starr and Daniel Stoll, *The Politics of Water Scarcity: Water in the Middle East* (Boulder, CO: Westview Press, 1988).

11   Solomon M. Hsiang, Marshall Burke and Edward Miguel, "Quantifying the Influence of Climate on Human Conflict," *Science*, Vol. 341, No. 6151 (September 13, 2013).

12   Ian Bannon and Paul Collier, "Natural Resources and Conflict: What We Can Do," in Ian Bannon and Paul Collier, eds., *Natural Resources and Violent Conflict: Options and Actions* (Washington, DC: World Bank, 2003), pp. 1–16; Paul Collier and Anke Hoeffler, "Resource Rents, Governance, and Conflict," *Journal of Conflict Resolution*, Vol. 49, No. 4 (2005), pp. 625–633; Matthias Basedau and Jann Lay, "Resource Curse or Rentier Peace? The Ambiguous Effects of Oil Wealth and Oil Dependence on Violent Conflict," *Journal of Peace Research*, Vol. 46, No. 6 (2009), pp. 757–776.

13   Collier and Hoeffler, "Resource Rents, Governance, and Conflict."

14   Basedau and Lay, "Resource Curse or Rentier Peace?"

15   Peter M. Haas, "Constructing Environmental Conflicts from Resource Scarcity," *Global Environmental Politics*, Vol. 2, No. 1 (2002), pp. 1–12.

16   Solomon M. Hsiang, Kyle C. Meng and Mark A. Cane, "Civil Conflicts Are Associated with the Global Climate," *Nature*, Vol. 476, No. 7361 (August 25, 2011), pp. 438–441; Hsiang, Burke and Miguel, "Quantifying the Influence of Climate on Human Conflict"; Peter H. Gleick, "Water, Drought, Climate Change, and Conflict in Syria," *Weather, Climate, and Society*, Vol. 6, No. 3 (June 2014), pp. 331–340.

17 John O'Loughlin et al., "Climate Variability and Conflict Risk in East Africa, 1990–2009," *Proceedings of the National Academy of Sciences of the United States of America*, Vol. 109, No. 45 (November 6, 2012), pp. 18344–18349; Frank D.W. Witmer et al., "Subnational Violent Conflict Forecasts for Sub-Saharan Africa, 2015–65, Using Climate-Sensitive Models," *Journal of Peace Research*, Vol. 54, No. 2 (2017), pp. 175–192; Adger et al., "Human Security."

18 Jan Selby, "Positivist Climate Conflict Research: A Critique," *Geopolitics*, Vol. 19, No. 4 (October 30, 2014), pp. 829–856; Halvard Buhaug et al., "One Effect to Rule Them All? A Comment on Climate and Conflict," *Climatic Change*, Vol. 127, Nos. 3–4 (December 2014).

19 Sebastian van Baalen and Malin Mobjörk, *A Coming Anarchy? Pathways from Climate Change to Violent Conflict in East Africa* (Stockholm: Stockholm University, 2016), p. 2.

20 Ibid., pp. 2–3.

21 Dimitrov, "Water, Conflict, and Security."

22 Adger et al., "Human Security," p. 775.

23 Alexander Carius, *Environmental Peacebuilding: Environmental Cooperation as an Instrument of Crisis Prevention and Peacebuilding: Conditions for Success and Constraints,* Paper submitted to the 2006 Berlin Conference on the Human Dimensions of Global Environmental Change (October 2006); Dennis Tänzler, Achim Maas and Alexander Carius, "Climate Change Adaptation and Peace," *Wiley Interdisciplinary Reviews: Climate Change*, Vol. 1, No. 5 (2010), pp. 741–750; Ken Conca and Jennifer Wallace, "Environment and Peacebuilding in War-Torn Societies: Lessons from the UN Environment Programme's Experience with Postconflict Assessment," *Global Governance*, Vol. 15, No. 4 (2009), pp. 485–504.

24 Katharina Wick and Erwin H. Bulte, "Contesting Resources: Rent Seeking, Conflict and the Natural Resource Curse," *Public Choice*, Vol. 128, Nos. 3–4 (2006), pp. 457–476.

25 Basedau and Lay, "Resource Curse or Rentier Peace?"

26 Macartan Humphreys, "Natural Resources, Conflict, and Conflict Resolution: Uncovering the Mechanisms," *Journal of Conflict Resolution*, Vol. 49, No. 4 (August 1, 2005), pp. 508–537.

27 Center for Naval Analysis (CNA), *National Security and the Accelerating Risks of Climate Change* (Alexandria, VA: CNA, May 2014); CNA, *National Security and the Threat of Climate Change* (Alexandria, VA: CNA, 2007); USAID, *Climate Change and Development: Clean Resilient Growth: USAID Climate Change and Development Strategy, 2012–2016* (Washington, DC: USAID, 2012).

28 Daniel Abrahams and Edward R. Carr, "Understanding the Connections Between Climate Change and Conflict: Contributions from Geography and Political Ecology," *Current Climate Change Reports*, Vol. 3, No. 4 (2017), pp. 233–242.

29 Idean Salehyan, "Climate Change and Conflict: Making Sense of Disparate Findings," *Political Geography*, Vol. 43 (2014), pp. 1–5.

30 Nicole Detraz, *Gender, Climate Change and Security: Linking Vital Issues*, Paper Presented at the Annual Meeting of the International Studies Association (Montreal, Canada, March 16, 2011), pp. 1–31; Detraz, "Environmental Security and Gender"; Christiane Fröhlich and Giovanna Gioli, "Gender, Conflict, and Global Environmental Change," *Peace Review*, Vol. 27, No. 2 (2015), pp. 137–146.

31 Detraz, *Gender, Climate Change and Security.*

32 Detraz, "Environmental Security and Gender," p. 350.

33 Farhana Sultana, "Gendering Climate Change: Geographical Insights," *The Professional Geographer*, Vol. 66, No. 3 (August 24, 2013), pp. 1–10; Farhana Sultana, "Living in Hazardous Waterscapes: Gendered Vulnerabilities and Experiences of Floods and Disasters," *Environmental Hazards*, Vol. 9, No. 1 (March 1, 2010), pp. 43–53; Sara Ahmed and Elizabeth Fajber, "Engendering Adaptation to Climate Variability in Gujarat, India," *Gender & Development*, Vol. 17, No. 1 (March 2009), pp. 33–50; Justina Demetriades and Emily Esplen, "The Gender Dimensions of Poverty and Climate Change Adaptation," *IDS Bulletin*, Vol. 39, No. 4 (January 26, 2008), pp. 24–31; Houria Djoudi and Maria

Brockhaus, "Is Adaptation to Climate Change Gender Neutral? Lessons from Communities Dependent on Livestock and Forests in Northern Mali," *International Forestry Review*, Vol. 13, No. 2 (June 2011), pp. 123–135.

34 Vandana Shiva, "Development, Ecology, and Women," in *Staying Alive: Women, Ecology, and Survival in India* (London: Zed Books, 2010), pp. 1–13.

35 Dianne E. Rocheleau, "Political Ecology in the Key of Policy: From Chains of Explanation to Webs of Relation," *Geoforum*, Vol. 39, No. 2 (2008), pp. 716–727; Dianne E. Rocheleau, Barbara Thomas-Slayter and Esther Wangari, "Gender and Environment: A Feminist Political Ecology Perspective," in Dianne E. Rocheleau, Barbara Thomas-Slayter and Esther Wangari, eds., *Feminist Political Ecology: Global Issues and Local Experiences* (London: Routledge, 1996), pp. 3–23; Demetriades and Esplen, "The Gender Dimensions of Poverty and Climate Change Adaptation"; Seema Arora-Jonsson, "Virtue and Vulnerability: Discourses on Women, Gender and Climate Change," *Global Environmental Change*, Vol. 21, No. 2 (May 2011), pp. 744–751.

36 Detraz, "Environmental Security and Gender," p. 349.

37 Ibid.

38 Geoffrey D. Dabelko et al., *Backdraft: The Conflict Potential of Climate Change* (Washington, DC: Wilson Center, 2013).

39 Julie Snorek, Fabrice G. Renaud and Julia Kloos, "Divergent Adaptation to Climate Variability: A Case Study of Pastoral and Agricultural Societies in Niger," *Global Environmental Change*, Vol. 29 (2014), pp. 371–386.

40 Starr, "Water Wars"; Gleick, "Water and Conflict."

41 Tobias Von Lossow, "Gender in Inter-State Water Conflicts," *Peace Review*, Vol. 27, No. 2 (2015), pp. 196–201, 197.

42 Ibid., p. 198.

43 Ibid.

44 Alex Loftus, "Water (in)Security: Securing the Right to Water," *Geographical Journal*, Vol. 181, No. 4 (2015), pp. 350–356, 351.

45 Karen Bakker, "Water Security: Research Challenges and Opportunities," *Science*, Vol. 337, No. 6097 (2012), pp. 914–915; Karen Bakker and Cynthia Morinville, "The Governance Dimensions of Water Security: A Review," *Philosophical Transactions of the Royal Society*, Vol. 371, No. 2002 (2013), p. 2.

46 Farhana Sultana, "Suffering for Water, Suffering from Water: Emotional Geographies of Resource Access, Control and Conflict," *Geoforum*, Vol. 42, No. 2 (2011), pp. 163–172.

47 Ben Crow and Farhana Sultana, "Gender, Class, and Access to Water: Three Cases in a Poor and Crowded Delta," *Society and Natural Resources*, Vol. 15 (2002), pp. 709–724; Leila M. Harris, "Gender and Emergent Water Governance: Comparative Overview of Neoliberalized Natures and Gender Dimensions of Privatization, Devolution and Marketization," *Gender, Place and Culture*, Vol. 16, No. 4 (2009), pp. 387–408; Sultana, "Suffering for Water"; Wendy Jepson et al., "Advancing Human Capabilities for Water Security: A Relational Approach," *Water Security*, Vol. 1 (2017), pp. 46–52; Farhana Sultana, "Gender and Water in a Changing Climate: Challenges and Opportunities," in Christiane Fröhlich et al., eds., *Water Security Across the Gender Divide* (Heidelberg: Springer, 2018), pp. 17–33.

48 Farhana Sultana, "Community and Participation in Water Resources Management: Gendering and Naturing Development Debates from Bangladesh," *Transactions of the Institute of British Geographers*, Vol. 34, No. 3 (2009), pp. 346–363.

49 Rhodante Ahlers and Margreet Zwarteveen, "The Water Question in Feminism: Water Control and Gender Inequities in a Neo-Liberal Era," *Gender, Place and Culture*, Vol. 16, No. 4 (2009), pp. 409–426; Barbara Louise Endemaño Walker and Michael A. Robinson, "Economic Development, Marine Protected Areas and Gendered Access to Fishing Resources in a Polynesian Lagoon," *Gender, Place and Culture*, Vol. 16, No. 4 (2009), pp. 467–484.

50 Sultana, "Suffering for Water," p. 167.

51 Ahlers and Zwarteveen, "The Water Question in Feminism"; Walker and Robinson, "Economic Development."

52 Ibid.

53 Bakker and Morinville, "The Governance Dimensions of Water Security," p. 10.

54 USAID, *Water and Conflict: A Toolkit for Programming* (Washington, DC: USAID, 2014), p. 9.

55 Ibid.

56 Ibid.

57 GTZ, *The Water Security Nexus: Challenge and Opportunities for Development Cooperation* (Eschborn, Germany: GTZ, 2010).

58 See, Edward R. Carr and Mary C. Thompson, "Gender and Climate Change Adaptation in Agrarian Settings: Current Thinking, New Directions, and Research Frontiers," *Geography Compass*, Vol. 8, No. 3 (March 4, 2014), pp. 182–197; Arora-Jonsson, "Virtue and Vulnerability"; Anna Kaijser and Annica Kronsell, "Climate Change Through the Lens of Intersectionality," *Environmental Politics*, Vol. 23, No. 3 (October 11, 2013), pp. 1–17; Djoudi and Brockhaus, "Is Adaptation to Climate Change Gender Neutral?" pp. 123–135; Ahmed and Fajber, "Engendering Adaptation"; Irene Dankelman and Willy Jansen, "Gender, Environment, and Climate Change: Understanding the Linkages," in Irene Dankelman, ed., *Gender and Climate Change: An Introduction* (London: Earthscan, 2010), pp. 21–54; Fatma Denton, "Climate Change Vulnerability, Impacts, and Adaptation: Why Does Gender Matter?" *Gender & Development*, Vol. 10, No. 2 (2002), pp. 10–20.

59 See, Hsiang, Burke and Miguel, "Quantifying the Influence of Climate on Human Conflict"; Solomon Hsiang and Marshall Burke, "Climate, Conflict, and Social Stability: What Does the Evidence Say?" *Climatic Change*, Vol. 123, No. 1 (October 17, 2014), pp. 39–55; M. Burke, S.M. Hsiang and E. Miguel, "Climate and Conflict," *Annual Review of Economics*, Vol. 7 (August 2015), pp. 577–617; Colleen Devlin and Cullen S. Hendrix, "Trends and Triggers Redux: Climate Change, Rainfall, and Interstate Conflict," *Political Geography*, Vol. 43 (2014), pp. 27–39.

60 Janani Vivekananda, Janpeter Schilling and Dan Smith, "Understanding Resilience in Climate Change and Conflict Affected Regions of Nepal," *Geopolitics*, Vol. 19, No. 4 (2014), pp. 911–936, 912; See also Abrahams and Carr, "Understanding the Connections Between Climate Change and Conflict."

61 Alvin Chandra et al., "Gendered Vulnerabilities of Smallholder Farmers to Climate Change in Conflict-Prone Areas: A Case Study from Mindanao, Philippines," *Journal of Rural Studies*, Vol. 50 (2017), pp. 45–59.

62 Jeffrey Stark, Christine Mataya and Kelley Lubovich, *Climate Change, Adaptation, and Conflict: A Preliminary Review of the Issues*, CMM Discussion Paper No. 1 (Washington, DC: USAID, 2009).

63 Adaptation Partnership, *Climate Change Adaptation and Peacebuilding in Africa* (Washington, DC: Adaptation Partnership, 2015).

64 Kirby Reiling and Cynthia Brady, *Climate Change and Conflict: An Annex to the USAID Climate-Resilient Development Framework* (Washington, DC: USAID, 2015), p. 16.

65 Ibid., p. 21.

66 Katie Peters and Janani Vivekananda, *Topic Guide: Conflict, Climate and Environment* (London: Overseas Development Institute and International Alert, 2014).

67 GTZ, *Climate Change and Security: Challenges for German Development Cooperation* (Eschborn, Germany: GTZ, 2010), p. 32.

68 USAID, *Building Resilience to Recurrent Crisis: USAID Policy and Program Guidance* (Washington, DC: USAID, 2012), p. 5.

69 Ibid., p. 9.

70 Ibid., pp. 11–12.

71 Fröhlich and Gioli, "Gender, Conflict, and Global Environmental Change," p. 143.

72 Edward R. Carr, "Men's Crops and Women's Crops: The Importance of Gender to the Understanding of Agricultural and Development Outcomes in Ghana's Central Region," *World Development*, Vol. 36, No. 5 (May 2008), pp. 900–915.

73 Fröhlich and Gioli, "Gender, Conflict, and Global Environmental Change," p. 143.

74 GTZ, *Climate Change and Security*, p. 32.

75 Fröhlich and Gioli, "Gender, Conflict, and Global Environmental Change."

76 Ibid., p. 143.

77 JICA, "Gender Issues in Conflict and Disaster: Supporting the Weak and Vulnerable in Our Society," *JICA's World*, Vol. 9, No. 3 (2017), pp. 2–3.

78 USAID, *Implementation of the United States National Action Plan on Women, Peace, and Security* (Washington, DC: USAID, 2012), p. 5.

79 USAID, *The Automated Directives System (ADS) Chapter 205* (Washington, DC: USAID, 2017), p. 28.

80 Ibid., p. 11.

81 Ibid., p. 28.

82 Ibid., p. 25.

83 See Andrew Natsios, *The Clash of the Counter-Bureaucracy and Development* (Washington, DC: Center for Global Development, 2010).

84 See Richard A. Schroeder, *Shady Practices: Agroforestry and Gender Politics in the Gambi* (Berkeley, CA: University of California Press, 1999); Dianne Rocheleau and David Edmunds, "Women, Men and Trees: Gender, Power and Property in Forest and Agrarian Landscapes," *World Development*, Vol. 25, No. 8 (1997), pp. 1351–1371.

85 See Jean-Christophe Gaillard, "Vulnerability, Capacity, and Resilience: Perspectives for Climate and Development Policy," *Journal of International Development*, Vol. 22, No. 2 (2010), pp. 218–232; W. Neil Adger, "Social and Ecological Resilience: Are They Related?" *Progress in Human Geography*, Vol. 24, No. 3 (2000), pp. 347–364; Carl Folke, "Resilience: The Emergence of a Perspective for Social-Ecological Systems Analyses," *Global Environmental Change*, Vol. 16, No. 3 (2006), pp. 253–267; Christopher B. Barrett and Mark A. Constas, "Toward a Theory of Resilience for International Development Applications," *Proceedings of the National Academy of Sciences of the United States of America*, Vol. 111, No. 40 (2014), pp. 14625–14630.

86 See Stephane Hallegatte, Jun Rentschler and Brian Walsh, *Building Back Better: Achieving Resilience Through Stronger, Faster, and More Inclusive Post-Disaster Reconstruction* (Washington, DC: World Bank, 2018).

87 Ibid., pp. 2–3.

88 Ibid., p. 27.

89 This is a point of growing concern in the literature on livelihoods. See Anthony Bebbington, "Capitals and Capabilities: A Framework for Analyzing Peasant Viability, Rural Livelihoods and Poverty," *World Development*, Vol. 27, No. 12 (1999), pp. 2021–2044; Edward R. Carr, "Livelihoods as Intimate Government: Reframing the Logic of Livelihoods for Development," *Third World Quarterly*, Vol. 34, No. 1 (2013), pp. 77–108.

90 Edward R. Carr et al., *USAID/Mali Climate Change Adaptation Activity (MCCAA) Behavioral Baseline Survey: Final Synthesis Report* (Washington, DC: USAID, 2016).

91 Snorek, Renaud and Kloos, "Divergent Adaptation to Climate Variability."

9

GENDER, HUMANITARIAN EMERGENCIES AND SECURITY

Tamara Nair

Natural disasters have many different causes, but they often generate similar human experiences – especially in terms of the human vulnerabilities, response capacities and power dynamics within affected societies. In every society, some people are more vulnerable to sudden disasters than others. Similarly, some members of society have relatively limited capacities for coping and recovering from crisis situations. These vulnerabilities and capacities are usually determined by factors such as economic class, race, age and gender. In this chapter, I examine the gender dimensions of humanitarian emergencies caused by natural disasters.

We have to begin by distinguishing between *natural disasters* and *humanitarian emergencies*. One might be tempted to use these terms interchangeably, but this would gloss over a fundamentally important issue. Natural events – such as earthquakes, tsunamis, floods, tropical storms and droughts – might be hazardous to the physical environment as well as flora and fauna, but they might not necessarily harm human beings. A natural disaster becomes a humanitarian emergency when human beings are affected. This might seem obvious, but it points to the heart of the matter: in order to understand how natural disasters become humanitarian emergencies, we have to understand how the affected human societies are constructed and organized – especially in terms of power dynamics in social, economic and political relations. The nature and magnitude of the physical events themselves are important, of course, but the human components of the equation are key: social, economic and political practices that are in place before, during and after an event will have a tremendous impact on the scale of the resulting disaster. Some scholars have argued that disasters are more a consequence of socio-economic than natural factors.[1]

The importance of gender in conflict settings has received a great deal of attention from activists and scholars, and this issue has been placed on the policy agenda through the adoption of United Nations Security Council Resolution (UNSCR)

1325 in 2000 and nine subsequent Women, Peace and Security (WPS) resolutions in the 2000s and 2010s. It is now widely recognized that women and girls face great and specific security threats in conflict situations. Scholars have demonstrated that there is a strong connection between a society's treatment of women and the peacefulness of that society.[2]

The gender dimensions of humanitarian emergencies have received much less attention from scholars and policymakers. Women and girls suffer disproportionately during most humanitarian emergencies, but the issue of gender-based suffering in these disasters is just beginning to be examined. And – just as the treatment of women in a society is correlated with the peacefulness of that society – gender bias in a society is an important barometer of how disastrous a humanitarian emergency is likely to be.

In most cases, most of the victims in humanitarian emergencies are women and girls. This is due to discriminatory social practices vis-à-vis women and girls: the effects of these events are not "natural" or due to nature; they are socially constructed. The high female mortality rates and the disproportionate, prolonged suffering of women after the 2004 Indian Ocean tsunami are examples of these problems.[3] The effects of these events on the lives of women, in turn, impacts the lives and experiences of many other people in societies. These second-order gender effects are important, but this kind of relational analysis is lacking in disaster studies.

More generally, scholars, analysts and policymakers need to examine gender norms and gender orders in pre-crisis social environments in order to develop a better understanding of the social constructs and social dynamics that will shape the disasters themselves. These inquiries are needed to develop inclusive, comprehensive response strategies, recovery plans and rebuilding policies.

There has been some policy progress, mostly at the international level. International aid organizations, governments, research institutes and local Non-Governmental Organizations have taken steps to pool knowledge about best practices and to carry out joint exercises. Problems remain, however. Transmission of best practices from the international level to regional and national levels has not been smooth or uniform. This has been due to cultural and institutional barriers, including the persistence of gender stereotypes in many policy circles. International rhetoric about gender mainstreaming has not led to the inclusion of gender dynamics in disaster policy on the ground.

In broader strategic terms, international actors continue to design disaster-response policies with the goal of restoring the status quo ante in the affected countries. They have not recognized that the social disruptions caused by natural disasters create openings for advancing gender equality. Although progressives and patriarchs might disagree on the intrinsic value of gender equality, one thing is clear: gender-equal societies are likely to be damaged less in disasters. Making progress on gender equality would therefore reduce the human dimensions of future disasters. Incorporating gender considerations into disaster prevention policies would be wise from a disaster prevention standpoint. Unfortunately, international actors continue to prioritize restoration over transformation. To put it bluntly, natural disasters have been wasted opportunities for change.

Looking ahead, global warming and climate change will present mounting challenges for humanity in the decades to come. The relationship between climate change and natural disaster events is complex. Scientists are increasingly worried that global warming, rising sea levels and changing climate patterns will generate increasing risks – in terms of both frequency and intensity – from tropical storms, coastal flooding, heat waves and wildfires, droughts and other problems.[4] These events, in turn, could lead to more substantial evacuations, longer-lasting population movements, unstable food production and food supplies, water management problems and other problems.[5] Given the very real possibilities of increased occurrences of disaster events, it would be wise to have stronger policies in place for humanitarian emergencies and disaster responses. It will also be essential for policy analysts and policymakers to do a better job of integrating the gender dimensions of disaster events into policy development and implementation planning.

This chapter assesses the state of research and policy on these issues. The first section of this chapter examines the social construction of humanitarian emergencies, focusing in particular on the gender dimensions of these emergencies. The second section looks at significant changes in disaster policy and the drivers of these changes. The third section analyzes obstacles to policy progress. The chapter concludes with suggestions for strategies that could strengthen the role of gender considerations in disaster policy deliberations. This could lead to better policy outcomes and, importantly, less suffering for women and their disaster-affected societies.

The gender dimensions of humanitarian emergencies

A natural event becomes a humanitarian emergency or disaster when it affects people. In addition, these events accentuate existing deficiencies in state capacities and magnify inequalities of class and gender. Katrina Lee-Koo has observed that disasters affect "the economy, development, international relations, and of course, the already complex relationships between state and civil society."[6] Humanitarian disasters are socio-economic constructs, and they reflect existing discriminatory elements in society. This includes the dominant power structures that exist in society. These structures determine the delineation between those who have access to resources, can acquire information and possess decisionmaking capabilities and those who do not. In a crisis, this can determine the level of suffering – or even life or death – of an individual. The level of suffering experienced by an individual during a natural disaster can depend on factors such as economic class, race, age and gender. This is especially true in developing countries, but it also shapes humanitarian emergencies in developed nations – as Hurricane Katrina revealed in the United States in 2005.[7]

A number of biological, social and economic conditions and processes make women more vulnerable to natural disasters.[8] From having limited options to begin with to prolonged suffering post-disaster, women are impacted more severely in these crises, and those who survive have longer physical and psychological recovery times.

However, not all women suffer disproportionately compared to men. Women who are educated, who are in higher socio-economic brackets or who are members of privileged racial or ethnic groups are much better off than men who are less educated or from lower economic classes, even in traditionally conservative societies with very distinct gender divisions. Similarly, not all men suffer less during and after natural disasters. The 2018 landslide triggered by Typhoon Mangkhut in the Cordillera Mountains in the Philippines killed a large number of young men who were prospecting for gold in the area.[9] In this case, the majority of victims were men who were trying to earn a living for themselves and their families. Dominant masculinity norms – including the pressure on men to provide for their families – can put men in harm's way.[10] This is an important and often-neglected gender dimension of humanitarian emergencies.

The gendered nature of suffering in humanitarian emergencies has been discussed at the highest levels in international policy circles. The disproportionate suffering of women in natural disasters is considered in the United Nations International Strategy for Disaster Reduction (UNISDR), which includes adoption of a gender policy for disaster risk reduction.[11] The importance of developing a gendered understanding of the impacts of natural disasters is also included in the Hyogo Framework for Action – the global blueprint for disaster risk-reduction efforts in 2005–2015 as well as the Sendai Framework for disaster risk-reduction that has been adopted for 2015–2030.

The development and integration of gender perspectives have not been strong in regional and national disaster polices. For example, the South Asian Association of Regional Corporation (SAARC) explicitly states in its disaster risk reduction framework that "progress in the area of gender and women's issues remains low and a number of countries accept that this is a gap.[12] Member states of the Association of Southeast Asian Nations (ASEAN) agree in their Agreement on Disaster Management and Emergency Response (AADMER) that women are a vulnerable group that requires further attention.[13]

Natural disasters are intensely disruptive in personal, economic and political terms. They open up the home: outsiders are allowed into domestic spaces that have become undone. The private sphere becomes visible. This can affect both men and women in disaster settings. Outsiders such as first responders can pass judgment on how things should be done. Resettlement camps – which are supposed to provide protection in emergencies – can become replicas and reproductions of existing power dynamics in societies, right down to resource allocation, domestic violence and access to health care. This can compromise security in the camps and further exacerbate existing inequalities.

Natural disasters also highlight the skewed gender norms and stereotypes about men and women that are prevalent in societies. Men are often perceived as leaders, aggressive go-getters and "undomesticated" individuals, in that they are minimally involved in the everyday grind of household duties. Women are often stereotyped as homemakers, nurturers and "weaker" individuals. These gendered norms and expectations can influence the formulation of disaster policies. Including a gender dimension in disaster policy should be contextual, since there are different practices and expectations in different parts of the world. Disaster policies often reflect this, but even in places where gender equality is more or less assumed (but not necessarily established) and where policies are supposedly gender neutral, women often suffer disproportionately in humanitarian emergencies. This was certainly true in the aftermath of Hurricane Katrina in the United States, where women – particularly women of color and women in lower income groups – faced especially severe challenges.[14] In 2018, Hurricane Florence in the Carolinas in the United States had different effects on women and men.[15]

Narratives about women almost always emphasize their victimhood – which is often attributed to social, political, religious or economic power systems that separate men from women and women from opportunities. Much less attention is paid to women's strengths – including their resilience and their ability to form informal networks almost immediately in crises. Kristine Aquino Valerio has written about the resilience of women during and after Typhoon Haiyan, which struck the Philippines in 2013.[16] In 2010 and 2011, destructive floods in Sindh, Pakistan, forced women to find food and medical care for their families and other victims while contending with numerous cultural restrictions on their freedom of movement.[17] Women affected by the devastating Australian bushfires of 2009 – the largest peacetime disaster to occur in Australia at that point in time – were active in creating "community cohesion through the organization of communal activities." They later moved on to lobbying politicians.[18] In crisis after crisis, women have engaged in multiple activities in the social sphere to safeguard the welfare of their families and their communities.

Narratives surrounding men and ideas of how men should behave and respond to crisis situations are also exaggerated. For instance, men are seen as being more "hardy" in crises. This downplays the many layers of insecurities men face before, during and after disasters strike, including psychological, economic and physical hardships. Men are displaced and disoriented during humanitarian crises, especially in terms of established power norms. Men are also upended by the increasingly militarized nature of humanitarian assistance, including the presence of both domestic and foreign military forces during disaster responses. These non-local military forces usually exclude the local "civilian male." When external military forces and first responders arrive and take charge of many aspects of local life, local men may be perceived – by themselves and others – as useless. This can be emasculating. These insecurities often lead to socially vile behavior, including domestic and intimate partner violence.

There is very little differentiation between developed and developing countries with respect to these masculinity issues and subsequent male misbehavior. After the 2011 earthquake in Canterbury, New Zealand, alcohol and drug addiction rates among local men increased. Domestic assaults by local men also increased.[19]

Domestic assaults by men also increased following the 2010 earthquake in Haiti.[20] Similar problems have developed in a string of other cases.[21]

At the international level, disaster response planning is carried out by institutions that are highly hierarchical and male-dominated, and they are usually overseen by a few powerful men. Although disaster response teams are multinational and complex, decisionmaking might be quite centralized – again, in the hands of a few men. These institutional structures and decisionmaking processes are well-established and rarely challenged.[22] It would certainly be difficult for local people who have been upended in a humanitarian crisis to challenge these institutional structures in the midst of a crisis.

External rescuers and humanitarian workers often assume that their efforts, backed by the power of science and technology, have universal applicability.[23] In reality, the effectiveness of humanitarian efforts is often determined by local access to resources such as safe drinking water, food, health care, safe passage and individual safety – before, during and after a crisis. Access to education and economic opportunities before a crisis can also determine how individuals cope with disasters and participate in restoration efforts. All of these access capacities vary widely in societies – they are not universal from person to person or from crisis to crisis – and they are strongly shaped by gender as well as by class, race and age. External rescuers and humanitarian workers generally do not take these local variations and variables into account. As a result, those who have the most leverage over response efforts have the least understanding of the vitally important social situation on the ground.

The increasingly militarized nature of disaster response focuses primarily on operations and logistics, along with an almost obsessive preoccupation with "Big Science" and technology.[24] Many disaster response planners view the core problems as "natural catastrophes," which leads them to focus on technical knowledge and interventions aimed at reducing risks and mitigating impacts. Most of their planning is geared toward informing military and civilian bureaucracies that will be involved in any response efforts.

Much less attention is paid to the "softer" human and social dimensions of humanitarian emergencies. Issues such as human rights and gender are afterthoughts – tangential to the military and technical issues that are seen as most important. It is not surprising, therefore, that humanitarian emergencies often lead to human rights violations and disproportionate levels of suffering by women. These issues have not been top planning priorities. Due to the neglect of human rights, women's rights and social justice issues in disaster planning and policies, disaster-affected societies face compounded social problems in the aftermath of disaster events. Policy neglect has policy – and human – consequences.

Significant changes and drivers for progress

There has been a turn in disaster research over the years, especially in the early to mid-2000s, as activists and scholars have observed and started to analyze the gendered nature of suffering in humanitarian emergencies. According to Elaine

Enarson and her colleagues, the theoretical foundations of disaster research have expanded, and the field has become more multidisciplinary.[25] In 2018, the journal *Disasters* devoted a special issue of the journal to gender and violence in humanitarian emergencies.[26] Most research on gender and disasters is based on a "social ecology approach, which examines how social actors are embedded in complex, multi-level social systems shaped by dynamic and historical processes that result in differential access to resources."[27]

In developed nations, disaster research has focused on the gendered division of labor and gendered opportunities.[28] In developing nations, much disaster research is rooted in development and gender equality.[29] Scholars have examined the differentiated effects of disasters on women, and several have highlighted the need for greater participatory planning and more inclusive decisionmaking in disaster policies. For example, a study on the triangular dynamics of female-headed households, economic vulnerability and climate variability in South Africa highlighted the importance of greater inclusion of women in flood and drought mitigation policies.[30] Another study examined 85 developing countries that combine fairly high levels of gender inequality with high levels of vulnerability to disasters. It found that economically secure women are less vulnerable to natural hazards, especially in light of climate variability.[31]

The development of innovative and effective disaster policies will depend on greater consideration of diverse voices and experiences. Policy developers should also pay greater attention to gender relations and how the experiences of one group affect others. These considerations are lacking in most disaster management policies around the world.

Although the policy world has lagged in important respects, scholars have been developing a more nuanced understanding of many critical issues, including the role of gender in disasters and humanitarian emergencies. Scholars have been examining male and female experiences in disasters, as well as institutional practices that maintain established patterns of gender domination. Scholars have also been advancing intersectional analyses of gender, class, race and sexuality. Not surprisingly, more attention is being paid to the nexus of climate change, conflict and gender inequality.[32]

Policy developers and policy actors have been slow to draw on and incorporate these new findings in their plans and programs. This is not to say that there have been no changes at the policy level. There are some signs of progress at the international level, especially in terms of coordinating efforts, identifying vulnerable groups and collecting data.

Many policy changes began to unfold in the 1990s. The dissolution of the Soviet Union and Yugoslavia along with economic liberalization in the early 1990s led several previously insular countries to open up. Throughout the 1990s and early 2000s, international actors launched humanitarian interventions in conflict zones and humanitarian actions for relief and recovery in natural disaster settings. For example, the 1999 Izmit earthquake in Turkey and the 1998 hurricane Mitch in Honduras and Nicaragua prompted an intense inflow of international relief.[33]

In both conflict and disaster settings, the suffering of women and girls was immense, and people around the world became more aware of these problems. Humanitarian actions generated field reports from soldiers, peacekeepers and humanitarian workers about the unique needs of women and girls in these crisis settings.[34] Growing awareness of these problems and growing momentum for action led to adoption of the Beijing Declaration and Platform for Action in 1995 and UNSCR 1325 and the WPS agenda in 2000.

In the early 2000s, international humanitarian actors began to focus on ways to provide more timely and predictable responses to humanitarian crises around the globe.[35] In 2005, the United Nations (UN) Under-Secretary General and Emergency Relief Coordinator (USG/ERC) in the United Nations Office for the Coordination of Humanitarian Affairs (UNOCHA) launched a comprehensive humanitarian reform process.[36] At the same time, a Central Emergency Relief Fund (CERF) advisory group was established to provide the USG/ERC with periodic policy guidance on the use of emergency relief funds. Membership criteria for the CERF group reflected both geographical and gender balance considerations.[37]

The 2005 reform effort introduced the Cluster Approach, which aimed to improve coordination, planning and proper prioritization in humanitarian efforts.[38] The Cluster Approach operates at two levels. At the global level, the new approach tries to strengthen system-wide preparedness and technical capacities to respond to humanitarian emergencies. Global Cluster leaders are appointed to ensure effective interagency responses in particular sectors and areas of concern. At the country level, the Cluster Approach aims to strengthen coordination and effectiveness of humanitarian actions by mobilizing clusters comprised of state agencies, Non-Governmental Organizations (NGOs) and non-UN organizations. The goal is to ensure involvement of all relevant national and local institutions and to fully utilize available resources.[39]

One key Area of Responsibility (AoR) for all humanitarian actors is prevention of and responding to Gender-Based Violence (GBV) in humanitarian crises. The GBV AoR was established in 2008. It stated that the goal of preventing and responding to GBV is to save lives. It directed that all humanitarian actors would have to address the issue with "adequate, comprehensive and coordinated action in humanitarian emergencies from the outset."[40] The United Nations Population Fund (UNFPA) has been the lead agency for the GBV AoR since April 2016. These were important, positive steps. Mentioning gender in humanitarian efforts – especially in terms of preventing and responding to GBV – was itself noteworthy. Establishing a formal area of responsibility for and designating leadership on GBV prevention were significant institutional actions. Even so, it is important to note that these initiatives still described and framed women in a victim narrative; women are not promoted as primary participants in the reform process or humanitarian actions more generally.

Since the 2000s, both the collection and sharing of humanitarian data have improved – leading to the development of more than 30 platforms for sharing data on humanitarian crises. UNOCHA has been promoting the regular and timely collection of sex-and-age aggregated data since 2012.[41] Unfortunately, data is collected in different ways by different agencies, and this obviously impedes cross-platform and cross-country analysis. One of the most serious data problems is that most of the available data is not disaggregated by gender. This is the case for both developed and developing countries.[42] This is an absolutely critical issue. Poor data inevitably leads to poor analysis and poor policy. Having data disaggregated by gender is essential for analyzing the gender dimensions of humanitarian crises and designing effective, gender-sensitive humanitarian actions.

An additional problem is that the type of data being collected is specific to the organizations involved in data collection. There is consequently little data sharing between government departments. In Southeast Asia – the most disaster-prone region in the world – the natural disaster management offices of ASEAN's ten member states collect types of data as required by various government departments. National data is ultimately shared among member states at the ASEAN Commission on Disaster Management. Unfortunately, different departments and different governments collect different forms of data, drawing on various criteria and methodologies. This of course impedes cross-issue and cross-country analysis.[43] In any event, these data collection efforts favor operational and technical information, as opposed to gender-relevant information.

ASEAN aspires to be a global leader in disaster policy. It has one of the world's most developed mechanisms for regional cooperation, and it has adopted the first region-wide, legally binding agreement on disaster responses – AADMER. Although AADMER is a step forward for coordinating disaster actions, it does not have a gender dimension apart from viewing women as disaster victims; this is one of its major shortcomings.[44]

In 2012, the UN Commission on the Status of Women (CSW) adopted resolution 56/2, which highlighted the disproportionate effects of natural disasters on women, and it noted the social and economic factors that contribute to these vulnerabilities. A key driver for adoption of the resolution was the growing awareness of these gender-based problems, due to the devastating effects of the earthquake in eastern Japan in 2011 and the international humanitarian efforts that followed. This was another case where on-the-ground experiences led to more information, more awareness and more action on the gender dimensions of humanitarian emergencies.[45] The CSW resolution stressed that further efforts in gender-responsive disaster management were needed.

In 2018, an initiative by the Australian government and ASEAN member states has started to connect the WPS agenda with humanitarian emergencies, which could pave the way for including gender perspectives in natural disaster policies.[46] There is increasing interest in involving women in natural disaster policy at the regional level. The issues of gender dynamics and gender norms are gaining some traction in policy circles in the region. The Australia-ASEAN partnership is pushing for progress in its own region. This might provide a good model for the rest of the world on these issues.

Obstacles to progress

As discussed previously, disaster policies have evolved in some respects with regards to women and girls. The key drivers of these changes have been the opening up of some countries and the increased incidence of humanitarian interventions since the end of the Cold War. International interventions have been especially important: "on-the-ground" observations and reports by an array of international, state and non-state actors have drawn much more attention to the plight of women and girls in humanitarian emergencies. There has also been a growing acknowledgement of the important role women can play in disaster management policies.

Even so, progress has been slow, limited and uneven. Scholars and experts at the international level have emphasized that large-scale disasters affect women disproportionately. They have stressed the importance of incorporating a gender perspective in disaster management and mitigation policies. Unfortunately, the urgency of these priorities has not been recognized in many humanitarian efforts, especially at the national level. Many national initiatives continue to focus on "upgrading" technical, operational expertise. This section examines persistent obstacles to greater inclusion of gender issues in disaster policy.

Many countries – especially in the developing world – have policies in place to advance gender equality, gender mainstreaming and capacity-building for women and girls. This is often due to development donor criteria, national efforts to reach the Sustainable Development Goals (SDGs) and pressure from domestic and international activists. Even so, there is often a disconnect between national policies on human rights, gender equality and social development, on the one hand, and disaster management policies, on the other.

There are two main reasons for this disconnect. First, national policymakers often feel that they have met established international standards to protect women. A lot has been done – especially since the adoption of the Convention on the Elimination of All Forms of Discrimination against Women (CEDAW) in 1979, the Beijing Declaration and Platform for Action in 1995 and the WPS resolutions starting in 2000. National governments have also made specific commitments to advance the rights, living conditions and safety of women and girls through adoption of the Millennium Development Goals (MDGs) in 2000 and the SDGs in 2015. National governments have taken steps to follow through on these commitments via National Actions Plans (NAPs) to advance the WPS agenda, as well as policies to reach specific MDG and SDG targets. Many of these initiatives focus on the role women play in the social development arena. Much less emphasis has been placed on advancing women's participation in national economic affairs and national security policy, which are directly connected to humanitarian crisis situations. In a humanitarian crisis, it would be valuable to have more women providing input on economic and national security matters.

The second problem is that women are still seen as victims in humanitarian crises. Women are not viewed as important participants in disaster responses: women are not viewed as having agency, ideas, valuable experiences and capacities for action. This outlook is widespread at the national level, especially in many developing countries. The reasons for ignoring and excluding women vary. In some cases, the experiential knowledge women have from their daily lives is not valued as much as the technical or scientific knowledge that men might have due to their educational advantages.[47] Countries that ignore or exclude women do not benefit from the valuable insights and experiences women could bring to the table. National policy deliberations and disaster policies are not as informed or effective as they could be. Crisis prevention and crisis mitigation efforts consequently suffer – and, more importantly, people and communities suffer. Ignoring women increases community vulnerability.

A related issue is that there is often a disconnect at the national level between social development policy and disaster policy. In many countries, social development policies pay at least some attention to women, children and minorities. But when disasters strike, disaster management and mitigation policies take over – and disaster policies generally pay little or no attention to social issues, including gender issues. The ASEAN Intergovernmental Commission on Human Rights (AICHR) found this disconnect to be quite glaring in Southeast Asia.[48] An important lesson is that paying some attention to gender issues some of the time is not enough. Gender issues should be mainstreamed and integrated into national policies across the policy spectrum. Occasional interests need to be developed into consistent and real policy actions.

In general, there are four main obstacles to further integration of women and gender perspectives into disaster policies, especially at the national and local levels. First, as discussed previously, women are often seen as victims and little else. They are not seen as policy actors or agents of change. Second, when women are seen as actors, they are often labeled as "agents of development," which confines their agency to the social development and development policy areas. This framing limits women's participation in disaster policy discussions. Third, there is a general disconnect between policies on human rights, gender equality and social development, on the one hand, and disaster management and mitigation policies, on the other. This also limits the role of women in disaster policy formulation and implementation. Fourth, when disasters happen, national disaster policies then supersede all other social policies. This pushes social issues to the side and elevates the technical orientations and actions favored in disaster policy circles.

These obstacles account for the limited understanding and inclusion of gender in disaster policies, and they persist for three main reasons. First, disaster policy is a male-dominated field. Disaster policy formulation and disaster policy implementation are undertaken by (male-dominated) national governments, often drawing very heavily on (male-dominated) national security agencies and military forces. Disaster policy is made by male-dominated decisionmaking structures that focus on masculinized knowledge – with overriding emphasis on technology, science, logistics and management. Social issues in general and gender issues in particular are peripheral to the conceptual frameworks of these policymakers. Second, many people and certainly many policymakers have a generalized, pervasive idea of "human" behavior derived from decades of gender-blind research and policies.[49] This way of thinking fails to differentiate between the experiences of men and women, fails to examine issues from women's points of view and fails to consider the specific nature of women's suffering in disasters. This understanding of "human" behavior, moreover, is knowledge gained "through men's eyes" and derived from men's experiences. This knowledge-formation and policy-formation process is highly problematic at best, and it can be dangerous in crises – where women are often in vulnerable positions, combined with relatively little social capital and capabilities.[50] Third, dominant groups (such as religious or political leaders) are willing to allow minor reforms aimed at superficial changes in technological systems and operations, but they resist fundamental changes in gender considerations, gender perspectives and gender roles in society.[51]

Strategies for progress

Jörn Birkmann and his colleagues have described post-disaster situations as "windows of opportunity" for change.[52] In theory, this could include policy initiatives, organizational reforms and broader social transformations – all made possible by major shocks to the status quo. In reality, major post-disaster changes are rare. Indeed, many of the examples of suffering discussed in this chapter are due to governments and societies failing to change in the aftermath of previous disasters.

One of the main arguments developed in this chapter is that disaster prevention and disaster responses will be enhanced if gender considerations are integrated comprehensively into policy processes. Women's vulnerability and safety issues need to be taken into account, women's voices need to be heard and women's roles in policy need to be expanded – significantly and systematically. Masculinity issues and the safety concerns of men also need to be examined carefully in inclusive gender assessments. This would be a step forward in social justice terms, but it would also be wise in public safety terms: gender mainstreaming and gender perspectives will lead to better disaster prevention and disaster response policies. This, in turn, will save lives in future crises.

The best way to advance these goals is to build on and strengthen connections to existing international frameworks, rather than attempting to create and adopt entirely new initiatives. Existing frameworks are already well-developed analytically, and they have already attracted considerable political support. Three international frameworks should be utilized: the WPS agenda, the "Building Back Better" formula and human rights mechanisms.

Strengthening links with the WPS agenda

UNSCR 1325 was adopted in 2000 due to a growing recognition of the "disproportionate and unique impact of armed conflict on women."[53] There have been calls for a UNSCR focused specifically on the suffering of women in disaster settings.[54] However, it is not necessary or optimal to have a new resolution focused on disaster issues. It would be better to draw on the framework developed for WPS issues to advance a Women, Disaster and Security agenda.

The WPS agenda is comprised of four main pillars: prevention, participation, protection, and relief and recovery. These four pillars should also be policy priorities for a more sophisticated, inclusive and effective conception of disaster policies.

Disaster management strategies should recognize the specific roles of women in disaster mitigation and response, as well as in relief and recovery. Women's concerns and women's participation should be expanded in risk identification and mitigation, disaster responses and into recovery and rehabilitation efforts. Drawing on the WPS framework, the goals should be prevention of harm, protection from harm, relief and recovery assistance in the event of a disaster and greater women's participation in every stage of the process. The latter should include participation of women in policy planning processes and policy implementation on the ground. Women's participation in these processes should be regular, systematic and extensive. In other words, it should be mainstreamed.

Similarly, to the WPS agenda and its call for the increased involvement of women in all stages of planning and implementation, it is particularly important to increase the number of female first responders. This will help to protect women and girls, especially in societies where men and women are often segregated. After the 2004 Indian Ocean tsunami, for example, Oxfam reported that some women in Aceh did not want to be rescued by unfamiliar men because the women's clothing had been torn or their headscarves had come off.[55] In most emergencies, most of the first responders are men, and the men often come from other communities and distant locations. The presence of more female first responders will help to save lives in places where these gender issues are pronounced. The presence of female security officers will also help to protect women and girls in emergency camps. This will make it safer for women to move around the camps and access essential resources such as water and food rations.[56] More generally, reform efforts should focus on recruiting and training more female staffers in all areas of disaster response and management, including medical teams.

One of the lessons learned from the WPS initiatives is the importance of collecting and compiling gender-disaggregated data. This lesson is certainly relevant in pre-disaster and post-disaster situations. Having gender-disaggregated data would provide policymakers with a more nuanced situational awareness of the effects of disasters. Having more women involved in data collection efforts would make these efforts more effective. In some cultural settings, women are much more likely to interact with other women than men, and some of the needed data might be personal in nature.

Many types of data should be collected. This should include information on all forms of violence, economic losses, and psychological or emotional trauma. The WPS Index, first launched in 2017 and updated in 2019, provides an excellent framework: it assesses women's well-being by examining 11 indicators across three dimensions – inclusion, justice and security.[57] Improved data collection efforts on disaster issues would provide stronger foundations for evidence-based research, leading to the incorporation of gender inequality as a component of the social construction of risk. Better data and more sophisticated, gender-based analyses should, in turn, lead to the development of better response, recovery and long-term rehabilitation policies.

Building back better – and differently

The Sendai framework for disaster risk reduction in 2015–2030 emphasizes the importance of incorporating gender considerations into disaster planning, and it calls for planners and responders to "Build Back Better" with respect to post-disaster reconstruction.[58] These are important priorities, but both of these Sendai formulations are framed in problematic ways.

Integrating gender considerations more systematically into disaster planning should be a priority at the international, national and local levels. The Sendai framework, however, calls for "empowering women and persons with disabilities to publicly lead and promote gender equitable and universally accessible response, recovery, rehabilitation and reconstruction approaches."[59] Although it would be good to elevate the roles of both women and persons with disabilities in disaster planning, it is highly problematic to lump these two groups together. This categorization reinforces the stereotype that women (and persons with disabilities) should be viewed mainly as victims. This traditional, simplistic characterization implicitly limits the role that women (and persons with disabilities) should play as active participants in planning, response and recovery efforts. It frames these groups as passive and helpless. It also states that women should take the lead in promoting gender equitable policies; it would be even better for women and men – everyone – to develop gender perspectives on these issues and mainstream these gender considerations in disaster planning.

The Sendai framework also notes that disasters provide critical opportunities for communities and countries to "Build Back Better." The idea is that reconstruction efforts should include measures that would prevent or reduce damage in future crises. This is reasonable and far-sighted. Disaster planners, however, almost universally frame this goal in terms of local and national "resilience" and "resilience building." According to the resilience formulation, the goal is for communities and countries to enhance their capacities to bounce back from disasters and restore the status quo ante – the way things were prior to the crisis. This might make sense for some elements of physical infrastructure, but it is more complicated in areas such as economic resilience, socio-ecological resilience and community resilience.[60] A UN report specifically states that the planning goal should be "the restoration of physical infrastructure and societal systems, and . . . the revitalization of livelihoods, economies, and the environment."[61]

Imbedded in the "Build Back Better" framework is the goal of restoring social systems. This is appropriate for societies that have already achieved high levels of social equality and justice, but it is not clear why unequal, unjust societies should be restored as they were – or why international actors would want to prioritize this as a goal. Indeed, the "Build Back Better" goal seems to apply only to physical infrastructure; when it comes to social structures, the goal seems to be "Build Back the Same."

The "Build Back Better" framework should be applied to broader social and gender considerations as well. In some cases, humanitarian emergencies might provide systemic disruptions and opportunities for fundamental changes and social progress. To move this forward, planners will have to do a better job of engaging in bottom-up consultation and assessing group vulnerabilities in risk-reduction planning.[62] They will have to talk with people in communities and analyze risks and dangers more carefully. This will be one of the keys to alleviating suffering – of women and men, of all disadvantaged groups – during and in the aftermath of disasters.

Empowering disadvantaged groups is a core political commitment in many international and national policy documents. Following through on these commitments will require examinations of existing power structures that influence decisionmaking and participation. Cultural, social and political institutions cannot be changed overnight. To make progress, international and national policymakers must establish several new priorities: (1) they must examine established norms and practices that frame women as victims; (2) they must follow through on their commitments to enhance the participation of women in policy formulation and implementation; (3) they must evaluate disaster policies in terms of their effects on women and other disadvantaged groups, and then change biased practices and policies; (4) they need to integrate gender assessments and true gender perspectives into policy planning efforts. These steps would lead to more effective disaster management and mitigation policies that would significantly reduce the disproportionate suffering of women during and in the immediate aftermath of disaster events. In a nutshell, policy planners should not only look to building back better, they should aspire to building back differently.

Utilizing human rights mechanisms

Human rights are abstract ideals, but they are also reflected in human insecurities such as economic insecurities, food insecurities, health insecurities and safety.[63] State negligence, both before and after natural disasters, contributes greatly to human insecurities. Vasselin Popovski argues that, when this happens, state negligence constitutes a human rights violation.[64]

I extend this argument to women's insecurities in natural disasters. Social behaviors such as gender ordering and gender norms find their way into political understandings of women's roles in society.[65] State policies, such as development and disaster policies, reflect these understandings to the detriment of women and girls. This is not always a conscious act to undermine women. Rather, it can be a form of institutional neglect on the part of decisionmakers. As a result, policies pertaining to women – including economic policies and disaster management policies – can be inherently discriminatory. In the 1990s, for example, a labor force survey conducted in Uganda showed that, when people were asked to include a "secondary" activity or job in addition to their "primary" activity or job, the number of workers soared from 6.5 million to 7.2 million, revealing 700,000 "missing" workers – the majority of whom were women.[66]

If complete data that reflects real-life situations is not collected before the occurrence of natural disasters, the extent of post-disaster damage cannot be accurately estimated. Women, in particular, might not be recognized for their work, including unpaid work, in informal economic sectors. This means that some groups of survivors may not be sufficiently compensated or left out of economic rehabilitation processes. Similarly, social safety nets might not be well-designed; women, again, might be disadvantaged as a result. The development of effective post-disaster policies depends on having comprehensive, inclusive pre-disaster data on economic and other matters. Governments need to have a complete picture of economic losses for all victims – men and women. However, if data collection is incomplete and discriminatory, then disaster management policies based on that data will create and compound human insecurities and human rights violations. Women are especially likely to be discriminated against and harmed in this regard in disaster settings.

CEDAW and other international human rights mechanisms such as the Convention on the Rights of the Child, the International Convention on the Elimination of All Forms of Racial Discrimination and the International Covenant on Economic, Social and Cultural Rights could be utilized to address mistreatment of women and girls in post-disaster situations, including victimization, prolonged suffering, health problems and threats to security. Individual women, women's groups and NGOs and international organizations could use these mechanisms to make the case for better state policies before, during and after disasters. They should link ineffective socio-economic and disaster policies to women's physical, economic, social and psychological suffering, making the case that these policies constitute human rights violations in disaster situations.

There are obstacles to adopting this strategy. Although human rights are supposed to be fundamental rights for all people and at all places, the understanding of human rights in practice is colored by "history, geography, culture, politics, and economics."[67] Even talking about human rights can set some people on edge in some places. The collection of accurate data can be marred by methodological difficulties. The effectiveness of domestic courts and legal systems varies widely, depending on political ideals and power dynamics in different societies. It is also dependent on whether the state is party to these human rights instruments in the first place. But for those that are, this is a possible route to justice and action.

Conclusion

Elaine Enarson has observed that, in "over fifty years of research on emergencies, disasters and catastrophes in the United States, a conspicuous silence around gender has been maintained – a looking away, perhaps a calculated blindness."[68] This is surprising and troubling. As a high-income country, the United States is relatively progressive on gender issues, at least compared to countries where women and girls are systematically deprived of basic rights such as education and health care. Enarson's observation reinforces an important point: policymakers around the world have a long way to go on these issues. Much more needs to be done to incorporate women and gender considerations into planning for humanitarian emergencies.

One priority is participation. Women must be more involved in decisionmaking at every level (community, provincial, national, international) and in every arena (the social, economic and political dimensions of policymaking). Women must be involved in assessing policy problems, and they must be influential in the decision-making and policy implementation that follows. A broader priority is taking gender considerations into account in policy analysis and policy development. For example, the economic importance of the female labor force needs to be highlighted in both the formal and informal sectors.

The life-and-death problems generated by humanitarian emergencies are likely to become more intense and widespread in the decades ahead: the world's population is projected to grow by approximately 60 percent in the first half of the 21st century, at a time when climate change is likely to make our natural world more volatile. It is therefore urgent and vital for policymakers to do a much better job of preparing for humanitarian emergencies. This will depend critically on the role of women and gender considerations in policy planning. Advancing these issues is in the interest not just of women and girls, but all of humanity.

Notes

1 Phil O'Keefe, Ken Westgate and Ben Wisner, "Taking the Naturalness Out of Natural Disasters," *Nature*, Vol. 260 (1976), pp. 566–567.
2 See chapters 2 and 3 in this book.
3 Oxfam, *The Tsunami's Impact on Women*, Briefing Note (Oxford: Oxfam, March 2005); Eileen Pittaway, Linda Bartolomei and Susan Rees, "Gendered Dimensions of the 2004 Tsunami and a Potential Social Work Response in Post-Disaster Situations," *International Social Work*, Vol. 50, No. 3 (2007), pp. 307–319.
4 See Intergovernmental Panel on Climate Change (IPCC), *Global Warming of 1.5°; Summary for Policymakers* (New York: UN Environmental Program (UNEP), October 2018); IPCC, *The Ocean and Cryosphere in a Changing Climate* (New York: UNEP, September 2019); Science Advisory Group, *United in Science* (New York: United Nations, September 2019).
5 Paul F. Herman, Jr. and Gregory F. Treverton, "The Political Consequences of Climate Change," *Survival*, Vol. 51, No. 2 (April 2009), pp. 137–148.
6 Katrina Lee-Koo, "Gender at the Crossroad of Conflict: Tsunami and Peace in Post-2005 Aceh," *Feminist Review*, Vol. 101, No. 1 (2012), p. 65.
7 See Shirley Laska and Betty Hearn Morrow, "Social Vulnerabilities and Hurricane Katrina: An Unnatural Disaster in New Orleans," *Marine Technology Society Journal*, Vol. 40, No. 4 (Winter 2006), pp. 16–26; Pam Jenkins and Brenda Philips, "Battered Women, Catastrophe, and the Context of Safety After Hurricane Katrina," *NWSA Journal*, Vol. 20, No. 3 (Fall 2008), pp. 49–68.
8 Kanchana Ginige, Dilanthi Amaratunga and Richard Haigh, "Tackling Women's Vulnerabilities Through Integrating a Gender Perspective into Disaster Risk Reduction in the Built Environment," *Procedia Economics and Finance*, Vol. 18 (2014), pp. 327–335.

9 Hannah Beech, "Philippine Miners Trapped in Typhoon: Drawn by Gold, Drowned in Mud," *New York Times* (September 17, 2018).

10 Elaine Enarson, "Human Security and Disasters: What a Gender Lens Offers," in Christopher Hobson, Paul Bacon and Robin Cameron, eds., *Human Security and Natural Disasters* (London: Routledge, 2014), pp. 37–56.

11 UNISDR, *Making Disaster Risk Reduction Gender-Sensitive* (Geneva: UNISDR, 2009).

12 The SAARC member states are Afghanistan, Bangladesh, Bhutan, India, Nepal, the Maldives, Pakistan and Sri Lanka. See SAARC Disaster Management Centre, *Post-2015 DRR Framework for SAARC Region (HFa2)* (New Delhi: SDMC, March 2014).

13 The ASEAN member states are: Brunei, Cambodia, Indonesia, Lao PDR, Malaysia, Myanmar, the Philippines, Singapore, Thailand and Vietnam. See ASEAN, *ASEAN Agreement on Disaster Management and Emergency Response* (Jakarta: ASEAN Secretariat, 2009).

14 See Laska and Morrow, "Social Vulnerabilities and Hurricane Katrina"; Jenkins and Philips, "Battered Women, Catastrophe, and the Context of Safety After Hurricane Katrina."

15 Richard Fausset, "At Water's Edge, a Hostage to Nature and Poverty After Storm," *New York Times* (September 19, 2018).

16 Kristine Aquino Valerio, "Storm of Violence, Surge of Struggle: Women in the Aftermath of Typhoon Haiyan (Yolanda)," *Asian Journal of Women's Studies*, Vol. 20, No. 1 (2014), pp. 148–163.

17 Julie Drolet et. al., "Women Building Lives Post-Disaster: Innovative Community Practices for Building Resilience and Promoting Sustainable Development," *Gender and Development*, Vol. 23, No. 3 (2015), pp. 433–448.

18 Ibid., p. 438.

19 See Jacqui True, "Gendered Violence in Natural Disasters: Learning from New Orleans, Haiti and Christchurch," *Aotearoa New Zealand Social Work Journal*, Vol. 25, No. 2 (May 2016), pp. 78–89; Cecile Meier, "Hurt & Hope: Post-Quake Addiction and Domestic Abuse Bring Cantabrians Down," *Stuff* (September 30, 2017, @ stuff.co.nz).

20 Louis Herns Marcelin, "Violence, Human Insecurity, and the Challenge of Rebuilding Haiti: A Study of a Shantytown in Port-au-Prince," *Current Anthropology*, Vol. 56, No. 2 (April 2015), pp. 230–255.

21 Debra Parkinson, "Investigating the Increase in Domestic Violence Post Disaster: An Australian Case Study," *Journal of Interpersonal Violence*, Vol. 34, No. 11 (2019), pp. 2333–2362; Alyssa Banford and Cameron Kiely Froude, "Ecofeminism and Natural Disasters: Sri Lankan Women Post-Tsunami," *Journal of International Women's Studies*, Vol. 16, No. 2 (2015), pp. 170–187; Robyn Molyneaux et al., "Interpersonal Violence and Mental Health Outcomes Following Disaster," *BJPsych Open*, Vol. 6, No. 1 (2020), pp. E1, 1–7; Sanaz Sohrabizadeh, "A Qualitative Study of Violence Against Women After the Recent Disasters of Iran," *Prehospital and Disaster Medicine*, Vol. 31, No. 4 (2016), pp. 407–412.

22 Kenneth Hewitt, "Foreword," in Elaine Enarson and Bob Pease, eds., *Men, Masculinities and Disasters* (London: Routledge, 2016).

23 See Anthony J. Marsella and Michael A. Christopher, "Ethnocultural Considerations in Disasters: An Overview of Research, Issues, and Directions," *Psychiatric Clinics*, Vol. 27, No. 3 (2004), pp. 521–539.

24 See Hewitt, "Foreword."

25 Elaine Enarson, A. Fothergill and L. Peek, "Gender and Disaster: Foundations and New Directions for Research and Practice," in Havidán Rodríguez, William Donner and Joseph E. Trainor, eds., *Handbook of Disaster Research*, 2nd ed. (Cham, Switzerland: Springer, 2017).

26 Disasters, "Special Issue: Gender, Sexuality and Violence in Humanitarian Crises," *Disasters*, Vol. 42, No. 1 (January 2018).

27 W. Peacock, H. Gladwin and B.H. Morrow, quoted in Enarson, Fothergill and Peek, "Gender and Disaster," p. 206.

28 See Elaine Enarson, *Women Confronting Natural Disasters: From Vulnerability to Resilience* (Boulder, CO: Lynne Reiner, 2012).

29 See Madhavi Malalgoda Ariyabandu and Maithree Wickramasinghe, *Gender Dimensions in Disaster Management: A Guide for South* Asia (Warwickshire: Practical Action Publishing, 2003); Elaine Enarson and P.G. Dhar Chakrabarti, *Women, Gender and Disaster: Global Issues and Initiatives* (New Delhi: Sage, 2009).

30 Martin Flato, Raya Muttarak and Andre Pelser, "Women, Weather and Woes: The Triangular Dynamics of Female-Headed Households, Economic Vulnerability and Climate Variability in South Africa," *World Development*, Vol. 90 (February 2017), pp. 41–62.

31 Kelly F. Austin and Laura A. McKinney, "Disaster Devastation in Poor Nations: The Direct and Indirect Effects of Gender Inequality, Ecological Losses, and Development," *Social Forces*, Vol. 95, No. 1 (September 2016), pp. 355–380.

32 Enarson, Fothergill and Peek, "Gender and Disaster." See also: Christiane Fröhlich and Giovanna Gioli, "Gender, Conflict, and Global Environmental Change," *Peace Review*, Vol. 27, No. 2 (2015), pp. 137–146; Nancy A. Omolo, "Gender and Climate Change-Induced Conflict in Pastoral Communities: Case Study of Turkana in Northwestern Kenya," *African Journal on Conflict Resolution*, Vol. 10, No. 2 (2010), pp. 81–102; Joane Nagel, "Gender, Conflict and the Militarization of Climate Change Policy," *Peace Review*, Vol. 27, No. 2 (2015), pp. 202–208; Michael J. Papa and Wendy Papa, "The Crisis in Darfur and the Social Structure of Global Climate Change, Race, and Gender," in Gil Richard Musolf, ed., *Conflict and Forced Migration: Studies in Symbolic Interaction*, Vol. 51 (Bingley, UK: Emerald, 2019), pp. 43–70.

33 See Alex K. Tang, *Izmit (Kocaeli), Turkey, Earthquake of August 17, 1999, Including Ducze Earthquake of November 12, 1999: Lifeline Performance* (Reston, VA: American Society of Civil Engineers, 2000); International Federation of the Red Cross (IFRC), *Hurricane Mitch Operations: Emergency and Transitions Appeal – 1998/1999 Global Report* (Geneva: IFRC, October 21, 1999).

34 Personal Communication, Alistair D.B. Cook Coordinator of the Humanitarian Assistance and Disaster Relief Programme, S. Rajaratnam School of International Studies, Nanyang Technological University, Singapore (January 2, 2019).

35 UNOCHA, *Update on Humanitarian Reform* (New York: UNOCHA, March 2006, @ unocha.org).

36 Ibid.

37 UN Central Emergency Response Fund, *CERF Handbook* (New York: UNOCHA, 2018), p. 7.

38 See UNOCHA, *What Is the Cluster Approach?* (New York: UNOCHA, March 2012, @ unocha.org).

39 GBV Area of Responsibility (AoR), *Handbook for Coordinating Gender-Based Violence Interventions in Emergencies* (Geneva: GBV AoR, 2019).

40 UNOCHA, *What Is the Cluster Approach?*

41 UNOCHA, *Gender Equality: A People-Centered Approach: Policy Instruction* (New York: UNOCHA, 2012), p. 3.

42 See UNOCHA, *Humanitarian Data Exchange* (@ data.humdata.org).

43 Personal Communication, Alistair D.B. Cook.

44 Tamara Nair, "Why ASEAN's Disaster Management Strategy Must Include Gender," *East Asia Forum* (June 3, 2016).

45 UN Commission on the Status of Women, *Report on the Fifty-Sixth Session* (New York: United Nations, 2012), p. 10.

46 Government of Australia, Department of the Prime Minister and Cabinet, *ASEAN and Australia Working Together to Deliver Women's Equality, Peace and Security in Our Region* (Canberra: Government of Australia, April 19, 2018).

47 See Frank S. Arku and Cynthia Arku, "I Cannot Drink Water on an Empty Stomach: A Gender Perspective on Living with Drought," *Gender and Development*, Vol. 18, No. 1 (2010), pp. 115–124.

48 AICHR, *Women in Natural Disasters: Indicative Findings in Unraveling Gender in Institutional Responses: An ASEAN Intergovernmental Commission on Human Rights*, AICHR Thematic Study (Jakarta: ASEAN Secretariat, July 2018), p. 2.

49 Enarson, *Women Confronting Natural Disaster*, p. 2.

50 Ibid.

51 Jörn Birkmann et al., "Extreme Events and Disasters: A Window of Opportunity for Change?" *Natural Hazards*, Vol. 55, No. 3 (December 2010), pp. 637–655.

52 Ibid.

53 "Women, Peace and Security," *UN Peacekeeping* (March 29, 2017).

54 For a discussion, see Payal K. Shah, "Assisting and Empowering Women Facing Natural Disasters: Drawing from Security Council Resolution 1325," *Columbia Journal of Gender and Law*, Vol. 15, No. 3 (2006), pp. 711–748.

55 See Oxfam, *The Tsunami's Impact on Women*.

56 Leni M. Silverstein, "Review of 'Guidelines for Gender-Sensitive Disaster Management' by Asia Pacific Forum on Women, Law and Development," *Reproductive Health Matter*, Vol. 16, No. 31 (2008), p. 157.

57 See Georgetown Institute on Women, Peace and Security (GIWPS) and Peace Research Institute Oslo (PRIO), *Women, Peace and Security Index* (Washington, DC and Oslo: GIWPS and PRIO, 2019).

58 UNISDR, *Sendai Framework for Disaster Risk Reduction 2015–2030* (New York: United Nations, 2015).

59 Ibid., p. 21.

60 See Fran H. Norris et al., "Community Resilience as a Metaphor, Theory, Set of Capacities, and Strategy for Disaster Readiness," *American Journal of Community Psychology*, Vol. 41, Nos. 1–2 (March 2008), pp. 127–150; Neil W. Adger et al., "Socio-Ecological Resilience to Coastal Disasters," *Science*, Vol. 309, No. 5737 (August 12, 2005), pp. 1036–1039; Adam Rose, "Defining and Measuring Economic Resilience to Disasters," *Disaster Prevention and Management*, Vol. 13, No. 4 (2004), pp. 307–314; Stephanie E. Chang, "Infrastructure Resilience to Disasters," *The Bridge*, Vol. 4, No. 3 (2014), pp. 36–41.

61 UN General Assembly, *Report of the Open-Ended Intergovernmental Expert Working Group on Indicators and Terminology Relating to Disaster Risk Reduction*, Seventy-First Session, A/71/1644 (New York: United Nations, 2016), p. 11.

62 See J.C. Gaillard and Jessica Mercer, "From Knowledge to Action: Bridging Gaps in Disaster Risk Reduction," *Progress in Human Geography*, Vol. 37, No. 1 (2012), pp. 93–114; Jessica Mercer et al., "Culture and Disaster Risk Reduction: Lessons and Opportunities," *Environmental Hazards*, Vol. 1, No. 2 (2012), pp. 74–95.

63 Enarson, "Human Security and Disasters."

64 Vasselin Popovski, "State Negligence Before and After Natural Disasters as Human Rights Violations," in *Human Security and Natural Disasters*, pp. 94–110.

65 UNISDR, *Making Disaster Risk Reduction Gender-Sensitive*.

66 C. MacDonald, "Is There a Sexist Data Crisis?" *BBC News* (May 18, 2016).

67 Popovski, "State Negligence," p. 95.

68 Enarson, *Women Confronting Natural Disaster*, p. 2.

10

GENDER, HUMAN RIGHTS AND SECURITY

Corey Levine and Sari Kouvo

Snapshot 1:

In March 2015, Farkhunda Malikzada was brutally killed outside a shrine in the center of Kabul. Farkhunda, a religious studies student, had stopped at the shrine on her way home where she found the shrine's attendant selling charms that were considered un-Islamic. After she criticized the attendant for selling the trinkets, he accused her of having burnt the Koran. A group of men that had gathered to watch the argument started beating and kicking Farkhunda and, finally, burnt her alive. The police who were watching did nothing to try and save her life.

In the immediate aftermath of her murder, when rumors were still spreading that Farkhunda burned the Koran, some religious leaders, parliamentarians and government officials came out in support of the killing. However, as the real story emerged, Farkhunda began to be hailed as a martyr by women's rights advocates who saw this horrifying incident as symbolic of the widespread and systemic nature of the gender-based violence that exists in Afghanistan, and the deep-seated social and political acceptance of this reality.

Snapshot 2:

On July 24, 2018, Oksana Schachko was found dead in her apartment in Paris, where she had been living as a political refugee. Ukrainian-born Oksana was one of the founding members of Femen, a feminist resistance movement that has become famous for its bare-breasted and politically bold manifestations against sexism, homophobia, authoritarianism and nationalism. Oksana had been arrested several times for her activism, including for staging a topless protest while Russian President Vladimir Putin was visiting Ukraine. During one arrest, security forces allegedly stripped the Femen activists naked, poured oil on them and threatened to set them on fire. Another time, Oksana was beaten so badly that she was hospitalized.

Oksana's death was ruled a suicide, but formal investigations have continued. Oksana's life is a clear testimony to the personal cost and real danger involved in challenging patriarchal power structures.

These two stories are gruesome reminders that human rights – included in international treaties or in national constitutions – provide little protection, especially in situations of weak governance, lack of rule of law and insecurity. Farkhunda and Oksana were both committed and outspoken young women, but their motivations and the contexts in which they lived were vastly different. Farkhunda was attempting to defend her religion in a country that is riven by ethnic and religious tensions, spurred on by the international fault lines that have opened up since 9/11 between western "liberal" ideals and "traditional" non-western values. Oksana was trying to resist all forms of oppression and authoritarian power, including religion, in a country that is still in a transition to democracy in the shadow of oligarchs and Russian occupation.

It is also important to point to the many similarities of Farkhunda's and Oksana's stories. Both women were exercising their human rights in countries that have ratified all the major international human rights treaties, and both countries have a significant international presence engaged in addressing both human rights and security. Yet, neither woman received the protection she deserved (and was entitled to) from the state. Both paid the ultimate price for their commitments and actions.

In relaying the stories of Farkhunda and Oksana, our goal is to illustrate the link between human rights, gender and security – the focus of this chapter. We examine key policy issues, assess progress to date and reflect on drivers, obstacles and strategies for change. This chapter builds on existing academic and civil society research in the field.[1]

We hope to highlight how, on the one hand, persistent lobbying and successful partnerships between women's rights activists, national governments and multilateral organizations have transformed international human rights and expanded the women's rights and gender agenda into new policy arenas, including security. On the other hand, this chapter also examines the challenges of turning the progress that has been made in law and policy into practice.

This chapter has four main parts. In the first part, we provide a brief outline of the developments in international human rights since World War II, with a focus on women's rights. We highlight how progress in human rights has been driven by political and security transformations. We also examine the progress that has been made with regard to the recognition of equality as a fundamental principle of international law and the legal acknowledgement of the systematic discrimination faced by women around the world. We discuss how limited the guarantees for human rights are in situations where states choose to ignore their obligations and where the international community lacks the political will or capacity to assert pressure on states who violate the rights of, or fail to protect, their citizens.

In the second part, we link human rights to the broader international gender agenda. This part focuses on the significant policy advances that have been made with regard to women's rights and gender issues from the 1990s onward. It also shows that progress has come at a cost: framing women largely as victims and subduing feminist voices seeking to challenge authority, particularly around the militarization of international engagement and the policy emphasis on security.

The third part focuses on the implications of gender, human rights and security as "lived reality" in one of the most complex and significant international interventions since World War II – Afghanistan. Documenting the socio-political changes since the international community arrived in the country shortly after 9/11, we illustrate how the Women, Peace and Security (WPS) agenda has been successfully used to open up public space for women as well as bring about legal and policy changes. However, this case study also highlights one of the key lessons learned by the Afghan women's movement: never let down your guard advocating for your rights, as progress can be easily halted or reversed.

The fourth part focuses on guidelines for action, examining the importance of strategic partnerships between women's rights activists inside and outside formal institutions to build on the progress that has been made within the challenging global political and security environment.

International law and human rights

The history of human rights and equality has been intimately intertwined with conflict-related societal change since the Enlightenment revolutions of the late 1770s. The American Declaration of Independence (1776) and the French Declaration of the Rights of Man and the Citizen (1789) sought to limit state power and protect the individual against abuses by the state. Exempt from protection were women, children, indigenous peoples and slaves. The fact that early human rights declarations excluded many human beings from the sphere of protection was an important springboard for both the abolitionist struggles and women's suffragette movements of the 19th and 20th centuries.

Human rights became an international norm in the 20th century, particularly after World War II. While certain aspects of human rights were reflected in the anti-trafficking and slavery treaties of the late 19th century, as well as in the conventions adopted by the International Labour Organization (ILO) after World War I; it was only after the atrocities of World War II that the political will was found to make the protection of human rights a significant part of the newly established United Nations (UN). The founders of the United Nations were conscious that there was a need to have some measure of intervening in the internal affairs of states; overriding national sovereignty in cases of extreme abuse by the state against its citizens, as the horrors of World War II and the Holocaust amply demonstrated. While national sovereignty is one of the fundamental principles of international law, it is not absolute when states violate the rights of individuals within their territory.

The UN Charter, adopted in 1945, identified international security, economic development and human rights as the three foundational pillars of the organization. Maintaining international security has remained the UN's main *raison d'être*, as demonstrated by the central position of the UN Security Council within the organization and the Council's mandate, which focuses on international peace and security. Human rights have been more modestly promoted as an aspirational principle. Even so, the Universal Declaration for Human Rights (UDHR), adopted at the third session of UN General Assembly in December 1948, was one of the UN's first major achievements, and it remains a significant document.[2] It laid down the foundation of the modern human rights regime for both civil and political rights, as well as economic, social and cultural rights. However, it is a declaration – not a treaty – so it is not a legally binding document. Although the importance given by states to the principle of sovereignty is one of the main reasons the UDHR did not become a binding treaty, there were member states (particularly South Africa, with its apartheid system) that objected to turning the concepts of human rights into binding laws. They were suspicious that international human rights law could be used to challenge national laws and policies.

When the UDHR was drafted, discussions arose about its relevance for women. Early versions of the Declaration consistently used male pronouns. Some of the female delegates worried that in many countries references to "mankind" and "his rights" would be taken literally and used to exclude women from the sphere of rights. As a result, the final version of the UDHR largely uses gender-neutral language.

Today, human rights is one of the few areas of international law that focuses on how states treat their citizens and others residing within their territories. Significant strides have been made in bringing the concepts of human rights and equality into a coherent international legal framework since the adoption of UDHR, although most of the progress has come in waves interlinked with political strife and conflict.

During the Cold War and the period of decolonialization from the 1950s to the 1990s, the UN's human rights work was largely focused on developing legally binding treaties for individual states to adopt and ratify. It was during this time, for example, that the International Covenant for Civil and Political Rights (ICCPR, adopted in 1966) and the International Covenant for Economic, Social and Cultural Rights (ICESCR, adopted in 1966) were drafted. The principle of equality between men and women is included as a basic right in both documents, including specific provisions prohibiting discrimination based on sex.[3]

However, it is important to point out that the equality model employed in the ICCPR and ICESCR – as well as the one used in the UDHR, including employing gender-neutral language – is based on promoting equal rights protections and prohibiting overly discriminatory laws and policies. Feminist legal scholars and gender experts have argued that, while this model may create the idea of equal opportunities, it does nothing to address the decades or centuries of systemic and structural discrimination and disadvantages that women have faced worldwide, irrespective of national or international laws that offer "protection" from human rights abuses.[4]

It was the third wave of the women's movement in the 1960s and 1970s in North America and Western Europe, which had already achieved some progress in legal equality, together with the process of decolonization that led to the political realization that addressing race-based and gender-based discrimination requires more than equal rights proclamations. Both movements recognized that, in order to achieve meaningful equality, there would need to be a fundamental social shift that addressed the nature of systemic discrimination. As a result, the United Nations (as well as regional human rights institutions) responded by adopting declarations and treaties that prohibited racial and gender discrimination and promoted women's human rights. The most well-known being the Convention on the Elimination of All Forms of Racial Discrimination (CERD, adopted in 1965) and the Convention on the Elimination of All Forms of Discrimination against Women (CEDAW, adopted in 1979).

CEDAW defines what constitutes discrimination against women and how equality can be achieved (Article 2) and, as such, it is a prescriptive document.[5] It acknowledges the failure of gender-neutral conventions to fundamentally address the historical and systemic nature of female oppression, recognizing that women and girls are oppressed in ways unique to their gender. It recognized that gender equality can only be achieved through "special measures" that address the inherent disadvantages between the sexes that exist in all societies.[6]

CEDAW is the only human rights treaty that targets culture and tradition as influential forces shaping gender roles and family relations (Article 5). However, CEDAW has remained a controversial addition to the UN treaty family, largely because of its far-reaching definition of state obligation to promote equality, as well as its non-discrimination clause that not only demands action against formal discrimination but also requires states to take action against indirect discrimination. It is the Convention upon which the highest number of reservations and objections have been placed.[7] It took 20 years for a complaint mechanism to be adopted to ensure that individual complaints could be addressed through CEDAW.

The CEDAW Optional Protocol, as the complaints mechanism is known, has led to a number of decisions against member states on such issues as domestic violence, parental leave and forced sterilization, as well as an investigation into the systematic killing of women in the Mexican city of Ciudad Juarez.[8] However the complaint mechanism is only available to individuals in those countries whose governments have specifically ratified the Optional Protocol. In addition, decisions taken by the CEDAW Committee after a complaint has been filed are not binding on member states. Ultimately, the implementation of a complaint decision depends on the member state and how it wants to be viewed on its human rights record – by national and international audiences.

The declarations and treaties adopted by the United Nations as well as regional institutions in the post-World War II era sought to ensure that governments, on the one hand, protected basic civil and political rights and, on the other hand, promoted economic, social and cultural rights. But while UN human rights institutions monitor and encourage compliance, as yet there are no international enforcement mechanisms in place. Governments have been willing to turn human rights into international laws, but they have not been willing to hand over powers to international institutions to ensure compliance of the human rights protections that states have signed on to. States are also allowed to derogate from their human rights treaty obligations, including on the grounds of national security, further weakening incentives for compliance. However, some rights are non-derogable, including the prohibition against discrimination, although what this means in practice is dependent on the culture and policies of the individual state.[9]

Since there are no binding enforcement mechanisms, states can choose to ignore their human rights and gender equality obligations, given that the biggest risk they face is censure from the CEDAW Committee, from other UN monitoring mechanisms, from other states in international policy debates or through bilateral engagements. The extent to which public criticism and encouragement works depends on what interests states have in being seen to promote, protect and enforce human rights. This depends on which interests are most important in national – and to a lesser extent – international politics.

Some states have chosen to systematically oppose specific rights because these are seen as contrary to their religious traditions or national culture. While most of the UN's key human rights treaties have been signed by the vast majority of UN member states, there are ongoing debates around the interpretation of human rights and their compatibility with differing values and norms; these are often presented as religious matters, but they frequently have cultural undertones.[10] The debate between "universalist" and "relativist" conceptions of human rights is most prominent when it comes to women's rights and is exemplified by differing national laws with regard to the legal age for marriage for girls and custody or property rights for women in divorce, as well as in the heated debates regarding honor crimes and female genital mutilation. It can also be found in the laws and policies for dress codes for women around the world: from the obligatory *abayas* in Saudi Arabia to the *burkini* bans in some cities in France.

The commitments to equal rights and non-discrimination that were encoded in UN human rights treaties have helped women's rights advocates around the world fight discriminatory legislation in their own countries. CEDAW and other women's rights documents have provided useful resources by pointing out areas where positive action is needed to fight systemic and structural discrimination. And just as the concept of human rights from the late 18th century onward provided a basis for emancipatory struggles at national levels, the international human rights system has been particularly responsive to women's equality. However, the same cannot be said for other areas of international law – particularly those policies related to international security, which have been more resistant to demands for women's rights and gender equality.

Rights, gender and international policy

The break-up of the Soviet Union and the end of the Cold War opened up new opportunities for promoting and transforming international concepts with regard to human rights and international security. The first major step was the Declaration and Programme of Action adopted by the World Conference on Human Rights in Vienna in 1993. The Vienna Programme, as the Declaration became known, attempted to address the universalist versus relativist debate by concluding that human rights are universal: if states have signed and ratified international human rights treaties, they need to comply with the obligations in them. The Vienna Programme explicitly acknowledged that while the international human rights system recognizes that some differences in national interpretation should be respected, states are not allowed to violate rights under the guise of cultural differences.

The Vienna Program went a step further in the struggle for gender equality by clearly articulating that the rights of women and girls are fundamental parts of universal human rights and that the eradication of discrimination against women should be a priority for the international community.[11] There was considerable mobilizing at the Conference under the slogan "Women's rights are human rights," with a focus on violence against women as a war crime.[12]

The fourth World Conference on Women held in Beijing China in 1995 – at the time, the largest UN conference ever held – broadened the concept of equality between men and women by shifting from a woman-centered approach to a gender-centered framework. The Beijing Platform for Action (PFA), which set out a comprehensive agenda for women's empowerment, concluded that in order to bring about real change for women, the international human rights framework needed to fundamentally address "equality between women and men [as] a condition for social justice and [as] a fundamental prerequisite for development and peace."[13] The change in language signified a shift from focusing mainly on women and the issues they face to examining how gender affects both women and men: this broadened the scope for understanding female oppression – not as separate from men, but in relation to how both men and women function in society. As the Mission Statement for the PFA notes: "A transformed partnership based on equality between women and men is . . . essential, so that women and men can work together for themselves, for their children and for society to meet the challenges of the twenty-first century."[14]

While international legal documents continue to mainly refer to women and sex, most contemporary policy documents now use gender-based language, promoting gender analysis as a tool for addressing imbalances and inequalities between men and women. However, the growing emphasis on gender also has its critics – both among women's rights advocates and their opponents. Some women's rights activists have criticized gender mainstreaming because it reduces attention on women's rights. Some religious and conservative activists have objected to the use of the concept of gender, particularly the idea that gender is a social construct; this is seen as a challenge to the male-dominated hetero-normative family as the basic unit of society.

The Beijing conference identified "women and armed conflict" as one its 12 "critical areas of concern." This was a milestone and an important step in the advancement of women's rights and a new security agenda.

With the fall of the Berlin Wall and the reorganization of the international system away from two dominant superpowers, international security concepts also evolved. A human security agenda focused on fundamental human rights gained traction in the academic and policy world. The Responsibility to Protect (R2P) doctrine transformed the concept of human security into a more ambitious normative framework. R2P sought "to narrow the gap between states' pre-existing obligations under international humanitarian and human rights law and the reality faced by populations at risk of genocide, war crimes, ethnic cleansing and crimes against humanity."[15]

The rise of the human security canon in the post-Cold War era gave women activists another tool to push the WPS agenda forward, which was formalized by the adoption in 2000 of United Nations Security Council Resolution (UNSCR) 1325 and nine subsequent WPS resolutions in the 2000s and 2010s. As a result of women's advocacy worldwide, the issue of women's rights and participation in public life – particularly in conflict, transitional and post-conflict situations – was part of the international security agenda.

While the early advocates of the WPS agenda sought to promote an anti-militarization agenda – one that was tilted more toward "women and peace" than toward "women and security" – over the years, the WPS agenda lost much of that revolutionary impetus. It focused less on challenging state-centered security (and its emphasis on military solutions) and more on making "wars safer for women." The attempts by the early advocates of the WPS agenda to challenge militarized security approaches and the defense industry never established a real foothold in the UN Security Council or with governments. Instead, much of the focus of the WPS agenda has been on ensuring women's participation in the military and in international peace and security missions.

In addition, the 9/11 attacks in 2001 and the "global war on terror" launched by the United States after the attacks, redirected attention of UN Security Council members away from human security and the WPS agenda to state security and counter-terrorism. The war on terror has significantly eroded the international human rights framework, especially rights related to due process, the treatment of detainees and the protection of privacy. It has taken many shapes and forms ranging from excluding certain individuals from the protection provided by the laws of war ("illegal combatants"), propagating torture and setting up illegal detention centers and enabling intrusive surveillance and profiling of civilian populations to installing stricter border controls. It has also increased global political tensions, with fragile and failing states becoming incubators for terrorist activity rather than development.

The war on terror also had a notable effect on gender policies in the 2000s and 2010s. Strict counter-terrorism laws and regulations to prevent money from being channeled to terrorist groups have affected the ability of local women's groups to access aid and international development spending in countries such as Syria and Iraq.[16] Many women and women's organizations felt as if they were being squeezed between a self-perpetuating cycle of terrorism and counter-terrorism. As Jane Huckerby and Lama Fakih have pointed out "human rights reports detail the significant human rights abuses that have occurred in the context of counter-ing terrorism without any reference to the gender of the victims, let alone any consideration of the differential impacts of counter-terrorism on women, men, and sexual minorities and the ways in which such measures use and affect gender stereotypes."[17] Martin Scheinin, the first UN Special Rapporteur on human rights and counter-terrorism, warned in a report to the UN General Assembly against the bartering of human rights in the name of countering terrorism. He noted that "overly broad counter-terrorism measures have unduly penalized individuals on the basis of gender, including for example, the activities of women's human rights defenders." He also stated that "abuses on the basis of gender are amplified through war rhetoric (such as with the 'war on terror') and increased militarization in coun-tering terrorism."[18]

While the shift in international thinking from human security to counter-ter-rorism has had a significant impact on the ability of civil society organizations to operationalize women's rights on the ground, at the same time the development of the policy framework for gender equality continued to expand through the imple-mentation of the Millennium Development Goals (MDGs).

The MDGs, adopted in 2000, were focused on poverty reduction and included commitments to promote gender equality and empower women by improving the ratio of girls to boys enrolled in school, the percentage of women employed outside the home, and the percentage of women in national parliaments.[19]

Although the MDG effort made great progress in reducing extreme poverty and advancing other priorities, much remained to be done. In 2015, the MDGs were superseded by the Sustainable Development Goals (SDG). Gender equality became an important stand-alone goal (goal 5). In addition, gender became a cross-cutting issue across all 17 goals. Member states recognized that "gender equality and the empowerment of women and girls will make a crucial contribution to progress across all the goals and targets."[20]

The SDGs are a major step forward in advancing women's rights and the links between gender equality, sustainable development and peace and security. That said, the issue of gender equality continues to remain on the periphery of the national and international security agendas. A large part of the problem is that the rhetoric of equality between men and women has yet to "trickle down" from the normative world of instruments and institutions to the "substantive" world of processes and programs. This remains true for the WPS resolutions and the SDGs.

International legal documents and the adoption of policy frameworks can be seen as progress, but they cannot themselves bring about effective societal trans-formations.[21] Laws and policies are tools that women's rights activists can use to advocate for change, but they do not in and of themselves constitute real change – especially not in fragile states and conflict-prone countries, where state structures are weak.

This is certainly true in Afghanistan – a country with varying and often markedly different political, cultural and religious positions and values, which often have a challenge co-existing. This makes change for girls' and women's rights slow and complicated.

A case study: Afghanistan

In response to the 9/11 terrorist attacks in 2001, the United States (US) and North Atlantic Treaty Organization (NATO) allies – invoking the right to self-defense – launched a military campaign against al Qaeda and the Taliban government that had harbored and supported the terrorist group.[22] At its height, more than 130,000 foreign troops were stationed in Afghanistan as part of the NATO-led International Security Assistance Force (ISAF), and the country had become the single largest recipient of aid in the world, accounting for 40 percent of the country's Gross Domestic Product.[23]

Integral to the international community's massive state-building intervention after the fall of the Taliban regime were efforts to promote the rights and improve the lives of Afghan women and girls.

The extreme forms of oppression against women under the Taliban did not dissolve with the fall of the regime. Years of conflict, migration (leading to a massive brain drain), lack of education and economic opportunities had made Afghanistan more impoverished and conservative – especially on women's rights – than it had been before the conflict. A senior woman in the Afghan government noted: "We are one of the few countries where children are more conservative than parents. We are a country where husbands let their wives work, but the sons forbid it, and parents let their daughters' study, but their brothers forbid it."[24]

The cause of Afghan women – and women's rights in general – became an objective for the United States and its international allies as they engaged on stabilization and reconstruction efforts.[25] Initiatives to "gender mainstream" the rebuilding of the country resulted in re-drafting laws and developing new legislation, integrating gender components into development and aid policy frameworks and highlighting the participation of women within Afghan structures and institutions. With international support, the December 2001 Bonn Peace Agreement established the Ministry of Women's Affairs. The 2004 Constitution recognized equality for women and men, along with the right to education. The Constitution also imposed gender quotas for Parliament. With the assistance of the international community, successive Afghan administrations adopted many policy and legal measures to bring about gender equality, including: the Elimination of Violence Against Women (EVAW) decree, which provided a comprehensive judicial and social service support framework to address this widespread systemic issue, as well as a WPS National Action Plan. Afghanistan also signed all the major UN human rights conventions, including

CEDAW, although it has held out on the individual complaint mechanisms, including CEDAW's Optional Protocol.

That said, international actors did not have a well-developed plan to support Afghanistan and its women's rights advocates to achieve sustainable change in a profoundly conservative and religiously driven country. Similarly, international actors did not question their underlying assumption – that Afghan women would have the ability, or desire, to serve as a buffer against radicalization. The laws and policies promoted and pushed by the international community constituted radical change. But there was also strong resistance to a western-imported gender agenda, propelled by religious leaders and some Afghan government officials.

As a result, the hard-earned rights of Afghan women were fragile, and they quickly eroded as conservative forces in Afghanistan regained the upper hand, winning political and popular support, while Western influence and support for women's rights declined.

The erosion of women rights includes a 2013 election law that reduced the number of quota seats for women in provincial councils. The tone for the new elections law had been set in 2012, when a few days before International Women's Day on March 8, 2012, the national Ulema (religious council) issued a statement that provided its vision for women's rights.[26] While affirming issues such as women's rights to inheritance, it also claimed that "men are fundamental and women are secondary," and it condoned the "harassment and beating" of women as long as there is a "Shariah-complaint reason."[27] The government chose not to distance itself from the statement, and the international community also remained quiet, contributing to a sense that women's rights were negotiable.[28] As a female Member of Parliament (MP) commented about the statement, "I think it's the beginning of taking women back to the dark period of the Taliban. It's an alarm for women in Afghanistan."[29]

One of the most telling signs of the rollback of women's rights came during a debate in Parliament to bring the EVAW decree, signed by the president, into a law passed by the country's national representatives. The debate was not a clash between those for and against violence against women, but rather about what EVAW was seen to represent. The debate between the two sides became so intense that the Speaker was forced to suspend the discussion. Sections of the law were described as "un-Islamic" and not compliant with Shariah law – convenient labels used by the political and religious ruling elites when traditions that promote and protect them are deemed to be under attack. One male MP from Urozgan argued against EVAW's minimum marriage age for girls (16), "citing historical figure Hazrat Abu Bakr Siddiq, a companion of the Prophet Muhammad, who married off his daughter at 7 years of age."[30] Other issues described as "un-Islamic" included the prohibition of forced marriage and unrestricted access to health care, education and women's shelters, which had also been facing attack as centers of "immorality" and "prostitution." The decree was not passed by Parliament.

Ultimately, the politicization of women's rights and the depiction of women's rights as a Western agenda divorced from the realities of Afghanistan played into the hands of conservative forces and those opposed to the international community's engagement in the country. Many Afghan men, as well as some women, came to view women's rights as a Western norm that was hostile to Islam and Afghan traditions. At the same time, international institutions that had been set up to promote and protect gender equality remained hollow shells – underresourced or sidelined.

While the early successes on Afghan women's rights were mostly due to the insistence of the international community, they aligned with the demands of Afghan women's rights defenders – both women and men – who were keen to see girls enrolling in school, mothers and infants receiving proper health care and women taking part in public life. Afghanistan has always had a strong women's movement and civil society continues to engage on all gender equality and WPS issues.

As the conflict began to flare up again in 2006, the international community began quietly turning its back on Afghan women and their political attention turned to the main reason they had gone into the country in the first place – the "war on terror." As the death toll mounted for both foreign civilians and security forces alike, rather than reassess their military commitments, international actors doubled down on their efforts to subdue Afghan insurgents through military force.

From 2005 onward, the focus was on security rather than on development, and women rarely, if ever, figured into this security agenda. As one women's rights defender noted, "[they are] using the insecurity to de-prioritize women's rights. It's an easy out."[31] A senior US State Department official confirmed the new priorities: "Gender issues are going to have to take a back seat to other priorities. There's no way we can be successful if we maintain every special interest and pet project. All those pet rocks in our rucksack were taking us down."[32] The consequences were described by a female Afghan Parliamentarian:

> There is a lack of commitment by the international community. At the start of the war, they talked about the importance of women's rights. All the gains we have made are very fragile. We can lose them easily without their support. [But] now they are saying leave everything to the Afghans and Afghan women can defend their rights. Yesterday they were bold in their statements but today they are quiet.[33]

It is, of course, not solely the international community's responsibility to change the situation for Afghan women, change must ultimately come from within. But the progress that has been made to date has been made in partnerships with international actors, the Afghan government and Afghan civil society.

As the role of international actors as promoters of women's rights has declined, the national political debate on women's rights in Afghanistan has also changed. This can be seen in the differing edicts provincial Ulemas released on women's rights a decade apart. In 2004, in the days when the international community was still strongly committed to a gender equality agenda for Afghanistan, the Kandahar Ulema (in one of the more conservative provinces in the country) issued a fatwah (religious edict) stating that it was the religious duty of the men of Kandahar to let their wives, daughters and mothers vote. In 2014 in the northern province of

Badghis – previously one of the more liberal regions of Afghanistan – the Ulema issued a decree warning "women and girls not to leave their homes to attend school or work in a co-ed environment with their male counterparts, calling it a 'prohibited' act."[34]

What the case study on Afghanistan shows is that the starting point in examining the nexus of gender, human rights and security should not be how equality is articulated in policies or laws, but how women themselves formulate what is important and what constitutes change for them. This does not mean that laws and policies are irrelevant, but that they are often just the first step. In the case of Afghanistan, how far the struggle for women's rights and gender equality has progressed needs to be understood in the broader context of the geopolitical and socio-economic developments that have taken place over the past several decades and which continue to shape the country. The fundamental difference between superficial changes and a sustained, systemic transformation is whether the change is largely home-grown. Although international laws, policies and actors can support change, they cannot be a substitute for national and local debate and action. It is at the national and local levels that the debates about what is necessary and possible need to be held. While many Afghan women are calling for change, the prospects for change differ depending on the individual woman and her location within Afghan society: her family situation and how much support she has from male family members, where she lives, what ethnic group she is from, her level of education and access to the outside world.

In complex conflicts where international and local interests in the political, economic and ideological spheres become intertwined, women's rights are all-too-easily transformed into nothing more than a strategic communication tool. While the various stakeholders, including donors, diplomats and recipient government officials recognize the political advantage of showcasing that they are defending women's rights – and often put a considerable amount of funding toward gender programming – the reality is that the resources put into women's rights and gender equality do not compare with the political and financial commitments to security, defense and counter-terrorism.

Conclusion

In the decade following the end of the Cold War, considerable progress was made in the international legal arena on women's rights. However, the "war on terror" in very concrete ways undermined core commitments to human rights. It also rekindled old tensions between the social value of equality, human rights and justice and the militarized interests of state-centered security.

The human security approach – with its emphasis on fundamental rights and sustainable living for all, and which helped lay the foundation for the WPS agenda – was replaced in the aftermath of 9/11 by security approaches focused on combating global terrorism. This development has undermined and eroded the international human rights framework, including the hard-won battles for women's human rights and gender equality. In times of transition, women's rights activists know that they need to be even more vigilant and strategic in their activism and advocacy, as progress can easily be derailed or reversed.

We started this chapter with an account of the brutal murder of Farkhunda, a pious young woman who stood up for what she believed in, and the death of Oksana, a feminist activist who challenged sexism and authoritarian power. Both women were attempting to apply the rights their countries had legally committed to, but both ended up as victims of the ongoing erosion of the international human rights system, symbolized by their states failing to live up to their obligations. These two brave women are only the beginning of a lengthy list of activists who have taken a stand for gender equality and justice, but who have suffered the ultimate consequences of their activism and resistance.

Obstacles to progress

After 9/11, states turned away from a human security agenda to a national security agenda, which focused on defending national interests and homeland security. This pushed the human rights agenda near the bottom of concerns of states. Although multilateral institutions and national foreign policies continued to espouse the WPS agenda, in practice it is clear there has been a reemergence of realist thinking with an emphasis on militarization and military actions.

The WPS agenda must now compete with the global war on terror in terms of resources (human, financial and material), political priorities and differing national and international interests. While a strong international policy and legal foundation have been established with regard to women's rights and gender equality, laws and policies need time to become part of the fabric of everyday life. As the case of Afghanistan shows, good policy intentions can remain just that without sustained commitments by the international community to support the transformation of legislative and policy instruments and without effective buy-in from local populations and institutions.

The gender equality and WPS agenda cannot fully succeed when national and international security is defined solely in military terms. A world in which human rights play a prominent role is by necessity a world that also pays attention to social and economic equity.

Drivers of progress

Although laws and policies to advance women's rights and gender equality do not in and of themselves necessarily bring about effective, sustainable change in the lives of girls and women, they still matter and are critical to moving these agendas forward. CEDAW, the Beijing Platform for Action and the WPS agenda have provided the institutional framework and laid the groundwork for mechanisms such as the Special Representative of the UN Secretary-General on Sexual Violence in Conflict, National Action Plans for the implementation of UNSCR 1325, as well as gender advisors and protection officers in many international and regional missions. These mechanisms translate international and national commitments into practical actions.

These advancements would not have been possible without the persistence of civil society and women's groups from around the world. Their sustained and persistent advocacy efforts ensured that women's voices and gender concerns were incorporated in each new international human rights instrument. The WPS agenda would not have seen the light of day without the tireless lobbying of activists and advocates. The ongoing advocacy by individuals and many civil society organizations ranging from the Women's International League for Peace and Freedom (which has been addressing gender, militarism, peace and security issues since 1915) to the UN Non-Governmental Organization (NGO) Working Group on Women, Peace and Security ensure that states and multilateral institutions continue to be held accountable to their commitments in this arena.

Strategies for progress

Given the powerful forces that continue to work against women's rights and the WPS agenda, several strategic guidelines should be kept in mind to safeguard the progress that has been made and to maximize the prospects for progress in the future.[35]

One of the major successes of the post–World War II human rights regime has been to include equality as a fundamental principle of international law. This has been the most important tool for working against overt discrimination through law or by state agents. While CEDAW, the UNSCR on WPS and other women-specific instruments go further in their attention to women's needs and experiences and provide substantive measures for fighting structural discrimination, the simple idea that we are all equal remains a powerful basis of modern international as well as national law. It will need safeguarding and defending in the current security-driven climate. This includes lobbying for the development and implementation of National Action Plans (NAPs) on WPS, continuing to support Non-Governmental Organizations and coalitions working on WPS issues and advocating for more women in leadership positions, both elected and appointed.

Beyond formal equality, legal and policy strategies for change must be carefully designed and take into account, local social, cultural and political contexts. Laws and policies need to be changed to reflect the needs and experiences of previously excluded groups. This does not mean that every cultural excuse for the differential treatment of women and men should be accepted. Rather, it means that there needs to be a real commitment to supporting women's own identified priorities and their visions of how to organize their societies. How this translates on the ground depends on local contexts. It can mean working within Shariah law and traditional mechanisms of justice. It can also mean introducing legislation and policies enabling positive discrimination and affirmative action to address the structural discrimination experienced by specific groups. In the latter case it is important that these measures are targeted and short-term, so that these measures intended to fight oppression do not themselves become discriminatory over time.

Change comes slowly. Trying to force change with guns blazing – literally – with time limits and little consideration for realities on the ground will not lead to sustainable change. It is important to allow time for consultation, for ideas to develop and for processes to settle. Taking time to assess, listening carefully and designing programs for the long-term is a more useful – and dare we say feminist – strategy in these times of distrust, quick fixes and militarized security.

Lastly, for change to be sustainable, international support is critical. This support needs to be sustained over the long-term, especially in cases of rebuilding countries that have been torn asunder by war. International actors should not allow women's hard-won rights to become negotiating chips in peace talks. Women rights, like human rights, are non-negotiable. Sustainable peace is possible only when women can fully participate and their rights are secured. It is a lesson that the international community must apply in every conflict in which it intervenes, so that the rhetoric of gender equality and the principles of the WPS agenda become a reality for all.

Notes

1 For an overview of feminist scholarship on international law, see Hilary Charlesworth and Christine Chinkin, *The Boundaries of International Law: A Feminist Analysis* (Manchester: Manchester University Press, 2000); Sari Kouvo and Zoe Pearson, eds., *Gender and International Law*, Vols. 1–4 (London: Routledge, 2014). For an introduction to feminist and gender perspectives on international relations and security, see Fionnuala Ní Aoláin et al., eds., *The Oxford Handbook of Gender and Conflict* (Oxford: Oxford University Press, 2018); Theodora-Ismene Gizelis and Louise Olsson, eds., *Gender, Peace and Security: Implementing UN Security Council Resolution 1325* (London: Routledge, 2015); Rosalind Boyd, ed., *The Search for Lasting Peace: Critical Perspectives on Gender-Responsive Human Security* (London: Ashgate, 2014).

2 See Johannes Morsink, *The Universal Declaration of Human Rights: Origins, Drafting and Intent* (Philadelphia, PA: University of Pennsylvania Press, 1999).

3 Article 3 of both Covenants state: "The States Parties to the present Covenant undertake to ensure the equal right of men and women to the enjoyment of all . . . rights set forth in the present Covenant."

4 See Lauri Hannikainen and Eeva Nykänen, eds., *New Trends in Discrimination Law: International Perspectives* (Turku, Finland: Turku Law School, 1999).

5 See Anne Hellum, ed., *Women's Human Rights: CEDAW in International, Regional and National Perspectives* (Cambridge: Cambridge University Press, 2013).

6 It is important to note that the category of "woman" is not monolithic. When talking about the barriers to gender equality, one has to be careful about sweeping generalizations. Gender discourse intersects with race, ethnicity, class, religion, citizenship, sexuality and age as well as other issues. In other words, "not all women are oppressed and/or subjugated in the same way or to the same extent, even within the same society at any given moment." See Nira Yuval-Davis, *Gender & Nation* (London: Sage, 1997), p. 8.

7 61 states have entered reservations. See the website of the Office of the UN High Commissioner on Human Rights (@ un.org).

8 Ibid.

9 See Ka Lok Yip, "Weakest Link: From Non-Derogation to Non-Existence of Human Rights," *Human Rights Law Review*, Vol. 17, No. 4 (December 2017).

10 See Abdullahi Ahmed An-Na'im, ed., *Human Rights in Cross-Cultural Perspectives: A Quest for Consensus* (Philadelphia, PA: University of Pennsylvania Press, 1992).

11 Paragraph 18 states: "The human rights of women and of the girl-child are an inalienable, integral and indivisible part of universal human rights ... and the eradication of all forms of discrimination on grounds of sex are priority objectives of the international community." See Donna J. Sullivan, "Women's Human Rights and the 1993 World Conference on Human Rights," *American Journal of International Law*, Vol. 88, No. 1 (January 1994), pp. 152–167.

12 See Sari Kouvo, *Making Just Rights: Mainstreaming Women's Human Rights and a Gender Perspective* (Uppsala, Sweden: Iustus Publications, 2004).

13 UN fourth World Conference on Women, *Beijing Declaration and Platform for Action* (New York: United Nations, September 1995).

14 Ibid.

15 See UN Office on Genocide Prevention and the Responsibility to Protect (@ un.org).

16 Jane Huckerby and Lama Fakih, *A Decade Lost: Locating Gender in U.S. Counter-Terrorism* (New York: New York University School of Law, Center for Human Rights and Global Justice, 2011).

17 Ibid., p. 13.

18 *Report from the Special Rapporteur on the Promotion and Protection of Human Rights and Fundamental Freedoms while Countering Terrorism*, A/64/211 (New York: United Nations, August 3, 2009), pp. 2, 10.

19 See the UN's Sustainable Development Goals (@ sustainabledevelopment.un.org).

20 UN General Assembly Resolution, *A/70/1 Transforming Our World: The 2030 Agenda for Sustainable Development* (New York: United Nations, October 21, 2015), para. 20.

21 See Sari Kouvo and Corey Levine, "Who Defines the Red Lines? Safeguarding Women's Rights and the Prospects for Peace in Afghanistan," in *The Oxford Handbook of Gender and Conflict*, pp. 485–496; "Law as a Placeholder for Change: Women's Rights and Realities in Afghanistan," in Kim Rubenstein and Katharine G. Young, eds., *En/gendering Governance: from the Local to the Global* (Cambridge: Cambridge University Press, 2016), pp. 195–216.

22 The right to self-defense is recognized in article 51 of the UN Charter. See also UNSCR 1368 of September 12, 2001, which condemned the terrorist attacks and paved the way for the military response; and UNSCR 1373 of November 12, 2001.

23 Roland Paris, "Afghanistan: What Went Wrong," *Perspectives on Politics*, Vol. 11, No. 2 (June 2013), pp. 538–548; Richard Hogg et al., "Afghanistan in Transition: Looking Beyond 2014," in *Directions in Development; Countries and Regions* (Washington, DC: World Bank, March 2013).

24 Interview conducted by Corey Levine with Afghan women's rights activist, Kabul, 2015.

25 Masuda Sultan, Corey Levine and Elizabeth Powley, *From Rhetoric to Reality: Afghan Women on the Agenda for Peace* (Washington, DC: Women Waging Peace Policy Commission, Hunt Alternatives Fund, February 2005).

26 The Ulema overlaps with the country's judiciary, which gives them an influential, quasi-governmental position with regard to Afghanistan's state institutions. Although the statement has no legal effect per se, this kind of political posturing – especially when religion is involved – carries a significant amount of weight.

27 English Translation of Ulema's Declaration on Women (@ afghanistananalysis.wordpress. com).

28 Kouvo and Levine, "Who Defines the Red Lines?" p. 486.

29 Fauzia Koofi quoted in "Afghan Concerns Over 'Guidelines for Women," *BBC World News* (March 6, 2012).

30 Sari Kouvo and Corey Levine, *From Bonn to Brussels: Delving into Fifteen Years of Afghan Women's Rights on the Agenda*, Unpublished Manuscript (2016).

31 Amnesty International, *Their Lives on the Line: Women Human Rights Defenders Under Attack in Afghanistan* (London: Amnesty International, April 7, 2015), p. 68.

32 Rajiv Chandrasekaran, "In Afghanistan, U.S. Shifts Strategy on Women's Rights as It Eyes Wider Priorities," *Washington Post* (March 6, 2011).
33 Farkhunda Zahra Naderi, quoted in Oxfam, *Behind Closed Doors: The Risk of Denying Women a Voice in Determining Afghanistan's Future*, Briefing Paper (Oxford: Oxfam, November 24, 2014), p. 12.
34 *Tolo News* (September 19, 2014, @ Tolonews.com).
35 These recommendations are adapted from Kuovo and Levine, "Who Defines the Red Lines?"

11

GENDER, GOVERNANCE AND SECURITY

Jacqui True and Sara E. Davies

It is well-established that women's status, including their public participation, contributes to political stability and state security.[1] Women's presence and gender balance in political and economic institutions may enhance good governance as well as national and international peace and security. However, women remain a minority or even absent from the governance and decisionmaking institutions of many states. The Middle East, Asia and Pacific regions have the most significant gender gaps in national governance, although gender imbalance in political and economic decisionmaking is a pattern across geographic regions, conflict-affected and relatively peaceful countries, state and non-state groups.[2] Political participation has brought major gains to social and economic equality over the past century: greater women's political participation could strengthen and improve democracy as well as achieve gender equality. Outside of national economic and political institutions in many states, there are equally strong demands to address gender gaps in foreign policy bureaucracies, international organizations, think tanks, media and development agencies.[3]

In this chapter, we define gender-inclusive governance as consisting of two major components: the meaningful participation of women and the presence of a substantive gender equality agenda.[4] As the numbers of women increase in governance institutions, the diversity of women's experiences can be articulated and translated into claims vis-à-vis the state, which may be facilitated by both women and men representatives. However, advocacy for temporary special measures such as quotas or campaigns for gender-balanced representation must be accompanied by institutional reform to ensure mainstreaming of gender analysis across political leadership, policy and practice.[5] The 1995 United Nations (UN) Beijing Platform for Action, which set forth the global agenda for gender equality, recognized that the equal political representation of women and men is a "necessary condition for women's interests to be taken into account.... Equality in political decisionmaking performs a leverage function without which it is highly unlikely that a real integration of the equality dimension in government policymaking is feasible."[6] Thus, temporary special measures such as gender quotas may help to transform situations of gender inequality, though this is not guaranteed as an automatic result of quotas. Three decades of feminist research into leadership and gender mainstreaming policy shows that advocating for women's presence in decisionmaking, and quotas to ensure it, will not in itself reform unequal structures, address rights abuses or create the necessary institutional change to enact policies that can achieve gender equality outcomes.[7] Mariz Tadros argues that quotas do not address all the barriers to women's participation in formal politics nor are they proxies for democratization or gender justice.[8] Women's presence in institutions is far more amenable to measurement, monitoring and evaluation than the mainstreaming of a gender perspective in governance, and this may be one of the reasons why it is often prioritized by states and international organizations. Yet gender equality has been touted as a solution to a range of global governance problems, including sustainable economic development, financial stability and the eradication of poverty, which require the integration of gender perspectives, analysis and evidence within policymaking.[9]

In this chapter, we discuss the broad rationales for gender-equal and inclusive governance in political, peace and security and economic domains. Second, we examine the common drivers and obstacles to gender-inclusive governance in national and international institutions, focusing on political institutions. We consider the implications of the broad knowledge base in political science and international relations about women's leadership in governance and how increasing the number of women in political institutions affects both the substance and the style of governance. Last, we explore successful strategies that have worked to promote gender balances and gender perspectives in policy and governance. We assess the likely impact of these strategies in the future, given current challenges and dynamics in global and local politics.

Rationale for gender-inclusive governance

Increasing women's participation in governance has become a global movement that began in Europe's former colonies in Oceania, Latin America and India and has spread to metropolitan Europe itself.[10] The 1995 Beijing Platform for Action called on a range of actors to encourage women's participation in all types of social, economic and political decisionmaking, including through the strategic use of positive action.[11] The Platform for Action defines "women's participation" in terms of a specific target of 30 percent women and focuses, albeit not exclusively, on political representation.[12] However, insufficient progress toward that target had been made by the Beijing + 15 review in 2010. In 2019, 125 years after women first achieved the suffrage in a nation-state (New Zealand), women's proportion of legislative seats has reached 25 percent globally.[13] We could see this as either a success or a failure depending on our expectations of the time frame for progress in women's political participation. At this rate, gender parity in political governance would be achieved in another century. The significant increases we have seen in the proportion of positions held by women in Latin America and many countries in Africa, notably Rwanda, as well as European states have been attributed by the United Nations to "affirmative and positive action policies, including quota systems or voluntary agreements and measurable goals and targets."[14]

Political strategies for advancing women's political participation have diffused from the national level to international politics with campaigns to appoint a female UN Secretary-General. UN Security Council mandates to increase women's presence in peace negotiations and security decisions are also relevant to engendering governance. United Nations Security Council Resolution (UNSCR) 1325, adopted in 2000, stresses the importance of women's "equal participation and full involvement in all efforts for the maintenance and promotion of peace and security" while subsequent Women, Peace and Security (WPS) resolutions call for the integration of gender perspectives in peace and security policies and operations, including peace processes and agreements.[15] Yet the 15-year review of UNSCR 1325 in 2015 identified a major implementation gap with respect to the presence of women in peace and security decisionmaking processes and institutions. Women are not consistently engaged in negotiating peace and are still frequently excluded from many peace processes.[16] The United States (US)-based Council on Foreign Relations has found that in all major peace processes between 1990 and 2017 just eight percent of mediators, eight percent of negotiators and five percent of witnesses and signatories to peace agreements were women.[17]

The lack of women's inclusion in peace and security decisionmaking has major implications for international relations. New research reveals the positive impact of women's participation on peace outcomes. This body of research notes that when women participate in civil society initiatives and in high-level mediation and peacemaking processes, better outcomes for security and the durability of peace are achieved.[18] This is supported by evidence showing that the presence of women at the highest levels of peace negotiations makes it 20 percent more likely that a peace agreement will be concluded and last at least two years, and 35 percent more likely that it will endure for at least 15 years.[19] The rationale for women's inclusion in peace processes is clear in scholarship – women's participation contributes to the prevention and resolution of conflicts, while the lack of women's participation undermines it.

Similar strategies to promote women's participation and leadership in governance have diffused from the realm of politics to the realm of economic power. Since the global financial crisis of 2007–08, there have been calls for more women and greater gender balance in corporate and financial governance from the trading floor to the boardrooms of firms, investment banks and regulatory authorities. Sparked by rigorous evidence connecting gender equitable representation in legislatures and corporate boards with less corruption, better policy outcomes and higher investment returns, the movement has rapidly spread over the last decade.[20] Research by Catalyst attributed increased financial returns to the magical number of "three" women present on the board of a firm, and research by Credit Suisse revealed that companies with women on their boards outperformed similar businesses with all-male boards by 26 percent worldwide.[21] Male-dominated economic governance has been shown to be suboptimal in terms of performance.[22] There is a robust relationship between higher levels of women's labor force participation and greater national economic competitiveness.[23] Governments under pressure to attract foreign investment are either regulating or encouraging improved business performance on gender equality from their workforces to the board level. Gender-inclusion is thus now an essential part of good economic governance as well as political governance.[24] One of the reasons why the business or "outcomes" case for gender-inclusive governance is so clear-cut is likely because women's meaningful participation in governance affects the substance and the style of that governance.

Toward gender-equal governance: drivers of progress

A body of evidence shows a demonstrable connection between the rise of women in public life – evident in the increase in women in decisionmaking leadership roles in legislative and executive branches of government – and the inclusion of pro-women policies on government agendas and greater public service responsiveness to female citizens.[25] More equal representation of women at the top is expected to deliver better results for citizens, states, employees and shareholders alike. But what are the drivers of progress toward gender-equal governance?

Gender quotas

Popular commentary has assumed that a critical mass of female representatives, usually estimated at 30 percent, can transform previously male-dominated organizations and enable women to advance gender-specific perspectives and policies. Current scholarship on national governance, however, is skeptical of the claim that women-friendly policies can only be achieved once women have reached a certain numerical level in legislatures.[26] At a global level, electoral and political party quotas – together with reserved seats – are significant drivers of progress in engendering governance. The majority of quota provisions have been adopted by individual political parties with a growing proportion involving changes to constitutions and electoral laws.[27] Quotas have contributed to a steady increase in women's share of parliamentary seats, although there is significant variation across regions and countries. Aili Tripp and Alice Kang's global study of gender quotas shows that the introduction of quotas has helped to overcome obstacles to women's political representation, such as economic underdevelopment, cultural influences and even electoral systems. In their analysis, the level of women's representation is explained by whether or not quotas have been introduced and whether the type of electoral system allows for greater candidate turnover (that is, party-list proportional representation systems).[28] Gender quotas, regardless of type, also improve perceptions of women's ability as political leaders in countries where they are present, according to Peter Allan and David Cutts.[29]

However, Drude Dahlerup and Lenita Freidenvall argue that the devil is in the details of the quota systems and their implementation.[30] Gender quotas may be merely symbolic without specifications of the provisions that match the electoral system in question, rules about the rank order of candidates, such as zipped candidate lists alternating male and female candidates, as well as sanctions for non-compliance.[31] Nomination procedures within political parties may mean that women are selected because they are loyal to the party or political leader (and not women as a group); stigmas may pertain to women elected in reserved seats undermining their political effectiveness, and often, attention to quotas in federal representation is higher than in local representation.[32]

Gender quotas, as Mona Lena Krook argues, represent only one demand-side solution to women's underrepresentation in politics.[33] Supply-side interventions – such as encouraging women to stand for election with capacity-building initiatives, campaign finance assistance and movement support – are important drivers of progress. There are also limits to these efforts, given male-dominated, patriarchal norms in politics. In Melanesian Island nations where women's political representation is minimal, women who are well-positioned to overcome the barriers to representation have chosen to remain outside of formal politics as an act of resistance. They seek to pursue programmatic reforms through women's movements and civil society alliances in parallel public spheres.[34]

Similarly, in Rwanda and Burundi, substantive rather than descriptive representation appears to be more important for women in their everyday lives. In both conflict-affected countries, women representatives have consistently exceeded 30 percent since the introduction of gender quotas and more women have joined the executive branches of government, yet this has not improved perceived political representation for women. None of the key government policies that women respondents mentioned in survey research have incorporated a gender perspective or analysis.[35] This reinforces the need to consider a substantive gender equality agenda as well as the representation of women as the two elements of gender-inclusive governance.

Women's movements and institutional spaces to advance gender perspectives

Women's participation and leadership can be transformative when accompanied by a substantive policy agenda that is informed by a gender analysis of priorities, needs and impact. Specialized parliamentary bodies on gender equality are an interstitial institutional space that promotes the development of a gender perspective.[36] They take different forms: standing committees, such as the FEMM Committee of the European Parliament, which have a formal institutionalized role in applying a gender lens to the legislative process, and women's caucuses, which are more informal bodies providing support to women members through capacity-building on policy issues and policymaking as well as mentoring and networking. The all-party parliamentary group on Women, Peace and Security (WPS) in the United Kingdom (UK) is an example of the latter.[37]

Very often a policy agenda that integrates a gender perspective is the product of political debates and alliances with women's movements. Women's formal and informal political participation is most often in the context of alliances, networks and coalitions. Those collective mechanisms for women's civil society participation and efforts to strengthen them are, thus, major drivers of progress toward gender-inclusive governance.

In 2001, Jacqui True and Michael Mintrom studied government adoption of gender mainstreaming policies between 1975 and 1998.[38] At the time, gender mainstreaming was a new phenomenon. It was only in 1995, at the fourth UN World Conference on Women, that the Beijing Platform for Action produced gender mainstreaming recommendations for governments to adopt. True and Mintrom found that the pace of the adoption of institutional mechanisms introduced at the national level to promote gender mainstreaming was rapid. Crucially, they did not attribute this progress to leadership at the executive government levels (which in many cases was lacking) or to quota provisions, but to the advocacy and effort of a network of women's civil organizations. The capacity for civil society organizations to meet, mobilize and network created a transnational feminist movement that supported local networks and those within national bureaucracies to campaign for domestic reform. Mala Htun and Laurel Weldon later found similar results when examining the emergence and strength of national violence against women policies.[39] In their comparative study of 70 countries over four decades, they pointed to "feminist mobilization in civil society" as the most significant factor associated with strong policies to address violence against women.

Women's organizing and campaigning as civic representatives also make it more likely that progressive gender mainstreaming policies and mechanisms will be sustained.[40] For example, the positive relationship between the women in positions of political power and the adoption of National Action Plans (NAPs) on WPS suggest strong potential for the integration of a gender-perspective on security governance with the greater presence of women leaders.[41] Substantive reform within institutions to address gender imbalances in leadership has been identified as essential to advancing gender mainstreaming in security policymaking.

Men's leadership

Gender-equal governance is not the sole responsibility of women. In many countries, new policy issues that reflect gender-equality perspectives typically only get onto political agendas when women have reached the highest level of government and have the political power to initiate such policies.[42] Policy issues such as the provision of early childhood education, the promotion of sexual health and reproductive rights and the agenda to eliminate all forms of violence against women and girls are of broad relevance to all of society. Some men have advanced these issues in their political leadership and governance roles.[43] Thus, a driver of progress in gender-inclusive governance is the empowerment of men as champions of gender equality and women's rights.

Men have a role to play in supporting and promoting gender equality in their organizations. Differences in values and attitudes toward gender and sexuality within and across countries divide national and global politics.[44] In this regard, men's leadership and attitudes are important since both men and women can hold pro-gender equality or feminist attitudes and support these ideas through their behavior in domestic and international governance.[45] Male champions of gender equality are particularly important when discrimination is entrenched. In the health sector, for example, women make up 70 percent of the global health workforce but hold only 25 percent of leadership positions. Leadership amongst senior male health professionals is essential to shift entrenched occupational segregation and discrimination at the local, national and global levels of health care delivery.[46]

New initiatives – such as former Australian sex discrimination commissioner, Elizabeth Broderick's "Male Champions of Change" network – aim to instigate concrete commitments and actions to support gender equality by individual male leaders in public and private sectors in a way similar to that of individual corporations under the UN's Women's Empowerment Principles program. "We need to focus on engaging men in transforming gender relations rather than as a reaction to the hard-won recognition of women's needs and rights, which thrives by obscuring deep gender inequalities."[47] But the turn to men – and masculinity – should be in addition to rather than a replacement for gender perspectives, although it can contribute to bringing about more gender-inclusive governance.[48]

In the area of foreign policy, former UK Foreign Secretary William Hague (a white middle-age Tory member of the UK Parliament) created the Prevention of Sexual Violence Initiative to elevate the issue as an international crime and a UK foreign policy priority. This remarkable choice indicates two things: that men can engage in gender security if they choose, and that they face no negative political consequences for doing so. (Hague stepped down with high approval ratings and no animosity from the Foreign Office.) Despite Hague's early engagement being protection-focused, his continued engagement with civil society actors in the WPS space produced a more gender-inclusive initiative that influenced the engagement of the Foreign Office and the Department for International Development on an ongoing basis.[49]

Political and economic upheaval as a result of conflict, disaster and financial crises

Conflict, disaster and financial crises create opportunities for contesting the normal, masculinist ways of governing, opportunities that are often lost when attention is diverted to blameworthy individuals rather than to structures of governance and policymaking. These ruptures challenge business as usual, which can provide openings for gender equality initiatives, women's leadership and more gender-inclusive governance.

One-third of the countries with 30 percent or more women parliamentarians are countries that recently experienced post-conflict or democratic transitions. This is in part due to UN mandates to support women's political representation. This gives women representatives an opportunity to bring new perspectives to shape the security and stability of their countries. In Kenya, women politicians from two different political parties – at the center of the conflict supported by women's civil society activism, the African Union (AU) and chief mediator, Graca Machel – came together and played major roles in integrating gender perspectives in the Kenya National Dialogue and Reconciliation process after the post-election violence in 2007–2008.[50] In Myanmar, the Alliance for Gender Inclusion in the Peace Process has been the lead organization in terms of ensuring women's attendance at annual peace conferences since the Nationwide Ceasefire Agreement was signed in 2015. After the 2016 national elections, the Asia Foundation attributed some of the ten percent (from four to 14 percent) increase in women's representation in federal parliament to these public campaigns on gender inclusion.[51]

In the case of the 2007–2008 global financial crisis, the lack of gender balance came to be seen as one of the explanations for the crisis itself.[52] Men dominated the lending institutions that contributed to the crisis. US Senate and UK select committee hearings revealed men to be not only at the top of the private banks and financial institutions, but also occupying leadership positions in most national regulatory and global economic and financial governance institutions.[53] The association between the financial sector's male dominance and near-system collapse demanded a response. The finance industry's skewed leadership called into question the reliability of the industry's governance and decisionmaking institutions. Space has since opened for women leaders to lead the charge in the makeover of these organizations.

Crisis responses may also perpetuate the gendered myth that women have inherent skills to solve crises, are inclusive, and more sympathetic to social welfare models. This may be a case of the "glass cliff," where women leaders are set up to fail; women are expected to produce policy and economic solutions that men have not been expected to achieve either with respect to corporate performance or electoral success.[54]

The feminist foreign policy movement

Another driver of progress toward gender-inclusive governance has been the emergence of a feminist perspective in foreign policy as reflected in several government statements and strategies.[55] As a feature of state branding, such a perspective is demonstrated by a leadership style that consciously balances power politics (and defense policy) with norms-driven, rule of law and consensus-based international relations. At the risk of reinforcing gender stereotypes, we might see this gendering of foreign and security policy as combining "hard" and "soft" power, "protection" and "prevention" policy intervention and "masculine" and "feminine" styles. As more women enter positions of foreign policy leadership, we are seeing feminine approaches to international relations that contrast with hyper-masculine and strongman approaches.[56] The scholarship on gender and leadership argues that a balance of men and women in leadership positions should enable gender differences (both masculine and feminine approaches) to come to the fore within the leadership styles of both women and men leaders.[57] That is, it is possible to combine good communication, consensus-building and even compassion with rational decisionmaking that fosters collective action and accepts the utility of force. Based on gender differences in voting and foreign policy opinion polling, women's greater expressed preferences for non-military, diplomatic solutions to insecurity and conflict are in some states being balanced against traditional military approaches, which (in public opinion polling) male citizens disproportionately embrace.[58] New networks of women leaders have emerged in the 21st century to provide mutual support and to mitigate the pressure on women leaders to adopt traditionally masculine policy agendas, including the use of force. In the late 1990s, Madeleine Albright began this trend when she created a caucus of female UN ambassadors and a network of female foreign ministers.[59] Most recently, a group of women leaders has formed to save multilateralism.[60] Such networks are key drivers of progress, enabling a more gender-inclusive style of leadership and governance.

At present, we mainly have individual case-study evidence of women leaders in the governance of domestic and foreign policy. However, in her study of ten democratic western states, Sylvia Bashevkin shows that there is a strong association between the position of women within their foreign policy elites and the levels of international aid targeted at women's empowerment in the Global South.[61] Tiffany Barnes and Diana O'Brien analyzed a dataset that includes more than 40 countries that have appointed women defense ministers.[62] They found that men are in the key defense positions in countries with large or rising military expenditures, which suggests a political climate "not conducive to changing norms" of gender inclusion. In 2017, however, the defense ministers of the largest European Union (EU) states (France, Germany Italy, Spain and the Netherlands) were all women; none had a military background. Based on these two studies, we can discern both a relationship between the presence of women in power and less militaristic defense policies as well as an obstacle to instituting gender-inclusive governance in the military and defense realm, where decisionmaking is characterized by masculine norms and male leadership.

The US case does not entirely follow this pattern, if we take account of the hawkish approaches of Madeleine Albright, Condoleezza Rice and Hillary Clinton as respective Secretaries of State; nor does the UK if we look at Margaret Thatcher's leadership style. However, Clinton (2009–2012) did aim to raise the resources for diplomacy. She initiated a strategic plan for the State Department and the US Agency for International Development (known as the Quadrennial Diplomacy and Development Review), which called for investments in long-term strategic planning in diplomacy and development. A long list of policy initiatives grew out of the Review related to health, nutrition, violence against women, data collection about women and child marriage.[63] Foreign policymaking, especially in the diplomatic, humanitarian and international development areas, may give women a freer rein than is possible in the highly masculinist realm of domestic politics. Women can be elevated and represent the nation in a way they may not be able to do comfortably at home. And they can maintain a militant approach to security and defense policy while taking up issues, such as human rights and gender equality, that generally do not receive strong support from their own parties.[64] Until more women hold these positions, it will be difficult to establish whether we are observing the emergence of a truly feminist approach to foreign and defense policy, grounded in feminist thinking, approaches and policy preferences.

Institutions matter

What are the drivers of progress in the instances where women are successfully leading reform in key policy areas? Institutions and their make-up, as well as informal logics of policy domains, matter greatly. The gender balance in the staffing profile of the public service in different policy portfolios – both with respect to seniority and sheer numbers – appears to affect progress toward gender-inclusive governance, preventing business-as-usual approaches. Also, concrete drivers of progress are measures to require leadership and accountability in the public service for promoting gender equality in policy development and for addressing gender equality in recruitment and employment practices, including reducing gender wage gaps and occupational segregation.[65]

With respect to the informal logics of policy domains, Htun and Weldon find that they vary across different policy domains with consequences for whether or not governments promote women's rights.[66] These informal logics can be both drivers and obstacles to the progress of gender-inclusive governance. In the violence against women and workplace equality policy areas, international norms are highly influential and enabling because of the logic of (international) status hierarchy among states. However, in domestic policies regarding family law or contraception, a logic of "doctrinal" politics within states dominates where institutional actors have significant influence in society and the public realm. Extending Htun and Weldon's analysis we might expect that in the security and defense policy domains, logics of power and secrecy operate to exclude women from leadership positions and to mask the glaring relevance of gender perspectives on armed conflict and terrorism, where male-only groups and norms of masculinity encourage and justify the use of violence.

The costly neglect of gender perspectives is clearly evident in the intelligence and analytics dedicated to counter-terrorism. In our study with UN Women on preventing violent extremism in Asia and the Pacific, we explored the relationship between attitudes characterized as "misogyny" or hatred of women, acts of violence against women and girls and violent extremism. In three countries in Asia (Bangladesh, Indonesia and the Philippines), we found that support for violence against women and hostile sexist attitudes are both stronger predictors of support for violent extremism than religiosity, which is commonly perceived to be the major root cause. In the aftermath of terrorist attacks across the world, we frequently hear that the attacker was known to police in part because of domestic violence charges, making these findings unsurprising but also highlighting the importance of evidence in showing the links between violent extremism and violence against women. Examining these gender-based factors in the support for violent extremism has the potential to better identify likely perpetrators of all kinds of extremist violence.[67]

Obstacles to progress

Despite evident progress, there are clear obstacles to advancing gender-equal governance. Many of the obstacles have already been mentioned. They are the counterparts to many of the drivers of progress, such as the adequacy of – or lack thereof – gender balance in expertise and gender-sensitive expertise in a particular policy area; the extent to which an issue or agenda is historically associated with men's leadership and masculine characteristics, which is the case with defense; and the extent to which men support or oppose gender equality, which affects their governance behavior and constrains the opportunities for women to govern. Also, "the glass cliff" phenomenon is a classic "opportunity versus obstacle" problem for women's leadership and gender-inclusive governance. Three other significant obstacles are worth discussing: the gendered nature of informal institutions (informal policies and practices within institutions), violence against politically active women and women in the public realm and gendered structural inequalities in the economy.

Gendered informal institutions

Informal policies and practices across institutions as well as logics of policy-making can reinforce gender inequalities and gender-based stereotypes and are oft-noted obstacles to women's meaningful participation and gender-sensitive policymaking. Even with an increasing proportion of women representatives in legislatures and the increasing visibility of successful women leaders, organizational cultures remain masculine and perpetuate male-as-norm informal rules and practices, such as when decisions get made in after-hours bars or during rounds of golf to which only men are invited.[68] Women do not get equal access to these types of informal "training" and recognition of "merit." These powerful informal practices need to be confronted if progress is to be made in gender-inclusive governance.[69]

In the context of unchallenged informal practices that are biased toward men, some women may adapt to masculine norms and scripts and effectively be co-opted within male power structures. There are many examples of women leaders becoming more "hawkish" than men in order to overcome a perceived gender bias which assumes that they are unfit to lead.[70] Increasingly, we have visible women leaders who represent alternatives to this approach to overcoming gender-bias and gender inequality.

Violence against women in politics

Violence against politically active women and women in the public realm is a major obstacle to gender-inclusive governance, since it has the effect of dissuading women from engaging in politics. The targeting of women in public life with threats, sexist abuse and physical attacks – often fueled by social media – while not a new phenomenon appears to be on the rise. Increased political participation of women has triggered backlashes, posing new obstacles to women's political, social and economic empowerment. Women are targeted for verbal and physical abuse in unique and gender-specific ways compared with men. US presidential candidate Hillary Clinton and former Australian prime minister Julia Gillard, for instance, received twice as many abusive tweets as male peers, Bernie Sanders and Kevin Rudd, during their leadership competitions.[71] In 2016, after she left politics, Gillard said that a woman in public view may expect to receive threats of violent abuse and rape almost daily.[72] This reflects a deeply ingrained sexism within western democracies.

This type of violence is much more widespread and underreported than generally thought. The rise of populism across the world has also mobilized misogyny and targeted politically active women for approbation, resentment and violence. Perpetrators include not only political opponents and criminals, but also community and religious leaders, state security forces and police and media and social media commentators. Many, if not the majority, of perpetrators are women's own party colleagues and family members. The drive to preserve traditional gender roles by preventing women from exercising their political rights means that even when violent acts are experienced at a very personal level, their implications are much broader – communicating the general message that *women as a group* should not participate in politics. Evidence shows that incidents of violence have discouraged female politicians in Asia, Europe and Latin America, making them less likely to stand for reelection and more likely to leave after fewer terms served (compared to male colleagues).[73]

The violence that politically active women experience may be physical, psychological, symbolic or economic violence. Economic violence against women includes degradation and coercion by controlling access to economic resources. In a political governance setting, this includes withholding campaign funds as well as destroying or damaging personal property or offices. In Kenya's 2017 election, a woman candidate who was running for a parliamentary position had her house torched and her bodyguard killed.[74] This act of violence undermined her campaign and led to the failure of her business, which had provided the funds for the electoral contest. Symbolic violence against women in politics takes the form of harm or defamation in the context of sexist media coverage of female politicians. A growing body of research on gender and social media shows how women are preferred targets for cyber aggression. Many Internet platforms post doctored images and spread false rumors about women, especially politically active women.[75] In the context of abuse and threats of violence, women are often encouraged to ally with male elites for protection (much like a husband in traditional societies), and their political agendas may be compromised as a result. These backlash dynamics are significant obstacles to gender-inclusive governance.

Gendered structural inequalities

Most efforts to promote women's participation neglect to address a major barrier: the gendered structure of the political economy. Globally, women are responsible for an unequal share of the paid and unpaid work of care and social reproduction. Social reproduction includes biological reproduction, unpaid production in the home (both goods and services), social provisioning (such as voluntary work directed at meeting community needs), the reproduction of culture and ideology and the provision of sexual, emotional and affective services in the household required to maintain family and intimate relationships.[76] The United Nations estimates that women's unpaid work is worth $10 trillion per year – or 13 percent of the global Gross Domestic Product (GDP).[77]

The gender division of labor in the family household affects the gender division of labor in the public realm, positioning women in "feminized" sectors and occupations that are typically the lowest paid, with the poorest working conditions and at the bottom of organizational hierarchies, due to women's frequent need to take on part-time and casual work in order to accommodate unpaid work responsibilities. This gender division of labor means that many women do not have the time to devote to leadership roles and to participation in national and international governance. Strategies for engendering governance across all domains must address gender divisions of care labor in the workforce and in households and communities.

Strategies for engendering governance

Strategies for engendering governance should respond to the major obstacles we have identified, especially masculine institutional cultures, violence and abuse targeted at politically active women and structural barriers in the political economy to women's governance participation.

A broad array of strategies is needed with respect to violence against women engaged in public life. Naming and shaming sexist political leaders and political candidates with serious allegations of rape, violence and sexual assault is a key tactic being taken up in the light of the *#metoo* movement. Directly challenging misogynist discourses by holding states to account under international law – drawing on the Convention on the Elimination of All Forms of Discrimination against Women and UNSCR 1325, which mandate women's participation in political decision-making – is an important strategy. Pushing for structural reform of the security sector and the judiciary to protect women's public access, security and political participation is needed to prevent violence directed against political women.

Reducing women's care burdens and distributing an equal care share to men is a strategy for engendering governance that could both challenge masculine institutional cultures and empower women by freeing up time to participate in governance. The UN's High Level Panel on Women's Economic Empowerment argues that care work "substantially limits [women's] participation and empowerment in political, social and economic spheres."[78] If care could be reduced and shared with men in individual households, this would remove a key structural barrier to women's meaningful participation. Canadian political scientist Jane Jenson argues, however, that what is needed to achieve gender equality is social investment in accessible and affordable care, which redistributes and reduces unpaid care as opposed to just sharing it with individual men.[79] Ensuring equal care and redistribution to men would involve changes to employment and employer policies, such as working hours as well as campaigns, individual behavior change and flexi-work. Recognizing and valuing the work of social reproduction as a crucial economic activity by supporting it through social redistribution and protection and pay equity for the caring sectors of the economy are important strategies as well.

Successful strategies for promoting gender-equal governance involve bottom-up societal and global campaigns, building alliances inside and outside institutions (including partnering with men) and amplifying the feminist foreign policy movement for social and political change.

Forging societal and global campaigns

Most concrete progress in the move toward gender-equal governance has been the result of bottom-up campaigns and transnational networked movements. In the social media age, these have been movements started by hashtags. Supporting these campaigns is a powerful strategy. For instance, the *#metoo* movement spread quickly, showing that the message of gender equality has broad appeal and that it resonates with ordinary people. It has resulted in powerful men losing their leadership positions and jobs, in organizations changing their policies and in societies becoming much more aware of the presence and impact of sexual harassment, abuse and violence – in workplaces and sectors from the political realm to government, the entertainment industry and businesses and universities. The US National Democratic Institute launched a global campaign – *#NotThe Cost* – to combat sexual harassment and raise awareness of the violence women face when holding or seeking office.

Challenging informal rules and practices through social movements such as *#metoo* also requires expert gender analysis. An academic-led *#womenalsoknow* social media movement has begun to challenge the universal prominence of male experts in media commentary and *#manels* in public events on politics and governance. Think tanks are of particular concern, as the research, ideas and media presence they cultivate have a major impact on policy agendas.[80] *#womenalsoknow* has spread around the world. It is raising awareness of the need to consult with women as well as male experts and to consider the impact of only talking to men.

Responding to violence against political women, former US Ambassador to the UN, Samantha Power, started a campaign called *#FreeThe20*. This campaign focused on 20 women who had been locked up by their governments for championing human rights or women's rights, including sexual harassment.[81]

Building alliances among women and with men

In addition to women's presence in elite peace processes, the likelihood of achieving a peace agreement with gender provisions increases when women's representation in national legislatures and women's civil society participation increases. One of the most important factors in achieving gender-sensitive peace agreements is women's civil society participation. Civil society participation includes women's freedom of speech, participation in civil society organizations and representation in the ranks of the media and academia. Civil society often provides women with their first opportunities to campaign and participate in talks and negotiations with government. In conflict-affected environments, the opportunity to participate safely and represent women's security concerns may only be possible through Civil Society Organizations (CSOs) that are able to advocate for women's human rights.[82]

The interchange among international organizations, member states and civil society is a key mechanism for integrating gender perspectives into peace agreements and international security policymaking. Case-study research documents the impact of local women's civil society activists and their efforts to lobby for inclusion in peace processes through the UNSCR1325 framework, and it shows that these efforts can inform and encourage activists in other countries. During Myanmar's ongoing peace process, the Alliance for Gender Inclusion in the Peace Process campaign instigated conversations about women's participation in traditionally "male" spaces such as conflict, security and peace.[83]

Expanding the feminist foreign policy movement

The feminist foreign policy movement is an important intervention in the logic of power, revealing an alternative logic of empowerment promoted through diplomacy that supports populations – women and men – to deliver peace and prosperity through principles of human rights and gender equality. This movement illustrates how formal attempts to address leadership in a male-dominated field, such as international relations, is producing substantive reform in diplomatic practice. In 2014, Sweden was the first country to stake out a feminist foreign policy, arguing that the pursuit of gender equality is not only a goal in itself but also a means of achieving other goals – such as peace, security and sustainable development. Sweden's feminist foreign policy has advanced principles of women's rights, women's equal representation and women's equal access to resources, which have influenced the country's choices of policy and alliances.[84] In this normative vision, the promotion of peacebuilding, conflict resolution and humanitarian responses are core activities of foreign policy. Former Foreign Minister Margot Wallström argued that "a feminist approach is a self-evident and necessary part of a modern view of today's global challenges."[85]

Justin Trudeau's government in Canada followed Sweden's lead, announcing in 2017 that it was embracing a feminist foreign policy focused on international assistance to women's rights organizations and sending more women soldiers to international peacekeeping operations.[86] Australia has also pursued a gender strategy, making gender equality and women's empowerment part of its core foreign policy objectives. As Foreign Minister, Julie Bishop increased the proportion of overseas development aid that must address gender equality as a primary or secondary objective from 50 percent to 80 percent. Like Canada, Sweden and the United States, Australia has established the position of a global ambassador for women to promote women's status abroad and across foreign policies. This provides an institutional mechanism for the development of normative feminist principles to inform foreign policy. The promotion of feminist foreign policies reflects a broader global shift in political power and a gradual power shift in gender relations as women's economic and political participation increases.

Conclusion

This chapter has examined the rationale for gender-equal and inclusive governance in the political, peace and security and economic domains. The obstacles to and drivers of progress in policy and governance were considered, followed by an examination of strategies to confront ongoing challenges in global and local politics.

Whether promoting parliamentary quotas or a feminist foreign policy, care must be taken in evaluating the net worth of such efforts. There is no reason why a feminist foreign policy must prove itself more worthy than existing strategic positions promoted by defensive realists. Male politicians do not need to justify what their maleness brings to a seat in parliament or government. There are still implicit and explicit assumptions that women must prove their worth and value.

Neither state legislatures nor the international system are preordained to be male or realist. These are social constructions that suited one group at the expense of another. We must challenge the presumption that politics and diplomacy have done a marvelous job until now simply because these institutions have been – historically – almost exclusively male. A feminist foreign policy is a normative project, but it is also a project about equal participation on just terms, as is parliamentary representation and institutional reform. Any benefit from participation is a positive outcome; the claim to participate should be a rights-based claim, not a cost-benefit claim.

When reviewing the arguments promoted in favor of women quotas in parliament or women's participation in peace processes, the persuasive line is often that women will do better and women will achieve more because women care, women are peaceful, and so on. These gendered assumptions may turn out to be false. Indeed, they may be potentially damaging to the cause. As this chapter has shown, gender stereotypes continue even after women have broken through glass ceilings. Women are often placed in impossible situations where the chances of success are steep for the few who have made it that far.

The present challenge for the demand for gender-equal governance is that it is operating in a time of rising misogyny and the scapegoating of women within and across states. That said, the social, economic and political momentum in favor of gender equality is too strong to ignore, as the *#metoo* movement has demonstrated. Moreover, the increased presence of women in powerful positions and the development of gender-mainstreamed policies seem to go together. Both sexes are, overall, benefitting from a changed status quo to gender norms. These changes are mutually enabling for women, men and people of unassigned sex. It is also changing the pathology of institutions – with changes to our collective expectations of who should be located in these institutions.

Former US Ambassador to the United Nations Samantha Power said that being the only woman on the UN Security Council made her a feminist.[87] By the end of her tenure as Ambassador, she was one of 37 women ambassadors leading their UN permanent mission in New York. In 2014, the UN Security Council nearly reached gender parity for the first time, with six women ambassadors on the 15-member Security Council. This shift was short lived: the number of women Ambassadors on the Council dropped to four in 2016 and to one in 2017.

A gender perspective on national and international governance must reflect substantive issues and agendas that relate to the intersection of inequality and injustice affecting women, especially particular groups of women, disproportionately. A gender perspective moves us beyond the fixation on counting the presence of women – although gender-balance and the presence of women are crucial ingredients in the mainstreaming of a gender perspective across all types and levels of governance.

Notes

1 See Valerie M. Hudson et al., "The Heart of the Matter: The Security of Women and the Security of States," *International Security*, Vol. 33, No. 3 (Winter 2008/09), pp. 7–45; Mary Caprioli, "Gendered Conflict," *Journal of Peace Research*, Vol. 37, No. 1 (January 2000), pp. 51–68; Erik Melander, "Gender Equality and Inter-State Armed Conflict," *International Studies Quarterly*, Vol. 49, No. 4 (December 2005), pp. 695–714.

2 See World Economic Forum (WEF), *The Global Gender Gap Report 2020* (Geneva: WEF, December 2019); International Parliamentary Union (IPU), *Gender Equality at a Glance* (Geneva: IPU, 2019).

3 Micah Zenko, "City of Men," *Foreign Policy* (July 14, 2011); Micah Zenko and Amelia Mae Wolf, "Leaning from Behind: Women in Foreign Policy and Media," *Foreign Policy* (September 24, 2015).

4 See UN Women, *Women's Meaningful Participation in Negotiating Peace and the Implementation of Peace Agreements* (New York: UN Women, May 2018), pp. 13, 44.

5 Mona Lena Krook and Pippa Norris, "Beyond Quotas: Strategies to Promote Gender Equality in Elected Office," *Political Studies*, Vol. 62, No. 1 (January 2014), pp. 2–20.

6 UN, *Beijing Platform for Action 1995*, UN Fourth World Conference on Women, para. 181.

7 See Kara Ellerby, *No Shortcut to Change: An Unlikely Path to a More Gender-Equitable World* (New York: New York University, 2017), pp. 101–127.

8 Mariz Tadros, "Introduction: Quotas – Add Women and Stir," *IDS Bulletin*, Vol. 41, No. 5 (September 2010), pp. 1–10.

9 World Bank, *World Development Report: Gender Equality and Development* (Washington, DC: World Bank, 2012); UN Development Programme (UNDP), *Powerful Synergies: Gender Equality, Economic Development and Environmental Sustainability* (New York: UNDP, 2012); Hillary Clinton, "Development in the 21st Century," *Foreign Policy* (January 6, 2010).

10 Ann E. Towns, *Women and States: Norms and Hierarchies in International Relations* (Cambridge: Cambridge University Press, 2010).

11 UN, *Beijing Platform for Action 1995*, paras. 189, 192, 194.

12 Ibid., paras. 184, 189.

13 See IPU (@ ipu.org).

14 See UN General Assembly Resolution, A/S-23/3, 2000, para. 22. See also International Institute for Democracy and Electoral Assistance, *Gender Quotas Database* (@ idea.int).

15 See UNSCR 1820 (2008); 1888 (2009); 1889 (2009); 1960 (2011); 2106 (2013); 2122 (2013); 2242 (2015); 2467 (2019); 2493 (2019).

16 Karin Aggestam and Isak Svensson, "Where Are the Women in Peace Mediation?" in Karin Aggestam and Ann E. Towns, eds., *Gendering Diplomacy and International Negotiations* (Basingstoke: Palgrave MacMillan, 2018), pp. 149–168.

17 Council on Foreign Relations (CFR), *Women's Participation in Peace Processes* (New York: CFR, 2018). See also Christine Bell, *Text and Context: Evaluating Peace Agreements for their Gender Perspective* (Edinburgh: Political Settlements Research Program, 2015).

18 Jana Krause, Werner Krause and Piia Bränfors, "Women's Participation and Peace Negotiations and the Durability of Peace," *International Interactions*, Vol. 44, No. 6 (August 2018), pp. 985–1016; Jacqui True and Yolanda Morales-Riveros, "Toward Inclusive Peace: Analysing Gender-Sensitive Peace Agreements 2000–2016," *International Political Science Review*, Vol. 40, No. 1 (January 2019), pp. 1–18.

19 Marie O'Reilly, Andrea Ó Súilleabháin and Thania Paffenholz, *Reimagining Peacemaking: Women's Roles in Peace Processes* (New York: International Peace Institute, 2015), p. 1. See also Thania Paffenholz et al., *Making Women Count – Not Just Counting Women: Assessing Women's Inclusion and Influence on Peace Negotiations* (Geneva: Inclusive Peace and Transition Initiative and UN Women, 2016).

20 McKinsey and Company, *Women Matter, Gender Diversity: A Corporate Performance Driver* (New York: McKinsey and Company, 2007); Kevin Daly, *Gender Equality, Growth and Global Ageing*, Goldman Sachs Global Economics Paper No. 154 (New York: Goldman Sachs, April 3, 2007); Jacqui True, "Counting Women, Balancing Gender: Increasing Women's Participation in Governance," *Politics and Gender*, Vol. 9, No. 3 (September 2013), pp. 351–359.

21 See Lois Joy et al., *The Bottom Line: Corporate Performance and Women's Representation on Boards* (New York: Catalyst, 2007); Deloitte Center for Corporate Governance, *Women in the Boardroom: A Global Perspective* (New York: Deloitte, November 2011); Credit Suisse Research Institute, *Gender Diversity and the Impact on Corporate Performance, 2005–2011* (Zurich: Credit Suisse, 2012).

22 Jacqui True, "The Global Governance of Gender," in Nicola Phillips and Anthony Payne, eds., *The International Political Economy of Governance* (London: Edward Elgar Press, 2014), p. 332.

23 WEF, *The Global Gender Gap Report*.

24 World Bank, *World Development Report*; World Bank, *Gender Equality as Smart Economics* (Washington, DC: World Bank, 2006).

25 See Sylvia Bashevkin, "Numerical and Policy Representation on the International Stage: Women Foreign Policy Leaders in Western Industrialised Systems," *International Political Science Review*, Vol. 35, No. 4 (September 2014), pp. 409–429; Lakshmi Iyer et al., *The Power of Political Voice: Women's Political Representation and Crime in India*, Working Paper (Cambridge, MA: Harvard Business School, July 29, 2011); Pilar Domingo et al., *Women's Voice and Leadership in Decision-Making: Assessing the Evidence* (London: Overseas Development Institute, 2015).

26 Karen Beckwith and Kimberly Cowell-Meyers, "Sheer Numbers: Critical Representation Thresholds and Women's Political Representation," *Perspectives on Politics*, Vol. 5, No. 3 (September 2007), pp. 553–565; Sarah Childs and Mona Lena Krook, "Critical Mass Theory and Women's Political Representation," *Political Studies*, Vol. 56, No. 3 (October 2008).

27 Mona Lena Krook and Pär Zetterberg, "Introduction: Gender Quotas and Women's Representation: New Directions in Research," *Journal of Representative Democracy*, Vol. 50, No. 3 (September 2014), pp. 287–329.

28 Aili Tripp and Alice Kang, "The Global Impact of Quotas: On the Fast Track to Increased Female Legislative," *Comparative Political Studies*, Vol. 41, No. 3 (2008), pp. 338–361.

29 Peter Allen and David Cutts, "How Do Gender Quotas Affect Public Support for Women as Political Leaders?" *West European Politics*, Vol. 41, No. 1 (May 2018), pp. 147–168.

30 Drude Dahlerup and Lenita Freidenvall, "Quotas as a 'Fast Track' to Equal Representation for Women: Why Scandinavia is no Longer the Model," *International Feminist Journal of Politics*, Vol. 7, No. 1 (2005), pp. 24–48.

31 Jacqui True, Nicole George, Sara Niner and Swati Parashar, *Women's Political Participation in Asia and The Pacific*, Conflict Prevention and Peace Forum Working Papers on Women in Politics No. 3 (October 2014), pp. 1–70.

32 Pär Zetterberg, "Do Gender Quotas Foster Women's Political Engagement? Lessons from Latin America," *Political Research Quarterly*, Vol. 62, No. 4 (2009), pp. 715–730.

33 Mona Lena Krook, *Quotas for Women in Politics: Gender and Candidate Selection Reform Worldwide* (Oxford: Oxford University Press, 2010).

34 Ceridwen Spark and Jack Corbett, "Emerging Women Leaders' Views on Political Participation in Melanesia," *International Feminist Journal of Politics*, Vol. 20, No. 2 (2018), pp. 221–235.

35 Andrea Guariso, Bert Ingelaere and Marijke Verpoorten, "When Ethnicity Beats Gender: Quotas and Political Representation in Rwanda and Burundi," *Development and Change*, Vol. 49, No. 6 (November 2018), pp. 1361–1391.

36 Joan Grace and Marian Sawer, "Representing Gender Equality: Specialised Parliamentary Bodies," *Parliamentary Affairs*, Vol. 69, No. 4 (2016), pp. 745–747.

37 Marian Sawer and Alicia Turner, "Specialised Parliamentary Bodies: Their Role and Relevance to Women's Movement Repertoire," *Parliamentary Affairs*, Vol. 69, No. 4 (October 2016), pp. 763–777.

38 Jacqui True and Michael Mintrom, "Transnational Networks and Policy Diffusion: The Case of Gender Mainstreaming," *International Studies Quarterly*, Vol. 45, No. 1 (March 2001), pp. 27–57.

39 Mala Htun and S. Laurel Weldon, "The Civic Origins of Progressive Policy Change: Combating Violence Against Women in Global Perspective, 1975–2005," *American Political Science Review*, Vol. 106, No. 3 (August 2012), pp. 548–569.

40 Anna Carella and Brooke Ackerly, "Ignoring Rights Is Wrong: Re-Politicizing Gender Equality and Development with the Rights-Based Approach," *International Feminist Journal of Politics*, Vol. 19, No. 2 (2017), pp. 137–152.

41 Jacqui True, "Explaining the Global Diffusion of the Women, Peace and Security Agenda," *International Political Science Review*, Vol. 37, No. 3 (June 2016), p. 320.

42 Mala Htun and S. Laurel Weldon, "When Do Governments Promote Women's Rights? A Framework for the Comparative Analysis of Sex Equality Policy," *Perspectives on Politics*, Vol. 8, No. 1 (March 2010), pp. 207–216.

43 Sara E. Davies and Jacqui True, "Norm Entrepreneurship in International Politics: William Hague and the Prevention of Sexual Violence in Conflict," *Foreign Policy Analysis*, Vol. 13, No. 3 (July 2017), pp. 701–721.

44 Pippa Norris and Ronald Inglehart, *Cracking the Marble Ceiling: Cultural Barriers Facing Women Leaders* (Cambridge, MA: Harvard University, 2008).

45 Elin Bjarnegard and Erik Melander, "Pacific Men: How the Feminist Gap Explains Hostility," *The Pacific Review*, Vol. 30, No. 4 (2017), pp. 478–493.

46 World Health Organization (WHO), *Delivered by Women, Led by Men: A Gender and Equity Analysis of the Global Health and Social Workforce* (Geneva: WHO, 2019).

47 Anne-Marie Goetz and Rachel Dore-Weeks, "What About the Men? Frankly, It Depends Why You're Asking," *The Guardian* (March 7, 2018).

48 Ibid.

49 Sara E. Davies and Jacqui True, "The Politics of Counting and Reporting Conflict-Related Sexual and Gender-Based Violence: The Case of Myanmar," *International Feminist Journal of Politics*, Vol. 19, No. 1 (April 2017), pp. 4–21.

50 Meredith Preston McGhie and E. Njoki Wamai, *Beyond the Numbers: Women's Participation in the Kenya National Dialogue* (Geneva: Centre for Humanitarian Dialogue, March 2011).

51 Transnational Institute, *No Women, No Peace: Gender Equality, Conflict and Peace in Myanmar*, Myanmar Policy Briefing No. 18 (Amsterdam: Transnational Institute, January 2016).

52 Aida A. Hozic and Jacqui True, *Scandalous Economics: Gender and the Politics of Financial Crisis* (New York: Oxford University Press, 2016); Elisabeth Prugl, "If Lehman Brothers Had Been Lehman Sisters...: Gender and Myth in the Aftermath of the Financial Crisis," *International Political Sociology*, Vol. 6, No. 1 (2012), pp. 21–35.

53 Hozic and True, *Scandalous Economics*.

54 See Michelle K. Ryan and S. Alexander Haslam, "The Glass Cliff: Evidence that Women are Over-Represented in Precarious Leadership Positions," *British Journal of Management*, Vol. 16, No. 2 (June 2005), pp. 81–90; Michelle K. Ryan, S. Alexander Haslam and Clara Kulich, "Politics and the Glass Cliff: Evidence That Women Are Preferentially Selected to Contest Hard-to-Win Seats," *Psychology of Women Quarterly*, Vol. 34, No. 1 (2010), pp. 56–64.

55 Suzanne Nosell, "A Feminist Foreign Policy: Hillary Clinton's Hard Choices," *Foreign Affairs*, Vol. 95, No. 2 (March/April 2016).

56 See Sylvia Bashevkin, *Women as Foreign Policy Leaders* (Oxford: Oxford University Press, 2018).

57 Deborah L. Rhode, *The Difference 'Difference' Makes: Women and Leadership* (Stanford: Stanford University Press, 2003).

58 Joshua S. Goldstein, *War and Gender* (Cambridge: Cambridge University Press, 2001); Ole R. Holsti and James N. Rosenau, "The Foreign Policy Beliefs of Women in Leadership Positions," *Journal of Politics*, Vol. 43, No. 2 (May 1981), pp. 326–347.

59 Jacqui True, "Mainstreaming Gender in Global Public Policy," *International Feminist Journal of Politics*, Vol. 5, No. 3 (2003), pp. 368–396.

60 Dulcie Leimbach, "Three Ex-UN Leaders Form a Women's Group to Save Multilateralism," *PassBlue* (February 21, 2019).

61 Bashevkin, "Numerical and Policy Representation," p. 425.

62 Tiffany D. Barnes and Diana Z. O'Brien, "Defending the Realm: The Appointment of Female Defense Ministers Worldwide," *American Journal of Political Science*, Vol. 62, No. 2 (January 2018).

63 Nosell, "Feminist Foreign Policy;" Valerie M. Hudson and Patricia Leidl, *The Hillary Doctrine: Sex and American Foreign Policy* (New York: Columbia University Press, 2015).

64 Jacqui True, "Gender and Foreign Policy," in Shahar Hamieri and Mark Beeson, eds., *Navigating International Disorder: Australia in World Affairs 2011–2015* (Oxford: Oxford University Press 2016).

65 See Organization for Economic Co-operation and Development (OECD), *Toolkit for Mainstreaming and Implementing Gender Equality* (Paris: OECD, 2018).

66 Mala Htun and S. Laurel Weldon, *The Logics of Gender Justice* (Cambridge: Cambridge University Press, 2018).

67 Monash Gender, Peace and Security Centre, *Building a Stronger Evidence Base: A Gender Sensitive Approach to Empowering Women for Peaceful Communities* (Bangkok: UN Women, 2019).

68 Georgina Waylen, "Informal Institutions, Institutional Change, and Gender Equality," *Political Research Quarterly*, Vol. 67, No. 1 (2014), pp. 212–223.

69 Louise Chappell and Georgina Waylen, "Gender and the Hidden Life of Institutions," *Public Administration*, Vol. 91, No. 3 (2013).

70 Carol Cohn, "Sex and Death in the Rational World of Defense Intellectuals," *Signs*, Vol. 12, No. 4 (Summer 1987), pp. 687–718; Nancy E. McGlen and Meredith Reid Sarkees, *Women in Foreign Policy* (London: Routledge, 1993).

71 Elle Hunt, Nick Evershed and Ri Liu, "From Julia Gillard to Hillary Clinton: Online Abuse of Politicians Around the World," *The Guardian* (June 27, 2016).

72 Ibid.

73 National Democratic Institute (NDI), *#Not the Cost: Stopping Violence Against Women in Politics* (Washington, DC: NDI, 2017).

74 Sarah Hewitt, "The Struggle for Women's Participation in Kenya," *Australian Outlook* (September 1, 2018).

75 See Karen Ross, *Gendered Media: Women, Men and Identity Politics* (New York: Rowman and Littlefield, 2010).

76 Catherine Hoskyns and Shirin M. Rai, "Recasting the Global Political Economy: Counting Women's Unpaid Work," *New Political Economy*, Vol. 12, No. 3 (2007), p. 300.

77 Jeni Klugman and Tatiana Melnikova, *Unpaid Work and Care*, A Policy Brief (New York: UN High Level Panel on Women's Economic Empowerment, 2016).

78 High Level Panel on Women's Economic Empowerment, *Leave No One Behind: Taking Action for Transformation Change on Women's Economic Empowerment* (New York and Washington, DC: United Nations and World Bank, 2017).

79 Jane Jenson, "Lost in Translation: The Social Investment Perspective and Gender Equality," *Social Politics: International Studies in Gender, State & Society*, Vol. 16, No. 4 (Winter 2009), pp. 446–483.

80 Melissa Conley Tyler, Emily Blizzard and Bridget Crane, "Is International Affairs Too 'Hard' for Women? Explaining the Missing Women in Australia's International Affairs," *Australian Journal of International Affairs*, Vol. 68, No. 2 (April 2014), pp. 156–176.

81 Stephanie Mitchell, "Samantha Power: The World in her Rearview Mirror," *The Harvard Gazette* (January 2018).

82 See Htun and Weldon, "The Civic Origins of Progressive Policy Change."

83 Erin Kamler, *Towards a Feminist Foreign Policy in Myanmar* (Berlin: Heinrich-Böll Stiftung, February 12, 2019).

84 Swedish Ministry of Foreign Affairs, *Handbook: Sweden Feminist Foreign Policy* (Stockholm: Government of Sweden, 2018).

85 Margot Wallström, "A Feminist Approach is Self-Evident and Necessary," *UNA-UK Magazine* (December 12, 2017).

86 Stephanie Fillion, "As Sweden and Canada Push Their Feminist Foreign Policy, Others Resist the Label," *Passblue* (February 12, 2018).

87 Jennifer Ryan, "Samantha Power: 'Being the Only Woman in the UN Made Me a Feminist'," *The Irish Times Women's Podcast* (November 13, 2017).

12

PROMOTING GENDER AND SECURITY

Obstacles, drivers and strategies

Chantal de Jonge Oudraat and Michael E. Brown

Gender and security have been two of the most central human preoccupations since the dawn of time, so it stands to reason that the connections between gender and security must be important as well. The contributors to this book have demonstrated that this is inarguably true and that the connections run both ways: gender affects security, and security problems affect gender issues. If you care about either of these issues, you need to think about both.

The connections between these two elemental human concerns received remarkably little attention from scholars or policymakers until the latter years of the 20th century. The impetus for security-gender analysis has come overwhelmingly from feminist and gender scholars, not the security studies community, which has been comprised mainly of men. Similarly, the impetus for policy action has come overwhelmingly from women's rights activists and the Women, Peace and Security (WPS) movement – not national or international security policy establishments, which have been and mostly still are dominated by men.

The good news is that scholars have made important strides in analyzing gender and security issues in the final decades of the 20th century and the first decades of the 21st century. There are established – or at least emerging – cadres of scholars and analysts working on all ten sets of issues examined in this book. As a result, progress has been made in advancing understanding of these issues.

The track record in the policy world is much more mixed – a combination of the good, the bad and the ugly. In some issue areas, progress has been made in establishing formal, aspirational goals for progress. The WPS agenda, which was supported by ten United Nations (UN) Security Council resolutions in the 2000s and 2010s, stands out in this regard. The UN Sustainable Development Goals (SDGs) for 2030 include a cluster of targets for advancing gender equality. Enunciating ambitious goals is not the same thing as achieving these goals, of course, but it is a good and necessary first step. International organizations, such as the United

Nations and the European Union (EU), have done a good job of embracing gender equality as a goal and understanding the importance of gender-security dynamics.

Policy progress has been much more limited elsewhere, especially at the national level. National security policy establishments continue to define security problems in traditional ways. The WPS agenda is, at best, a secondary concern for national security policymakers. Moreover, national security establishments generally do not understand gender or the connections between gender and security, as the chapters in this book demonstrate. Most national security policymakers still define gender and security issues as "women's" issues, which, in addition to being conceptually misguided, provides another mechanism for treating these issues as secondary priorities.

Progress has also varied a great deal from country to country. In 2014, Sweden adopted an explicitly feminist foreign policy, making it a global leader on gender issues in general. Canada, France and Mexico have taken steps in this direction as well.[1] At the other end of the spectrum, in 2019 Saudi Arabia announced that women will be allowed to travel outside the home without the permission of a male guardian – a step toward gender equality, but still several quantum leaps behind most of the world.

What is especially worrisome is that the goals of advancing gender equality and elevating gender in security policy have been subject to increased pushback and experienced more setbacks in the 2010s. The prospects for the gender and security agenda in the 21st century is far from certain. What is certain is that smooth and steady progress is not in the forecast. The balance between the good, the bad and the ugly will continue to evolve.

Given this picture, it is especially valuable to examine three sets of factors that have shaped and will continue to shape gender and security progress: *obstacles to progress, drivers of progress* and *strategies for progress*. The contributors to this book have focused on these three factors in their analyses of gender-security dynamics in ten issues areas. In this concluding chapter, we draw on the insights presented in these studies and develop some general assessments.

Although there is variation from issue to issue, and especially from country to country, there are two striking commonalities when it comes to gender-security dynamics in the 20th and 21st centuries: the main obstacles to progress and the main drivers of progress are the same.

The main obstacles to progress have been men and the male-dominated political, economic and social institutions – patriarchies – that have been running most of the world for most of human history. These deeply entrenched institutions have engaged in multi-generational efforts to perpetuate their positions as well as targeted campaigns to halt, minimize or reverse advances toward gender equality. Men and male-dominated institutions have employed a panoply of time-tested tactics to oppose steps toward gender equality, ranging from tokenism and marginalization to outright violence. The precepts of patriarchies are especially pronounced, powerful and resistant to change in national and international security matters.

The main drivers of progress have been women activists and women's rights organizations that have focused on security problems. Women and women's organizations have been the initiators and the prime movers behind every campaign in every issue area. They have been politically and strategically wise in building alliances with men and other organizations, mobilizing support in their home countries and across international civil society and building support within national governments and international organizations.

Although the demographics are not perfectly black and white – many women support patriarchal systems; many men are feminists – these obstacles and drivers are highly gendered, and this is not surprising. Gender is fundamentally about power. Changing gender balances involves changes in existing balances of power. One of the basic features of politics – at the international, national and local levels – is that established powers rarely surrender their privileged positions voluntarily. The campaign for gender equality has been and will continue to be a multi-decade, multi-generational power struggle. With this political context in mind, we present five main long-term strategies for progress in this chapter's final section. We first examine the policy track record, the main obstacles to progress and the main drivers of progress to date.

The track record: the good, the bad and the ugly

The good: The UN was founded on three interconnected pillars – peace and security, human rights and economic development. The UN Charter recognized that human rights and gender equality are basic conditions for peace and security as well as economic development. The Charter's preamble specifically affirmed "the equal rights of men and women."[2] The adoption of the Universal Declaration of Human Rights in 1948 further consolidated the notion of equal rights.

As Corey Levine and Sari Kouvo point out, efforts to advance human rights have gone through several phases since the 1940s. The UN's human rights work from the 1950s to the 1990s was largely focused on the development of legally binding agreements that included equality between men and women as a basic human right. In the 1960s and 1970s, it became clear to activists that addressing gender-based discrimination would require "more than equal rights proclamations." Attaining real equality would have to address "the nature of systemic discrimination."[3] This led to the adoption of the Convention on the Elimination of all Forms of Racial Discrimination (CERD) in 1969 and the Convention on the Elimination of all Forms of Discrimination against Women (CEDAW) in 1979.

Jeni Klugman reviews the development community's evolution from a Women in Development (WID) paradigm to a Gender and Development (GAD) approach in the 1980s. The GAD approach was based on the recognition that "a holistic approach to gender relations" would be needed to empower women in the long-term. It was understood that policies needed "to tackle the underlying sources of women's subordination, while considering the power dynamics between women and men." This new approach focused on institutional forms of gender discrimination alongside concerns about equity and parity in participation in development programs. The adoption of the Millennium Development Goals in 2000, and especially the adoption of the SDGs in 2015, further strengthened and institutionalized the gender equality agenda.[4]

Although the first UN Women's Conference in Mexico in 1975 and the UN Decade of Women (1975–85) were initially focused on the role of women in economic development, the UN's efforts gradually expanded to include the role of women in peace and security matters. The fourth UN Women's Conference (held in Beijing in 1995) recognized the important role of women as actors in advancing international peace and security. The 1995 Beijing Declaration and Platform for Action established ambitious goals for gender equality, development and peace. The Executive Director of UN Women, Phumzile Mlambo-Ngcuka, has noted that the Beijing Declaration and Platform "became for the women's movement what the UN Charter is to UN member states: a place of historic, consensual agreement that we can lean on in the face of disagreements and changing administrations. It instigated a global network of gender activists that formed across every corner of the world on every issue."[5]

After intense lobbying from women's organizations in the late 1990s, the UN Security Council developed a normative framework that further recognized women's vulnerabilities in armed conflicts and the importance of women's participation in peace and security processes. The adoption of UN Security Council Resolution (UNSCR) 1325 (2000), along with nine other resolutions in the 2000s and 2010s, are now known as the WPS agenda. WPS implementation efforts and gender mainstreaming policies have become established, with ongoing initiatives at many international organizations, including the UN, the African Union (AU), the EU and the North Atlantic Treaty Organization (NATO).

As Jacqui True and Sara Davies point out, the adoption of gender mainstreaming policies and mechanisms at the national level has also been rapid.[6] Many states have government ministries dedicated to women's empowerment and gender equality issues. As of 2020, 83 states have developed National Action Plans (NAPs) to implement UNSCR 1325. The Scandinavian countries and many other countries in Europe have declared that the advancement of gender equality is a primary objective of their domestic and foreign policies. As noted, Sweden adopted a feminist foreign policy in 2014. Some countries, including Canada and France, have made gender balancing a core principle of their staffing policies in national governance.

The number of women in parliaments across the world doubled between the late 1990s and the late 2010s; it increased from 17 percent to 24 percent in one decade (2009–2019).[7] As of 2019, 127 countries have adopted constitutional, electoral or political party quotas.[8] These quota mechanisms have helped to advance women's participation in governance.[9]

The expansion of women's participation and leadership in governance has extended to the corporate world. True and Davies emphasize that higher levels of women's representation in both politics and corporate boards are linked to "less corruption, better policy outcomes and higher investment returns." They write:

"Male-dominated economic governance has been shown to be suboptimal in terms of performance. . . . Gender-inclusion is thus now an essential part of good economic as well as political governance."[10] It is no longer a social policy add-on, but "smart economics" to promote women's participation in governance.

The bad and the ugly: Although the list of public declarations in support of gender equality has grown, implementation has been slow, limited and uneven. Gender inequalities persist. Gender perspectives have been misunderstood, poorly integrated or left out altogether in security policy analyses.

Jane Freedman argues that gender should be central in the analysis and development of migration policies but, unfortunately, sophisticated gender perspectives are lacking. The result is an array of migration misconceptions and flawed migration policies worldwide. For example, while in the past the typical profile of a migrant was a man, half of migrants today are women, and many of these women are not part of family migrations; they are migrating on their own. For many of these women, gender inequalities in their home countries are part of their motivations to migrate. Freedman emphasizes that gender "influences who migrates, how and why they migrate, and their experiences during migration."[11] Unfortunately, there have been no systematic policy initiatives to reduce the gendered insecurities that abound in migration populations.

Gender perspectives are also poorly developed in both terrorism research and counter-terrorism policy. Jeannette Gaudry Haynie highlights that the gender dimensions of terrorism remain marginalized and are not widely understood or accepted in research and policy. Significantly, little comparative analysis has been done on the radicalization paths of men and women. The deficiencies are even greater in the policy world. National security establishments and counter-terrorism agencies have narrow, simplistic conceptions of the role of gender in terrorist organizations. As Haynie explains, counter-terrorism "programs often use female stereotypes to counter terrorism while remaining blind to the way masculinities can shape terrorist narratives."[12] In comparison, terrorist organizations such as the Islamic State in Iraq and Syria (ISIS) have developed relatively sophisticated gender-based strategies for recruiting men and women. If you are less advanced than ISIS in thinking about gender, you are not in a good place.

The lack of gender perspectives in the field of environmental security is similarly detrimental to the development of effective policies. Edward Carr shows how nuanced and intersectional framings of gender in the area of water security have helped to demonstrate "who is made insecure in the face of resource stress and conflict, and when and where insecurities emerge." In Bangladesh, for example, many women, along with poor and marginalized men, are excluded from water management decisions. Research on climate change and security have focused on the general relationship between climate change and conflict, but analysts have not focused on the "important question: when and for whom does climate variability and change contribute to conflict?"[13]

This is also a critical question in humanitarian emergencies. Tamara Nair emphasizes that "humanitarian disasters are socio-economic constructs and they reflect existing discriminatory elements in society." Countries with highly gendered societies are therefore likely to experience many gendered problems during and after natural disasters. As in other issue areas, policy establishments fall far short in addressing the gender dimensions of humanitarian emergencies. Nair argues: "International rhetoric about gender mainstreaming has not led to the inclusion of gender dynamics in disaster policy on the ground."[14]

Although the UN and member states made bold commitments in 2015 to reach an elaborate set of SDGs by 2030, SDG 5 – on the promotion of gender equality and women's empowerment – is off to a weak start. In 2019, the UN reported that insufficient progress had been made on the root causes of gender inequality, "including legal discrimination, unfair social norms and attitudes, decision-making on sexual and reproductive issues and low levels of political participation."[15] If these trends continue, SDG 5 will not be realized in 2030.

The WPS agenda has been one of the most prominent gender-security initiatives in the 21st century, but problems abound even in this area. Policy progress has fallen short of stated goals in all four pillars of the WPS agenda: protection, participation, prevention, relief and recovery. Kathleen Kuehnast argues that, although the issue of conflict-related sexual violence has received high-level attention, little progress has been made in preventing violence or in bringing perpetrators before international or national courts. The 2019 report of the UN Secretary-General lists 50 parties that have committed or are responsible for conflict-related sexual violence. The UN and its member states have also been unable to deal effectively with the issue of Sexual Exploitation and Abuse (SEA) committed by UN peacekeepers.[16]

Although there has been some success in integrating women and women's organizations into the peace negotiations in Colombia, women have been absent or marginalized in most peace negotiations and peace operations. In their case study of Afghanistan, Levine and Kouvo show how lofty international ideals about gender equality can backfire and how the "hard-earned rights of Afghan women were fragile, and they quickly eroded as conservative forces in Afghanistan regained the upper hand ... while Western influence and support for women's rights declined." As the conflict has gone on, international actors in Afghanistan have begun to de-emphasize the gender agenda, leaving women in increasingly precarious positions.[17]

Policy apathy, neglect, misunderstanding and failure are bad enough, but a growing, active opposition to the gender-security agenda – and gender equality in general – is downright ugly. A surge in patriarchal ideology in both authoritarian governments and some democracies, along with corresponding attacks on women's rights in many countries, are worrisome new developments in the 21st century.

Anne Marie Goetz and Rob Jenkins show that a new wave of pushback against the gender agenda has led to mounting setbacks.[18] In Russia, the Duma decriminalized many cases of domestic violence in 2017.[19] In China, the government has opposed and jailed feminist activists, as well as members of the #*metoo* movement.[20] In the United States, the federal government and many states are restricting access to safe and legal abortions. Access to safe and legal abortions has also been a growing issue in Europe – most notably in Lithuania, Poland, Slovakia and Spain.[21] In 2018, the Hungarian government revoked accreditation and funding for gender studies programs. A spokesman for the Hungarian government stated: "The Government's standpoint is that people are born either male or female . . . and we do not consider it acceptable for us to talk about socially-constructed genders, rather than biological sexes."[22]

A wave of neo-patriarchs came to power in the 2000s and 2010s – most notably, Vladimir Putin in Russia, Xi Jinping in China and Donald Trump in the United States, countries that control three of the five permanent seats on the UN Security Council. These leaders have framed their positions as a defense of the traditional family and used this as cover to push back against women's rights. Traditional worldviews have promoted traditional gender stereotypes, in which women may be revered for their reproductive capacities, but only as long as they stay at home and remain subordinate to men. Efforts to curtail women's rights include limitations on reproductive rights and campaigns to deny legal rights to safety – in particular, women's safety from domestic violence. The societies that the neo-patriarchs seek to preserve or re-create are ones in which gender inequality is a basic principle. In this worldview, furthermore, there are only two genders: men and women. There is no room in this binary, hierarchical structure for other genders or orientations. Many women have also been supporters of these patriarchal beliefs and gender stereotypes.

In this context, it is not surprising that women who have run for and attained political offices have frequently been threatened with and subjected to violence. A 2016 study of 39 countries across five regions found that 82 percent of women Members of Parliament (MP) had experienced psychological violence; 44 percent had received threats of death, rape, beatings or kidnapping; 26 percent had experienced physical violence while serving in parliament; and 47 percent feared for their own security and the safety of their families.[23] During the 2017 elections in Kenya, dozens of women were raped by police officers and men in uniforms. In Egypt, women protesters have been sexually assaulted and raped. In Pakistan, women have been barred from voting by traditional councils and baton-wielding men at polling stations. In Canada, Haiti and Tunisia, women parliamentarians have reported sexual harassment and assault by other MPs.[24] A 2018 study showed that violence against women in politics is also rampant in Europe: 85 percent of women MPs reported psychological violence; 47 percent have been threatened with death, rape or beating; and 58 percent reported being the target of sexist attacks on social media networks.[25]

Goetz and Jenkins show how neo-patriarchs are trying to roll back women rights not only at the national level, but at the global level.[26] For example, a new WPS resolution (UNSCR 2467) was brought to the UN Security Council in 2019 for consideration. The Trump administration threatened to veto the resolution if it mentioned sexual and reproductive health, including safe termination of pregnancies for survivors of conflict-related sexual violence. As a result, all references to health services for rape survivors were deleted from the resolution. The resolution was subsequently adopted by the UN Security Council but, significantly, this was the first time a WPS resolution was not passed unanimously: Russia and China abstained from the vote, indicating their declining support for the WPS agenda overall.

As Freedman points out, the increased prioritization of "state security over human security" in the 2000s and 2010s has added another overarching set of pressures to security calculations in many countries.[27] Negative narratives about migration, fears of transnational terrorism, and increasingly vocal populist movements – led and exploited by opportunistic politicians – have agitated many countries. This has pushed human security issues into the background in many places. Rising tensions between some of the major powers have reinforced the growing emphasis on national security. This has added to the challenges facing the gender equality and gender-security agendas.

The chapters in this book show that the track record in advancing gender equality and the gender-security agenda is mixed. There has been notable progress, but problems still abound. The surge in patriarchal ideologies and neo-patriarchal actors in the 21st century is even more problematic.

Obstacles to progress

There are many obstacles to advancing progress on gender-security issues and, ultimately, to achieving gender equality. These obstacles are more formidable in some countries than others, and they vary in form from one issue area to another. The organizations involved in counter-terrorism are not identical to those that provide humanitarian relief in emergencies, for example. Although the specifics vary from place to place and over time, there are powerful patterns that are common to all of the issue areas studied in this book. Five main obstacles to progress stand out.

Patriarchy: First and foremost, the vast majority of human societies and institutions have been created and structured as patriarchies – male-dominated entities that seek to perpetuate established gender hierarchies. The starting points for all patriarchies are ideational, social, cultural and institutional: the idea that men should be in charge of all important matters is inculcated, reinforced and perpetuated through social units such as families and communities, group cultures, as well as religious and national institutions. Valerie Hudson argues that the sexual order established within societies is the first political order that molds all other orders within society.[28] Hudson explains: "For most of human history, leaders and their male subjects forged a social contract: Men agreed to be governed by other men in return for all men ruling over women."[29] Similarly, Cecilia Ridgeway has argued that the "lack of deep change in the structure of the family has been a powerful force that pushes back against gender change in the public sphere."[30]

These ideas are formalized, routinized and strengthened in organizations and institutions – small and large, at the local, national and international levels – and they are mutually reinforcing. Organizations define the roles group members should have, the power capacities they may (or may not) enjoy and the ways individuals interact. Organizations formalize all of this through established rules, procedures and processes. They perpetuate these structures and power relationships through education, training and organizational cultures. These formal mechanisms are reinforced by informal institutions, norms, networks and practices. Individual positions and interpersonal relations are highly gendered in the vast majority of human institutions and organizations.

This is especially prominent in military organizations. As Ellen Haring explains: "National military organizations are quintessentially masculine constructs that rely on notions of men as warrior-protectors and women as the protected. . . . Within this conception there is no room, or accommodation, for women who want to join national militaries. The result is that when women have joined, they have generally been confined to support roles, are rarely the focus of recruiting efforts, are not promoted at the same rate as men and suffer from marginalization, discrimination and harassment."[31] Countless other organizations and professions are similarly gendered, although the rules and policies may be less formal in other organizational structures.

It is important to remember that, when feminists and gender activists are pushing for gender equality, they are working to change existing patriarchies that are based on intensely gendered, deeply entrenched belief systems, cultures and institutions that are, in turn, framed by established laws and policies and backed by formidable power resources. Patriarchal systems (like other privileged and autocratic systems) are intensely focused on preservation and survival. They are very effective at responding to changing circumstances, defeating new threats and preserving their privileged positions. Goetz and Jenkins observe that "efforts to involve women directly in post-conflict peacebuilding have faced perennial obstacles" over the first two decades of the 21st century.[32]

The foundational sources of gender problems are the patriarchal interests, systems and power structures that guide human relations. Similarly, the foundational obstacles to progress in the gender-security realm are the patriarchal systems that operate in specific issue areas.

Resistance: The second obstacle to progress is that change provokes resistance – general inertia and active opposition.

At the individual and group level, established belief systems are highly resistant to change and dismissive of evidence that contradicts prevailing views. This is one of the core findings of cognitive psychology, and it is a recognized problem in national security decisionmaking.[33] Patriarchy is fundamentally an idea – the idea that men should dominate leadership positions in human societies at every level. It is an idea that has been adopted by much of humanity for most of human history, and it is therefore deeply entrenched. Patriarchy has developed into a belief system that, like all belief systems, is highly resistant to change, especially when they are reinforced by self-interests; these "motivated misperceptions" are doubly durable.

Patriarchy, moreover, is a belief system that has become highly institutionalized – informally in families and through group cultures and formally in social, economic, political and governmental organizations. One of the core findings of organization theory is that organizations are also highly resistant to change, due to both general inertia and the active opposition of those who benefit from the status quo.[34] Organizational resistance to change becomes increasingly pronounced when organizations are large, formal and hierarchical. This describes most businesses and corporations, government institutions at every level and, especially, military organizations and national security agencies. Military history is filled with cases of military organizations that held onto old technologies well beyond their obsolescence. Patriarchies would be highly resistant to change even if everyone was equally vested in these systems. Equal opportunity is not a prominent feature of patriarchies, however.[35]

The perseverance of patriarchies over time and around the world is due in large part to the active, self-serving efforts undertaken by male leaders and male-dominated institutions to preserve the established order. These efforts are widespread, sustained, intense and, above all, intentional. The protectors of patriarchies employ several sets of tactics to weaken gender equality campaigns, minimize women's participation in institutions and preserve the status quo. (See Table 12.1.)

At the most general level, the protectors of patriarchies try to sideline, stall and derail gender equality and gender-security agendas. One way this is done is by prioritizing other national security interests, such as great-power politics or the counter-terrorism campaigns following the September 2001 terrorist attacks in the United States.[36]

It is also common for political leaders to make grand pronouncements about advancing gender equality and gender-security initiatives without providing the sustained commitments, resources or policy actions needed to bring about real change. As the saying from the sports world goes, leaders are "talking the talk, not walking the walk" when it comes to these issues. Paying lip service to an ideal is a common way of stalling and resisting change, without paying the political costs of doing so openly.

A policy idea that works to preserve the status quo is the growing emphasis in policy circles on social and institutional "resilience" in the face of humanitarian disasters, climate change, terrorism or other sources of social turmoil.[37] It is certainly wise to design physical infrastructure and governmental institutions so that they will be able to function in the aftermath of hurricanes, tsunamis, earthquakes and attacks. However, embedded in the idea of "resilience" is a commitment to preservation and restoration – restoring both physical infrastructure and social orders to the status quo ante. Since most social institutions are male-dominated constructs, the enshrinement of resilience as a general policy goal has the hidden, added effect of making patriarchies more resilient.

Many of the tactics employed by protectors of patriarchies are deployed within institutions, such as military, national and international organizations, as well as businesses and corporations. For many patriarchal institutions, the starting point has been total exclusion of all women from participation. This has been done, more in previous centuries than the current one, through formal laws and policies. Informal social and cultural barriers can also work to exclude women from participating in institutions large and small. If exclusion is outlawed or becomes politically

TABLE 12.1 Gender Policy Tactics of Patriarchs and Progressives

Patriarchs	*Progressives*
Sidelining the gender agenda	**Mainstreaming the gender agenda**
Prioritizing other organizational or national interests	Institutionalizing gender equality as a central, constant, normal, legitimate policy priority
Talking the talk	**Walking the walk**
Making public pronouncements and paying lip service to gender equality, without providing the resources or effort for real change	Insisting that grand pronouncements are matched by sustained action, substantial resources, policy implementation, real progress
Preservation and restoration	**Reformation and transformation**
Working to preserve the status quo in times of change; working to restore the status quo ante after conflicts or disasters; emphasis on resilience	Advancing gender equality in times of turmoil and post-crisis settings via new laws, policies, norms; emphasis on "building back better" in terms of gender
Exclusion	**Inclusion**
Preserving male hegemony via laws and formal policies; via informal social and cultural barriers	Promoting female participation via new laws and policies, legal actions; via political and social action
Tokenism	**Gender Balancing**
Preserving male dominance by admitting small, controlled numbers of women into professional and policy circles; superficial inclusion	Promoting gender equality by achieving statistically and politically meaningful levels of female participation; equal numbers plus equal power
Marginalization	**Empowerment**
Keeping female members of a group weak and peripheral	Elevating women into decisionmaking and policymaking positions; building capacities
Restricting the pipeline	**Expanding the pipeline**
Preserving male dominance by restricting female education, recruitment, retention, promotion	Expanding women's opportunities via education, recruitment, retention, promotion
Know-who	**Know-how**
Relying on "old-boy networks" – literally – for professional support and advancement	Instituting merit-based personnel processes; expanding gender expertise in academic, professional and policy settings
Setting up for failure	**Setting up for success**
Providing insufficient support for women; assigning impossible tasks to women (glass cliffs)	Supporting women via mentors and networks; providing leadership training and promotion paths
Violence promotion	**Violence prevention**
Trying to intimidate activists, pioneers and political women via threats and use of violence; instigating and allowing violence against women	Charging and punishing those who employ, encourage or allow violence against women; changing laws, policies and cultures as needed
Sweeping under the rug	**Naming, shaming and jailing**
Preserving male dominance by ignoring or concealing illegal or improper actions and by protecting violators	Establishing and strengthening whistleblower mechanisms; exposing cover-ups, identifying wrongdoers, prosecuting criminals
Closing ranks	**Building the ranks and extending the flanks**
Men working with men within institutions to preserve male homogeneity and dominance	Expanding networks of alliances among civil society organizations, governments and international organizations – vertically and horizontally

untenable, tokenism and marginalization are the fallback positions. Patriarchies then admit the smallest possible number of women into their staff, professional or policy ranks, thereby reducing the legal and political heat. But they restrict women to junior, subordinate and peripheral positions, preserving male domination of high-level deliberations and decisionmaking.

Patriarchies reinforce this process by restricting women's access to educational, professional and leadership training programs, thereby limiting the number of women who are qualified for institutional positions. Institutions also control the pipeline via gender-biased recruitment, promotion and retention policies. These formal actions are reinforced by continued reliance on informal networks of contacts – old-boy networks (literally) – for hiring and promotion recommendations. And, when women are admitted into institutions, they are often set up for failure. In addition to receiving disproportionately little training and support, they are often given impossible tasks – they are placed on "glass cliffs" – that might doom their own professional prospects while giving more ammunition for patriarchs to use in the future.[38]

The vilest of all of the tactics employed by protectors of patriarchies is violence. Patriarchal violence was one of the original instruments of male dominance in human relations, and it is pervasive across human institutions today. Patriarchal violence takes many forms – from threats and harassment to assault, rape and murder. Patriarchal violence is carried out against women and girls in all sorts of settings: against activists for women's rights, against women pioneers in male-dominated institutions and against women who seek or hold political offices. Patriarchal violence takes place against individuals and on a massive scale. Patriarchal institutions often tacitly allow or even encourage violence. And, when acts of violence are carried out or complaints are registered, patriarchal institutions generally cover up male crimes, sweep problems under the proverbial rug (a rare instance of men cleaning up), and work to preserve male dominance and the established hegemonic order. Although acts of violence are usually carried out by individual men or groups of men – who should be held accountable for their crimes – it is important to recognize the broader institutional dimensions of the problem. At best, patriarchal institutions are complicit in violence that takes place in their domains. At worst, patriarchal institutions design and carry out campaigns of gender-based violence against women and girls, as seen in armed conflicts and genocides from Bosnia to Rwanda to Myanmar. As True and Davies note, the "pathology of institutions" in gender-security issues is multidimensional, and the pervasiveness of violence in patriarchal institutions is especially ugly.[39]

Misconceptions: The third obstacle to progress in gender-security matters, especially when national and international security organizations are involved, is that policymakers underestimate and misunderstand gender. Most national and international security establishments are dominated by men. They focus on traditional security threats that are analyzed through traditional lenses and familiar policy frameworks. For many in the national security communities, the international system is seen as composed of unitary and genderless states in competition with each other. A state's power and place within the international system is defined by its military and economic resources. This state-centric and military-centric view of the world remains a dominant view, especially in the national security establishments of the major powers.

Starting in the last decade of the Cold War and especially since the end of the Cold War, some scholars and international actors have advocated for a more expansive view of the security agenda. The human security conception of security emphasizes an important array of non-military security problems, including economic security, food security, health security and environmental security. The human security framework also emphasizes the importance of security at the personal and community level – not just the national level.[40]

Adding to this, feminist and gender scholars have demonstrated how an analysis of gender and gender hierarchies is critical for understanding security challenges – in terms of both traditional, state-centric, military-centric concerns and non-traditional, human-centric, non-military concerns.[41] They have shown, for example, that societies with gender inequalities are more prone to violence, corruption and instability, including higher levels of both intra-state conflict and conflict with other countries.[42] Unfortunately, these insights have not been integrated into the frameworks and threat assessments of national security policy establishments.

In addition, on the infrequent occasions when the members of national security communities think about gender, they automatically translate *gender* into *women*, and often use the two terms interchangeably. This is problematic in several respects. It immediately leads policymakers (mostly men, along with some women) to downgrade the importance of the issues. It reinforces gender stereotypes, including the traditional tendency to think of women in passive, protective terms: women are seen as victims, not as decisionmakers and participants in security deliberations. Consequently, it leads men (and some women) to not only ignore gender, but to also conflate "women and children," "women and girls" and "women and youth." These are common formulations in national and international policy circles that infantilize women and deny their agency.

These common misconceptions highlight a deep flaw in most security policy deliberations: most security policy analysts and security decisionmakers are deeply ignorant about what a true "gender perspective" entails and what it would add to national and international security deliberations and outcomes. For most security policy analysts and decisionmakers, having a gender perspective means thinking about what a problem means for women or, even worse, getting a woman's point of view on the matter. This is an almost universal problem in national security policy establishments. Although the United Nations, the EU and NATO have made some efforts to develop gender expertise and incorporate gender perspectives into policy analyses, this is still a problem in these and other international organizations.

The 2015 UN reviews of the WPS agenda, UN peacekeeping operations and the peacebuilding architecture acknowledged that UN member states and the UN Secretariat have insufficiently integrated gender perspectives in their peace and security analyses and processes.[43] These reviews also recognized that, for many UN member states as well as many in the UN Secretariat, gender continued to be seen as an "add-on."[44] These national and international security actors continue to see gender as a peripheral issue – if it is in their field of vision at all.

A 2016 survey by New America found that the majority of US national security policymakers had little knowledge or understanding of gender. Most policymakers equated gender with women and were not familiar with the WPS agenda. A majority of policymakers believed that an "add women and stir" approach – that is, adding a token number of women to security deliberations – would be sufficient. Most policymakers believed that gender is relevant only for a handful of subjects that involve women and girls, such as sex trafficking, sexual violence and sex slavery in ISIS. They did not see gender as relevant to national defense in general or to issues such as economics and trade.[45] A follow-up survey in 2018 generated similar results. Core issues, such as gender mainstreaming and the WPS agenda, were either unfamiliar to the respondents or they evoked hostile reactions.[46]

This lack of appreciation and understanding – about the nature of gender and its importance to a wide range of important national and international security problems – is not restricted to US policymakers. Most experts and decisionmakers in security policy communities worldwide do not think about or understand gender or the gender-security nexus. This weakens security policy deliberations and leads to bad national and international security outcomes. It is also a major obstacle to advancing gender equality and the gender-security agenda.

Money: A fourth obstacle to progress is that gender equality and gender-security initiatives have been consistently and woefully underfunded. Grand policy pronouncements have not been matched by the levels of resources that would be needed for policy implementation and real progress. The EU, for example, has identified gender equality as a priority. Narrowing the gender gap in the EU could generate 10 million new jobs and boost the EU's economic output by 3.15 trillion Euros by 2050. Even so, it has been estimated that less than 1 percent of the EU's Structural and Investment Funds for 2014–20 were dedicated to gender equality measures.[47] Stated goals are not being supported by commensurate resource commitments.

Similarly, over the 2016–17 period, only four percent of the development aid generated by the 30 members of the Organization for Economic Co-operation and Development (OECD) Development Assistance Committee (DAC) was specifically dedicated to gender equality and women's empowerment programs; 62 percent of the aid was gender blind.[48] The average funding share of the 26 private philanthropic organizations that focus on gender equality and report their activities to the OECD/DAC was not much higher – five percent of overall funding went to initiatives that featured gender equality as a primary goal.[49]

Moreover, only a fraction of this money reaches non-governmental women's organizations – key actors on the ground. Over the 2015–16 period, OECD/DAC states allocated an annual average of $464 million to women's organizations (governmental and non-governmental). Only $225 million of this total went to Non-Governmental Organizations (NGOs) and only $38 million went to women's organizations in developing countries.[50] Given that women organizations are powerful drivers for gender progress, these are disappointing figures.

More generally and fundamentally, "few advanced countries and none of the G-7 countries have adopted a comprehensive legal framework to support gender-responsive budgeting practices."[51] In other words, few countries have adopted procedures that track how public expenditures are actually helping women and men. As a result, most governments have no idea of how well or even if their budget allocations are addressing gender inequalities and advancing their professed goals. They are flying blind. Among the G-7 countries, only Canada, France and Japan publish gender budget statements. Similarly, few countries worldwide produce gender impact statements.[52]

In sum, most national governments – the key funders of policy actions worldwide – have not allocated enough resources to gender equality and gender-security priorities. They have generally done a poor job of earmarking funds specifically for gender priorities; they have done a poor job of directing funds to women's NGOs; and they have done a poor job of assessing the impact of the allocations they have made. In public policy, one of the keys to turning grand declarations into actual accomplishments is dedicating sufficient amounts of funding to the tasks at hand. In this issue area, the gap between propounding and funding is enormous.

Data: A fifth and final obstacle to progress on gender equality and gender-security initiatives might seem mundane, but it is fundamentally important: poor data. Scholars, policy analysts and policymakers do not have enough of the right kind of data to assess gender problems and devise better gender-based policies. It is difficult to collect information on wartime sexual violence, for example, for understandable reasons.[53] A more general and widespread data problem is that data sets on many issues do not differentiate by sex.[54] This makes quantitative analysis of gender issues difficult, if not impossible.

Data gaps are acute in all of the issue areas examined in this book. Data about the numbers and percentages of women in national parliaments and federal executive branches is generally available, but there is very little data about the numbers and percentages of women who hold government positions at provincial and local levels. On the economic front, while many countries publish sex-disaggregated data on unemployment, labor force participation and education, few countries produce sex-disaggregated data on the informal economic sector – where women are disproportionately active. Data on violence against women, particularly domestic violence, is very limited; most of the available data undoubtedly underestimates the incidence of violence.

A report on the availability of gender data in Africa showed that data problems were huge in terms of the availability of sex-disaggregated data; no sex-disaggregated data was available for 48 percent of gender-related indicators. Data problems were also widespread in terms of categories such as age, income and racial or ethnic status; better data in these areas would enable researchers to analyze gender dynamics in greater detail. In addition, the report noted that data collection is infrequent and data analysis is slow.[55] As Klugman points out, "only 13 percent of the world's countries have a dedicated budget for collecting and analyzing gender statistics, and data is available for less than one-quarter of key gender indicators across the SDGs."[56]

Data collection efforts have been hindered by other problems as well. Data should be timely and regular. Few countries have statisticians who have been properly trained to recognize gender biases in data collection and data analysis.[57] Moreover, different countries have very different data definitions and data collection practices, which makes cross-country comparisons difficult.

Although some NGOs and some international organizations – including the United Nations, the World Bank and the OECD – have started gender data initiatives, it will take a concerted effort to close the gender data gap. It is especially important for national governments – which have more resources and better access to their citizens – to collect sex-disaggregated and gender-specific data. Many governments do a poor job in this regard. Data collection is essential: it provides the information needed for policy assessment which, in turn, reveals whether or not policies are actually working and progress is actually being made.

Drivers of progress

Although the forces of social inertia and entrenched patriarchies are formidable, progress has been made in advancing gender equality since the beginning of the 20th century and in advancing gender-security priorities since the end of the Cold War. Progress never "happens" on its own, and this is especially true in social, economic and political arenas where vital interests are at stake and established powers will work intensely and relentlessly to preserve their privileged positions. Established patriarchies have done this for eons, and they will continue to do so in the future. Progress has happened in this arena because other actors have worked intensely and relentlessly – and often very courageously – to get gender equality issues placed on international, national and local policy agendas. This, in a nutshell, is the story of the struggle for gender equality. In the issue areas examined in this book, five drivers for progress stand out.

Activists: First and foremost, women and women's rights activists have led the charge. They have worked together in non-profit, non-governmental, civil society organizations, national and transnational networks and coalitions – including support from men – and building capacities for further political mobilization. They have worked at the grass-roots level in local communities, in national capitals and at the headquarters of international organizations. They have figured out what needed to be done, they have put issues on policy agendas and they have pushed energetically and effectively for decisions and action. This is a common pattern across all of the issue areas studied in this book.

Kuehnast argues that the impetus for progress has come from non-governmental actors: "Civil society organizations have been the key drivers leading to the adoption of gender-inclusive language in international commitments and the WPS agenda."[58]

True and Davies conclude that women's formal and informal participation through civil society organizations, networks and coalitions have been the "major drivers of progress toward gender-inclusive governance." They note that other scholars have similarly concluded that feminist mobilization in civil society has been "the most significant factor" in advancing policies to address violence against women.[59] The campaign for gender equality, they argue, has been driven primarily by activists and civil society organizations in a bottom-up process: "Most [of the] concrete progress in the move toward gender-equal governance has been the result of bottom-up campaigns and transnational networked movements. In the social media age, these have been movements started by hashtags."[60]

The end of the Cold War combined with advances in information technologies generated by the digital revolution created more political space for NGOs and civil society actors, as well as enhanced capacities for communication, mobilization and transnational networking. A key component of civil society action has been strategically and politically astute engagement with international organizations, national governments and individual national leaders to advance these causes. Civil society actors have strengthened their bases of support through coalition building, alliance formation and multi-level action. They have worked with and through these international and national actors. This has been one of the keys to their success.

International organizations: A second driver for progress has been the effort undertaken by international organizations – the United Nations most notably, but also the World Bank, as well as regional organizations such as the EU. The decisions and actions taken by international organizations are complicated, of course, because they are not fully autonomous actors. These organizations were created by their member states, and key decisions are taken by member states. Even so, it is fair to say that these international organizations have played a key role in advancing progress on gender equality and gender-security issues. Women's rights activists and civil society organizations have engaged the United Nations, in particular, to develop policy initiatives and place these ideas on the organization's agenda. Prodded by civil society, the United Nations has played a prominent role in elevating these issues and establishing norms and policy standards for the world.

The international conferences organized by the United Nations during the UN Decade for Women (1975–85) helped to build and consolidate a global feminist network. The adoption of CEDAW in 1979 was an important milestone in the advancement of women's rights. The UN's fourth World Conference on Women held in Beijing in 1995 brought together more than 30,000 delegates. Starting in 1995, the United Nations began to prioritize gender mainstreaming as a method for advancing gender equality within the organization and in the organization's work. The idea was that the UN's policy deliberations should include equal participation of women and a gender perspective. The EU endorsed gender mainstreaming in the late 1990s.[61] NATO has also adopted policies and action plans on Women, Peace and Security. It calls on its member and partner states to report on gender mainstreaming within military forces and military organizations.[62] The G-7 has hosted annual W-7 summits – convening women's rights activists, scholars and political leaders from G-7 countries and around the world – in conjunction with its regular summits.

The work of international organizations in gender and gender-security issues has been amplified by the establishment of special offices and positions, which has institutionalized these issues within these organizations. Within the United Nations, the establishment of the Office for the Special Representative of the UN Secretary-General on Sexual Violence in Conflict has helped to raise the global profile of this issue. The establishment of the UN Women office in 2010 consolidated and elevated the UN's work on gender issues and created a new cadre of gender advocates within the organization. Individual UN departments and agencies have added gender advisors, and most UN peace operations are now required to have gender advisors. In 2012, NATO appointed a new Special Representative for WPS. The AU appointed a Special Envoy on WPS in 2014. In 2015, the EU's External Action Service appointed an ambassador to advise the organization on gender and the implementation of UNSCR 1325. The creation of these posts has been important in elevating gender equality and gender-security issues within these organizations.

National governments: The third driver for progress has been a set of progressive national governments that have adopted and championed gender equality and gender-security initiatives. Here, too, Non-Governmental Organizations and civil society activists have played a key role in prodding and working with national leaders and governments. That said, some progressive governments have themselves moved into leadership positions on these issues.

In 2009, the United States appointed an Ambassador-at-Large for Global Women's Issues. Sweden formally adopted a feminist foreign policy in 2014.[63] Canada adopted a feminist international development policy in 2017 and named its first Ambassador for WPS in 2019. France took steps in this direction in 2019, with the government stating: "Gender equality now needs to become a great global cause."[64] Western donor states and the EU have provided financial and technical support to states in the developing world to support gender equality legislation, WPS National Action Plans and women's empowerment programs. Donor states have also put pressure on less progressive states to promote gender equality and take steps on gender-security initiatives.

Individual national leaders have played key roles in national-level deliberations and decisions. In 2012, United Kingdom (UK) Foreign Minister William Hague worked with UN Special Envoy Angelina Jolie to raise global awareness and promote the prevention of conflict-related sexual violence. In 2014, Margot Wallström became Sweden's Foreign Minister and launched the government's feminist foreign policy, which prioritizes the promotion of gender equality and is centered around women's rights, representation and resources.

At the national level another important impetus for change has been the emergence of compelling governmental and national needs. As Haring notes, national military organizations in the 20th century occasionally took steps to allow women into previously prohibited positions because of dire demographic needs: they did not have enough men to do the jobs. In these cases, where national security was very much at stake, national governments took steps to promote gender equality, not because they had become enlightened, but because it was an operational imperative. The United States (US) military also took steps to expand the scope of operations undertaken by female soldiers in Afghanistan and Iraq in the 2000s and 2010s because of operational necessities: it needed to have female soldiers on the ground to get information from local women who would not speak to foreign men. Need-driven change has been an important driver of gender progress for many national military organizations.[65]

Norms and laws: A fourth driver of progress has been the development of normative frameworks that, in turn, have led to the adoption of UN resolutions and international laws, as well as national-level laws, policies, rules and regulations. The formalization of norms and laws has been the result of efforts from civil society activists and progressive governments; these norms and laws, in turn, have become drivers of further progress. Once they are established, norms and laws put pressure on other actors to comply with the newly decreed standards.

Levine and Kouvo show how human rights became an international norm in the 20th century and how international accords, such as the Universal Declaration of Human Rights, continue to set important standards for international behavior. CEDAW has set standards and framed the agenda for promoting gender equality and prohibiting discrimination on the basis of sex and gender.[66] The number of resolutions and declarations, including the WPS resolutions, further strengthen these norms. Administrative directives and regulations have operationalized these instruments within international organizations and national governments. The UN Security Council's WPS resolutions have prompted states to develop National Action Plans for the advancement of these goals.

True has highlighted the importance of language and concepts in this context:

> Words and concepts literally make it possible to think and to see what was previously unthinkable or hidden. Powerful slogans such as "democracy without women is no democracy," "women's rights are human rights and human rights are women's rights," "sexual harassment" and "violence against women" have changed the way we see and think about the world around us.[67]

The presence of language on gender equality in international and national policy documents has established gender equality as a legitimate objective. Gender equality language has also generated goals and metrics that international organizations and their member states should meet. International reporting requirements attached to CEDAW, the Beijing Platform for Action, the WPS agenda and the SDGs have helped to reinforce these standards, hold member states accountable and promote progress. These formal processes also provide additional entry points and mechanisms for civil society organizations and supportive member states to engage international organizations and national governments in the advancement of gender goals.

Scholars: A fifth and final driver of progress has been the academic community. Starting in the final decades of the 20th century and expanding in the first decades of the 21st century, scholars and analysts have played a vital role in researching the multidimensional nature of gender inequality and developing a better understanding of the complex linkages between gender and security issues. Our collective understanding of the linkages between gender and armed conflict, for example, has improved vastly over the past several decades. Whereas women were previously seen only as victims of armed conflict, we now know that gender inequalities are powerfully associated with the onset of violence. We now also know that female participation in peace negotiations and peace operations is powerfully correlated with successful peace processes and peace itself. These intellectual advances are due to the hard work of feminist and gender scholars.[68]

This work has had important effects beyond the academy. Kuehnast describes how feminist and gender scholars developed the intellectual case for the WPS agenda.[69] Scholars and analysts have made important contributions to international action in many other issue areas as well – education and health, economic development, population movements, environmental problems, humanitarian emergencies, human rights, governance and traditional national security matters. Academic research and insights have helped to shape effective, just policies.

Support for research on gender inequality and gender-security issues has come from many sources, including UN agencies, the World Bank, progressive national governments (the Nordic countries, in particular), as well as foundations and universities. In gender studies and the gender-security area, scholars and researchers have added to knowledge, strengthened norms and contributed to better policy.

Strategies for progress

The problems of gender inequality have deep roots in human society, and the gender-security issues examined in this book have correspondingly deep and complex lineages. The ongoing campaigns to promote gender equality and advance progress in the gender-security area will undoubtedly continue for a very long time to come. These will be multi-decade, multi-generational propositions. This chapter, therefore, will not conclude with policy recommendations for near-term actions. Rather, it will adopt a long-term time frame.

As discussed throughout this book, campaigns to advance gender equality and enlightened gender-security policies have been arduous precisely because of entrenched patriarchal interests and patriarchal obstruction of progress. This has been, and will continue to be, a conflict between opposing interests and powers. What is needed, therefore, is a set of ideas grounded in strategic thinking more than policy planning.

Some strategic advice is generic and could guide action in many issue areas. Strategic actors, for example, should focus on both the long term and the near term at the same time. If one is engaged in a multi-decade campaign, it is essential to maintain a focus on long-term challenges (such as changing patriarchal cultures) and long-term goals (achieving gender equality). But it is also valuable to rack up near-term victories, build capacities and gather momentum over time. Similarly, strategic actors must be able to play defense and offense at the same time. It is important to defend against near-term setbacks while taking advantage of opportunities to make gains and change power balances over time. In addition, strategic actors should develop both top-down as well as bottom-up initiatives. The latter are especially important in gender-security issues, where local contexts are key.[70] This might sound common-sensical, but it is ignored by many policymakers – with predictable, unfortunate results.

We conclude this chapter by outlining five strategic principles that should guide those who are fighting for gender equality and progress in the gender-security arena: people, parity, perspectives, policy and power.

People: Promoters of progress should be explicit and systematic in framing the agenda in terms of *gender* – gender equality and gender-security issues – and not just in terms of *women*.

It is certainly true that the core problem created by patriarchy has been discrimination against women and girls (and gender minorities). Women's rights activists and feminist scholars have been exactly right to raise awareness about these inequities and to push for actions that would advance women's equality and empowerment. The WPS agenda has been formally framed in terms of women; it has been very valuable, and it is not going to be repackaged by the UN Security Council. Women's rights, WPS and other women's issues will continue to require attention – and they will frequently be framed as women's issues – going forward.

At the same time, framing these issues as women's issues has several conceptual and political drawbacks.[71] A headline featuring "women" makes it easier for men to think of women's inequality as "somebody else's problem" that doesn't directly engage their own interests.[72] In addition, as discussed previously, it makes it easier for male-dominated policy establishments to treat these issues as secondary issues, compared to other national security problems.

Framing these issues in terms of gender has several corresponding advantages. A gender framework automatically integrates men and masculinities into analyses of the relevant issues.[73] "Mainstreaming men" helps with both diagnostics and prescriptions. Employing a gender framework also reinforces the idea that everyone has a stake in these issues: after all, every human being is gendered in one way or another. This, in turn, makes it more difficult for men and male-dominated policy establishments to compartmentalize, downgrade and neglect these issues. A gender framework that mainstreams men may also make it easier for gender equality and gender-security advocates to find allies and build the coalitions that will be needed to change the balance of power and bring about substantial change. A gender framework also provides a better framework for integrating LGBTQ issues into analysis and advocacy.

Women's rights activists, feminists and gender scholars are well aware of the advantages and disadvantages of the alternative framing options. This is not a new issue. Women's rights activists do not want to undercut any of the gains that have been made, and they do not want to take steps that could downgrade the importance of women's issues. These are valid, important points.

Even so, the balance of advantages tips in favor of a gender framework in the gender-security area. It is essential to mainstream the gender-security issues that have been examined in this book; this will be more difficult to do if they are framed solely in terms of women. It is essential to mainstream gender perspectives in analyses of these issues; this will be more difficult to do if the issues are formally framed in terms of women. It is essential to mainstream men on these issues, as well; this will be more difficult to do if women alone are in the headline. It is critical to shape the narrative about gender equality and gender-security issues; this will be easier if men and boys are already included in the table of contents.

Parity: A second strategic principle is promoting and ultimately achieving equitable gender participation – gender parity – in national and international security matters, as well as in public policy and human affairs more generally. This is the right thing to do in terms of providing equal rights and opportunities for every human being. It is also the smart thing to do at the local, national and international levels. Communities must develop and utilize all of their human capital if they are to maximize communal well-being. At the national level, for example, countries will not be able to maximize national prosperity, national power and national security – core concerns of realists and national security traditionalists – if women are not fully and equally engaged in the lives of their nations.

Moving toward participation parity will also be one of the keys to promoting comprehensive gender equality in societies. After all, if men were inclined to bring about gender equality on their own, this would have already happened. The inclusion of more and more women in social, economic and political affairs will be the result of progress toward gender equality, but it will also be a driver for further progress. This will be an iterative, sequential process.

As discussed earlier, the protectors of patriarchies start with a preferred policy of totally excluding women from participating in protected areas. This has often been enshrined in formal laws, rules and policies, and reinforced by informal social and cultural practices. If pushed to open a few doors, patriarchal fallback positions are tokenism and marginalization. Proponents of progress will have to counter all of these tactics. They will have to campaign for inclusion and statistical balances by fighting for new laws, rules and policies and by working to change social and organizational cultures over time. Cultural change, in particular, is a long-term, multi-generational project. Instituting quotas might be a way of helping to advance and institutionalize these participation goals. True gender balancing – 50/50 participation rates in every aspect of security policy – should be the ultimate goal of gender-security advocates.

These will be important steps, but they will not be sufficient. It is essential for numerical gains in women's presence to be accompanied by women's empowerment and equal participation. This means having not just growing numbers of junior and mid-level staff jobs but equal representation at top-level decisionmaking and policymaking positions. It means having equal power, equal status and equal roles in professional and policy circles.[74] The goal is not just a token presence or even statistical equality but political equality within institutions – a true balance of power. As Jeannette Gaudry Haynie points out, it is especially important for women to be in the top leadership ranks of their organizations, as this is one of the keys to promoting and consolidating diversity. This, in turn, is one of the keys to having rich, multi-faceted and effective policy deliberations.[75] Institutions and policies should be evaluated in terms of these gender-inclusive standards.

In addition to changing laws, rules and policies in a top-down fashion, it will also be vital to enhance education of girls, as well as professional and leadership training for women. This will expand the pipeline from the bottom up, build capacities and create the demographics for sustainable change. Along with formal education and training, women will benefit from better mentoring mechanisms and stronger support networks: old-boy networks should be neutralized by wise-women networks. This will help to position women for success. Activists should also push for merit-based, gender-sensitive hiring, promotion and retention policies as well as open paths to leadership positions across the public and private sectors. The goal should be for women to be valued for their expertise regardless of their professional fields. They should not be treated as tokens, and they should not be valued solely for their perspectives on women's and gender issues.

As discussed previously, violence is the most odious and horrific tactic employed by individual men and, more systemically, by patriarchies. Gender equality activists must continue to work for stronger violence prevention, protection and prosecution measures. As in other areas, this will require better laws, rules and policies, as well as social and cultural change. More specifically, it means strengthening mechanisms for charging, prosecuting and punishing those who employ, encourage or allow violence against women. Naming and shaming are not enough; prosecuting and jailing must become standard operating procedures. This must also apply to those who cover up crimes of violence. The problem is not just bad individuals, but inherently bad institutions: patriarchies tacitly and often openly encourage violence against women. Institutions committed to gender equality, gender parity and women's full participation must tackle the issue of violence directly and tenaciously.

Taking steps toward gender parity – not just numerically, but in terms of equal participation and institutional leadership – will entail fundamental changes in gender relations in gender-security affairs. Moving toward gender parity will also necessitate changes in institutional balances of power, and this will inevitably be met with sustained resistance. Patriarchies will oppose these kinds of changes, in particular, because gender parity would transform the essential nature of the patriarchies themselves. Gender equality and gender-security advocates will have to think strategically and politically about building numbers, capacities and power positions in institutional arenas.

Perspectives: Feminists and gender scholars have stated repeatedly (and correctly) that it is essential to include gender perspectives in security policy analyses, security policy deliberations and security policy actions. This is a third strategic principle for devising better policies in gender-security issues areas and security matters in general.

Unfortunately, national security policy establishments usually agree with this only occasionally and often reluctantly. On the all-too-rare occasions when national security agencies open their deliberations to include gender perspectives, they almost always misunderstand what this should entail. The default approach is to reduce "including gender perspectives" to "focusing on women's issues momentarily" or, all too often, "getting a woman's point of view" on the issue of the day. It is no exaggeration to say that most national security agencies worldwide are clueless about what a true gender perspective is and what it would add to security policy deliberations. This is unfortunate for a multitude of reasons, but most paradoxically and sadly because national security suffers as a result.

A proper gender perspective is a broad-based, sophisticated analysis of the gender-security issues at hand. It should examine all of the relevant gender issues, as well as gender relations and gender dynamics operating in all contexts. It should consider how security issues affect gender issues, as well as the ways gender issues might affect security problems. It should examine the ways gender is considered in policy responses and policy implementation. At its best, a gender perspective transcends traditional security policy silos and assesses the complex ways gender and multiple security issues are interconnected. A gender perspective can also illuminate intersections with other inequalities, such as those generated by race, ethnicity, class, education, religion, disability, sexual orientation or age.[76]

Proponents of the gender-security agenda should focus on three priorities. First, it is important to expand the ranks of professionals – women and men – who have broad, deep gender expertise. This should be based on expanded educational and training programs at national military academies and intelligence schools, as well as colleges and universities in general. There has been some growth in gender and gender-security programs in colleges and universities in Europe and North America in the first two decades of the 21st century. There has been less emphasis on building gender expertise in the military and intelligence communities.

Second, it is important to mainstream the idea that gender perspectives are not just useful; they should be essential elements of every security policy deliberation. They should not be thought of as special sets of analytic tools that are deployed only on rare and special occasions. They should be normal, automatic, constant, required components of security policy deliberations for scholars and analysts – and especially for policymakers.

Third, it is important to build gender expertise and intellectual capacities everywhere. Although some progress has been made in the academic world and in international organizations, such as the United Nations and the EU, more intellectual capacities are needed elsewhere. National security establishments just about everywhere are woefully uninformed about the nature and importance of gender perspectives and gender-security interconnections.[77] Government-affiliated academies and training programs around the world should make this a top priority.

Policy: Although the development of good ideas has been an important driving force in human progress in general, and in the promotion of gender equality, this is only a first step. A fourth strategic principle for progress is to focus intently on policy – policy agendas, policy formulation, policy implementation and policy outcomes, in particular. "Talking the talk" has value, but "walking the walk" in terms of policy action is the ultimate goal. Five priorities merit sustained attention.

First, raising general awareness about gender inequalities and gender-security issues will continue to be important for the foreseeable future, but it is essential for awareness-raising efforts to cross the policy threshold and develop into agenda-setting, policy decisions and policy actions. Placing and keeping gender equality and gender-security issues on policy agendas will be ongoing priorities – at the international, national and local levels. This is not a one-time proposition; it will be a continuing challenge. The goal is to mainstream the gender equality and gender-security agendas: these priorities should be institutionalized as central, constant, legitimate goals and integrated automatically into policy analyses and deliberations.

An important element of this process is codification of norms and aspirations in international and national law. International laws – even non-binding UN resolutions – put pressure on national governments. National laws put pressure on government agencies at the national, provincial and local levels. Passing laws and adopting resolutions will not be sufficient by themselves, of course, but they help to shift discourses and power balances in the direction of action. This, in turn, will help to mainstream gender-security issues as policy priorities.

Second, proponents of progress should be sensitive to every opportunity to make progress. In particular, they should be cognizant of the fact that times of great turmoil might generate possibilities for great progress. As former White House advisor Rahm Emanuel once put it, "You never want a serious crisis to go to waste."[78] Tamara Nair observes that natural disasters are massively disruptive events, not just in terms of infrastructure but in terms of social relations – including gender relations. They consequently create opportunities for societies to break with the past and build new and more equitable futures. When natural disasters generate humanitarian crises, Nair argues that "policy planners should not only look to building back better, they should aspire to building back differently."[79] Carr notes that climate change and growing environmental challenges will generate more and more turmoil and disruption in the decades ahead. In post-crisis settings, he argues, policymakers "must ask if the status quo (or a return to the status quo) is an appropriate goal."[80] Instead of emphasizing resilience and restoration – in terms of physical infrastructure as well as social relations – policymakers should be alert to opportunities for social transformation and progress.

Third, although new laws, policies and pronouncements about gender equality and gender-security priorities will continue to be important steps forward, they will not be sufficient. Policy actions, policy implementation and on-the-ground outcomes are the ultimate goals. Transparency will be important to ensure that policy deliberations are not undercut by hidden agendas. Strengthening whistle-blower mechanisms and protections will help in this regard.

Fourth, allocating sufficient budgetary resources is absolutely essential. Budget allocations should not be one-time propositions, but ongoing, regular line items with measurable actions that should be tracked and assessed: follow the money.

Last, a key to successful policy will be better data, including improved data collection, data analysis and data distribution efforts. If governments are to devise and assess gender equality and gender-security policies, they must generate sex-disaggregated data, gender statistics and gender indicators that are systematic across issue areas, timely, regular and open to examination. The United Nations should put more pressure on national governments to collect and share data on gender equality and gender-security issues, ideally using internationally standardized data categories and definitions. Generating better data, in turn, will be one of the keys to better policy assessment – determining which policies are working and which ones are falling short – as well as more effective "lessons learned" units inside governments.[81]

Power: Many gender equality and gender-security problems are analytical. Having better data, for example, would support better analyses of gender problems and the development of more effective policies. The fundamental problem, however, is profoundly political: gender is all about power. Established patriarchies want to preserve the status quo. The champions of gender equality and gender-security agendas seek to change existing power distributions.

The final strategic principle for future action is that proponents of progress must always be aware that initiatives to promote gender equality and gender-security priorities are profoundly political campaigns to change existing balances of power. When scholars and policymakers look at gender in any issue area, it is essential for them to focus on power, the nature of existing power dynamics and possible avenues for changing these power balances. Power relations and power dynamics must be at the center of analysis, policy development and policy implementation. Gender advocates should not assume that data, analysis and sweet reason will be sufficient to bring about the changes they seek. They should always be thinking of ways to change the balance of power in their favor.

Proponents of progress must be prepared to play defense at all times. Patriarchies will inevitably work to preserve their positions. This will happen at every level, in every institution and in every issue area. Gender advocates should try to anticipate and neutralize patriarchal pushback against new initiatives. Gender advocates should also focus on consolidating any and all gains that have been made. Patriarchies will try to reverse gender equality gains whenever they can. In addition to the steady-state, default level of patriarchal action, the 2010s have seen a surge of neo-patriarchal energy from major powers such as Russia, China and the Trump administration in the United States; religious and quasi-religious fundamentalist organizations such as ISIS; white supremacist and right-wing militants, including neo-Nazis; as well as the intensely misogynist ideology and terrorism of the Incel (involuntary celibate) movement.[82] The common ideological thread connecting these diverse actors is misogyny, and the common policy thread is pushback against the gender equality and gender-security agendas. This is likely to continue, at a minimum, and it may intensify in the years ahead. Gender advocates should re-double their efforts to consolidate gains and prepare for policy assaults.

Proponents of progress must also continue to play offense. This will entail building capacities at all levels. At the individual and community levels, this means expanding education for girls and women and providing advanced education and leadership training for women in the workforce. It also means working with boys and men and connecting with communities and societies more generally through schools, mass media and social media. Education – in terms of individual students, local communities and the general public – will continue to be key.[83] The prospects for promoting gender equality will depend to a large degree on the communication of narratives that will win the hearts and minds of people that, in turn, will bring about a shift in the number of people committed to gender equality – as opposed to throwback patriarchies.

Women's rights organizations and civil society have been primary drivers of most of the gender equality advances that have materialized since the 1970s, and it will therefore be essential to continue building these organizational capacities in the decades ahead. This means generating higher levels of financial, organizational and technical support for these organizations and protecting them from the mounting attacks they are likely to face.

Building capacities at the group level must also involve the formation of stronger networks, coalitions, partnerships and alliances among women's and gender-ori-ented organizations, with other civil society organizations and with government agencies and international organizations, including the United Nations in particu-lar. Gender equality and gender-security advocates should work to broaden and deepen these connections, institutionalize these relationships over time and build institutional capacities for the long haul.

Adopting the strategic perspective developed here will strengthen the capaci-ties of gender equality and gender-security champions to advance these important priorities in a political context that may become much more challenging over the first half of the 21st century. Focusing on these five strategic priorities – people, parity, perspective, policy, power – will help proponents of progress to build institu-tional capacities, shape the ideational narrative, and change the demographic space. These gains, in turn, will shift and ultimately tip the balance of power away from established patriarchies.

Changing a balance of power is never easy. The campaign to promote gender equality is an effort to change the most deeply entrenched, institutionalized and pervasive power structure in human affairs. It is a contest to change the ultimate balance of power.

Notes

1 See Lyric Thompson and Rachel Clement, *Defining Feminist Foreign Policy* (Washing-ton, DC: International Center for Research on Women, 2019) and Jamille Bigio and Rachel Vogelstein, *Understanding Gender Equality in Foreign Policy*, White Paper (New York, Council on Foreign Relations, Spring 2020).

2 *United Nations Charter*, Preamble.

3 See chapter 10 in this book, p. 200.

4 See chapter 7 in this book, p. 136.

5 Phumzile Mlambo-Ngcuka, Madeleine Albright Development Lecture, Aspen Institute (August 1, 2019).

6 See chapter 11 in this book.

7 Data from the Inter-Parliamentary Union (IPU).

8 Data from the *Gender Quotas Database*.

9 For more on the value and limitations of quotas, see chapter 11 in this book.

10 Ibid, pp. 216–217.

11 See chapter 6 in this book, p. 115.

12 See chapter 4 in this book, p. 73.

13 See chapter 8 in this book, pp. 162–163.

14 See chapter 9 in this book, pp. 177–178.

15 See United Nations, *Sustainable Development Report 2019* (New York: United Nations, 2019).

16 See chapter 2 in this book.

17 See chapter 10 in this book, p. 206.

18 See chapter 3 in this book.

19 See Indra Ekmanis, "After Decades in the Shadows, Russia's Feminists Grab Their Spotlight," *PRI's the World* (June 5, 2019).

20 See Leta Hong Fincher, *Betraying Big Brother: The Feminist Awakening in China* (Brooklyn, NY: Verso, 2018).

21 See Sonia Elks, "Women Rights Under Attack in Europe, Say Feminist Parties," *Thomas Reuters Foundation News* (May 20, 2019).

22 Lauren Kent and Samantha Tapfumaneyi, "Hungary's PM Bans Gender Study at Colleges Saying 'People Are Born Either Male or Female'," *CNN World* (October 19, 2018).

23 See IPU and Parliamentary Assembly of the Council, *Sexism, Harassment and Violence Against Women Parliamentarians*, Issues Brief (October 2016). See also UN Women, *Expert Group Meeting: Report and Recommendations* (New York: UN Women, March 8–9, 2018).

24 Cited in Gabrielle Bardall and Emily Myers, *Violence Against Women in Politics: A Barrier to Peace and Security*, US Civil Society Working Group on WPS Policy Brief (May 2018).

25 See IPU and Parliamentary Assembly of the Council of Europe, *Sexism, Harassment and Violence Against Women Parliamentarians*, Issues Brief (October 2018).

26 See chapter 3 in this book.

27 See chapter 6 in this book, p. 113.

28 See Valerie Hudson, *The First Political Order: Sex, Governance, and National Security* (New York: Columbia University Press, 2020).

29 Quoted in Peter Bernard, "The New Authoritarians Are Waging War on Women," *The Atlantic* (December 12, 2018).

30 Cecilia Ridgeway, *Framed by Gender: How Gender Inequality Persists in the Modern World* (Oxford: Oxford University Press, 2011), p. 159.

31 See chapter 5 in this book, p. 90.

32 See chapter 3 in this book, 48.

33 See Leon Festinger, *A Theory of Cognitive Dissonance* (Stanford: Stanford University Press, 1957); Irving L. Janis, *Victims of Groupthink: A Psychological Study of Foreign Policy Decisions and Fiascoes* (Boston: Houghton Mifflin, 1972); Robert Jervis, *Perception and Misperception in International Politics* (Princeton, NJ: Princeton University Press, 1976).

34 See James G. March and Herbert A. Simon, *Organizations* (New York: Wiley, 1958); Richard M. Cyert and James G. March, *A Behavioral Theory of the Firm* (Englewood Cliffs, NJ: Prentice-Hall, 1963).

35 See L. Jenkins and Georgina Waylen, *Understanding Institutional Change from a Gender Perspective*, University of Manchester Working Papers in Gender and Institutional Change No. 1 (2014).

36 See chapter 10 in this book.

37 See chapters 8 and 9 in this book.

38 On glass cliffs, see chapter 11 in this book.

39 See Ibid, p. 230.

40 For more discussion on human security, see chapter 1 in this book.

41 See Carol Cohn, ed., *Women & War* (Cambridge: Polity Press, 2013); Cynthia Enloe, *Bananas, Beaches, and Bases: Making Feminist Sense of International Politics*, 2nd ed. (Berkeley, CA: University of California Press, 2014); Swati Parashar, J. Ann Tickner and Jacqui True, eds., *Revisiting Gendered States* (Oxford: Oxford University Press, 2018); Laura Sjoberg, *Gendering Global Conflict: Toward a Feminist Theory of War* (New York: Columbia University Press, 2013); Laura Sjoberg, *Gender, War and Conflict* (Cambridge: Polity Press, 2014); J. Ann Tickner, *Gendering World Politics* (New York: Columbia University Press, 2001); J. Ann Tickner, *A Feminist Voyage Through International Relations* (Oxford: Oxford University Press, 2014).

42 See Mary Caprioli, "Gendered Conflict," *Journal of Peace Research*, Vol. 37, No. 1 (2000), pp. 53–68; Mary Caprioli, "Primed for Violence: The Role of Gender Inequality in Predicting Internal Conflict," *International Studies Quarterly*, Vol. 49, No. 2 (June 2005), pp. 161–178; Erik Melander, "Gender Equality and Intrastate Armed Conflict," *International Studies Quarterly*, Vol. 49, No. 4 (December 2005), pp. 695–714; Valerie M. Hudson et al., *Sex and World Peace* (New York: Columbia University Press, 2012); Jeni Klugman and Mariana Viollaz, *Gender Inequality and Violent Conflict: A New Look* (Washington, DC: Georgetown Institute for Women, Peace and Security, 2017); Patrick M. Regan and Aida Paskeviciute, "Women's Access to Politics and Peaceful States," *Journal of Peace Research*, Vol. 40, No. 3 (May 2003), pp. 287–302.

43 See UN Women, *Preventing Conflict, Transforming Justice, Securing Peace: A Global Study on the Implementation of UN Security Council Resolution 1325* (New York: UN Women, 2015). See also *Report of the High-Level Independent Panel on Peace Operations*, UN Document A/70/95 and S/2015/446 (June 17, 2015); *The Challenges of Sustaining Peace: A Report of the Advisory Group of Experts for the 2015 Review of the United Nations Peacebuilding Architecture*, UN Document S/2015/419 (June 29, 2015).

44 See Eli Stamnes and Kari M. Osland, *Synthesis Report: Reviewing UN Peace Operations, the UN Peacebuilding Architecture and the Implementation of UNSCR 1325* (Oslo: Norwegian Institute of International Affairs, 2016); Security Council Report, *Women, Peace and Security: Closing the Security Council's Implementation Gap* (New York: Security Council Report, February 2017).

45 See Heather Hurlburt, Elizabeth Weingarten and Carolina Marques de Mesquita, *A Guide to Talking Women, Peace, and Security Inside the U.S. Security Establishment* (Washington, DC: New America, 2017).

46 See Heather Hurlburt, Elizabeth Weingarten and Elena Souris, *National Security: What We Talk About When We Talk About Gender* (Washington, DC: New America, December 10, 2018); Heather Hurlburt et al., *The Consensual Straitjacket: Four Decades of Women in Nuclear Security* (Washington, DC: New America, March 2019).

47 See European Institute for Gender Equality, *Gender Budgeting: Mainstreaming Gender into the EU Budget and Macroeconomic Policy Framework* (Luxembourg: European Union, 2018), p. 7.

48 OECD, *Development Finance for Gender Equality and Women's Empowerment: A Snapshot* (Paris: OECD, January 2019); OECD, *Aid in Support of Gender Equality and Women's Empowerment: Donor Charts* (Paris: OECD, March 2019).

49 See OECD, *Development Finance for Gender Equality and Women's Empowerment*.

50 See OECD/DAC, *Aid to Gender Equality and Women's Empowerment: An Overview* (Paris: OECD/DAC, July 2018).

51 IMF, *Gender Budgeting in G7 Countries* (Washington, DC: IMF, April 19, 2017).

52 Canada, France and the United Kingdom produce gender statements on a regular basis. See IMF, *Gender Budgeting in G7 Countries*. See also Ileana Steccolini, "New Development: Gender (Responsive) Budgeting," *Public Money and Management*, Vol. 39, No. 5 (2019), pp. 379–383; European Institute for Gender Equality (EIGE), *Gender Budgeting* (Vilnius, Lithuania: EIGE, April 2019).

53 See Dara Kay Cohen, Amelia Hoover Green and Elisabeth Jean Wood, *Wartime Sexual Violence: Misconceptions, Implications, and Ways Forward* (Washington, DC: US Institute of Peace, February 2013). See also Robert Ulrich Nagel, *The Known Knowns and Known Unknowns in Data on Women, Peace and Security*, London School of Economics, WPS Working Paper Series No. 19 (2019).

54 For more on sex-disaggregated data and gender statistics, see UN Statistics Office, *Gender Statistics Manual: Integrating a Gender Perspective into Statistics* (New York: United Nations, May 14, 2013).

55 See Data2X.org, *Bridging the Gap: Mapping Gender Data Availability in Africa: Key Findings and Recommendations* (Washington, DC: Data2X.org, March 2019).

56 See chapter 7 in this book, p. 138. See also United Nations, *Noting Major Gaps in Gender Statistics, Speakers Say Data Collection Must Ensure All Groups Are Represented*, Commission on the Status of Women, Meetings Coverage ECOSOC/CSW 11th Meeting WOM/2178 (New York: United Nations, March 18, 2019).

57 See Data2X.org, *Bridging the Gap*.

58 See chapter 2 in this book, p. 40.

59 See chapter 11 in this book, p. 219.

60 Ibid, p. 227.

61 The EU's Treaty of Amsterdam, adopted in 1997, stated that promotion of equality between men and women would be a fundamental task of the Union. It required EU members to eliminate gender inequalities. See also EU, *Women, Peace and Security: Council Resolutions*, 15086/18 (December 10, 2018); *EU Action Plan on Women, Peace and Security (WPS) 2019–2024*, 11031/19 and EEAS (2019) 747 (July 5, 2019).

62 See NATO/EAPC, *Women, Peace and Security: Policy and Action Plan* (Brussels: NATO, 2018). See also Chantal de Jonge Oudraat et al., *The 1325 Scorecard: Gender Mainstreaming: Indicators for the Implementation of UNSCR 1325 and Its Related Institutions* (Brussels: NATO, 2015).

63 Ministry of Foreign Affairs, *Handbook: Sweden's Feminist Foreign Policy* (Stockholm: Government of Sweden, 2019).

64 Jean-Yves Le Drian and Marlene Schiappa, "Feminist Foreign Policy," *France Diplomatie* (March 8, 2019).

65 See chapter 5 in this book.

66 See chapter 10 in this book.

67 Jacqui True, "Mainstreaming Gender in Global Public Policy," *International Feminist Journal of Politics*, Vol. 5, No. 3 (2003), p. 374.

68 See chapter 2 in this book.

69 Ibid.

70 On the importance of local contexts, see chapters 7 and 10 in this book.

71 See Chantal de Jonge Oudraat and Michael E. Brown, *WPS+GPS: Adding Gender to the Peace and Security Equation*, WIIS Policy Brief (Washington, DC: Women In International Security (WIIS), November 2017).

72 Douglas Adams, *Life, the Universe and Everything* (London: Pan Books, 1982).

73 See Terrell Carver, "Men and Masculinities in International Relations Research," *Brown Journal of World Affairs*, Vol. 21, No. 1 (Fall–Winter 2014), pp. 113–126.

74 See chapter 11 in this book.

75 See chapter 4 in this book.

76 See European Institute on Gender Inequality (EIGE), *Intersecting Inequalities: Gender Equality Index* (Luxembourg: European Union, 2019).

77 Sweden is a notable exception to the general rule.
78 Emanuel quoted in Jack Rosenthal, "A Terrible Thing to Waste," *New York Times Magazine* (July 31, 2009).
79 See chapter 9 in this book, p. 190.
80 See chapter 8 in this book, p. 169.
81 On "lessons learned" efforts, see chapter 4 in this book.
82 See chapter 3 in this book. See also Shannon Zimmerman, Luisa Ryan and David Duriesmith, *Recognizing the Violent Extremist Ideology of 'Incels'*, WIIS Policy Brief (Washington, DC: WIIS, September 2018).
83 See chapters 6, 7 and 10 in this book.

INDEX

#*FreeThe20* 227–228
#*manels* 227
#*metoo* movement 227
#*NotThe Cost* 227
#*womenalsoknow* 227

9/11 80–81
75th Ranger Regiment 107
2030 Agenda for Sustainable Development 11

abortion 51, 144, 146, 240–241
academic community 254
Action for Peacekeeping (A4P) 93
activists 250–251, 255–256, 257
Adger, Neil 155
Afghanistan 95, 97, 149, 205–208, 240
Agreement on Disaster Management and
    Emergency Response (AADMER) 179
Albright, Madeleine 222
Alexievich, Svetlana 93
Allan, Peter 217
alliances 228
al Qaeda 77, 80
Amos, James 105
anarchy 30
Anderlini, Sanam 20
Andrijasevic, Rutivica 119
Angola 60
Aquino, Benigno 55
Arab Spring 34
Arendt, Hannah 32
armed conflict: Beijing Conference and
    203; continuum of 32, 33; definition

of 28; drivers of progress 39–40;
environmental security and 156–158;
gender in 33–38; human rights and 203;
literature on 28–29; obstacles to progress
41–42; onset of 29–33; policy responses
to sexual violence 38–39; post-conflict
challenges 48–49; power relations and
33; psychological and social impact
of wartime sexual violence 37–38;
scholarship on sexual violence 35–38;
sexual violence and 34–38, 240, 241;
state militarism 31; strategies for progress
42–43; war and peace dichotomy 32–33;
see also military organizations
ASEAN Agreement on Disaster
    Management and Emergency Response
    (AADMER) 179, 184
Asian Infrastructure Investment Bank
    (AIIB) 60
Aspin, Les 95
Association of Southeast Asian Nations
    (ASEAN) 179, 184, 186
asylum 122–123, 126, 127; *see also* refugees
Atta, Mohamed 80–81
Australia 126, 180, 229
authoritarianism: illiberal hegemony and
    58; misogyny and 52

Baader-Meinhof 76
backdraft 160
Baird, Sarah 149
Bakker, Karen 162
Bangladesh 148, 239

Bardou, Florian 57
Barnes, Tiffany 222
Barnett, Jon 155, 156
Basedau, Matthias 158
Bashevkin, Sylvia 222
Beijing Conference 1, 7, 12, 29, 38, 61, 183,
    185, 202, 203, 214, 215, 238
Berry, Marie 34
biological/essentialist view 6
Birkmann, Jörn 187
Bishop, Julie 229
Bjarnegard, Elin 31
blind resistance 99
Boko Haram 56, 77, 78
Bolsonaro, Jair 57
borders 117, 118
Bosnia 34, 38
Bourgois, Philippe 32
Brazil 54, 57
Broderick, Elizabeth 220
Brown, Michael E. 1, 235
Brundtland Report 156
building back better 169, 189–190
Bulte, Erwin 158
Buzan, Barry 8

campaigns 227–228
Campbell, Kristen 36
Canada 93, 98, 126, 229, 238, 252
Caprioli, Mary 31
care work 226–227
Carr, Edward 22, 155, 170, 239, 259
Castles, Stephen 116
Catholicism 57, 58
C-Fam (Center for Family and Human
    Rights) 52
Chandra, Alvin 163
Chaney, Paul 60
change: difficulty of 6–7; resistance to 99,
    243–246
childbirth 137
China 52, 59–63, 240
China-Pakistan Economic Corridor
    (CPEC) 61
Chowdury, Anwarul 12
civil society participation 228, 250–251
climate change 123–124, 163–165, 178
"Climate Change and Security" (GTZ)
    164, 166
Clinton, Hillary 222, 225
Cluster Approach 183
Cockburn, Cynthia 30
Cohen, Dara Kay 36
Cohn, Carol 33, 100

Cold War: human rights and 199; security
    and 8–9, 10
collective action 150
Collier, Paul 157
Colombia 58, 65, 240
Combat Exclusion Policy 96
Commission for the Status of Women
    (CSW) 12, 184
conflict: climate change and 163–164;
    definition of 30; water security and
    161–163; see also armed conflict
"Conflict, Climate, and Environment"
    (DfID) 164
conscription 97
constructivist view 6
Convention on the Elimination of All
    Forms of Discrimination against Women
    (CEDAW) 1, 12, 23n1, 185, 200, 237
Convention on the Elimination of All
    Forms of Racial Discrimination (CERD)
    200, 237
Convention Relating to the Status of
    Refugees 114, 122, 123, 131n4
Correa, Sonia 58
counter-terrorism (CT) 73
Cross, Robin 91
cultural change 106
Cultural Support Teams 91, 97
Cutts, David 217

Dahlerup, Drude 218
data: incomplete 17–18, 249–250; sharing
    of 183–184; strategies for progress
    and 260
David, Emmanuel 123
Davies, Sara 22, 35, 214, 238, 251
Declaration and Platform for Action 1, 7,
    12, 183, 185, 238
defense ministers 222
de Jonge Oudraat, Chantal 1, 235
Democratic Republic of the Congo 14, 34
demographics 32
den Boer, Andrea 32
Denmark 19
Detraz, Nicole 160
development: changing norms 146–148;
    collective action 150; drivers of change
    145–150; education 148–149; gender
    equality and 137; gender, importance
    of 136–138; humanitarian emergencies
    and 182; international discourse
    135–136; leadership and 149–150; legal
    reforms 145–146; obstacles to progress
    139–145; patterns of disadvantage

138–139; strategies for progress 145–150;
Sustainable Development Goals (SDGs)
136–137

Disasters (journal) 182

discrimination: by region *143*; social
institutions and 142; *see also* inequalities

drivers of progress: activists 250–251; armed
conflict 39–40; development 145–150;
environmental security 165–166;
governance 217–224, 223; humanitarian
emergencies 181–184; human rights
209–210; international organizations
251–252; military organizations 96–98;
national governments 252–253; norms
and laws 253; peacebuilding 64–66;
scholars 254; security 237; terrorism
83–84

Duterte, Rodrigo 54, 55–56, 62

Economic and Social Council (ECOSOC)
(UN) 12

economic leadership 216–217

economic restrictions 3, 248–249

education 137, 138, 144, 148–149, 150, 257

Egnell, Robert 106

Egypt 241

Eight-Stage Change Process 102

eldercare 144–145

Elected Ten 66

Elimination of Violence Against Women
(EVAW) 205, 206

El Salvador 36

Elsie Initiative on Women in Peace
Operations 93

Emanuel, Rahm 259

empowerment 147, 189, 190, 219–220

Enarson, Elaine 182, 191

environmental security: armed conflict and
156–158; climate and 163–165; drivers
of policy progress 165–166; gender and
160–161, 239; introduction 156–159;
obstacles to policy progress 166–168;
policy frameworks and 159; scarcity and
157, 158; strategies for progress 168–170;
water security 157, 161–163

equality: in Afghanistan 205; armed conflict
and 33; Convention on the Elimination
of All Forms of Discrimination against
Women 200; GDP and *141*; gender
discourse and 211n6; in governance
215; parity and 256; peace and 32; in
political participation 214–215; in
Sustainable Development Goals 204; *see
also* inequalities

Erdogan, Tayyip 55

essentialist view 6, 7

Ethiopia 147

European Union (EU): Common European
Asylum System 126–128; *Global Strategy
for Foreign and Security Policy* 11; policy
perspectives 25n40; Policy Plan on Legal
Migration 126

Fakih, Lama 204

Fausto-Sterling, Anne 6

female empowerment 147

Female Engagement Teams 91, 95

feminist foreign policy movement 221–223,
228–229

feminist masculinities theory 37

feminization 116

food security 163

France 130, 238, 252

Francis (Pope) 57

Freedman, Jane 22, 113, 239, 242

Freidenvall, Lenita 218

Fröhlich, Christiane 166

funding 248–249, 260

Gabriela party 56

gender: defining 6–8, 53, 75; as social
construct 33, 202–203; terminology
and 53

Gender and Development (GAD) approach
136, 237–238

gender-based violence (GBV) 183; *see also*
violence against women and girls

Gender Equity Movement in Schools
146–147

gender hierarchy 30, 34

gender ideology 53, 57, 58

gender-security agenda 4–5

Ghana 166

Gillard, Julia 225

Gioli, Giovanna 166

girls clubs 147

"glass cliff" 221, 224, 246

global campaigns 227–228

Global Compact for Safe, Orderly and
Regular Migration 130

Global Compact on Refugees 130

Global Framework for Disaster Risk
Reduction 169

Global Strategy for Foreign and Security Policy
(EU) 11

Global Study 15

Goetz, Anne Marie 21, 47, 240, 241

Goldstein, Joshua 30, 90

governance: alliances 228; campaigns
227–228; crises and 220–221; drivers
of progress 217–224, 223; economic
leadership 216–217, 238–239; feminist
foreign policy movement 221–223,
228–229; institutional spaces 218–219;
institutions and 223–224, 224;
men's leadership 219–220; obstacles
to progress 224–226; peace and
security decisionmaking 216; political
participation 238–239; proportion of
legislative seats 215–216; quotas 214,
215, 217–218, 229, 238; rationale for
gender-inclusivity 215–217; strategies
for engendering 226–229; structural
inequalities 226; violence against women
in politics 225–226; women's movements
and 218–219; *see also* political
participation
Greece 128, 129
greed proposition 157, 159
Green, Amelia Hoover 36
grievance proposition 157–158
Group of Friends of the Family 52
group resistance 100–101
Grzebalska, Weronika 52
guiding coalition 103

Hague, William 220, 252
Haiti 181
harassment 98
Haring, Ellen 21, 90, 243, 252
Haynie, Jeannette Gaudry 21, 72, 239, 257
health 144
Herzegovina 34
hierarchies: armed conflict and 36; at
international level 30; in military
organizations 90, 102; in organizations
101; robustness of 34; in terrorism 78
High-Level Panel on Threats, Challenges,
and Change 10–11
Hoeffler, Anke 157
Hollaback! 150
Homer-Dixon, Thomas 158, 159, 161
Hsaing, Solomon 157
Htun, Mala 219, 223
Huckerby, Jane 204
Hudson, Valerie 31, 32, 242
Human Development Report (UNDP) 10
humanitarian emergencies: building back
better 189–190; changes in research
181–184; climate change and 178;
constructs of 178; data sharing 183–184;
definition of 176; drivers of progress

181–184; gender-based violence (GBV)
183; gender dimensions of 178–181,
239–240; human rights mechanisms and
190–191; interventions 185; obstacles
to progress 185–187; policy and 182,
185, 186–187; response efforts 181;
risk-reduction strategies 179; strategies
for progress 187–191; women and girls
in 177, 185–186; WPS agenda and
187–189, 188
human rights: in Afghanistan 205–208;
C-Fam (Center for Family and Human
Rights) 52; counter-terrorism and
84–85; drivers of progress 209–210; in
humanitarian emergencies 190–191;
international law and 198–201;
international policy and 202–205;
obstacles to progress 209; strategies
for progress 210–211; track record
237; United Nations and 11, 198–201;
Universal Declaration of Human Rights
11; universalist vs. relativist conceptions
of 201, 202; World Conference on
Human Rights 38
human rights defenders 51–52
human security framework 10
human security school of thought 9
Humphreys, Macartan 159
Hungary 241
Hunter, Lori M. 123
Hurricane Florence 180
Hurricane Katrina 180
Hyogo Framework for Action 179

identity markers 6
ideological resistance 99, 100
ideology of gender 53, 57, 58
illiberal drift: among regional powers
53–63; erosion of norms and 50–53
Incel 81
inclusion 138
India 64, 148, 150
Indian Ocean tsunami 166, 177, 188
inequalities: armed conflict and 33; causes
of 3–4; economic 3, *141*, 142; in
education 144, 148–149; gender norms
and 142; in health 144; in leadership
49; legal reforms and 145–146; in
legal rights 3; most glaring 137–138;
patterns of 138–139; in pay 3; in political
participation 3, 32; sexual violence and
35–36; state militarism and 31; structural
226; violence and 31; *see also* equality
Informal Experts Group (IEG) 15, 16, 65

institutional spaces 218–219
institutions 101, 102, 223–224, 224, **245**
Intergovernmental Panel on Climate
    Change (IPCC) 158
International Covenant for Civil and
    Political Rights (ICCPR) 199
International Covenant for Economic, Social
    and Cultural Rights (ICESCR) 199
International Criminal Tribunal for
    Rwanda (ICTR) 36, 38
International Criminal Tribunal for
    Yugoslavia (ICTY) 36, 38
international law, human rights and
    198–201
International Masculinity and Gender
    Equality Survey (IMAGES) 37
International Organization for the Family 57
international organizations 251–252
International Protocol on the
    Documentation and Investigation of
    Sexual Violence in Conflict 39
inter-state conflict 28, 39
intra-state conflict 28, 31, 39
Iraq 95
ISIS 16, 34, 77, 239
Israel 93, 97, 99
Issawi, Salim 72
Italy 128

Japan International Cooperation Agency
    (JICA) 166
Jenkins, Rob 21, 47, 240, 241
Jenson, Jane 227
Jolie, Angelina 39, 252
justice, as well-being indicator 138

Kang, Alice 217
Keegan, John 90, 108
Kenya 147, 150, 221, 225, 241
Khaled, Leila 72, 82
Khashoggi, Jamal 53
Klugman, Jeni 22, 31, 135, 146, 237, 250
Kolodziej, Edward 10
Kotter, John P. 106
Kouvo, Sari 22, 196, 237, 240, 253
Kovats, Easzter 52
Krook, Mona Lena 218
Krylova, Anna 93
Kuehnast, Kathleen 21, 28, 240, 250, 254
Ku Klux Klan 77
Kurdistan Workers' Party 77

language 253
Lay, Jann 158

leadership: development and 149–150;
    expansion of 238–239; in foreign policy
    221–222; humanitarian emergencies and
    192; importance of 257; inequalities in
    49, 149; male 219–220; peacebuilding
    and 49; *see also* governance
Lee-Koo, Katrina 178
legal rights 3
Levine, Corey 22, 196, 237, 240, 253
Libya 119, 128
Li, Li 146
Lionesses 91, 95
Loftus, Alex 161
Lund, Kristin 99

Machel, Graca 221
Macklin, Audrey 126
Mai, Nicola 119
mainstreaming: adoption of 219, 238; in
    Afghanistan 205; definition of 7; of
    gender perspectives 258; men 255; track
    record 16–20, 251; within the UN 12
Male Champions of Change 220
Malikzada, Farkhunda 196, 197
Marchand, Marianne 117
marital systems 32
masculinity: humanitarian emergencies and
    179–180; militaristic practices and 30;
    nostalgia for 33; sexual violence and 37;
    social constructions of 37; toxic 29
maternity/paternity leave 98
Matfess, Hilary 32
Mawdsley, Emma 59
McDermott, Rose 32
Mearsheimer, John 9
Melander, Erik 31
MenCare campaign 148
migrant women's associations 129
migration/migrants: *see* population
    movements
Miles, Rosalind 91
military organizations: best practices
    107–108; change in 99–102,
    252–253; common approaches 108;
    communicating change vision 104;
    drivers of progress 96–98; emergence
    of 8; empowerment 104–105; gains,
    consolidating 106; guiding coalition
    103; inter-state problems and 9; new
    approaches 106–107; obstacles to
    progress 98–102; as obstacle to progress
    243; short-term wins 105–106; strategies
    for progress 102–108; urgency 102–103;
    US military 95–96; vision and strategy

103–104; women's participation 91–96, **94**; *see also* armed conflict
Millennium Development Goals (MDGs) 16, 185, 204, 238
Miller, Mark 116
Millward, James 60
Minassian, Alek 81
Mintrom, Michael 219
misconceptions 246–248
misogyny 52, 55–56, 57, 81–82, 225
missing women 137
Mlambo-Ngcuka, Phumzile 15, 238
Mobjörk, Malin 158
Monitoring and Evaluation (M&E) frameworks 167–168
Morinville, Cynthia 162
Myanmar 2, 34, 63, 221, 228

Nair, Tamara 22, 176, 239–240, 259
Narodnaya Volya 76
National Action Plans (NAPs): increase in 238; migration and 130; nature of 19–20; number of 2, 19; women's leadership and 219
natural disasters 123, 176; *see also* humanitarian emergencies
neo-patriarchs 241
Nepal 150
New People's Army (NPA) 83
New Zealand 180
Nicaragua 148
Niger 142
Nigeria 54, 56–57
Nordas, Ragnhild 36
norms: armed conflict and 30, 33, 91; changing 7, 146–148; as driver of progress 253; humanitarian emergencies and 179, 180; inequalities and 142; in military organizations 91; perpetuation of 6; strategies for progress and 259; terrorism and 78–79
norm-spoiling 52
North Atlantic Treaty Organization (NATO) 94, 107
Norway 97, 99

O'Brien, Diana 222
obstacles to progress: armed conflict 41–42; data 249–250; development 139–145; environmental security 166–168; governance 224–226; humanitarian emergencies 185–187; human rights 209; military organizations 98–102; misconceptions 246–248; money

248–249; patriarchy 242–243, 244–246, **245**; peacebuilding 48–50, 63–64; population movements 128–129; resistance 243–246; security 236, 242–250; terrorism 82–83
On Violence (Arendt) 32
organizations 101, 251–252
Özler, Berk 149

Pakistan 54, 61–62, 241
parity 256–257
patriarchy: after wars 34; armed conflict and 30; marital systems and 32; neo-patriarchs 241; as obstacle to progress 242–243, 244–246, **245**; strategies for progress 256; violence and 246
pay gaps 3
peace and security affairs: underrepresentation of women 18, 216, in peace and security affairs; "women and peace thesis" 31
peacebuilding: among regional powers 53–63; drivers of progress 64–66; funding 49; illiberal drift 50–53; leadership 49; obstacles 48–50, 63–64; politics and 50–63
peacekeepers 17, 60, 96, 97
Pennington, Reina 93
perspectives 257–258
Peto, Andrea 52
Philippines 54, 55–56, 62, 83, 179, 180
physical security, armed conflict and 31
Platform for Action (PFA) 61, 202, 214, 215
policy frameworks: climate change and 164; environmental security and 159, 165–168; feminist foreign policy movement 221–223; gender dynamics and 7–8; humanitarian emergencies and 182, 185, 186–187, 190–191; human rights and 202–205; illiberal drift 50–53; informal logics of 223; on migration 125–126, 130–131; military framework and 9; misconceptions and 248; nature of 3–4; progress in 235–236; resilience and 165; strategies for progress and 259–260; terrorism and 79–80, 84, 239; WPS agenda 11–16
political participation: in Afghanistan 206; armed conflict and 31; effects of 214; humanitarian emergencies and 192; increase in 238; strategies for 216; underrepresentation of women 3, 32; violence and 225–226, 241; *see also* governance

political resistance 99
political violence 32, 35
politics, peacebuilding and 50–63
polygyny 32
Pope Francis 57
Popovski, Vasselin 190
Popular Front for the Liberation of
  Palestine (PFLP) 72
population movements: borders and 117,
  118, 128; causes of 114, 115, 116–117;
  climate change and 123–124; Common
  European Asylum System 126–128;
  feminization of 116; gender and
  115–117, 239; gendered representations
  124–125; migrants, defined 114; numbers
  of 114, 120, 122; obstacles to progress
  128–129; policy frameworks 125–126;
  politicization of 116; public attitudes
  129; security and 114–115, 117–119,
  127–128; strategies for progress 128–131;
  trafficking 119–120
populism 52–53, 225
power: armed conflict and 30, 33;
  environmental security and 156;
  exclusion from 138; gender and 6, 7;
  humanitarian emergencies and 178, 181;
  political violence and 32; redefining of
  30; strategies for progress and 260–261;
  structural relations of 33; water security
  and 162
Power, Samantha 227, 230
Prevention of Sexual Violence Initiative
  (PSVI) 17, 39, 220
prevention pillar 20
Program H 147–148
PT protest 100
Putin, Vladimir 241

Qualification Directive 127
quotas 214, 215, 217–218, 229, 238

Race and Religion Protection Laws 63
Raduha, Nina 99
Rajapaksa, Mahinda 62
Rapoport, David 74
Reception Directive 127
refugees 114, 120–123; *see also* asylum;
  population movements
Regional Action Plans (RAPs) 2
relief and recovery pillar 18
reproductive rights 51
resilience 165, 244
resistance to change 99, 243–246
Resolution 56/2 184

Resolution 1325 on Women, Peace and
  Security (WPS) 1, 2, 12, **13**, 14–15, 40,
  41, 93, 96, 187, 203, 216, 226
Resolution 1820 38
Resolution 2242 15–16
Resolution 2467 51, 241–242
RESOLVE network 84
resource curse 157
Responsibility to Protect (R2P) 203
Revolutionary Armed Forces of Colombia
  (FARC) 91
Rice, Condoleezza 222
Ridgeway, Cecilia 242
Rodger, Elliot 81
Rohingya 2, 34, 63
role models 150
roles 6, 7
Roman Catholicism 57, 58
Romania 146
Rome Statute of the International
  Criminal Court 34, 38
Rothschild, Emma 8, 10
Ruddick, Sara 33
Rudd, Kevin 225
Russia 52, 92, 240
Rwanda 34, 36, 148

Saleyhan, Idean 159
Sanders, Bernie 225
SASA! 148
Saudi Arabia 53, 236
Scales, Robert 100
Schachko, Oksana 196–197
Scheinin, Martin 204
Scheper-Hughes, Nancy 32
scholars 254
schooling: *see* education
security: defining 8–11; demographics and
  32; drivers of progress 237; non-military
  considerations 30; obstacles to progress
  236, 242–250; opposition to 240;
  parity in 256; priorities 258; progress in
  235–236; setbacks 236; state vs. human
  242; track record 237–242; as well-being
  indicator 138
self-defense 205, 212n22
Self-Employed Women's Association 150
Sendai Framework 179, 189
Serrano, Lauren 99
sexual violence: conflict-related 34–38, 240,
  241; as crime against humanity 17; gender
  inequality and 35–36; group behaviour
  and 36; international level 17–20; legal
  regimes and 36–37; masculinity and 37;

migration and 118, 120; peacekeepers and 17; policy responses 38–39; psychological and social impact 37–38; scholarship on 35–38; trafficking 119, 120; as war tactic 17

Sexual Violence in Armed Conflict (SVAC) 36

Sierra Leone 34

Singer, Debra 126

Sirisena, Maithripala 54

Sjoberg, Laura 30

Slovenia 99

Snorek, Julie 161, 170

Social Institutions and Gender Index (SIGI) 35, 142, *143*

social power 162

social reproduction 226

societal campaigns 227–228

Solidarity for African Women's Rights (SOAWR) 150

Somalia 58–59

South Africa 97

South Asian Association of Regional Corporation (SAARC) 179

South Korea 63

South Sudan 2

Soviet Union 9, 92–93

Sri Lanka 36, 54, 62–63

state militarism 31

stereotypes: hierarchies and 6; migration and 124–125; neo-patriarchy and 241; patriarchy and 33; in terrorism 73, 77, 82, 84; of violence 17

Stop Street Harassment 150

strategies for progress: armed conflict 42–43; development 145–150; environmental security 168–170; humanitarian emergencies 187–191; human rights 210–211; military organizations 102–108; overview 254–255; parity 256–257; people 255–256; perspectives 257–258; in policy 259–260; political participation 216; population movements 128–131; power 260–261; terrorism 84–85

Sudan 14, 166

Sultana, Farhana 162

Sustainable Development Goals (SDGs) 2, 16, 136, 145, 185, 204, 238, 240

Sweden 2, 97, 98, 228, 236, 238, 252

Syria 2, 34

Tadros, Mariz 215

Taliban 78

Tamil Tigers 36, 77

terrorism: 9/11 14; case studies 80–82; causes of 74–75; community support 77–78; defining 74–75; drivers of progress 83–84; gender and 75–80, 78, 78–79, 239; hierarchies in 78; human rights and 203–204; individual terrorists 76–77; ISIS 16; obstacles to progress 82–83; policy implementation and 79–80; strategies for progress 84–85; women's roles in 76–77

Thatcher, Margaret 222

threat multiplier approach 159

Tickner, J. Ann 11, 30

traditionalist school of thought 9

trafficking 119–120

Tripp, Aili 217

Trudeau, Justin 229

True, Jacqui 22, 35, 214, 219, 238, 251, 253

Trump, Donald 51, 241

turf protection 100–101

Turkey 58–59, 128

Typhoon Haiyan 180

Typhoon Mangkhut 179

Uganda 147, 148, 150, 191

Ulema 206, 207, 208, 212n26

Ullman, Richard 8, 10

underrepresentation of women: in peace and security affairs 2, 18, 216; in political participation 3, 32

United Kingdom 39, 50, 92, 130, 252

United Nations: *2030 Agenda for Sustainable Development* 11; China and 60–61; Commission for the Status of Women 12; as driver of progress 251–252; female ambassadors in 230; Group of Friends of the Family 52; High-Level Panel on Threats, Challenges, and Change 10–11; humanitarian emergencies and 183; human rights and 11, 198–201; human security framework 10; migration and 130; peacebuilding and 47; peacekeepers 17, 60, 96–97; proclamations 1–2; on protection of women 125–126; role of women and 238; Universal Declaration of Human Rights 11, 199; women in the military 93–94, 96–97; women's office *see* UN Women;

United Nations International Strategy for Disaster Reduction (UNISDR) 179

United Nations Office for the Coordination of Humanitarian Affairs (UNOCHA) 183, 184

United Nations Security Council: conflict-related sexual violence 15, 38–39; Elected Ten 66; Informal Experts Group (IEG) 65; resolutions *see* UNSCR; sexual violence 17; terrorism and 79–80; WPS principles in 65–66

United States 50, 95–96, 96, 126, 240, 252

Universal Declaration of Human Rights 11, 253

unpaid work 137, 144, 226

UNSCR: Resolution 1325 1, 12, **13**, 14–15, 93, 177; Resolution 1820 38; Resolution 2242 15–16; Resolution 2467 51; Women, Peace and Security *see* Women, Peace and Security (WPS);

UN Women 15

Uppsala Conflict Data Program 139

USAID 165, 166–167

US Army Rangers 107

US Civil War 92

US Institute of Peace 84

US Marine Corps 96, 100–101, 103, 104, 105

Valerio, Kristine Aquino 180

Van Baalen, Sebastian 158

Vienna Programme 202, 212n11

violence: economic 225; migration and 117; patriarchal 246; political 32, 225–226; sexual *see* sexual violence; as social process 33

violence against women and girls: in conflict settings 2, 17; gender norms and 142; in humanitarian emergencies 183; migration and 118, 127–128; numbers of 137, 139; in politics 225–226, 241; in refugee camps 121; SDG target 145; sexual violence *see* sexual violence; trafficking 119–120; WPS index *140*

violent extremism 74

Viollaz, Mariana 31

Vivekananda, Janani 163

von Lossow, Tobias 161

Wallström, Margot 228, 252

Waltz, Kenneth 9

Water and Conflict Toolkit 162

water security 157, 161–163

Weiss, Cora 20

Weldon, Laurel 219, 223

well-being 138

West, Candace 6

Wick, Katharina 158

Women, Business, and the Law (World Bank) 142

Women in Development (WID) approach 136

Women, Peace and Security (WPS): acceptance of 238; adoption of 1, 38; definition of gender and 7; as driver of progress 65; effects of 40, 253; humanitarian emergencies and 187–189; migration and 129; passage of 12; pillars of 14–15, 18–19, 20, 25n55, 188; problems in 240; resolutions 1, 2, 12, **13**, 14–15, 40, 41, 177; terrorism and 72–73, 79–80; women in the military and 93

Women Protection Advisors 39

"women's" issues 4, 5

women's movements 65, 200, 218–219

women's organizations 219, 237, 248–249

Women's Peace and Humanitarian Fund 49

Wood, Elisabeth 36

World Conference on Human Rights 38, 202

World Conference on the Status of Women 1

World Conference on Women 12, 29, 38, 61, 202

World Congress of Families 52

World War I 92

World War II 92

WPS index 138, 139, *140*, 188

Xi Jinping 61, 241

Youth-to-Youth clubs 147

Yugoslavia 36

Zimmerman, Don 6